ROUSSEAU

The Arguments of the Philosophers

EDITOR: TED HONDERICH

Grote Professor of the Philosophy of Mind and Logic,
University College London

The purpose of this series is to provide a contemporary assessment and history of the entire course of philosophical thought. Each book constitutes a detailed, critical introduction to the work of a philosopher or school of major influence and significance.

*available in paperback

ROUSSEAU

Timothy O'Hagan

London and New York

First published 1999
by Routledge
11 New Fetter Lane, London EC4P 4EE

Simultaneously published in the USA and Canada
by Routledge
29 West 35th Street, New York, NY 10001

Typeset in Garamond by RefineCatch Limited, Bungay, Suffolk
Printed and bound in Great Britain by
MPG Books Ltd, Bodmin, Cornwall

British Library Cataloguing in Publication Data
A catalogue record for this book is available from the British Library

Library of Congress Cataloging in Publication Data
O'Hagan, Timothy.
Rousseau / Timothy O'Hagan.
p.   cm.
Includes bibliographical references and index.
(hbk. : alk. paper)
1. Rousseau, Jean-Jacques, 1712–1778.   I. Title.
B2137.037   1999
194 – dc21   98–13945
CIP

ISBN 0–415–04443–X

FOR MY MOTHER,
BETTY O'HAGAN

CONTENTS

CONTENTS

CONTENTS

Acknowledgements

My greatest debt is to Martin Hollis, friend and critic, who died on 27 February 1998. For nearly a quarter of a century he was generous with his time, exacting in his standards and unfailing in his support and encouragement. Other old friends who have helped with discussion and critical reading are Nicholas Bunnin and Angus Ross.

Nicholas Dent read the penultimate version of the whole manuscript with great care. He showed how I could make useful changes in its structure and presentation. If I had made all the improvements he suggested, I should have written a new and better book. But I hope I have responded to at least some of his criticisms.

I have had much help from newer friends too. Daniel Schulthess converted a rough-hewn draft of 'La morale sensitive de Jean-Jacques Rousseau' into impeccable French, and also guided me in improving its structure. Chapter I of this book is a somewhat longer version of that article, rendered into English. Since then I have exploited Daniel Schulthess's rich philosophical culture on many occasions. I am also grateful to Rüdiger Bittner for casting a sceptical eye over the chapters on religion.

During the course of writing the book I have enjoyed the hospitality of members of the Philosophy Department, University of Geneva, in particular Kevin Mulligan, and of Richard Glauser and Daniel Schulthess, of the Philosophy Seminar, University of Neuchâtel. In Geneva I benefited from the presence of Jean Starobinski and Bronislaw Baczko. I am also indebted to Charles Wirz, of the Institut et Musée Voltaire, Geneva, for his scholarship and kindness alike. Maryse Schmidt-Surdez, conservatrice des manuscrits, Bibliothèque publique et universitaire, Neuchâtel, was a friendly guide to the Rousseau manuscripts in the Library, and also kindly supplied the page of Rousseau's handwriting reproduced on the cover.

I owe much to the pitiless responses of my students, particularly those at the University of East Anglia and the State University of New York, Binghamton, to whom I presented earlier versions of many chapters of the book. Students in Neuchâtel and in China demanded yet more clarifications.

I signal my debts to the published work of modern Rousseau scholars repeatedly in the notes, and I apologize to any whose works I may have inadvertently failed to acknowledge.

My thanks, as always, go to Mary Robinson for ceaseless secretarial help.

I am grateful to Jerry Goodenough for help in preparing the index and in proof-reading, and to Alice Stoakley for the most careful copy-editing an author could hope for.

Finally I wish to acknowledge my gratitude to the following institutions for their financial support of a period of research in the Suisse romande: the Pro-Helvetia Foundation and the Fonds national de recherche scientifique, Switzerland, and the British Academy.

INTRODUCTION

Rousseau: the life and the work[1]

(A)   Geneva: an eccentric upbringing (1712–28)

Jean-Jacques Rousseau was born in the Calvinist city state of Geneva in 1712. Both his parents were citizens, from the class of the *moyenne bourgeoisie*, which included independent artisans, clergymen, intellectuals and minor political figures. His mother, Suzanne Bernard, was the daughter of a *roué* who died when she was nine. She was then adopted by a 'pastor . . . a luminary of the Academy of Geneva and a man of property'.[2] She was considerably richer than her husband, Isaac Rousseau. He was a watchmaker and an unsuccessful dancing master, the descendant of French Huguenots long established in Geneva. Jean-Jacques' mother died a few days after his birth. He was then raised by an aunt and by his cultivated but feckless father. The latter left Geneva in 1722, abandoning his ten-year-old son, after an ignominious confrontation with an officer in the French army, an affair of insults and 'honour', which did not quite result in a duel. He entrusted Jean-Jacques to his wealthy brother-in-law Gabriel Bernard, who in turn sent him to be tutored in rural Bossey by the pastor Lambercier (1722–4). The pastor's daughter was put in charge of the young Jean-Jacques' discipline. As a result, he acquired from her a taste not only for country life, but also for the delights of being spanked by a good-looking young woman, thus adding a significant strand to what would be a disordered sexual life.

After this rustic idyll, Jean-Jacques returned to Geneva to spend four years (1724–8) in miserable apprenticeship, first as a legal clerk [*greffier*], then as an engraver.

(B)   Savoy and France: discovery and loss of love (1728–42)

The evening of 14 March 1728 marked a turning-point in Rousseau's life. Finding himself locked out of the city after curfew, Jean-Jacques made his way to Annecy in the Catholic Duchy of Savoy. There he was inveigled, with little resistance, into exchanging Protestantism for Catholicism by the religious but erotic Mme de Warens. She arranged for him to be instructed and baptized into the Catholic faith in Turin. After his return, he established himself in Mme de Warens' household, and with her embarked on his first and deepest romantic attachment. There followed years of errancy and haphazard employment, including a term as tutor to the de Mably family (1740–1). On the basis of that brief experience he wrote an early sketch of his educational theory. The passionate affair with Mme de Warens terminated unhappily in 1738, when Jean-Jacques was displaced by her factotum Wintzenried.

(C)   Paris, with Venetian interlude: formation of a writer, subverting the Enlightenment 'from within' (1742–55)[3]

Rousseau devoted much of his time in the early 1740s to his life-long passion for music. He moved to Paris in 1742. There he presented his 'Project concerning new musical notation' to the Academy of the Sciences, which granted it a certificate, and his first published work on music appeared in 1743. Moving in circles of considerable power and privilege, Rousseau's career now took another change of tack, when he was posted as secretary to the French Ambassador to Venice, an appointment which lasted less than a year (1743–4). Jean-Jacques parted from his employer amid acrimony and recriminations, a pattern which would be repeated many times in his later life. Though a personal and professional disaster, his brief diplomatic career taught him much about the realities of political power and about relations between unequal individuals.

After returning to Paris, Jean-Jacques encountered Thérèse Levasseur (1745), and embarked on the only personal relationship which would last for the rest of his life. This bizarre alliance with a barely literate laundress has been analysed and criticized by countless commentators, friends and enemies alike. In particular, the fact that the author of the *Emile*, the most revolutionary treatise on child-raising of its time, should have consigned his five children from Thérèse to the Foundlings Home, made him the butt of ceaseless ridicule, a caricatural figure of hypocrisy, embodying the failure to unite theory and practice.

2

Rousseau's world at this time was that of the *philosophes*, the intellectual élite of Europe. All of them were freethinkers, some were deists, some were atheists, some were sceptical empiricists, some were dogmatic materialists. They were united by a belief in human progress, summarized thus by Condorcet in the twilight of the Enlightenment: 'the moral goodness of man, the necessary consequence of his constitution, is capable of indefinite perfection like all his other faculties . . . nature has linked together in an indissoluble chain truth, happiness and virtue. . . .'[4] Within the Enlightenment camp divergent political positions were represented, but most of the *philosophes* preferred to put their trust in enlightened despots, rather than in radical democrats, to deliver a new, tolerant order embodying 'truth, happiness and virtue'.

In this, as in much else, Rousseau was in disagreement with his natural allies.[5] From the beginning he was an outsider in their world. He fell in love with one cultivated, educated, rich woman after another, while remaining in unmarried wedlock with someone they took to be his maid. He was a Genevan in Paris, a religious believer among religious sceptics, an egalitarian among élitists, a sceptic about culture among believers in culture.

It was as critic of culture from within that Rousseau composed the first work that would establish his reputation, the *Discourse on the Sciences and the Arts*, written in response to the question set by the Academy of Dijon in 1749, 'whether the restoration of the sciences and the arts has contributed to the purification of morals'. Walking through the forest to visit Diderot, then imprisoned in the Château de Vincennes, and reflecting on this question, Rousseau underwent a moment of illumination, 'a sudden inspiration', in which he claimed to have seen the guiding thread of all his future work:

> if I had ever been able to write a quarter of what I saw and felt under that tree, how clearly would I have made all the contradictions of the social system seen, with what strength would I have demonstrated that man is naturally good and that it is from these institutions alone that men become wicked. Everything that I was able to retain from these crowds of great truths which illuminated me under that tree are scattered about in my three principal writings . . . (LMa 1135/575)

The moment of insight revealed to Rousseau that the answer to the Academy's question was 'no'. Diderot encouraged Rousseau in developing that provocative response, which challenged the received wisdom of the established order and of its *bien pensant* critics alike.

In the foreword to a collection of his works published in 1763 Rousseau commented on it:

> What is celebrity? Here is the unfortunate work to which I owe mine. Certainly this piece, which won me a prize and made me famous, is at best mediocre, and I dare add that it is one of the slightest of this whole collection. (Seuil 2.52/CW 2.3)

Whatever its weaknesses, the *First Discourse* launched Rousseau as the *enfant terrible* (albeit a somewhat aging *enfant*) on the Parisian stage.

A period of intense creativity followed (1751–5). The opera *Le devin du village* was composed and performed before the King and greeted with acclaim. In the *Letter on French Music* (1753), Rousseau defended Italian opera against French, melody against harmony, simplicity against complexity. He returned to Geneva in 1754 to be readmitted formally into the Protestant church. In the same year he was writing the *Second Discourse*, the text in which he came closest to the *philosophes*. His approach to history was wholly naturalistic, and he kept a sceptical distance from theological speculation. Yet he was infinitely more radical than any of his contemporaries in his criticism of the inegalitarian order of his day. The *Second Discourse* was published in 1755, and, in the same year, the *Third Discourse*, the *Political Economy*. In the latter, Rousseau sketched several themes of his political philosophy, including the general will, the distinction between government and sovereign, the Lawgiver, patriotism and civic virtue. The *Third Discourse* is generally seen as the most 'liberal' (and least 'totalitarian') of Rousseau's political writings. But it is interesting that it also makes the most radical egalitarian claims. In it Rousseau argued that the government must take measures to prevent the 'continual increase of inequality of fortunes' (3D 276/168), and that it should use the taxation system to do this (3D 271–2/164).

(D)   Montmorency, Montlouis: the maturing of a genius (1756–62)

Accompanied by Thérèse and her mother, Rousseau withdrew from Paris in 1756 to the relative seclusion of Montmorency, where he was installed by the powerful Mme d'Epinay in her property, the Ermitage. In the two years he spent there, Rousseau broke finally with the circle of the *philosophes*. He inveighed against Voltaire in his letter on providence, and quarrelled with Grimm and Diderot, as well as with his patron Mme d'Epinay and his beloved Sophie d'Houdetot. Having left the Ermitage in a sulk, Rousseau managed to attract other rich protectors, including M. Mathas, agent of the Duke of Condé, and the Maréchal and Maréchale de Luxembourg. From Mathas' cottage in Montlouis, near Montmorency, Rousseau sealed the break with the *philosophes* in his *Letter to d'Alembert*. In it, he denounced d'Alembert's proposal that a theatre should be founded in Geneva, and indulged in an intemperate tirade against the acting profession and against modern women. Amidst all these distractions, Rousseau was working feverishly on his three masterpieces. The epistolary novel *Julie, ou la Nouvelle Héloïse* was published in 1761, the *Emile* and the *Social Contract* in 1762. In retrospect, this appears as the pinnacle of Rousseau's career. It was also the moment of crisis, the beginning of the end.

(E)   Switzerland, England, France: years of exile (1762–70)

The *Emile* was immediately outlawed for its explicit rejection of original sin, a central doctrine of Christian theology, both Catholic and Protestant. In France it was condemned by the civil authority of the Parlement de Paris and by the religious authority of Charles de Beaumont, Cardinal Archbishop. A warrant was issued for its author's arrest, but there was no refuge for him in his native Geneva, where both the *Emile* and the *Social Contract* were also condemned. The dramatic story of Rousseau's flight and exile has been told many times, first by Jean-Jacques himself in the *Confessions*, and then by a legion of biographers. The period falls into three phases: the Swiss exile, the English exile and the internal exile, back in France.

(i)   The Swiss exile (1762–6)

Jean-Jacques found a brief refuge in Yverdon in the canton of Bern. Expelled from there by the local authorities who bowed to pressure from Geneva, he established himself in Môtiers, located in Neuchâtel, then ruled by Prussia. There he would enjoy the protection of its governor, the Lord-Marshal George Keith, and, at one remove, that of the enlightened despot Frederick the Great. From Môtiers he published two polemics. The first was the *Letter to de Beaumont* (1763), a detailed response to the Archbishop's *Mandement* condemning the *Emile*. In May 1763, after the Genevan authorities had bowed to French pressure and decreed that the *Letter* should not be reprinted in the city, Rousseau renounced his Genevan citizenship publicly and defiantly. In the second polemic, the *Letters Written from the Mountain* (1764), Rousseau replied to the *Letters Written from the Country*, published anonymously by the Genevan attorney-general Tronchin, in which the lawyer had defended the actions of the oligarchic Petit Conseil of Geneva and its condemnation of Rousseau's two books. In his nine *Letters*, Rousseau re-worked the central theses of his *Social Contract*, discussed the political system of Geneva in detail, arguing that its democratic heritage had been betrayed by an oligarchic faction, and provided a laborious defence of his own conduct. Following the publication of the *Letters Written from the Mountain*, even the remote haven of Môtiers became unsafe. After a moment's peace on the Ile de Saint Pierre on the Lake of Bienne, immortalized in the Fifth Walk of the *Reveries of a Solitary Walker*, Rousseau finally left Switzerland. With the help of Hume, he embarked on his second phase in the wilderness.

(ii)   The English exile (1766–7)

England promised to be a place of welcome and relaxation for the troubled Jean-Jacques. His reputation was at its height and he had many admirers in that country. The political climate of tolerance towards dissenters and hostility towards French power was benign. Yet Rousseau transformed that friendly environment into a threatening and hostile one. Because of his prickliness about receiving charity, his relationship with Hume was doomed from the start. As he began work on his *Confessions*, he was descending ever deeper into an obsession that he was the victim of a conspiracy engineered by his former friends among the *philosophes*, to whose machinations Hume now seemed to be party. Biographers have laboured to distinguish paranoia from reality, for there were elements of both. Since he was singularly devoid of a sense of humour, the *philosophes'* malicious practical jokes only plunged him further into the abyss. The worst of these was the letter, written by Horace Walpole, supposedly from the King of Prussia, offering Jean-Jacques asylum in his territory. How could a man in his state see the joke in Walpole's sally, originally dreamed up, perhaps, by Hume: 'If you go on racking your brains to discover new misfortunes, choose them according to your preferences; I am King and can provide you with such misfortunes as you wish; and, unlike your enemies . . . I shall cease persecuting you when you cease taking a pride in being persecuted. Your good friend, Frederick'.[6] Through Hume's good offices, Rousseau was offered a pension by George III of England. By now demented by hatred of Hume, Rousseau refused the pension for fear of incurring the slightest obligation to the one who had once been *'le bon David'*. In May 1767 he returned to France.

(iii)   Internal exile back in France (1767–70)

Eighteenth-century absolutism was despotic, but it was also neg-
ligent, even forgiving. After leaving England, Rousseau spent three
years in the French provinces, returning to his life-long love of
botany, and undergoing a strange charade of the marriage ceremony
with Thérèse. By the end of this period of wandering, he had completed most of his *Confessions*, though he hesitated to publish them
for fear of the 'calamities' they would cause him.

(F)   Return to Paris: a life withdrawn (1770–8)

Rousseau returned to Paris in June 1770, and lived out his last years
in retirement in the rue de la Plâtrière, renamed rue Jean-Jacques
Rousseau by the Commune of Paris in 1791. During these last years,
Rousseau's obsessive behaviour became ever more marked. But his
prose style remained limpid and precise. He was able to produce the
Considerations on the Government of Poland, on commission, in 1772. In
them, he worked through central theoretical conclusions of the
Social Contract, modified them and applied them to the empirical
circumstances of the case presented to him. They betray no signs of a
deranged mind. Rather, they suggest an author whose intellectual
powers are undimmed and who is capable of reacting with sensitiv-
ity and assurance to a challenging assignment. Throughout most of
this time, Rousseau was also engaged in the demanding daily grind
of music copying which was now, once again, his main source of
income.

Having completed his *Confessions*, Rousseau gave readings from
them to influential individuals. In response, Mme d'Epinay galvan-
ized Jean-Jacques' former friends who were pilloried in their pages
to prevent their further dissemination. From the side of the authorities, the arrest warrant issued against Rousseau in 1762 had not
been cancelled. With good reason, he felt himself surrounded by
threats from all sides: 'The idea of the plot . . . was strongly based
in reality and it would be an abuse of psychiatry to try to explain
the whole of Rousseau's personality by the ready-made categories
of delirium of interpretation and delirium of persecution'.[7] In
this mood, Rousseau embarked on his last works of self-defence.
Rousseau, Judge of Jean-Jacques, written in 1772–6, was a massive coda
to the *Confessions*. In this elaborate dialogue, the common reader (*'le
français'*) is educated by 'Rousseau' to abandon the prejudices deeply
entrenched in his mind by the propaganda of *'ces messieurs'*, and to
reach a measured judgment of that ill-used genius 'Jean-Jacques'.[8]
The dénouement was bizarre. After lengthy planning, Rousseau

attempted to deposit the manuscript of *Rousseau, Judge of Jean-Jacques* at the high altar of the Cathedral of Notre Dame, to be read, he imagined, by the King of France. There he found access to the altar blocked by the 'unforeseen obstacle' of a grill.[9] At first deterred by this 'sign', Rousseau subsequently responded by making further copies of the manuscript and distributing them to more or less reliable recipients, including Condillac and a young Englishman, Brooke Boothby, who published the first Dialogue in London after Rousseau's death in 1780.

Despairing of confession and of dialogue as forms of apologia, Rousseau retreated finally to reverie. Even in his last work, the *Reveries of a Solitary Walker*, Rousseau did not abandon the hope that he might produce the definitive justification of his life, but his writing was now infused with a sublime note of withdrawal from society and identification with nature, a mystical stoicism anticipated in many of his previous works, but now reaching a point of condensation. The *Reveries* were left uncompleted on 12 April 1778, Palm Sunday. Two months later Rousseau made his last retreat to the country, this time to Ermenonville, as guest of the Marquis de Girardin, and there he died on 4 July 1778.

(G)   Sickness and solitude[10]

Throughout his life Rousseau suffered from a painful retention of urine combined with a degree of incontinence. According to his own testimony, his health was so poor that he was frequently near death. While there is no reason to disbelieve him, we should bear in mind Starobinski's caution that 'however rich Rousseau's medical dossier may be, it contains almost nothing but the patient's own declarations'.[11] Rousseau tells an agonizing story of a condition which grew increasingly grave, and which, as his trust in doctors diminished, he treated himself by self-administered catheters. As he portrays the disorder, it intensified under conditions of stress, particularly when he was called on to appear at public occasions. According to Rousseau's own self-analysis, his retreats to the country, along with his adoption of the loose 'Armenian costume', were as much a response to his medical condition as an expression of disillusion with the world of high society.

In his meticulous summary of the evidence, Starobinski concludes that we can reach no definitive judgment on the nature or cause of Rousseau's illness. The calumny that he suffered from a venereal disease was put about by his enemies, including Voltaire. Rousseau was so concerned to rebut this that he wrote in his will in 1763:

The strange illness that has consumed me for many years, and which to all appearances will end my days, is so different from all other illnesses of the same kind that I think it is important for public utility that it should be subjected to post mortem examination. That is why I wish my body to be opened up by skilled people, if that is possible, and I append a note on the nature of my illness which may be able to guide them in performing the operation. (OC 1.1224–5)

But the autopsy left this mystery, like many others in Rousseau's life, unresolved, as the assembled surgeons failed to find any abnormality in the organs.

(H)   The three axes of Rousseau's thought

Rousseau's published and unpublished work now fills over 60,000 pages of the *Oeuvres complètes*,[12] and the *Correspondance complète*, comprising letters to and from the author, runs to 49 volumes. The secondary literature, in many languages, is massive, and increases by the day. The present book is selective. It covers a limited number of themes in Rousseau's thought, and it concentrates on just three of his texts, the *Discourse of Inequality* (the *Second Discourse*), the *Emile* and the *Social Contract*. These three constitute the axes of Rousseau's idea of formation. The formation of the human race is the axis of the *Second Discourse*, the formation of the individual that of the *Emile*, and the formation of the citizen that of the *Social Contract*. The three axes are linked by Rousseau's insight that 'we must study society by men and men by society. Those who want to treat politics and morality separately will never understand anything about either of them' (Em IV.524/235).

Rousseau is an unreliable guide to the value of his own works. In his letter to Malesherbes of 12 January 1762 (LMa 1136/575) he refers to the *First Discourse*, the *Second Discourse* and the *Emile* as his 'three principal writings'. Admittedly, the *Social Contract* was still uncompleted at that date, and that would explain its omission. Writing four years later to the Rev. Hugh Blair, Hume says that he thought *Julie, ou la Nouvelle Héloïse* was 'his Master-piece . . . tho' he himself [Rousseau] told me that he valu'd most his *Contrat sociale* [*sic*]; which is as preposterous a judgment as that of Milton, who preferd the Paradise regaind to all his other Performances'.[13] In the end, as a commentator, one must rely on one's own estimate of the value of the texts, rather than on the author's. I increasingly agree with Hume, and many of Rousseau's eighteenth-century readers, that *Julie, ou la Nouvelle Héloïse* is not only the most enjoyable of

Rousseau's writings, but also the one in which he develops his psychological insights in the most subtle and delicate form. The epistolary novel is the perfect vehicle for bringing out the ambiguities and conflicts within the hearts of men and women. It gives the author the rare occasion to avoid the pitfalls of dogmatism and rhetorical overkill, and leaves the reader disturbed and intrigued, without being hectored. But to expound the novel as a philosophical text would demand more familiarity with this literary genre than I possess. I have therefore used *Julie, ou la Nouvelle Héloïse* to illustrate themes which run through my three chosen texts, rather than as an object of extended exegesis.

My decision to make relatively little use of the *First Discourse* needs more justification. I have already indicated its importance as a rhetorical statement of Rousseau's critique of culture. As such, it constitutes an almost caricatural counterpoint to the received wisdom of the Enlightenment, encapsulated in Condorcet's formula of the 'indissoluble chain of truth, happiness and virtue'. Against this, Rousseau claimed, provocatively, that there is no such chain, and that 'happiness and virtue' are both undermined rather than fostered by 'the restoration of the sciences and the arts'. Important as it is as a rhetorical statement, I have little to add to the analyses made of the *First Discourse* by others,[14] and so in this case I have followed Rousseau's judgment on his own work, that it is 'mediocre' and 'slight'. He was even more dismissive of the *First Discourse* in the *Confessions*:

> this work, full of warmth and strength, is absolutely lacking in logic and order; of all the ones that have come from my pen it is the weakest in reasoning and the poorest in unity and harmony . . . (Conf VIII.352/295)[15]

(I)   Hume's generous judgment

With a degree of flattery, Hume wrote to Rousseau, before the unhappy dénouement of their relationship: 'you are the person whom I most revere both for the Force of your Genius and the Greatness of your mind. . . .'[16] I hope that readers of this book will be persuaded of the soundness of that judgment, and that they will conclude that Rousseau deserves if not reverence, at least respect, for the qualities which Hume recognized in him on 2 July 1762.

I

Rousseau's Divided Thought: the Morality of the Senses and the Morality of Duty

(A)   *Two themes in tension*

In his *Confessions*, Rousseau provides us with a remarkable résumé of a book which he never wrote:

> Looking within myself and seeking in others the factors upon which these different states of being rested [*tenoient*], I discovered that they depended [*dépendoient*] to a great extent on the prior impression of external objects, and that, we, being continually modified through the agency of our senses and our organs, bore the effects of these modifications, without being aware of it, in our thoughts, our feelings, and even our actions. Numerous striking examples that I had collected put the matter beyond all dispute; and thanks to their physical basis they seemed to me capable of providing an external régime which, varied according to circumstances, could put or keep the mind in the state most conducive to virtue. From what errors would reason be preserved, and what vices would be choked even before birth, if one knew how to compel the brute functions to support the moral order which they so often disturb? . . . it seemed to me an easy task to put it into a book which would be as pleasant to read as it was to write. I made very little progress with this work, however, the title of which was *The Morality of the Senses* or *The Wise Man's Materialism*. Distractions of which the cause will soon be clear took my attention away from it. (Conf IX.409/ 343–4)

Even if Rousseau abandoned the project of writing a book with that title, the theme of *The Morality of the Senses* runs throughout

11

his work, though it is in constant tension with another equally important theme, that of the irreducible struggle between duty and inclination. The latter is an austere deontology, in which virtue is understood as a 'state of war' against the passions. The tension is one between a naturalistic morality of unity and a Kantian morality of division. Some commentators have argued that Rousseau resolved the tension by replacing naturalism by deontology, moving from a starting point close to the *philosophes* to an end point close to Kant. Against them I shall maintain that the tension between the two themes remains unresolved to the end of Rousseau's life, and provides the dynamic of his most challenging work.

In the passage with which we started, Rousseau summarizes the doctrine of the morality of the senses in a few condensed sentences. In them he sketches some components of a theory of psychological 'dependence' (rather than determinism), according to which our 'different states of being depend to a great extent on the prior impression of external objects'. He does not explain in any detail how 'we' (as totalities) are 'modified . . . through the agency of our senses and our organs', and bear 'the effect of these modifications in our ideas, our feelings and even our actions'. The morality of the senses has a 'physical basis', but Rousseau does not provide any physical model of the mechanism of modification and dependence. We can speculate why he avoids detailed theorizing in this domain. Is it that he is opposed to any kind of systematic work, as he sometimes says himself, whether because of his natural laziness, or because he has a more principled dislike for the 'spirit of system'? It is true that Rousseau says of himself:

> I take pleasure in meditating, in searching, in inventing. Putting things in order disgusts me. The proof that I have less reasoning power than wit is that it is the transitions that always cost me the most effort, and that would never happen if the ideas were all connected in my head. (MP 1128–9)

But, despite these self-deprecating remarks, Rousseau applies himself systematically to many philosophical problems. So the cause of his reluctance to push deeper into questions of mind and matter needs to be investigated. The explanation must be that he was on the one hand attracted by a monistic, physicalist model of human psychology, but on the other hand he envisaged that any investigations into that model would lead inevitably to the iron determinism espoused by La Mettrie, d'Holbach and the materialists of the *Encyclopédie*. And since he held that freedom of choice is both an irreducible given of introspection and also a necessary condition of our moral life, he preferred either to sit on the fence or else to reach only the most tentative conclusions concerning the mind/body problem.

As psychologist, in Book II of the *Emile*, Rousseau promises to deliver a model which looks more materialist than dualist. It will describe:

> the cultivation of a sort of sixth sense called common sense, less because it is common to all men than because it results from the well-regulated use of the other senses, and because it instructs us about the nature of things by the conjunction of all their appearances. This sixth sense has consequently no special organ. It resides only in the brain, and its sensations, purely internal, are called perceptions or ideas . . . It is the art of comparing them among themselves that is called human reason. (Em II.417/157–8)

Rousseau goes on to describe the progress of reason as the development of this sixth sense:

> Thus what I call the reason of the senses [*raison sensitive*] or childish reason consists in forming simple ideas by the conjunction of several sensations, and what I call intellectual or human reason consists in forming complex ideas by the conjunction of several simple ideas. (ibid.)

There is no trace of dualism here. Transition from one stage of reason to another is channelled through the sixth sense, a physical function of a physical organ, the brain.

But as a moralist Rousseau finds himself driven into a metaphysical dualism of substances, propounded explicitly in the 'Profession of Faith of the Savoyard Vicar', for whom 'man is free in his actions, and, as such, animated by an immaterial substance' (Em IV.586–7/281). From the supposedly evident premiss that human beings are free agents capable of thought, Rousseau, through the Vicar, rapidly derives the conclusion that a dualism of substances, material and immaterial, must be true. He had already rejected Locke's hypothesis, enthusiastically adopted by Voltaire in the thirteenth of his *Philosophical Letters*, that matter might be capable of thinking (Em IV.584–5/279).[1] When writing in his own persona, rather than the Vicar's, for instance in the letter to Jacob Vernes of 18 February 1758 (CC 5#616, p. 33), Rousseau retreats from the argument to a position which he admits will be labelled 'prejudice' by his opponents. His response is that his 'prejudice' is 'more persuasive' than their reason when reason leads to the counter-intuitive conclusion that one should 'prefer to give feeling to stones rather than accord a soul to man.'

None of this is serious philosophy. I mention it only to mark off a debate into which Rousseau is drawn against his better judgment, and which he could have left alone without prejudicing the valuable insights of the morality of the senses. In the passages from Book II of the *Emile*, the physical *sensus communis* plays the active role of coordinating sensations and ideas. In the passages from the 'Profession of Faith' in contrast, Rousseau is driven towards dualism by the imperative to defend the active, autonomous nature of the human being. In the latter, Rousseau, using the Vicar as his spokesman, attributes the active role to the soul, the passive to the body. He glosses over the problems of interaction between soul and body, and ignores the sophisticated engagements with that problem which had been at the heart of philosophical investigation since Descartes.[2] Having raised the problem, he simply abandons it, and indeed it is a problem in which he should never have become involved at the beginning, since his own views on the psychology of social interaction, on pedagogy, on the formation of the personality and on political evolution are all independent of the problem of interaction and of the metaphysics of substance.

Rousseau's own theory might better be labelled 'the wise man's realism' (rather than 'the wise man's materialism'). What he outlines is not a mechanistic determinism, but rather a theory of the affective field in which the moral agents are situated and make their choices. Rousseau describes the physiological, psychological and social constituents of this field with precision. He assigns a greater importance to the passions than some of his rationalist predecessors, but here he differs little from most of his contemporaries, including Hume. Where he shows true originality is in anticipating elements of a theory which would later be rigorously elaborated by Gestalt psychologists. The ideas of the *environment* and of the *imagination* are the keys to Rousseau's theory, according to which one encounters, and at the same time constructs, one's identity by interacting with one's environment. In the educational programme of the *Emile*, this environment should consist first of a natural world, governed by causal laws, which only later comes to be inhabited by other moral agents. One begins by encountering one's environment as a given, which one then transforms and enlarges as one interacts with one's fellow men and women. In this interaction the imagination plays a key role. One can become enslaved by one's imagination, or one can master it, and so take some active part in re-figuring the foreground and background of one's Gestalt.

Despite his hostility to professional philosophers and to the 'spirit

14

of system', Rousseau poses himself a formidable array of philosophical tasks which will require systematic solutions. He will
undertake to instruct the public in the elements of the moral life, to
construct a psychological model of the nature of men and women, of
the ways in which that nature is formed and transformed, and finally
a model of the social and political institutions within which different types of personality prosper or perish. This last model leads
Rousseau to meta-theoretical reflections on the interaction between
the individual and society. To say that Rousseau addresses this array
of problems is not to say that he solves them, or even that he orders
them in a wholly coherent framework. But the morality of the senses
provides the guiding thread through much of his thought.

(B)   'Man is a naturally good creature'

The fundamental principle of all morality, about which I have
reasoned in all my works . . . is that man is a naturally good
creature, who loves justice and order; that there is no original
perversity in the human heart, and that the first movements of
nature are always right. I have made clear that the single passion
with which man is born, namely love of self, is in itself indifferent
with respect to good and evil, and that it becomes good or evil
only by accident, in the circumstances in which it develops . . .
(LdeB 935)

Here Rousseau defends his work in the letter to Charles de
Beaumont, Archbishop of Paris, who had banned the *Emile* for its
heretical denial of original sin. Far from withdrawing that denial,
Rousseau calls it the fundamental principle of all morality, and
proceeds to expound it in detail. So far, the principle is identical
with the morality of the senses and has no metaphysical implications. But it soon develops into a metaphysical dualism according to
which:

Man is not a simple creature; he is composed of two
substances. . . . That demonstrated, it emerges that love of self is
not a simple passion, but has two principles, that of intelligence
and that of sensation [*un être intelligent et un être sensitif*], and the
well-being of each of these is not the same. The appetite of the
senses tends to the well-being of the body, the love of order to the
well-being of the soul. (LdeB 936)

But in this Letter, as elsewhere, the morality of the senses is
independent of the metaphysics:

15

[The love of order], when developed and made active, is called conscience, but conscience develops and becomes active only as men become enlightened. . . . When . . . men come to cast their eyes on their neighbours, they also begin to see how they are related to them and to things, and they formulate ideas of convenience, justice and order; they become aware of moral beauty, and conscience becomes active. Now they have virtues, and if they also have vices, it is because their interests clash with one another and their ambition awakens at the same time as their enlightenment increases. But so long as there is less opposition between their interests than there is convergence between their enlightened minds, men are essentially good. (ibid.)

All the central ideas of the morality of the senses are here. Reason and enlightenment are morally neutral. They develop only in society, where conscience is called upon to identify and motivate virtuous behaviour when duty and interest clash. The world in which the environment is arranged so that such clashes are rare is one in which our natural goodness can survive. In all other circumstances conscience and virtue will be needed.

(C) 'That great maxim of morality'

Describing the behaviour of his tender-hearted but feckless father, Rousseau writes that he derived from it:

that great maxim of morality, perhaps the only one that is of any practical use in morality, to avoid situations which put our duties in opposition to our interests and which show that our good resides in the misfortune of others. For I am sure that in such situations, however sincere the love of virtue which we apply, sooner or later we weaken without noticing it. We become unjust and wicked in fact, though we have not ceased to be just and good in our souls. (Conf II.56/47)

For all the hypocrisy of the conclusion, the 'great maxim' itself embodies the central idea of the morality of the senses. Rousseau explains the maxim in a note, written in his own voice, to *Julie, ou la Nouvelle Héloïse*:

Despite ourselves, our different situations determine and change all the affections of our hearts: we shall be vicious and bad insofar as we have an interest to be so, and unfortunately the chains with which we are burdened make it ever more in our interest to be so.

The effort of correcting the disorder of our desires is nearly always vain, and is rarely true: it is not so much our desires that need to be changed, but the situations which produce them. If we want to be good, let us remove the relations which prevent us from being so. (JNH III.20. Note added by Rousseau to Rey's 1763 edition, quoted in OC 2.1558)

The pragmatic comment that 'the effort to correct the disorder of our desires is nearly always vain' is followed by a moral judgment that it is 'rarely true'. For those who must constantly 'correct' such 'disorder' could never live integrated or authentic lives.

(D)   Contradiction

The goal of the morality of the senses is the self-reconciliation of the individual: 'Make man one [*Rendez l'homme un*], and you will make him as happy as he can be' (PolFr VI.3.510/41). In lamenting the loss of unity, Julie expresses Rousseau's profoundest aspiration: 'Is it not shameful [*indigne*] in a man never to be able to live in harmony with himself . . .' (JNH III.18.362/298). Rousseau encounters a world whose inhabitants live in contradiction with themselves, and returns in all his works to investigate the different modalities of that contradiction, which sets our state against our desires, our duties against our inclinations, our institutions against our nature.

(E)   Imagination and amour-propre

The fundamental modality of contradiction, that of our state against our desires, precedes all morality, and is produced by every social order. It is a commonplace that we all have ambitions which outstrip our capacities. Rousseau transforms this into an interesting thesis by locating it within a complex psychological model. That in turn contains an element of stoicism, an aspiration to regain the condition of the 'savage', who 'lives within himself' (2D 193/66). After the transition to the social world, that goal is never achieved automatically. Imagination develops, and leads us into an ever-expanding imaginary world, the 'world of chimeras'. It becomes the source of many of our miseries, from which we can be delivered only if we work on their source. Early in the child's education, this means that we should strive to restrict its imagination: 'The real world has its limits, the imaginary world is infinite. Unable to enlarge the one, let us narrow the other . . .' (Em II.305/81). But later, the imagination must be correctly channelled and focused. Like our other faculties, it is, in itself, morally neutral. While it can lead to psychological enslavement and dependence, it is also the key to a healthy socialization, putting us in our neighbours' place and allowing the development of compassion. The social world is, and must be, one of mutual recognition, in which we find ourselves in the eyes of others. Without imagination we could not enter that world.

The second modality of contradiction, which sets our duties against our inclinations, marks the world of morality. Rousseau does not make a sharp distinction between moral and psychological questions. He registers it as a fact that once individuals have left infancy and humanity has left the pure state of nature, they are condemned to live together, in society: 'Must we destroy Societies, annihilate thine and mine, and go back to live in forests with the Bears? A conclusion in the manner of my adversaries . . .' (2D noteIX.207/ 79). There is no 'return' for Rousseau. Now that we live together, we must regulate our inclinations in relation to those of others, from the most intimate circle, that of the family, through the political order of the state, to humanity as a whole. *Amour-propre*, fed by the imagination, is the dangerous but unavoidable source of good and evil in society. Our duties lay down the limits to the legitimate play of the imagination.

The third modality of contradiction, setting our nature against our social institutions, structures the political domain. There, one's freedom of choice is regulated by that of one's neighbours. Each individual functions within a field of objects of choice, arrayed by the imagination. A well-ordered system of institutions limits that field so that we are not presented with objects of choice which will lead us beyond the bounds of legitimate interaction.

(F)   Three strategies of identification

Throughout his work Rousseau seeks for strategies[3] whereby individuals can identify themselves with different totalities larger than they, and to find in them a resolution of the contradictions which tear them apart. Society, nature and the divine order are three such totalities. The starting point of all these strategies is self-love [*amour de soi*], which we extend beyond our immediate selves by means of compassion, that innate repugnance at seeing a fellow creature suffer (2D 154/36):

> when the force of an expansive soul makes me identify myself
> with my neighbour, and I feel my own self, so to speak, in him,
> then it is in order not to suffer myself that I want him not to
> suffer. I am interested in him out of love for myself, and the reason
> for the precept is in nature itself which inspires in me the desire

18

for my own well-being in whatever place I feel myself to exist.
(Em IV.523.Fn/235Fn)

(i) Identification with society

This first strategy calls for fundamental political change if it is to be
realized, and Rousseau is only rarely optimistic about the chances of
its success. Here the apparently negative drive of *'repugnance* at seeing a fellow creature suffer' can be transformed by well-ordered
social institutions into something more positive. When one sees
one's duties and interests harmonizing, one's particular identity
begins to enlarge: 'I take an interest in him (my neighbour) out of
love for myself'. Rousseau's political theory specifies the conditions
in which a rational consensus may arise. When those conditions are
realized, citizens 'will be able to come to identify themselves in some
way with this larger whole' (3D 259/155), and the general will finds
expression. Such consensus is derived from each man's preference for
himself and consequently from the nature of man (SC II.4.373/149).
But the preferences of individuals coincide with the common good
only in specific circumstances, that is when all citizens are free and
relatively equal (SC II.11), and there are no political factions (SC
II.4). In other circumstances, when the necessary conditions are not
realized, that is to say in most existing societies, there is no basis for
a rational consensus, particular interests and the common interest do
not coincide, and individuals cannot identify themselves with society. According to this reading, Rousseau's political theory is to be
understood as an extension of the morality of the senses. If it is
correct, then identification is no longer to be understood as a
mystical fusion of the individual with the whole, but rather as the
outcome of a transformed social environment which would
encourage individuals to recognize their shared interests. This
does not mean that the political theory is rendered simple or that
the problem of totalitarianism is resolved. But it makes the goal
of Rousseau's aspirations for the new political order more com-
prehensible, even if it does not ultimately make them more
palatable.

(ii) Retreat from society: identification with the natural order

Where the first strategy is one of forward movement, demanding the
transformation of the social world, both the second and the third
strategies represent a retreat from society, a transformation of the
self, not of the world. The second strategy amounts to a reversal of
the first. The languor, which had always been a recurring mood of

19

Rousseau's works, comes to dominate his last ones, in particular the *Reveries of the Solitary Walker*. By then Rousseau has abandoned all hope that the social world could be transformed. Reacting to the *Encyclopédistes'* plot against him, part real, part imagined, Rousseau judges that he was 'never really made for civil society' (Reveries VI.1059/103). That is an extreme judgment, for Rousseau is distancing himself not only from the corrupt world, dominated by factions, but from all 'civil society, where everything is difficulty, obligation and duty'. In escaping from that world, Rousseau seeks to retreat into the natural world, where:

> earth in the harmony of her three kingdoms offers man a living, fascinating and enchanting spectacle, the only one of which his eyes and his heart can never grow weary. . . . The more sensitive the soul of the observer, the greater the ecstasy aroused in him by this harmony. At such times his senses are possessed by a deep and delightful reverie, and in a state of blissful self-abandonment he loses himself in the immensity of this beautiful system, with which he feels himself identified. (Reveries VII.1062–3/108)

The terms are the same, feeling, identification, system or order. But Rousseau now translates them into a different idiom, that of the romanticism of nature. At this point in his work, and not before, Rousseau can rightly be called a romantic.

(iii)   Religion: identification with the divine order

Where the first two strategies are exclusive, the second displacing the first, the third coexists with both the first two. Having parted company with the *Encyclopédistes* after the *Second Discourse*, Rousseau spends much of the rest of his life fighting atheism on two fronts. The first front is the one established by his enemies, the traditional arguments of reason for and against the existence of God. As we shall see, Rousseau takes those arguments seriously, and puts into the Savoyard Vicar's mouth serious, if not wholly convincing, arguments of a conventional kind. Rousseau's conclusion is that on the basis of reason alone no decisive victory is possible between believers and unbelievers. Absolute atheism, he holds, is no less dogmatic than the religious dogmatism it opposes. Leaving that stalemate unresolved, Rousseau proceeds to the second front, that of his own choosing, what he calls in his letter to Voltaire the 'proof from feeling' [*preuve de sentiment*]: 'It is inhumane to trouble peaceful souls, and bring despair to men for no purpose, when what you want to teach them is neither certain nor useful'. The 'proof from feeling' is close to the morality of the senses: 'a thousand preferences draw me to the side of greater consolation and add the weight of hope to the scale of reason' (LV 1070–2). Consolation and hope are the feelings on which the proof depends. Sceptical critics would point out that duty and interest would coincide only in the hereafter. One might also ask whether troubled souls who rely on this proof could find in it a means to reconcile themselves to their lives on earth. The Savoyard Vicar claims to have found in it some respite from 'that continual alternation' which put him 'always in contradiction with himself' (Em IV.602/291). Rousseau goes beyond the Vicar's cautious position when he puts into Julie's mouth a near-mystical identification with the divine order: 'It is in contemplating this divine model that the soul purifies and raises itself' (JNH III.18.358/295). She continues with what must be a heretical *reductio* of the proof from feeling: 'even if the great being with which we are concerned did not exist, it would still be good for us to be ceaselessly concerned with it, in order for us to be more masters of ourselves, stronger, happier and wiser' (JNH III.18.359/295). In other words, if God did not exist, it would be better to invent Him!

(G)   Julie's 'Elysium': dialectic of nature and art

[On entering Julie's 'Elysium'] I was struck by a welcome sensation of freshness coming from the vivid greenery, from the flowers on every side, from the babbling of running water and from the song of a thousand birds, which touched my imagination as much as my senses. At the same time I believed that I was looking at the wildest, the most solitary place in nature. I seemed to be the first mortal to have penetrated that deserted spot. Surprised, struck, transported by this unexpected sight, I stood for a moment motionless and let out an involuntary cry of enthusiasm: '. . . Julie, the end of the earth is at your doorstep!' 'Many people have the same impression as you,' she replied with a smile, '. . . But you know, the grass here used to be quite dry, the trees were quite sparse and scattered and gave little shade, and there was no water. Now you see it fresh, green, decked out, adorned, flowery and watered. How much effort do you think it has cost me to put it into that state? . . .'
'Good heavens,' I said, 'you only needed to neglect it. The place is charming, I agree, but it is rustic and abandoned. I see no human labour in it. You have shut the gate; the water has reached here somehow or other; nature alone has done all the rest. You yourself could not have done it as well as she.'
'It is true,' she replied, 'that nature has done it all, but under my

direction, and there is nothing here that I have not ordered.'
(JNH IV.11.471/387–8)

This exchange between Julie, calm and masterful, and her former lover, St Preux, gushing and naïve, condenses Rousseau's attempt to realize the morality of the senses within an imperfect world. There we are to recover the four basic elements of human nature, freedom, self-preservation [*amour de soi*], compassion and perfectibility, and to channel them through a reformed education and politics, by a careful modulation of *amour-propre*. Rousseau envisages a society whose members would be equal and autonomous, and from which exploitation would be banished. Without the necessary channelling, degeneration is inevitable. So far, the metaphor of Julie's Elysium is not hard to translate. But, when we press it further, difficulties emerge. If we use artifice to make a 'natural' garden, we encounter technical and aesthetic problems, but no moral ones. But the latter appear as soon as we leave the garden for the realm of human relations. Rousseau tells us that 'one must use a great deal of art to prevent social man from being totally artificial' (Em IV.640/317). If one person succeeds in 'preventing' another from being something, it would seem that the former must be manipulating and denying the autonomy of the latter, and so breaking Rousseau's fundamental moral imperative. If, on the other hand, one attempts to 'prevent oneself' from being something, one would seem to be embarked on a strategy of bad faith, in which one must deceive oneself in order to succeed. We now sketch a response to the charge that the morality of the senses must lead to one or other of these unacceptable strategies.

(H) The perils of manipulation and bad faith

(i) Manipulation in education: the tutor and the pupil

Rousseau advises the tutor to 'take an opposite route with [his] pupil' (Em II.362–3/120). The conventional route is one in which the adult argues, cajoles, reasons and threatens the child. Rousseau argues that such an approach is useless because the child soon learns to play the game of interaction and finally masters the teacher. Rousseau proposes to replace this frustrating game by what he calls 'negative education', which is appropriate for the pre-adolescent child. The tutor here acts as stage setter rather than as interactive participant. His task is to keep clear the field of choice for his pupil, to limit the range of intentional objects available to him. At this stage the child is to encounter the world as a world of material objects governed by natural laws, not as a world of human beings endowed with wills to be manipulated. This would allow the young child to develop his autonomy, free of domination by 'caprices' which have not been 'fomented'. From this starting point, the child will become an adolescent, and the adolescent an adult, while still remaining 'master of his will' once he has entered the dangerous world of political and moral relations. As one makes the passage to that world, one's imagination begins to flourish, as one discovers oneself as the subject of *amour-propre*. Those who have been well schooled by the morality of the senses will continue to master their imaginations. The rest, badly raised in the 'school of the world', will remain trapped in the vicious play of domination and subordination. Everything depends on *timing*, on the educator's ability to intervene (or refrain from intervening) at the right moment, neither too early nor too late. Already in Book I of the *Emile*, Rousseau is warning the tutor to prepare from afar the realm of freedom (Em I.282/63). The scene must be properly set if the adult is to perform as a free agent upon it.

(ii)   Manipulation in politics: the Lawgiver and the people

A central figure in Rousseau's political theory is the Lawgiver [*légis-lateur, nomothetes*]. A first reading of *Social Contract* II.7 suggests a sinister, totalitarian figure, who manipulates the people. In apparently élitist fashion, Rousseau marks off the 'superior intelligence' of the Lawgiver from the 'passions' of the people, which the Lawgiver sees, but does not experience. Initially, the very existence of such a figure seems incompatible with the normative requirement that legitimacy derive from, and only from, the general will of the people. The paradox of the Lawgiver, like that of the educator, can be resolved if we again take seriously the importance of *timing*, which now needs to be combined with the distinction which Rousseau makes between 'principles of right', the conditions of legitimacy, universally applicable, and 'maxims of politics', to be realized in the political institutions of particular societies. The task of the Lawgiver is to lay out maxims of politics, fundamental laws or constitutional conventions suitable for a given people. Rousseau himself tried to fulfil the role of Lawgiver by writing constitutional documents for two societies, Poland and Corsica, but he gives only a brief theoretical explanation of that role in the *Social Contract*. There the Lawgiver remains a mysterious figure. But it is clear that he is not supposed to deprive the people of its sovereign will. Instead he is to discern the field within which that will may be most effectively expressed. He must have confidence in his own mastery of *timing*, be prepared 'to work in one century and enjoy the reward in another', just as Emile's tutor forms the mind and body of the child, so that he may be able to exercise his freedom as an adult. The tutor then retires from the scene.

According to this reading, the tutor and the Lawgiver set the scene for the working of the adult will, but do not manipulate it after the scene is set.

(iii)   Bad faith

Starobinski levels the following charge against the morality of the senses:

> The use of the psychological effects of the world of the senses is an artifice which compromises freedom. One and the same man cannot, without bad faith, construct a magical stage setting and passively abandon himself to its magic. He cannot fail to know that he himself voluntarily put together the very thing which he now wants to undergo as though it were an involuntary influence. If he has deliberately submitted to the influence of external things . . . he must recognize that he can equally freely withdraw from that influence. The strategy of the morality of the senses reveals that Rousseau has decided to give himself up absolutely to things, while immediately forgetting that his decision was taken in full freedom.[4]

The objection is a powerful one, but it may not have reached the two central elements of the morality of the senses as it has been interpreted here, the idea of *timing* and the idea of the intentional *field* of choice confronting the agent. On this interpretation, one may arrange one's field of choice oneself, in advance, in such a way that certain objects of choice may be present or absent in the future. It is not evident that one who sets the scene thus is necessarily guilty of bad faith. It would of course be impossible to be consistent if one tried to change the set and to act out one's role at the same time. Such an attempt would impose an intolerable strain on the individual. But it would be wrong to think that anyone who engages in such stage-setting must slip from the active to the passive mode from one moment to the next. In the course of one's life one is formed, first by others, then by oneself, and during that formation the phenomenological presentation of one's world changes. As the imagination develops, threatens to dominate us, submits to our control, and, thus controlled, serves to liberate us in the social world, figure and ground change places in our Gestalt. The individual can be liberated from the 'world of chimeras' only within an ordered and

24

disciplined framework, and there alone are 'the limits of the possible less narrow than we think' (SC III.12.425/189). Starobinski concludes his objection thus:

> The morality of the senses is supposed to free the mind from the strain of reflection. Its aim is to set up automatic mechanisms which will turn a life of immediate experience into a life of virtue. It would succeed perfectly if we could deliver ourselves naïvely to our sensations while forgetting that those very sensations have been put to work by reflection.[5]

To this we might respond that there are parallels to the morality of the senses in other kinds of training. The dancer, the skier or the painter all undergo long periods of disciplined apprenticeship in which the teacher imposes on the pupils, and then the pupils on themselves, drills which involve artifice and reflection, so that, at the end, the good learners will be able to execute their movements naturally, without reflection, concentrating their attention directly on the task to be performed. This process of physical training, which passes from the pre-reflective via the reflective to the final stage of the 'post-reflective', does not involve bad faith. Rousseau's morality of the senses suggests that moral training could involve a similar process.[6]

(I)   'Virtue is a state of war'

The morality of the senses is to be understood as the search for the reconciliation of the individual with society, with God, with oneself, for a new harmony of our duty with our interest, of our reason with our passions, of our soul with our body. In the real world, such harmony is always beyond our reach, and our moral life is marked by constant conflict.

In propounding the morality of the senses, Rousseau regards psychological conflict with alarm, as a symptom of the insuperable division, even disintegration, within the individual, to be deplored and, if possible, avoided.

But Rousseau is also drawn to a more strenuous morality of virtue and duty. In propounding it, he rates the moment of conflict more positively, as the necessary route to self-knowledge and self-mastery. It provides the dynamic for our moral formation and realizes our capacity for perfectibility. On her deathbed Julie sees the end of moral conflict as the end of the desire to live:[7]

> this little room contains all that is dear to my heart, and perhaps

all that is best on earth; I am surrounded by everything that interests me, the whole universe is here for me . . . I see nothing that extends my being, and nothing that divides it; it is present in everything around me, and no portion of it is distant from me; my imagination has nothing to do, I have nothing to desire; for me to feel and to enjoy are the same thing; I live at every moment in everything I love; I am sated with happiness and life. Death, come when you want to. I no longer fear you. I have lived. I have anticipated you. I no longer have any new feelings to experience. You no longer have any secrets to hide from me. (JNH VI.8.689/ 566)

From this point of view, the successful morality of the senses would be down-graded to the *negative* status of mere chance coincidence, yielding no principled guidance for moral choice: 'there is no virtue in following your inclinations and indulging your taste for doing good just when you feel like it; virtue consists in subordinating your inclinations to to the call of duty . . .' (Reveries VI.1052–3/ 96). In the course of his extended homily to Emile, as the pupil finally reaches adulthood, the Vicar expounds the idea of virtue as struggle in these words:

The word *virtue* comes from *force*; force is the basis of all virtue. Virtue belongs only to a'being who is feeble in his nature and strong in his will . . . What, then, is the virtuous man? It is he who knows how to conquer his affections; for then he follows his reason and his conscience; he does his duty; he keeps himself in order, and nothing can make him deviate from it. (Em V.817–8/ 444–5)[8]

St Preux expresses the same thought (with a degree of humbug, perhaps) to Julie in an epigram: 'Dear friend, don't you realize that virtue is a state of war, and that, to live in it, one always has some combat to wage against oneself?' (JNH VI.7.682/560).

But just as Rousseau's political theory tells us that a social order based on force is by definition illegitimate, so, in his understanding of the human soul, he is never fully reconciled to the morality of virtue and duty. His unease surfaces in the rhetoric of *Rousseau, Judge of Jean-Jacques*, which goes beyond force to violence: 'virtue is nothing but labour and combat. . . . But should one put oneself in these violent situations from which such cruel duties arise?' (RJJJ 2D.823/126).[9]

There are three moments of Rousseau's thought on this topic: (i) a moment of positive utopia, where he believes that the morality of the senses can be realized in a transformed environment; (ii) a Kantian moment, where he stresses the merit of overcoming one's inclinations; and (iii) a moment of resignation, where he despairs of the possibility of either of the first two moments and seeks harmony by retreat, by isolation, by a policy of avoidance rather than confrontation. These three moments are not precisely linked to a chronological development of Rousseau's thought. Elements of each of them are present from the earliest to the latest works. The first two moments are both present in *Julie, ou la Nouvelle Héloïse*, the *Emile* and the *Social Contract*. The third becomes increasingly dominant in the posthumous autobiographical works, particularly clearly in *Rousseau, Judge of Jean-Jacques*, where Rousseau says of Jean-Jacques that he prefers to flee temptations rather than have to vanquish them, since he has little confidence in his success in such a combat. (RJJJ 2D.855/151). Such comments, it is true, are presented anecdotally to highlight peculiarities of the author's own character. But they also constitute a strategy open to others to adopt in the face of the recalcitrance of the real social world, one that is consistent with the morality of the senses in that it links external conditions to psychological possibilities.

But Rousseau holds that conscience, whose task it is to identify our duty, is itself a kind of feeling. So, even when he is apparently furthest from the morality of the senses, and closest to a morality of virtue and duty, he does not establish the same clear distinction between the two as Kant and later deontologists would do. To understand this, we note Rousseau's reaction to the Abbé Cahagne's reading of *Julie, ou la Nouvelle Héloïse*, according to which it is a drama of duty versus passion.[10] The Abbé is a subtle reader, who wants to reconcile his enthusiasm for the novel as a work of passionate fiction with the requirement to interpret it in a fashion acceptable to religion. He finds within it not one, but two, struggles between duty and passion. As man of the cloth, he praises the author for describing this combat of duty and honour against love, how religion alone could make duty triumph. But as man of the heart, he finds Julie unfaithful to another duty, her duty towards Love, and finds his heart murmuring against that betrayal. In his reply to the Abbé, Rousseau brushes off Julie's betrayal of love, which, he says, remains with her in its entirety. As to the struggle with conventional duty, Rousseau simply denies that Julie's motivation should be thus construed. Rather he wanted to depict Julie as faithful to her character. By that he means that Julie had to pose feeling against feeling, rather than feeling against duty. Could she survive the realization that her conduct, having caused the death of her mother, risked causing that of her father too? Here is Rousseau's reply:

> Whenever in a novel one depicts a particular action one is not concerned with the moral question but with the imitation of nature. It is not a question of knowing whether Julie acted rightly or wrongly in marrying, but whether, acting freely in the given situation and consistently with her character, the decision she had to take was either to obey her father or, having seen him on his knees in floods of tears, to hold out against his despair, never allowing herself to be deflected. (Letter to the Abbé Cahagne, 3/4 March 1761, CC 8#1336, p. 203)[11]

Rousseau suggests that this is the perspective of a novel, rather than that of a moral treatise, but the distinction cannot be absolute. For, as we noted above, Rousseau holds that there is nothing in our moral life that is wholly beyond feeling, since conscience is a feeling, innate within us, unlike reason, which is acquired. It is an active feeling, which, when enlightened by reason, can be pitted against the passions, drives which, too often, hold us, as passive victims, in their grip (Em IV.600/290). So even when they are considered in the most deontological fashion, conflicts within the hearts of moral agents between duty and inclination are fought out as conflicts between feeling and feeling.

(J)   The fate of the morality of the senses

On a Kantian reading, the morality of the senses represents only a phase, and a relatively unimportant phase, in Rousseau's thought. Thus Robert Osmont, editor of *Rousseau, juge de Jean-Jacques*, writes: 'Rousseau finally understood that his work must rise above the materialism of the wise man in order to show us the true destination of his being',[12] a destination which is the Kantian realm of virtue. On our reading, the latter morality did not displace the former in Rousseau's thought. Rather, the two moralities remained in constant tension within it. If Rousseau abandoned the project of theorizing the morality of the senses early in his life, its theme returns to dominate his last works. In books II and III of the *Emile* he distinguishes two stages of reason, first 'reason of the senses' (*raison sensitive*), and subsequently 'intellectual reason'. Moral education in turn passes through three phases, each governed by its own law, first that of necessity, then that of utility, and finally that of morality proper, 'that which is suitable and good' (Em III.429/167). It is tempting to think that the morality of the senses is restricted to the first two phases, and is displaced by a Kantian morality in the third phase. But Rousseau is investigating a story of development and tension, rather than one of displacement. Ideally, as our interests develop, we come to identify them with the common interest. Because that ideal is never realized, virtue remains a 'state of war'. Rousseau has little hope for victory in that war. He would prefer to find peace in the morality of the senses. But he has even less confidence that it will be possible to reform the corrupt society in which we live, so that it will provide a suitable environment for a rational consensus. All that remains is retreat, to religion or to nature, where solitary human beings might regain paradise, lost for ever by those in society.

(K)   Romanticism and reason: two perspectives on the morality of the senses

In 'La méthode de M. de Wolmar' (1932), Etienne Gilson wrote:

> Since all direct intervention by reason is condemned in advance [by Rousseau], the only moral pedagogy suitable for *an essentially passive being* [italics added] must be brought to bear on that being from outside. Since man is made by his milieu, why not use his milieu to make him? In other words, instead of directly reforming the soul by rational prescriptions and commands, a procedure which would be doomed to certain failure and would only lead to evil, the task is to use the external world and with it fashion the sentient soul [*l'âme sensible*] by choosing, varying and measuring out . . . the external influences to be applied to that soul.[13]

Gilson rightly recognized the importance of the morality of the senses and of the idea of the environment, or milieu, in Rousseau's work. But he was wrong, I think, to conclude that from this perspective one becomes, as an individual, merely the passive outcome of one's environment. As I have interpreted him in this chapter, Rousseau does not intend the morality of the senses to show that human beings are 'essentially passive'. Rather, he takes seriously both the irreducible presence of the environment, and the ability of individuals to respond actively to that environment, as they figure and re-figure its foreground and background.

In another brilliant work also published in 1932, *The Question of Jean-Jacques Rousseau*,[14] Ernst Cassirer bent the interpretative stick in the opposite direction. Reading Rousseau as anticipator of Kant, he avoided the mistake of ascribing to him a passive view of human beings, and attacked what he saw as a 'romantic' caricature of Rousseau's thought:

> If we start from the premise that Rousseau's essential achievement lies in setting the cult of feeling against a limited and one-sided

rationalist culture, we are faced with a strange anomaly in regard
to the foundation and development of his ethics . . . For . . . the
remarkable fact becomes apparent: Rousseau – in opposition to
the predominant opinion of the century – eliminated feeling from
the foundation of ethics.[15]

Cassirer's Rousseau anticipates Kant as critic of the dominant
'eudaemonism', the 'psychological optimism of the eighteenth century'.[16] He shares with the optimists the view that human beings are
fundamentally good, but for this Kantian Rousseau, goodness is

> not an original quality of feeling but a fundamental orientation
> and . . . destiny of man's will. This goodness is grounded not in
> some instinctive inclination of sympathy, but in man's capacity
> for self-determination. Its real proof lies . . . not in the impulses of
> natural good will but in the recognition of an ethical law to which
> the individual will surrenders voluntarily.[17]

Cassirer did not wish to discount the importance of feeling for
Rousseau and correctly stressed Rousseau's distinction, within feeling, between merely passive sensations, those of associationist
psychology, and active sentiments, particularly the sentiment of
conscience.

Cassirer found in Rousseau's model of self-determination and the
purified will a rough draft of Kantian practical reason:

> Although all our ideas come to us from outside, the sentiments
> evaluating them are within us, and it is by them alone that we
> know the compatibility or incompatibility between us and the
> things we ought to seek or flee. (Em IV.599/290)

It is an active feeling, 'a particular sentiment of my existence' [*un
sentiment propre de mon existence*] (Em IV.570–1/270) which allows me
to establish my own identity, to find myself as 'not simply a sensitive and passive being [*un être sensitif et passif*] but an active and
intelligent being' (Em IV.573/272), and, in an ideal political world,
to prescribe a law to myself. For Cassirer,[18] the goal of Rousseau's
pedagogy is to train children to be psychologically and intellectually
autonomous, to master each stage of skill and of socialization for
themselves; the same is true of his philosophy of religion, the Protestant ideal of autonomous interpretation of scripture, and of his
political theory, the civic ideal of a *polis* of free citizens, identifying
themselves with the general will, itself the outcome of properly
channelled individual wills.

Cassirer was right to stress that the ideal of autonomy is different from the ideal of happiness, in any straightforward sense. He was also right to stress the deep continuity between Rousseau's and Kant's projects in attempting to realize the former ideal in both theoretical and practical domains. Key elements of their moral philosophies are indeed the same. Both stress the radical difference between reason and passion, duty and happiness, general and particular interests. Both hold that these elements are in constant conflict within most people. The image of the divided self underlies the figure of the categorical imperative. Yet there is an equally radical shift between the two approaches. Kant's rigorous deontology systematically puts the opposition between the elements in the foreground. He aspires to a world which would transcend those conflicts, but that world is a shadowy background defined by religion: 'the existence is postulated of the cause of the whole of nature . . . which contains the ground of the exact coincidence of happiness and morality.'[19] For Rousseau too the self is divided and 'virtue is a state of war'. But for him the foreground is occupied by the tragic psychological reality of that division, whose causes, whether social, political or pedagogical are to be explained by the morality of the senses, and whose reconciliation is always to be sought: 'You must be happy, Emile' (Em V.814/442), he declaims, and that duty is as incumbent as the duty to be virtuous.[20]

Since the oscillation between the morality of the senses, on the one hand, and deontology, on the other, constitutes a *Leitmotiv* of Rousseau's investigations into all aspects of human life, it is impossible to assign him definitively to either of the camps marked romantic or rationalist. Rousseau, unlike Kant, is not concerned to keep ethical questions about our duties strictly quarantined from psychological questions about the drives of the heart. In addressing those questions he always looks beyond them to the material conditions of the order of things which can foster the reconciliation of the divided self.

In his later work, *Rousseau, Kant and Goethe,* Cassirer recognized this divide between Rousseau and Kant, but assessed it entirely to the detriment of Jean-Jacques: 'Rousseau was destined by fate to the very syncretism Kant . . . condemns. He set up a strict and lofty ideal of virtue, but he demanded, as the price of serving it, the fulfilment of his yearning for happiness'.[21]

In this book I follow Cassirer in opposing the image of Rousseau as high priest of 'the cult of feeling'. I stress that there is within Rousseau's work a constant tension between feeling and reason on the one hand, and between ethical naturalism and deontology on the other. I follow Rousseau's twisting path between romanticism and rationalism, not seeking a specious reconciliation, but hoping to find something more fruitful in the tension than an artificial 'syncretism'.

II

The *Discourse on the Origin of Inequality Among Men*

In 1753 the Academy of Dijon announced in the *Mercure de France* the question for the prize essay: 'What is the source of inequality among men, and whether it is authorized by natural law?' In response to it, Rousseau re-phrased the question, replacing 'source' by 'origin', and wrote his *Discourse on the Origin and Foundations of Inequality among Men*[1] in the following year.

Unlike its predecessor, the *Discourse on the Arts and Sciences*, this *Second Discourse* did not win the prize. In his *Confessions*, Rousseau dismisses his failure to win the prize with characteristic sour grapes: 'I was certain in advance that it would not get it, knowing well that it is not for work of this kind that Academy prizes are established' (Conf VIII.388–9/326).

The *Second Discourse* is the most sophisticated work of Rousseau's *Encyclopédiste* phase.[2] Making audacious thought-experiments, Rousseau starts from the present to explain how things must have been in the past. He develops a model of homo sapiens located in a natural environment, and explains how the species developed as its innate properties were stimulated and shaped by external, contingent causes. He concludes that the present corrupt and inegalitarian order of things has no legitimate basis, but is the outcome of historical accidents. He thus exploits the iconoclastic, naturalistic approach of the *Encyclopédistes*, and applies it to the most sensitive political problem of his day. His concluding call for a new, egalitarian order is more radical than anything envisaged by those writers.[3]

Rousseau's judgment that the *Second Discourse* is 'a work of the greatest importance' (ibid.) is accurate. Claude Lévi-Strauss entitled his 1962 tribute 'Jean-Jacques Rousseau, founder of the sciences of man',[4] boldly claiming that 'Rousseau did not simply anticipate ethnology, he founded it; first, in a practical fashion, in writing this

Discourse . . . which poses the problem of the relationship between nature and culture, and which constitutes the first treatise in general ethnology'.

(A)   Time and 'the sciences of man'

In the Preface, Rousseau plunges into the central methodological problem of the *Discourse*, which he captures in a memorable image, wrenched without acknowledgement from the end of Plato's *Republic*. Plato, having proved that the soul is immaterial and immortal, describes how it is contaminated by association with the body:

> We must use reasoning [*logismos*] to gaze at the soul, as it is when purified, not as we now look on it, mutilated by association with the body. Then you will find it more beautiful by far. . . . We have correctly described the soul as it appears at present. However, we were looking at it in the same way as the people who saw the sea-god Glaucus. They could not easily see his original nature because some of the old parts of his body were broken off, others were crushed and utterly mutilated by the waves, while other things had grown on him – shells, seaweed and stones, so that he looked more like some kind of wild beast than what he was by nature. That's just how we see the soul, subjected to countless evils. And so we must look elsewhere. . . . To the soul's love of wisdom, and see how the soul, through its kinship with the divine and immortal and eternal, seeks to touch and converse with them. Think what it might become if it followed that path wholeheartedly, and were lifted by that impulse out of the sea in which it now is, and stripped clean of the stones and shells, which through its earthly entertainments and its so-called happy feastings, are now grown on to it, numerous earthy, stony, wild things. Only then might one see the soul's true nature. . . .[5]

And here is Rousseau's version:

> how can the source of inequality among men be known unless one begins by knowing men themselves? And how will man manage to see himself as Nature formed him, through all the changes that the sequence of times and things must have produced in his original constitution, and to separate what he gets from his own stock from what circumstances and his progress have added to or changed in his primitive state? Like the statue of Glaucus, which time, sea and storms had so disfigured that it looked less like a God than a wild Beast, the human soul, changed for the worse

within society by a thousand continually renewed causes, by the acquisition of a mass of knowledge and errors, by changes that occurred in the constitution of the Bodies and by the continual impact of the passions, has, so to speak, changed its appearance to the point of being nearly unrecognizable; and instead of a being acting always by fixed and invariable Principles, instead of that heavenly and majestic simplicity which its Author had imprinted on it, one no longer finds anything except the deformed contrast of passion which believes it reasons and understanding in delirium. (2D 122/12)

At a first glance, the similarities between the two texts are striking. Many elements have been taken over, some are reproduced almost verbatim. Both writers contrast the way the soul was, in its natural form, with the way it is now, disfigured and mutilated by countless ills, overlaid by grotesque accretions. In both texts, the soul now looks more like a beast, beneath humanity, than a god, above it, and it is difficult (but presumably not impossible) to recognize it.

But the differences are equally interesting. Rousseau has replaced the sea-god by a statue. He may thus be anticipating the developmental story of Part II of the *Discourse*, drawing an analogy between three stages of the model (raw material of wood or stone, the newly carved statue, the old disfigured statue) and three stages of the history of humanity (pure state of nature, youth of the world, depraved civil society).[6]

Though Rousseau, like Plato, talks of the soul, he does not here or elsewhere in the *Second Discourse* hold that the body causes the degeneration of the soul. Rather society corrupts both body and soul alike, 'through the acquisition of a multitude of pieces of knowledge and error'.

In order to distinguish social accretions from natural endowments, Plato teaches us to ascend from the world of appearances to the pure world of abstract ideas, by means of reasoning. Rousseau's method is different. He bids us rely as much on the heart ('the pure heart') as on the head, in order to discover within ourselves the natural drives of human beings, in particular the drive of compassion.

Both Plato and Rousseau use the temporal vocabulary of then and now, but Rousseau alone is concerned with the qualitative, irreversible changes in humanity, as it undergoes the bombardment of 'several extraneous causes'. In telling this historical story, he engages in some complex model-building, constructing and testing possible worlds.

For Rousseau, then, human nature is 'nearly unrecognizable', but can none the less be discovered under experimental conditions. But, asks Rousseau, 'What experiments would be necessary to achieve knowledge of natural man? And what are the means of making those experiments in the midst of society?' (2D 123–4/13).

Rousseau's tone in the Preface is tentative, even hesitant: 'I began some lines of reasoning. I ventured some conjectures, less in the hope of resolving the question than with the intention of clarifying it and reducing it to its genuine state' (2D 123/13). But, as we shall see in a moment, when Rousseau says that he is proceeding by conjecture, he is not modestly disclaiming his ability to achieve knowledge. Rather, he envisages conjecture as the only available method of constructing a model to explain events which took place in the past and which cannot be repeated.

The essay question set by the Academy contained two parts, the first concerning the source (or origin) of inequality, the second concerning natural law. Rousseau devotes most of the text to answering the first part of the question. He gives no direct response to the second part until the last pages of the *Discourse*. But, without answering it directly, he engages with the natural law tradition in the Preface. In an initially puzzling passage, he first appears to dismiss all versions of natural law theory for failing to take sufficiently seriously the difficulty of the question of origins:

> for it is no light undertaking to separate what is original from what is artificial in the present Nature of man, and to know correctly a state which no longer exists, which perhaps never existed, which probably never will exist, and about which it is nevertheless necessary to have precise Notions in order to judge our present state correctly. (ibid.)

In particular, he criticizes 'the Roman jurists [who] subject man and all other animals indifferently to the same natural Law' (2D 124/13–14). Their mistake was to confuse two senses of law, the prescriptive sense of law as command, and the descriptive sense of law as statement of 'the general relations established by Nature among all animate beings for their common preservation' (2D 124/14). The 'Moderns', in contrast, are mistaken in being too restrictive, since they, in 'recognizing under the name Law only a rule prescribed to a moral being . . . intelligent, free, and considered in his relations with other beings, consequently limit the competence of natural Law to the sole animal endowed with reason, namely man'. They wrongly presuppose 'enlightenment which only develops with great difficulty and in very few People in the midst of society itself' (2D 125/14). In stating his own position on the next page Rousseau seeks to recover that strand in the 'ancient' tradition, going back through Montesquieu to the Stoics, in which natural law is the way in which all creatures endowed with feeling (thus both humans and 'lower' animals) participate in the natural order through the drives of self-preservation and compassion. At the same time the 'Moderns', despite their erroneous rationalism and abstraction, are correct in seeing that positive law is exercised over and by human beings alone, creatures endowed with free wills, which can ultimately be fused into a general will.[7]

Rousseau's recurring criticism of his predecessors is that they have been insufficiently radical in their attempts to distinguish the natural from the social. They have remained at the level of the empirically given: 'All of them . . . have carried over into the state of Nature ideas they had acquired in society: they spoke about savage man and they described Civil man' (2D 132/19). This led them to confuse cause and effect, as in the case of Hobbes, whose 'mistake . . . is not that he established the state of war among men who are independent and have become sociable, but that he supposed this state natural to the species and gave it as the cause of the vices of which it is the effect' (GM 288/81).

In Rousseau's system, in contrast, the state of nature is an ideal type, which he constructs artificially by abstracting from every social factor, that is from the different ways in which men and women have lived in ordered relations, however minimal the order, however transitory the relations. Rousseau pushes against the limits of the conceivable in conducting his thought experiment. What sense does it make to hypothesize the existence of pre- or sub-social human beings when all human beings do in fact live in societies? Scientists studying other species allow that some species are, and some are not, essentially social. So why should we not assume, as Aristotle and the natural law tradition assumed, that human beings, like ants, simply are essentially social? As I understand him, Rousseau is arguing that we should cast sceptical doubt on at least two received doctrines concerning essential human characteristics, the Aristotelian assumption of natural sociability and the Hobbesian assumption of natural aggression. Instead we should adopt the working hypothesis that the human raw material is almost totally malleable by its social environment. Empirical evidence of social diversity, relayed in travellers' tales and studied by ethnologists, suggests, but no more than suggests, the malleability thesis. But Rousseau is not asserting that the raw material is totally malleable. The stone of the statue of Glaucus subsists through all transformations. The ethnologist's task is to uncover that raw material and explain the ways in which it interacts with its environments.

But now a paradox presents itself. Lévi-Strauss was right to hail Rousseau as a (if not the) 'founder' of the human sciences, and Rousseau himself claims to address that branch of knowledge which is 'the most useful and the least advanced, that of man' (2D 122/12). Yet he also tells us that he is 'leaving aside . . . all scientific books which teach us only to see men as they have made themselves' (2D 125/14), and that we should 'begin by setting all the facts aside, for they do not affect the question' (2D 133/19). But what kind of scientist discards scientific books and ignores the facts? We can respond that the books Rousseau bids us discard are those of the natural lawyers, who allege that human beings are endowed by nature with reason and a sense of justice, although these can only be the outcome of social life. We can say that the 'facts' to be ignored are those recounted in the Old Testament about the origin of humanity. This exhortation can be seen, in part, as a tactical move, forced on Rousseau to avoid a charge of heresy, which a realist reading of his story must yield:

> Religion commands us to believe that since God Himself took Men out of the state of nature, they are unequal because He wanted them to be so; but it does not forbid us to form conjectures drawn solely from the nature of man, and the Beings surrounding, about what the human Race might have become if it had remained abandoned to itself. (ibid.)

But Rousseau is distancing himself not only from Biblical narrative, but from all history understood as mere narrative, as the story of 'facts' or events succeeding one another in time, but not explained or connected within a general theoretical framework.[8]

Lévi-Strauss finds in Rousseau a forerunner of structuralist, synchronic explanation, based on a non-historical category of 'reversible' time:

> Ethnology invokes 'mechanical' time, i.e. reversible and non-cumulative . . . The time of history, on the other hand, is . . . not reversible and is oriented in a given direction. An evolution leading contemporary Italian society back to the Roman Republic is . . . inconceivable . . .[9]

Lévi-Strauss envisages a choice between two conceptions of time. The one suited to the ethnologist is 'reversible', in the sense that there is nothing inscribed in any social form which determines the direction of its development. Historical time, in contrast, is not only 'irreversible', it is also teleological, 'oriented in a given direction'. But though that understanding of time is central to Lévi-Strauss's thought, it provides a distorted mirror of Rousseau's own conception of time in the *Second Discourse*, which does not correspond to either of Lévi-Strauss's conceptions. For in this text, Rousseau is sketching a hypothetical history of a series of irreversible, qualitative changes which have developed and consolidated inequality among human beings:

> Precisely what . . . is at issue in this Discourse? To indicate in the progress of things the moment when, Right taking the place of Violence, Nature was subjected to Law; and to explain by what sequence of marvels the strong could resolve to serve the weak, and the People to buy an imaginary repose at the price of real felicity. (2D 132/18)

And when he recalls the guiding thread of the *Second Discourse* in the *Confessions*, he highlights the progress of time, and its irreversible effects:

> wandering deep in the forest I sought and found the vision of those primitive times, the history of which I proudly traced. I demolished the petty lies of mankind; I dared to strip man's nature naked, to follow the progress of time and trace the things which have distorted it; and by comparing man as he had made himself with man as he is by nature I showed him in his pretended perfection the true source of his misery. (Conf VIII.388/326)

In the *Second Discourse* Rousseau is not excluding historical time. Indeed throughout Part II, each stage of development is marked as an irreversible turning point, and it is that theme which gives the narrative its sombre rhetorical power. The first three transitions, as well as the development of language within Stage II, are brought about by accidental, external causes. The subsequent transitions are triggered by factors which are increasingly internal to human agency.

While there are moments of nostalgia for an imagined earlier epoch, in particular for the 'Youth of the World' (2D 167ff/45ff), the *Second Discourse* is not a call for a 'return':

> What then? Must we destroy Societies, abolish thine and mine, and return to live in the forests with the bears? An inference in

the manner of my adversaries, which I prefer to anticipate rather than leave them the shame of drawing it. (2D note IX.167/79)

Writing with hindsight in *Rousseau, Judge of Jean-Jacques*, he is decisive: 'But human nature does not go backward, and it is never possible to return to the times of innocence and equality once they have been left behind' (RJJJ 3Dial.935/213).

(B)   'Nascent man' in the 'pure state of nature'

Rousseau elaborates an *'histoire raisonnée'*.[10] He attempts to show how things must have been in the past in order for them to be the way they are today, repeatedly using modal verbs to refer to 'changes that must have come about' (2D 134/20). This procedure involves 'reasonings', 'conjectures', 'experiments . . . necessary to achieve knowledge of natural man' (2D 123–4/13), thought experiments conducted 'within society' – where else? And within society Rousseau constructs the model of the 'forest' to represent the polar opposite of society. What is the forest? It is a hypothetical world with a minimum of needs (2D 135/21) and shared interests and a maximum of dispersal (2D 146–7/29–30):

> wandering in the forests, without industry, without speech, without domicile, without war and without liaisons, with no need of his fellows, likewise with no desire to harm them, perhaps never even recognizing anyone individually. . . . (2D 159–60/40)

Rousseau devotes the whole of Part I of the *Second Discourse* to describing this hypothetical world of the pure state of nature. It is a circular, self-reproducing state in which all needs are satisfied and the 'goad of necessity' is absent (2D 144/28).

In the pure state of nature, Rousseau strips human beings down to their pre-social 'hard-wiring'. According to his model, the species homo sapiens consists of physical bodies endowed with four properties: (1) a drive to self-preservation; (2) pity or compassion, 'a natural repugnance to see any sensitive Being perish or suffer, principally those like ourselves' (2D 126/14–15); (3) free will (2D 141/25–6); and (4) perfectibility (2D 142/26). All four are present in the pre- or sub-social state.

In the Preface, Rousseau refers to the properties of self-preservation and compassion as 'two principles anterior to reason' (2D 125–6/14–15). He returns to self-preservation in Part I, which he begins with an examination of the 'Physical Man', 'an animal less strong than some, less agile than others, but all things considered the most advantageously organized of all' (2D 134–5/20). Like every other animal, the human is 'an ingenious machine to which nature has given senses in order to revitalize itself and guarantee itself' (2D 141/25). But the human being is more than that. In addition to the 'Physical Man', there is 'the Metaphysical and Moral side' (ibid.). In making the distinction, Rousseau focuses on self-preservation as the mark of the physical, and on free will as the mark of the moral. A human being is identical with other animals as a self-preserving machine, but differs from them in that 'man contributes to his operations as a free agent'. As human beings are free, they are also conscious of acting freely. So freedom brings with it self-consciousness, or at least the capacity for it: 'it is above all in the consciousness of freedom that the spiritual nature of one's soul shows itself' (2D 142/26).

Later, in criticizing Hobbes, Rousseau returns to compassion, that 'innate repugnance to see one's fellow creature suffer', and says of it that it is 'so Natural that even Beasts sometimes give perceptible signs of it' (2D 154/36). We pause here to note that Rousseau reaches different conclusions about compassion in different texts. In the *Essay on the Origin of Languages*, he holds that:

Pity, although natural to man's heart, would remain forever inactive without imagination to set it in motion. How do we let ourselves be moved to pity? By transporting ourselves outside ourselves; by identifying with the suffering being. We suffer only to the extent that we judge him to suffer; it is not in ourselves but in him that we suffer. (EOL ch.9.395/261)

The Savoyard Vicar is given the same view to enunciate in the *Emile* Book IV:

who does not pity the unhappy man whom he sees suffering? Who does not want to deliver him from his ills if it only cost a wish for that? Imagination puts us in the place of the miserable man rather than in that of the happy man. (Em IV.503–4/221)

In these texts compassion, though present in the human heart, remains dormant until stimulated by the imagination. In the *Second Discourse*, in contrast, it appears to be both present and active in the pure state of nature, before the advent of imagination or reflection. This latter view is also found in *Rousseau, Judge of Jean-Jacques*, particularly clearly in the Second Dialogue, where Rousseau contrasts 'the man of nature' with the 'virtuous' man. The former lacks imagination and reflection, but is naturally compassionate

41

(RJJJ 2Dial.864/158). Starobinski's final judgment is that Rousseau's changing perspectives on the relation between compassion and imagination 'do not belong to different periods of this thought and are not evidence of any chronological development'.[11]

Starobinski's judgment suggests that there is no finished picture of compassion to be found in Rousseau's writings, despite the key role which it plays in most of his investigations. Although it would not correspond to a literal reading of all the texts, one might seek to synthesize them by holding that there are four innate, pre-social properties of human beings according to the *Second Discourse*, of which both self-preservation and compassion are shared with other animals, both being active in the pure state of nature. To reconcile the texts, we should then need to distinguish two stages in the development of compassion. The first stage would be the physical experience of squeamishness, the distress one suffers when faced by another's pain. This seems to be the thought behind Rousseau's formulation 'an innate repugnance to see one's fellow creature suffer' (2D 126/15). But we are not necessarily moved by that 'repugnance' to help the suffering individual. We may simply want to run away and avoid the source of the distress.[12] We would move to the next stage of compassion only with the advent of imagination and reflection. With reflection we would manage to master and distance ourselves from our own distress, and with imagination put ourselves in the other individual's place, with the result that 'it is not in ourselves but in him that we suffer' (EOL ch9.395/261).

As we have seen, free will and perfectibility are specific to the human species, and both of them await the 'goad of necessity' to activate them. Perfectibility in particular remains entirely dormant until human beings begin to interact. It then emerges as the key to the development of the species, which comes about as free creatures learn from experience and transmit their accumulated knowledge to their successors. That development is benign if and only if the drive to self-preservation is generalized, and one identifies oneself with one's neighbour, so that self-interest and compassion combine, rather than conflict (2D 156/37–8). In contrast to the natural law tradition, Rousseau does not include reason in the list of 'natural' properties. By this he must mean that reason is present in the pure state of nature only as an untriggered capacity, a 'virtuality', and that the power to reason develops only as individuals are driven to satisfy needs, which are, by definition, absent from the model.

Endowed with these four innate characteristics, what kind of creatures are human beings in the pure state of nature? Part of the answer is that they represent the mirror image of the inhabitants of present-day civil society. Each developed human trait of our world finds its opposite counterpart in the pure state of nature.

We approach the model (see Figure 1), *Through the Looking Glass* fashion, by displaying in the left-hand column the dominant traits of men and women in civil society. Rousseau then elicits the pure state of nature as it were by distillation, negating the social traits and collecting the residue. The thought experiment is extended and elaborate because Rousseau seeks to depict each moment of the distillation process in a vivid image of a possible, albeit never realized, world.

Figure 1

CIVIL SOCIETY	PURE STATE OF NATURE
(1) Human beings interact.	(1) Human beings are dispersed.
(2) Human beings, tied by morality, are bearers of virtues and vices.	(2) Human beings are amoral, neither good nor bad.
(3) Human beings, initially united in society, come to be isolated from their species as reason, reflection, imagination and *amour-propre* are triggered.	(3) Human beings, initially separated in the forest, come to identify with their species through compassion. Reason, reflection and *amour-propre* are untriggered.
(4)* Human beings interact through *amour-propre*.	(4)* Human beings are ignorant of or indifferent to others' opinions.
(5) Human beings are aggressive and anxious.	(5) Human beings are timid, but without anxiety.
(6) Human beings are industrious.	(6) Human beings are indolent.
(7)* Communication takes place through developed language.	(7)* There is little communication beyond cries of warning, etc.
(8)* Sexuality is mediated through the family.	(8)* Sexuality consists of haphazard couplings.
(9) Inequalities are important.	(9) Inequalities are unimportant.

The Figure depicts some, but not all, of the oppositions which Rousseau establishes in the *Discourse*. Three of them, asterisked in the table, will be addressed in separate chapters later in this book. So for the moment we shall simply indicate the strategic role they play, alongside the other oppositions, rather than investigate Rousseau's detailed treatment of them.

(1) The forest is the model of dispersal. Human beings are 'scattered in the Woods among the animals' (2D 146/29), 'wandering in the forests, without industry, without speech, without domicile, without war and without liaisons, with no need of his fellows, likewise with no desire to harm them' (2D 159–60/40). Since the forest is also a plentiful provider, at least of the elementary things needed for biological survival, the 'goad' [*aiguillon*] of necessity, which may

drive individuals into society as they seek mutual help in adversity, is lacking (2D 144/28).

(2) 'It seems at first that men in that state, not having among themselves any moral relationship or known duties, could be neither good nor evil, and had neither vices nor virtues . . .' (2D 152/34). Yet Rousseau had told us a few pages earlier to consider 'the Metaphysical and Moral side' of human beings in the pure state of nature (2D 141/25), and links that 'side' to their freedom and perfectibility. It is in virtue of those characteristics that human beings, unlike other animals, are moral beings, since they alone have the capacity for moral agency. But that capacity is not realized until they engage with one another socially. In that sense the pure state of nature is a pre-moral world, since it is inhabited by people who have only the untriggered capacity for moral agency. So they are neither good nor bad, neither virtuous nor vicious. In civil society they live in moral relations with one another, governed by undertakings and expectations corresponding to those undertakings. Their behaviour is now virtuous or vicious, as they fulfil or fail to fulfil their duties. Rousseau's style is teasing in this passage. 'It seems at first . . .', he writes, suggesting that it may seem different after due consideration. In the end, it turns out that the first impression was correct, but Rousseau cannot resist the temptation to compare our present corrupt society unfavourably with the pure state of nature, bidding us 'beware of our Prejudices, until one has examined with Scale in hand whether there are more virtues than vices among civilized men'. But that leaves untouched the basic insight that the pure state of nature is a world *without* morality, in the sense we elaborated above, whereas civil society is a world *of* morality, even if it is a world in which vice constantly outweighs virtue.

(3) Self-preservation and compassion are linked in the pure state of nature through identification. Each of us has 'an innate repugnance to see a fellow creature suffer', a repugnance which is no more than an extension of our desire to avoid suffering ourselves. As we come into contact with more members of our species (and other species close to our own), we identify ourselves increasingly with them:

> commiseration will be all the more energetic as the Observing animal identifies himself with the suffering animal . . . this identification must have been infinitely closer in the state of Nature than in the state of reasoning [*état de raisonnement*]. It is reason which engenders *amour-propre* and reflection which fortifies it. (2D 156/37)

In the pessimistic story of the *Second Discourse*, as we become social-ized, our feelings become distorted through *amour-propre*, the prod-uct of reasoning and reflection. Rousseau is insistent that human beings in the pure state of nature do not reason. Thus the precepts of natural law must be based on feeling and not presuppose 'enlighten-ment [*lumiéres*] which only develops with great difficulty and in very few People in the midst of society itself' (2D 125/14). Without reflection and imagination we are also without anxiety, particularly about illness and death. In this sense, says Rousseau, with character-istic hyperbole, 'the state of reflection is a state contrary to Nature and . . . the man who meditates is a depraved animal' (2D 138/23). Starobinski points out that this is a provocative inversion of Diderot's counter-rhetoric that 'Anyone who does not reason renounces his humanity [*qualité d'homme*], and must be treated as a denatured animal'. And he argues, correctly, that Rousseau is not advocating a return to the pure state of nature, but is rather pointing to the high price we pay for the passage from (natural) animality to (social) humanity.[13] Imagination too remains inactive until the pas-sage to society. 'His imagination portrays nothing' to the savage (2D 144/28): hence his equanimity in the face of danger and death, which he need not experience many times, as socialized people do, in anticipation. In his recapitulation of this passage in the *Essay on the Origin of Languages*, Chapter 9, the relation between compassion, on the one hand, and imagination and reflection, on the other, shifts.[14] Imagination and reflection negate compassion in the *Second Discourse*, whereas in the *Essay*:

> Social affections develop in us only with our enlightenment. Pity, though natural to the human heart, would remain eternally inactive without the imagination which brings it into play. How do we allow ourselves to be moved by pity? By transporting ourselves, by identifying ourselves with the suffering creature. We suffer only insofar as we judge that it is suffering; it is not in us but in it that we suffer. (EOL ch.9.395/261)

Starobinski talks of the 'double status of pity in Rousseau, on the one hand prior to reflection and immune to its influence, on the other hand "brought into play" by reflection and imagination'. The key to the ambiguity lies in the first sentence of the passage. The stage at which compassion must await reflection and imagination to trigger it is the stage at which we have already entered society, the stage of 'social affections'. The instinct of compassion is indeed innate and pre-social, it no longer shows itself automatic-ally. The essentially social activities of reflection and imagination, for all their fatal consequences in badly ordered societies, are necessary as the triggers of compassion in the well-ordered one: the recurring theme of '*le remède dans le mal*', highlighted by Starobinski.[15]

(4) Rousseau devotes an important note (2D noteXV.219–20/ 91–2) to the distinction between *amour de soi* and *amour-propre*. We shall return to this distinction later and locate it in Rousseau's complex images of *amour-propre*, as they develop from the *Second Discourse* to the *Emile*. At this stage, we restrict ourselves to the schematic opposition between the natural, pre-social drive to preserve oneself, which is *amour de soi*, and the transformation of that drive in society, where we find ourselves locked into degrading battles for relative distinction and for recognition in the eyes of others, in short, in the play of *amour-propre*. In keeping with his generally negative judgment on our present social life, Rousseau passes a negative judgment on the essentially social drive of *amour-propre*. All that will change with the *Emile*. But in the *Second Discourse* Rousseau traces a development towards a degenerate end point, the present. In contrast to that, the Savage, who, unlike ourselves, 'lives within himself' (2D 193/66), appears admirable. A major theme of Part II of the *Second Discourse* is the emergence and development of *amour-propre* step by step with inequality. Even in this pessimistic story, some stages of *amour-propre*, particularly in the Youth of the World, are benign. Only in retrospect can we see them as leading to the fatal outcome.

(5) Against Hobbes, Rousseau argues that human beings, far from being naturally aggressive ('intrepid' 2D 136/21), are timid creatures. But though they are timid, they are not anxious. As we have seen, anxiety is the outcome of the imagination, which is inactive in the pure state of nature:

> the only evils he knows are pain and hunger. I say pain and not death because an animal will never know what it is to die; and knowledge of death and its terrors is one of the first acquisitions that man has made in moving away from the animal condition. (2D 143/27)

Timidity turns into aggression only when individuals find themselves threatened by other individuals in their struggle for survival. Driven in society by *amour-propre*, that struggle for survival turns into a zero-sum game for pre-eminence, as one's badly socialized ego survives only at the expense of that of one's neighbour. All the aggression generated by sexuality makes itself felt only in society, as passion is channelled is through *amour-propre*:

love itself, like all the other passions, has acquired only in society that impetuous ardor which so often makes it fatal for men; and it is all the more ridiculous to portray Savages continually murdering each other to satisfy their brutality as this opinion is directly contrary to experience. . . . (2D 158/39)

(6) 'Alone, idle, and always near danger, Savage man must like to sleep, and be a light sleeper like animals . . .' (2D 140/25). Rousseau develops the contrast between the industry of the socialized human being and the idleness of the savage at the very end of the *Second Discourse*:

Savage man and Civilized man differ so much in the bottom of their Hearts and inclinations that what constitutes the supreme happiness of one would reduce the other to despair. The former breathes only repose and freedom; he wants only to live and remain idle . . . the Citizen, always active, sweats, agitates himself, torments himself incessantly in order to seek still more laborious occupations; he works to death, he even rushes to it sometimes in order to get in condition to live. . . . (2D 192/66)

Like their other properties, the idleness of human beings in the pure state of nature is ideal-typical. Despite his many joking comments on his own laziness, his 'active heart and lazy nature' (RJJJ 2Dial.816/120), Rousseau is not advocating that we should 'return' to that state of idleness, but is using it to highlight the frustrating character of work in the contemporary world. Here it systematically fails to bring satisfaction to agents who find themselves locked in a struggle for comparative eminence and who seek only to outdo their competitors with the results of their industry, rather than to enjoy the process and products of work as values in themselves. Rousseau will attempt to instil a work-ethic of just that kind in his pupil in the *Emile*, teaching him to ply an honest trade, enjoyable in itself, and to produce artefacts useful in themselves.

(7),(8) In depicting human beings who lack both language and kinship structures, Rousseau pushes his ideal type to the limits of the conceivable. We shall examine both these hypotheses in later chapters. The two themes are linked because it seems immediately plausible that children would 'naturally' take their first steps in learning a language from their parents, in a family setting (2D 146/30). Rousseau will argue that neither language nor the family (any kind of family) is part of the hard-wiring of the human being. Both are products of society. Both are socially tainted and both need to be socially reformed.

Against the received wisdom, Rousseau holds that:

> Man's first language, the most universal, most energetic, and only language he needed before it was necessary to persuade assembled men, is the cry of Nature . . . elicited only by a kind of instinct in pressing emergencies, to beg for help in great dangers, or for relief in violent ills. . . . (2D 148/31)

That 'language', Rousseau will show, is at most a form of sub-linguistic communication, not a language proper. The transition from the one to the other comes about only with the transition to a society of 'assembled men'.

Without a developed language, without socially established cues to memory:

> Males and females united fortuitously, depending on encounter, occasion and desire, without speech being a very necessary interpreter of the things they had to say to each other; they left each other with the same ease. . . . (2D 147/30)

Again, Rousseau is not advocating that society should replace the family by sexual anarchy. Once the pure state of nature is left, the only solution to our present disorders is to replace the demands of nature by an equally demanding social order. In the case of human sexuality, the counter-model offered to the corrupt family structure of present-day society turns out not to be a recovery of natural equality, transformed into social equality, but rather to be a radic-ally inegalitarian relationship between the sexes, endorsed by social sanctions.

(9) In the Exordium to the *Discourse* Rousseau distinguishes:

> two sorts of inequality in the human Species: one, which I call natural or Physical, because it is established by Nature and consists in the differences of ages, health, Bodily strengths, and qualities of Mind or Soul; the other, which may be called Moral or Political inequality, because it depends upon a sort of convention and is established, or at least authorized, by the consent of Men. (2D 131/18)

'Moral or Political inequality' exists only insofar as it is recognized and sustained by social norms. It is also a zero-sum relation, which 'consists in the different Privileges that some men enjoy to the prejudice of others' (ibid.). In society, one person's superi-ority is bought at the expense of another person's inferiority. In summarizing Part I of the *Discourse*, Rousseau claims to have 'proved that Inequality is barely perceptible in the state of Nature, and that its influence there is almost null' (2D 162/42). He reiterates that result at the end of Part II, concluding that:

> inequality, being almost null in the state of Nature, draws its force and growth from the development of our faculties and the progress of the human Mind, and finally becomes stable and legitimate by the establishment of property and Laws. (2D 193/67)

In the Finale to the *Discourse* Rousseau applies that conclusion in passing judgment on present-day society and in making a recommendation for its reform.

(C)   Emergence from nature via the 'combination of several extraneous causes' (2D 162/42)[16]

'There was neither education nor progress; the generations multiplied uselessly . . . each generation always starting from the same point . . .' (2D 160/40). The pure state of nature would have reproduced itself eternally, had it not been for the irruption of contingent, catastrophic events. These events would be contingent at least in the explanatory framework of the social scientist, even if the natural scientist might be able to locate them as the necessary outcome of some sequence of natural events. They would be catastrophic in that they would bring about sudden, irreversible changes in humanity with surprising speed.

The vocabulary of external, contingent causes combines two somewhat different versions of the idea that changes in natural species and in humanity are determined by chance. The two versions are not inconsistent, but they are invoked to explain changes of different kinds.

In the first version, Rousseau explains that the statue of Glaucus depicts 'the human soul, changed for the worse [*altérée*] within society by a thousand continually renewed causes' (2D 122/12).[17] It depicts determination by 'several' [*plusieurs*], 'various' [*diverses*] causes, all of which are separately 'trivial' [*trés-légeres*], but which, in 'combination' [*concours*] have 'a surprising power when they act without interruption' (2D 162/42). In this version, which could be called 'cumulative' determination, the effect is brought about by a kind of accumulation of small changes over an immensely long period of time. The first great transition, from 'nascent man' to elementary cooperation (Figure 2: 0 → I) was brought about by

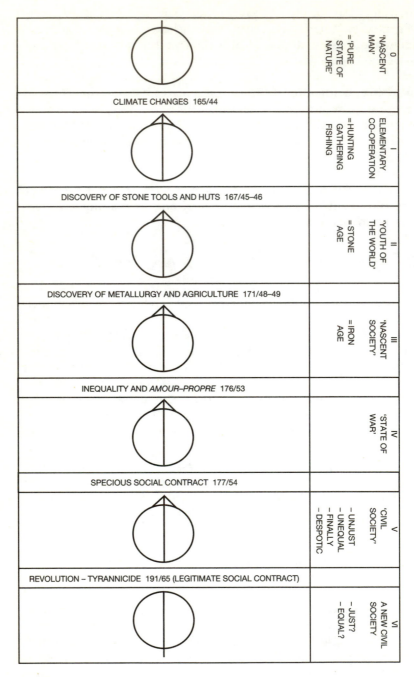

	0 'NASCENT MAN' = 'PURE STATE OF NATURE'
CLIMATE CHANGES 165/44	
	I ELEMENTARY CO-OPERATION = HUNTING GATHERING FISHING
DISCOVERY OF STONE TOOLS AND HUTS 167/45–46	
	II 'YOUTH OF THE WORLD' = STONE AGE
DISCOVERY OF METALLURGY AND AGRICULTURE 171/48–49	
	III 'NASCENT SOCIETY' = IRON AGE
INEQUALITY AND *AMOUR–PROPRE* 176/53	
	IV 'STATE OF WAR'
SPECIOUS SOCIAL CONTRACT 177/54	
	V 'CIVIL SOCIETY' – UNJUST – UNEQUAL – FINALLY – DESPOTIC
REVOLUTION – TYRANNICIDE 191/65 (LEGITIMATE SOCIAL CONTRACT)	
	VI A NEW CIVIL SOCIETY – JUST? – EQUAL?

Figure 2 Emergence from the pure state of nature

climatic changes, 'barren years, long and hard winters, and scorching Summers' (2D 165/44). With the plural nouns ('years', 'winters', 'summers') Rousseau seems to suggest that this was the result of 'cumulative' determination. The discovery of fire was equally fortuitous, but the result of a single chance occurrence, 'Lightning, a Volcano, or some happy accident' [*quelque heureux hazard*], rather than of an accumulation of such events.

Rousseau signals a 'first revolution', which brought human beings from elementary cooperation to 'the youth of the world' (Figure 2: I → II). This too was inaugurated by a single chance discovery:

> they discovered some kinds of hatchets [*quelques sortes de haches*] of hard, sharp stones, which served to cut wood, scoop out earth, and make huts from branches . . . this was the epoch of a first revolution, which produced the establishment and differentiation of families. . . . (2D 167/45–6)

We shall return to the 'youth of the world' when we examine *amour-propre*, sexuality and language in Chapters VII, VIII and IX below. For the moment we note simply that Rousseau regards it as the stage at which the seeds of future discord are sown. From social interaction come 'the first duties of civility, even among Savages'. As people came to recognize each other as persons, acting freely and intentionally, 'any voluntary act became an outrage, because along with the harm that resulted from the injury, the offended man saw in it contempt for his person . . .' (2D 170/48). But despite this, Rousseau's verdict on the 'youth of the world' is positive, even lyrical:

> this period of the development of human faculties, maintaining a golden mean between the indolence of the primitive state and the petulant activity of our *amour-propre*, must have been the happiest and most durable epoch . . . the least subject to revolutions, the best for man. . . . (2D 171/48)

Why should this epoch be 'the best for man'? Perhaps it is because it is the fine point at which individuals have begun to depend on one another, and have thus entered into moral relations which involve trust and *amour-propre*, but those relations are not yet based on major inequality of wealth and power. That will come only at the next stage, with the discovery of metallurgy and settled agriculture, and the development of the division of labour and of the monetary economy.[18] Rousseau explains the development of language in the 'youth of the world' by cumulative determination:

one can conjecture . . . how various [*diverses*][19] particular causes could have spread language and accelerated its progress by making it more necessary. Great floods or earthquakes surrounded inhabited Cantons with water or precipices; Revolutions of the Globe detached and broke up portions of the Continent into Islands. One conceives that among men thus brought together and forced to live together, a common Idiom must have been formed sooner than among those who wandered freely in the forests on solid Ground. (2D 168–9/46–7)

The next transition, from the youth of the world to 'nascent society', was inaugurated by the discovery of metallurgy and agriculture, which caused a 'great revolution' (2D 171/49) (Figure 2: II → III). Their discovery was the result of 'some fatal accident' [*quelque funeste hazard*] (2D 171/48). The origin of metallurgy could have been 'the extraordinary circumstance of some Volcano which, by throwing up metallic materials in fusion, would have given Observers the idea of imitating this operation of Nature' (2D 172/ 49). Once again Rousseau conjectures that a single chance event, which human beings observed, interpreted and applied, triggered the revolution. Rousseau does not find an external, chance cause, whether single or cumulative, for the transition to settled agriculture. He suggests that even in the pure state of nature people would have observed the elements of propagation, and that they would then have come to apply its principles systematically when driven by need, as the division of labour developed with metallurgy, when 'some men were needed to smelt and forge iron, other men were needed to feed them' (2D 173/50). Nascent society brought with it private property and law, 'the first rules of justice' (ibid.). Most importantly, it fostered economic inequality, itself the unintended consequence of the new productive system, based on an increasingly sophisticated division of labour. It was thus no less contingent than the previous changes:

Things in this state could have remained equal if talents had been equal, and if, for example, the use of iron and the consumption of foodstuffs had always been exactly balanced. But this proportion, which nothing maintained, was soon broken; the stronger did more work; the cleverer turned his to better advantage; the more ingenious found ways to shorten his labor; the Farmer had greater need of iron or the blacksmith greater need of wheat; and working equally the one earned a great deal while the other barely had enough to eat. Thus does natural inequality imperceptibly manifest itself along with contrived inequality; and thus do the differences among men, developed by those of circumstances, become more perceptible, more permanent in their effects, and begin to have a proportionate influence over the fate of individuals. (2D 174/51)

As nascent society grows, so too do both inequality and *amour-propre*. We shall return to *amour-propre* later. For the moment we note only the ghastly dénouement in which 'Nascent Society gave way to the most horrible state of war: the human Race, debased and desolated, [was] no longer able to turn back or renounce the unhappy acquisitions it had made . . .' (2D 176/53). The transition from nascent society to the state of war is marked in the Figure in the same way as the previous transitions, by vertical lines suggesting a catastrophe point (Figure 2: III → IV). But Rousseau does not here describe any particular turning point which would correspond to the previous three. The transition comes about through a gradual increase in inequality and *amour-propre*, the later stages of nascent society slowly collapsing into the early stages of the state of war. Little space is devoted to the state of war. It is still a form of social life, but one which lacks agreed forms of legitimation. It is ruled by clashing war lords, each of whom is 'destitute of valid reasons to justify himself and of sufficient forces to defend himself' (2D 177/53), and so it rapidly descends into anarchy.[20]

(D)   *Civil society, the specious contract and despotism*

The next break described in the *Second Discourse* (Figure 2: IV → V) inaugurated civil society, that is the political world which we now inhabit, unjust, for the moment relatively stable, but no less prone than its predecessor to collapse into anarchy or despotism.[21] The transition to civil society is marked by a social contract, not the legitimate social contract Rousseau was to describe in the book of that name, but a specious agreement, based on deception. The context of this agreement was the state of war, a disorderly sub-society, marked by great differences in wealth and power but no settled political or legal system. The specious contract was devised by 'the rich, pressed by necessity [who] finally conceived the most deliberate [*réfléchi*] project that ever entered the human mind' (ibid.). The terms of the specious contract are, of course, persuasive: 'Let us unite,' it begins, 'to protect the weak from oppression, restrain the ambitious, and secure for everyone the possession of what belongs to him'. This rhetoric conceals the fact that in insuring the security of property by the force of the laws, it is insuring a grossly unequal distribution that has already been made. Its terms are also vague, providing no guarantee that citizens will be entitled to participate in political decision making. In these two respects the specious contract contrasts with the legitimate one of the *Social Contract*. The latter presupposes the equality of the contracting parties and guarantees the continuing sovereignty of the people, expressed through the general will. The specious contract of the *Second Discourse* thus provides a rational reconstruction of the ideological basis of the real societies we now inhabit: 'all ran to meet their chains believing they ensured their freedom'. The genuine contract provides a blueprint of the moral grounding of the ideal society we can aspire to.

Immediately after the description of the specious contract, 'a surprise awaits the reader . . .' Rousseau abandons the narrative style, leaves the world of facts and enters the world of right and principles '. . . addressing the foundations which should have been given to the institution of civil society in order to make it fully legitimate',[22] in other words Rousseau bids us now 'test the facts by right' (2D 182/58). In what follows he anticipates some of the opening moves of the *Social Contract*, subjecting previous theories of political obligation to criticism. He rejects two alleged sources of obligation, 'conquests by the more powerful, or union of the weak' (2D 179/55). The former would amount to might rather than right, and would not therefore be a genuine basis of obligation. The latter is intrinsically implausible, once it is seen that 'the weak', in the sub-political, but already social world envisaged by the theorists, are in fact 'the poor', and since they have 'nothing to lose except their freedom, it would have been great folly for them to give away voluntarily the sole good remaining to them.' Rousseau follows Locke in rejecting 'paternal authority' (2D 182/57). He concludes:

> I limit myself, in following common opinion, to consider here the establishment of the Body Politic as a true Contract between the People and the Chiefs it chooses for itself: a Contract by which the two Parties obligate themselves to observe Laws that are stipulated in it and that form the bonds of their union. (2D 184/59–60)

This is not yet the 'pact of association' of the *Social Contract*, in which the people forms itself into a sovereign body. Since the parties to it are the people on the one side and 'the Chiefs' on the other, it still follows the schema of the 'pact of submission',[23] though its outcome is something close to the general will of the *Social Contract*:

> The People, having, on the subject of Social relations, united all their wills into a single one, all the articles on which this will is

explicit become so many fundamental Laws obligating all members of the State without exception. (2D 184–5/60)

It also differs from the agreement of the *Social Contract* in that it presupposes relations of inequality from the start. This brings the normative digression back to the historical narrative, since 'the various forms of Governments derive their origin from the greater or lesser differences to be found among individuals at the moment of Institution' (2D 186/61). From that starting point Rousseau traces 'the progress of inequality', in which:

> the establishment of the Law and of the Right of property was the first stage, the institution of the Magistracy the second, and the third and last was the changing of legitimate power into arbitrary power . . . the status of rich and poor was authorized by the first Epoch, that of powerful and weak by the second, and by the third that of Master and Slave, which was the last degree of inequality and the limit to which all the others finally lead, until new revolutions dissolve the Government altogether or bring it closer to its legitimate institution. (2D 187/62)

Rousseau paints a dramatic picture of the contemporary world of extreme inequality, riven by disordered *amour-propre*. As so often, he draws up a balance sheet, since even this nightmare world brings with it certain benefits, even if they are outweighed by losses. 'If this were the place to go into details', he says:

> I would point out how much that universal desire for reputation, honors and preferences, which devours us all, trains and compares talents and strengths; how much it multiplies and stimulates passions; and making all men competitors, rivals, or rather enemies, how many reverses, successes and catastrophes of all kinds it causes daily by making so many Contenders race the same course. I would show that to this ardor to be talked about, to this furor to distinguish oneself, which nearly always keeps us outside of ourselves, we owe what is best and worst among men, our virtues and our vices, our Sciences and our errors, our Conquerors and our Philosophers – that is to say a multitude of bad things as against a small number of good ones. (2D 189/63)

The motor of contemporary society is competition, which is in itself morally neutral. As we shall see when we turn to the *Emile*, in a well-ordered educational system, competition can be harnessed to good ends, as we encourage children to excel in virtue. But even there it is a dangerous instrument, since those trained to contend, in any contest whatsoever, often finish by valuing their skill as competitors over the value of the goal they are competing to attain. Within our society, the goods for which we compete are all zero-sum, so that 'the powerful and rich men . . . prize the things they enjoy only insofar as the others are deprived of them . . . [and] would cease to be happy if the People ceased to be miserable' (2D 189/63). Inequality, which began as an accidental and unintended consequence of our socialization, has become a value, indeed the most important value, pursued by the rich and the powerful.

In the face of growing inequalities the law becomes powerless, and anarchy ensues, as the mighty, lacking any restraint, engage in a fight to the death, drawing the weak and the poor into the carnage. When one of them is finally victorious, the result is despotism.

Despotism, 'the extreme point which closes the Circle . . . touches the point from which we started' (2D 191/65). The mathematical image stands not for a literal 'return', but for an end point which is a grotesque parody of the starting point. It 'restores' equality, but now it is an equality of misery. It 'restores' the absence of law, because there is now no law 'except the will of the Master':

> Here everything is brought back [*se ramene*] to the law of the stronger, and consequently to a new state of Nature different from the one with which we began, in that the one was the State of Nature in its purity, and this last is the fruit of an excess of corruption. (ibid.)

In these circumstances violent revolution, even tyrannicide, is justified:

> the Contract of Government is so completely dissolved by Despotism, that the Despot is Master only as long as he is the strongest, and as soon as he can be driven out he cannot protest against violence. The uprising that ends by strangling or dethroning a Sultan is as Lawful an act as those by which he disposed, the day before, of the lives and goods of his Subjects. (ibid.)

Rousseau deflects the charge that he is instigating insurrection on his own doorstep by conveniently replacing a Western absolutist monarch by an oriental 'Sultan'. But the disguise must have been threadbare. The metaphor of the circle completes the rhetorical conclusion, as 'Force alone maintained him, force alone overthrows him. Everything thus occurs according to the Natural order . . .'.

In the Figure I mark a final transition at this point (Figure 2: V → VI), joining to the insurrection of the *Second Discourse* the legitimate contract of the *Social Contract*. This is speculative, since Rousseau does not link the two in either text. The narrative of the *Discourse* comes to an abrupt end with the insurrection. The ideal type of the legitimate social order whose terms are spelled out in the *Social Contract* I.6 presupposes, as we shall see, a particular context, but not the dramatic revolutionary context of the pages we have just read. Since Rousseau's unshaken belief in human free will does not allow for any 'iron laws' of history, neither the insurrectionary dénouement nor the normatively grounded fresh start are inevitable, still less a necessary connection between them. The V → VI transition is a possibility, no more than that.

(E) Finale

In a rapid Finale, Rousseau first summarizes the differences between natural and social human beings, focusing on the emergence of *amour-propre*:

> the Savage lives within himself; the sociable man always outside of himself, knows how to live only in the opinion of others; and it is, so to speak, from their judgment alone that he draws the sentiment of his own existence. (2D 193/66)

Then, in the last paragraph, he eventually responds to the second half of the Academy's question. There he draws together the results of his investigations in the *Discourse* to assert as a premiss that, as a matter of *fact*:

> inequality, being almost null in the state of Nature, draws its force and growth from the development of our faculties and the progress of the human Mind, and finally becomes stable and legitimate by the establishment of property and Laws. (2D 193/67)

From that he draws the *normative* conclusion that: 'moral inequality, authorized by positive right alone, is contrary to Natural Right whenever it is not combined in the same proportion with Physical inequality' (2D 193–4/67). In order to make sense of this conclusion, we must understand the term 'Physical inequality' as standing not for bodily inequality, but for 'natural inequality of talents', as Starobinski glosses it (OC 3.lxix). That principle might appear to generate a ruthless meritocracy, which could turn out to be as

57

inegalitarian as the system it is designed to replace. But if we accept the factual premiss, as Rousseau hopes to have persuaded us by now that we should, then we accept that 'Physical' inequalities between individuals, those inequalities with which they are born, rather than those which they acquire through socialization, are minimal. And if that is the case, then the normative conclusion follows that 'moral' inequalities, those bestowed by society in rank, riches and power, should also be minimal.[24]

III

The *Emile*

(A)   Introduction. Rousseau's judgment on the Emile

The *Second Discourse* had stressed the immense distance between the pure state of nature and civil society, and left it to the 'pure heart' to rescue our natural drives from social corruption. In the *Emile* Rousseau strives to translate that aspiration into reality, showing how corruption can be postponed, or even prevented, by a meticulous educational formation, a process which demands an acute sense of timing on the part of the educator. As he presents this programme, Rousseau refines the natural/social opposition. He ties together moral and scientific education. He elaborates, in often eccentric detail, the mechanisms, tricks and manipulations which are needed to produce that rare outcome, the autonomous adult.

The *Emile* is part pedagogical treatise, part novel. It combines general principles of psychology and education with a fictional account of the raising of Emile by his tutor from infancy to adulthood.[1] Interweaving anecdotes and arguments, Rousseau presents a revolutionary pedagogy, embedded in a theory of developmental psychology, and we shall concentrate on this in the present chapter. He also propounds an innovatory theory of human interaction and domination (*amour-propre*), a theory of language-acquisition, a disturbing account of sexuality, a summary of political theory and a self-contained treatise of natural theology which forms part of the 'Profession of Faith of the Savoyard Vicar'.[2] We shall consider each of these topics in separate chapters.

According to Rousseau's own judgment in *Rousseau, Judge of Jean-Jacques,* the *Emile* provided the key to all of his work:

From my first reading, I had felt that these writings proceeded in

59

a certain order which it was necessary to find in order to follow the chain of their contents. I believed I saw that this order was the reverse of their order of publication, and that going backward from one principle to the next, the Author reached the first ones only in his final writings. To proceed by synthesis, then, it was necessary to begin with these, which is what I did, by focusing first on the *Emile*, with which he finished. . . . (RJJJ 3Dial.933/211)

But he was disappointed by the gap between the public reception given to the *Emile* and his own estimate of its importance within his *oeuvre*:

The publication of this book did not occur with that burst of applause that followed the publication of all my writings. Never did a work have such great private praise, but so little public approbation. What was said to me about it, what was written to me about it by the people most capable of judging it, confirmed to me that this was the best of my writings, as well as the most important. But all this was said with the most bizarre precautions, as if it were important to keep secret the good one thought about it. (Conf XI.573/480)

Yet that timid response is hardly surprising, since the *Emile* was rapidly condemned by the Faculty of Theology of the University of Paris and then by the Paris Parlement, which ordered its author's arrest. We have already followed the story of Rousseau's subsequent flight and exile.[3] In the course of that flight he stayed briefly in Yverdon, until the Genevan authorities ordered that both the *Emile* and the *Social Contract* be burnt, 'as foolhardy, scandalous, impious, tending to destroy the Christian religion and all governments'.[4] In August 1762, when Rousseau had retreated to Môtiers, the *Emile* came under fire yet again, this time from Charles de Beaumont, Archbishop of Paris, who issued a *Mandement* 'bearing condemnation of a book entitled *Emile, or on Education* by J.-J. Rousseau, citizen of Geneva'.[5] Rousseau published his reply, the *Letter to Christophe de Beaumont*, a year later, in which he responded to the Archbishop's edict paragraph by paragraph, clarifying many parts of his educational theory and of the theology of the 'Profession of Faith'. In it he made particularly clear that he rejected the doctrine of original sin, and so laid himself all the more open to the charge of heresy. Having incurred the wrath of religious and political authority both in France and in Geneva, Rousseau endured unhappy exile in England, quarrelled with his benefactor Hume, and returned to France to live out the rest of his life in relative isolation. All this followed from the publication of the *Emile*.[6]

(B) The form of the treatise/novel

Rousseau was master of many genres, including the novel, the philosophical discourse, the autobiography and the rhetorical polemic. He was no purist, and rarely kept elements of those different genres strictly separate. The *Emile* embodies a particularly striking mixture of genres, a strange amalgam of pedagogical treatise and novel. The scholarship of P. D. Jimack has thrown light on its formation.[7] He has shown that the *Emile*, as Rousseau originally conceived it and sketched it in the *Manuscrit Favre*, was to be a work of impersonal theory, in which the individual character of Emile did not appear. In the published version of the book Rousseau explains its form like this:

> at first I have spoken little of my Emile, because my first educational maxims, although contrary to those that are established, are so evident that it is difficult for any reasonable man to refuse his consent to them. But in the measure I advance, my pupil, differently conducted than yours, is no longer any ordinary child. He requires a way of life special to him. Then he appears more frequently on the scene, and toward the last times I no longer let him out of my sight for a moment until, whatever he may say, he has no longer the least need of me. (Em I.265/51)

Jimack judges that here Rousseau 'was indeed telling part of the truth. But he was also trying to cover up the evolution of the work from a treatise into a kind of a novel, an evolution which was neither complete nor entirely satisfactory.'[8]

(C) Natural and social

(i) No original sin

Rousseau regarded the doctrine of original sin as both false and wicked.[9] He proclaims his rejection of it in the opening words of the *Emile*: 'Everything is good as it leaves the hands of the Author of things; everything degenerates in the hands of man' (Em I.245/37). Rousseau intends to trace the source of that degeneration:

> Let us set down as an incontestable maxim that the first movements of nature are always right. There is no original

perversity in the human heart. There is not a single vice to be found in it of which it cannot be said how and whence it entered. (Em II.322/92)[10]

(ii) Nature: an elusive term

The opening pages of the *Emile* are dense. In them Rousseau plays elusively on *nature* and *natural*, terms which will play an important role throughout the book, but which he will never definitively pin down. Here he starts from a typology of *sources* of our education, which 'comes to us from nature or from men or from things' (Em I.247/38). At this point he allots a narrow educational role to nature, limiting it to the 'internal development of our faculties and organs'. From men we learn the 'use that we . . . make of this development'. While 'the education of things' is 'what we acquire from our own experience of the objects which affect us'.

The typology of sources leads him to define the goal of education as the formation of the person 'in whom they all coincide at the same points and tend to the same ends'. Only such a person 'reaches his goal and lives consistently'.

The three sources of education are subject to different degrees of control: 'that of nature does not depend on us at all; that of things depends on us only to a certain extent; that of men is the only one of which we are truly masters.'

Putting these more or less axiomatic starting points together, Rousseau outlines his educational programme: 'Since the conjunction of the three educations is necessary to their perfection, the two others must be directed towards the one over which we have no power.'

At this point Rousseau pauses, aware that he has reached a schematic conclusion which depends on the strange restriction of nature to the 'internal development of our faculties and organs', by which he seems to mean physiological processes like 'the impulse of the inner parts of the body which tend towards growth' (Em I.254/43).[11] But since much of the *Emile*, in particular the first two books, is devoted to controlling the child's physical environment so as to allow his body, constantly exercised, to grow and develop freely and spontaneously, Rousseau cannot continue to identify the *natural* with the *physiological* (even with the physiology of 'the inner parts') since one's physiology is affected for good or ill by human intervention.

Nearer the heart of Rousseau's shifting ideas of nature in this context is the following account of infant development:

(1) 'We are born with the capacity to sense' [*nous naissons sensibles*] (Em I.248/39).
(2) We acquire 'consciousness of our sensations' (ibid.); that is our awareness of ourselves increases, as we become increasingly able to distinguish between our sensations and the objects that cause those sensations.
(3) We learn to avoid objects which cause us pain and to pursue those which cause us pleasure.
(4) Then a more complex process sets in, as we *reflect* on 'the conformity or lack of it that we find between us and those objects', and make '*judgments* . . . about them on the basis of the *idea* of happiness or of perfection given us by *reason*' (ibid.: italics added).
(5) This process solidifies into 'dispositions', which are 'extended and strengthened as we become more capable of using our senses and more enlightened' [*plus sensibles et plus éclairés*] (ibid.).
(6) But at the same time those dispositions can be 'more or less corrupted' [*s'altèrent plus ou moins*] (ibid.).
(7) 'Before that corruption they [the dispositions] are what I call in us nature' (ibid.).

According to this definition (7), our nature (what is natural to us), is the totality of our uncorrupted dispositions to use our senses in promoting our happiness. This definition would be less narrow than that of 'the impulse of the inner parts', and would allow for 'the education of men' to be applied to our physiology, both 'outer' and 'inner', as noted above. If we follow (7), we shall also be able to see how a 'natural' human being, so defined, could survive in society.

On the basis of (7) Rousseau proclaims that 'it is to these primary dispositions [*dispositions primitives*] that everything must be related' (ibid.). By 'everything', he refers to the three educations which he hopes to harmonize. Such harmony would be possible 'if our three educations were only different from one another. But what is to be done when they are opposed?' (ibid.). He is far from confident that success can be attained because corruption of the primary dispositions, the transition from (5) to (6), is hard to avoid in the corrupt world we inhabit, and indeed it is almost impossible under the regime of the mistaken educational systems ('of men') which are presently practised. 'All that one can do by dint of care is to come more or less close to the goal, but to reach it requires luck' (Em I.247/38).

As so often, Rousseau is torn between a deep pessimism, as he regards the world as it is, and a degree of optimism, as he develops his own counter-theory. These two attitudes give rise to two different responses to the question whether the demands of nature and of society can finally be reconciled.

(iii)   The two demands and Rousseau's two responses

We have seen that nature and society can, and usually do, impose conflicting demands on the individual. In his more pessimistic moments, Rousseau sees these demands as polar opposites:

> Natural man is entirely for himself. He is the numerical unity, the natural whole, related only to himself or to his fellow creature. Civil man is only a fractional unity, dependent on the denominator; his value consists in his relation to the whole, that is the social body. Good social institutions are those that are best able to denature man, to deprive him of his absolute existence in order to give him a relative one and to transport the *I* into the common unity; so that each particular individual no longer thinks of himself as one, but as a part of the unity and no longer feels except within the whole. . . . He who in the civil order wants to preserve the primacy of the sentiments of nature does not know what he wants. Always in contradiction with himself, always floating between his inclinations and his duties, he will never be either man or citizen . . . (Em I.249–50/39–40)[12]

More optimistically, he envisages a possible reconciliation:

> I will be told that I abandon nature. I do not believe that at all. It chooses its instruments and regulates them according to need, not to opinion. Now needs change according to the situation of men. There is a great difference between the natural man living in the state of nature and the natural man living in the state of society. Emile is not a savage to be relegated to the desert. He is a savage made to inhabit cities. (Em III.483–4/205)

Commentators have found it remarkable that Rousseau should try to 'recreate natural man in society' in Book III having declared that to be impossible in Book I.

A response to the objection might be that in Book I Rousseau is describing the ideal type of social integration outlined, with all its totalitarian dangers, in the *Social Contract*. According to that model, ideal citizens, transformed by the constitutional provisions of the ideal Lawgiver,[13] would come to identify their particular interests with the public interest in the decision-making process of the general will. Public education, as supposedly practised in Geneva and as

envisaged for Poland,[14] would provide more or less concrete illustra-
tions of the kind of education Rousseau had in mind.

In the utterly imperfect political and social environment of contemporary France, the education of the 'savage made to inhabit the
cities' would be the best that could be attained, a realistic *pis-aller*.[15]
This is the approach that Rousseau adopts throughout most of
the *Emile*. There he is pessimistic about the possibility of political
and social change, but relatively optimistic in holding that a good
individual, properly educated, can flourish even in an imperfect
world.

(D)   Negative education and the art of timing

Rousseau's most provocative pedagogical idea was that of 'negative
education'. He introduces it by name near the beginning of Book II
of the *Emile*, where he applies it specifically to 'the most dangerous
period of human life . . . that from birth to the age of twelve':

> the first education ought to be purely negative. It consists not at
> all in teaching virtue or truth but in securing the heart from vice
> and the mind from error. If you could do nothing and let nothing
> be done, if you could bring your pupil healthy and robust to the
> age of twelve without knowing how to distinguish his right hand
> from his left, at your first lessons the eyes of his understanding
> would open up to reason. (Em II.323/93)

He reiterates the principle at the start of Book III:

> Remember always that the spirit of my education consists not in
> teaching the child many things, but in never letting anything but
> correct [*justes*] and clear ideas enter his brain. Were he to know
> nothing, it would be of little importance to me provided he made
> no mistakes. I put truths into his head only to guarantee him
> against the errors he would learn in their place. Reason and
> judgment come slowly; prejudices come in crowds; it is from
> them that he must be preserved. (Em III.435/171)

As so often, Rousseau is carried by his provocative rhetoric beyond
what he advocates in practice. Thus Book II, which takes Emile from
infancy to the end of childhood at about age twelve, contains several
positive lessons. With the help of the gardener Robert, the tutor
teaches the elements of property (Em II.331–3/98–9). As we shall
see later, he uses the running race (Em II.393–6/141–3) to teach
both moral and theoretical lessons, and by the end of Book II Emile

will have acquired quite advanced skills in draughtsmanship through practical instruction (Em II.397–400/143–6).

In short, the aim of the negative education is not to avoid positive teaching altogether (whatever Rousseau may say in his wilder epigrams), but to achieve a proper timing, a match between the stages of the child's development, physical, emotional and intellectual, and the kinds of instruction to which it is susceptible at those stages.[16] Rousseau encapsulates the theory in the *Letter to de Beaumont*:

> What I call positive education is that which tends to educate the mind beyond its age and to give the child knowledge of the duties of the man. What I call negative education is that which tends to perfect the [sense] organs which are the instruments of our knowledge before giving us knowledge itself and which prepares us for reason by exercising our senses. Negative education is not lazy, far from it. It does not give us virtues, but it prevents vices; it does not teach truth, but it preserves us from error. It disposes the child towards what may lead it to truth when it is able to understand it, and towards the good when it is able to love it. (LdeB 945)

Rousseau summarizes the stages of development at the start of Book III (Em III.428–9/167) in terms of the kind of rules that the child can understand. During infancy and childhood (Books I and II, up to the age of twelve), 'we have known no law other than that of necessity'. It is a world of contrived necessity, in which the tutor sets the scene so that the pupil *encounters* the world as though it contained only natural obstacles. Between childhood and puberty (Book III) 'we are dealing with what is useful'. From there 'we gradually approach moral notions which distinguish good and bad'. This last stage is inaugurated by the onset of sexuality in Book IV.

So in postponing Emile's full entry into society Rousseau is also postponing his development into a fully moral being:

> keep away from your pupil's mind all notions of social relations which are not within his reach. But when the chain of knowledge forces you to show him the mutual dependence of men, instead of showing it to him from the moral side, turn all your attention at first toward industry and mechanical arts which make men useful to one another. (Em III.456/185–6)

In particular Rousseau is anxious to postpone the acquisition of an inappropriate moral vocabulary, since 'before the age of reason one cannot have any idea of moral beings or of social relations. Hence so far as possible words which express them must be avoided . . .' (Em II.316/89).

But the necessity-utility-morality division is schematic. Rousseau always associates morality with society. The gradual approach to morality through utility has already started in Book II, as Emile encounters the gardener Robert not as a force of nature, but rather as a *person*, with interests of his own which he is prepared to defend.

Here, I think, Rousseau's sense of timing is precise. We learn about justice, he suggests, by encountering injustice, injustice committed against ourselves. Children complain 'that's not fair' (rather than 'that hurts', or 'that's uncomfortable') remarkably early, as they encounter injustice, whether real or imagined, inflicted on them by parents, brothers and sisters. Thus:

> Our first duties are to ourselves; our primary sentiments are centered on ourselves; all our natural movements relate in the first instance to our preservation and our well-being. Thus the first sentiment of justice does not come from the justice we owe but from that which is owed us . . . (Em II.329/97)

It is the entirely selfish awareness of unjust treatment meted out to us that prompts us to take the first step towards formulating a comprehensive sense of justice which will extend beyond the first step so far that we will end up not by negating the duty we owe to ourselves, but by expanding the idea we have of ourselves, as we increasingly identify our partial interests with more general interests.[17]

In Rousseau's story, Emile, under the tutor's supervision, plants his beans, 'mixes his labour' with their cultivation. He tends them daily and waters them until 'with transports of joy we see them sprout'. Ever manipulative, the tutor intervenes: 'I increase this joy by saying to him "This belongs to you"' (Em II.329/98). In the dramatic dénouement, the gardener Robert (like the conjuror, an accomplice of the tutor) uproots the beans: 'The young heart is aroused. The first sentiment of injustice [N.B.] comes to shed its bitterness in it . . .' (Em II.331/98–9). But the gardener's case is unanswerable. It is based on the right of the first occupier and mixer of labour:[18] 'What sirs? Is it you who have thus ruined my work? I had sown Maltese melons there. . . .' In the ensuing conversation, the unctuous tutor apologizes for his pupil's unwitting misdeed. The gardener proceeds to develop the 'labour theory of property', anchored in the experience of the peasant smallholder. The property system he advocates requires little policing by civil society under normal conditions of minimal external intervention: 'No one touches his neighbor's garden. Each respects the labor of others so that his own will be secure' (Em II.332/99). As in the best fairy stories all ends happily, as Robert allows Emile to cultivate a corner of his garden. Yet both parties remain outside full civil society. This is a stage at which property exists, but is defended by the force of the individual, not of the law: 'Remember that I will go and plough up your beans if you touch my melons', concludes the gardener.

(E)   Reason and reasoning[19]

Rousseau's differing conceptions of reason and reasoning are hard to tie down. He himself admits, in a footnote to the *Emile*, that his language, though not his thought, on the topic is inconsistent:

> One time I say children are incapable of reasoning; another time I make them reason quite keenly. I do not believe that with that I contradict myself in my ideas; but I cannot gainsay that I often contradict myself in my expressions. (Em II.345/108)

We shall see how far we can unravel the ideas from the expressions. For Rousseau, whereas our feelings or sentiments are innate, our reason is acquired. It is 'one of the acquisitions of man, it is even one of the most slowly acquired' (LdeB 951). In Julie's words: 'it is only at the end of several years that reason begins to form' in children (JNH V.3.562/461).

In some contexts Rousseau marks off reason [*raison*] from reasoning [*raisonnement*] or the art of reasoning [*l'art de raisonner*]. When he does so, he presents reasoning as epistemologically and morally neutral, against reason, which is ordered towards the true and the good.[20] He makes the distinction most clearly here, in the *Lettres morales*:

> The art of reasoning [*L'art de raisonner*] is not reason. It is often the abuse of reason. Reason is the faculty of ordering all the faculties of our soul in conformity with the nature of things, and in conformity with the relation of things to us. Reasoning [*Le raisonnement*] is the art of comparing known truths in order to construct on their basis other truths of which we were previously ignorant and which this art [of reasoning] enables us to discover. But it does not teach us to discover those basic truths [*ces vérités primitives*] which serve as the core of other truths. And when in the place of truths we put our opinions, our passions and our prejudices, far from illuminating us, it blinds us. It then does not elevate the soul, but enervates and corrupts our judgment which it ought to perfect. (Lmor 2.1090)

In her letter on education, Julie develops this theme at length, linking it to the schema of the stages of the acquisition of reason (first the reason of the senses, then 'human' reason[21]), and to Rousseau's criticism of Locke. There Julie follows Emile's tutor in warning us not to reason with young children, since they will pick up the tricks of argumentation by imitation [*raisonnement*], without acquiring the knowledge of the proper objects of argumentation [*raison*]:

> as soon as you have put one thing to their judgment, they will claim to judge everything. They will become sophistical and subtle, full of bad faith, fertile in nitpicking distinctions, always seeking to reduce to silence those who are feeble enough to expose themselves to their meagre enlightenment. (JNH V.3.573/470)

Whenever Rousseau makes the distinction between reason and reasoning it is to the detriment of the latter. In the previous passages he criticizes those who would teach children reasoning at an age when they cannot yet recognize the proper moral-epistemological objects of reason. But, as he himself recognizes in the footnote to the *Emile*, Book II, he also attributes quite sophisticated and legitimate powers of reasoning to children. The 'idea' behind Rousseau's inconsistent 'expressions' must be that reasoning is appropriate and legitimate provided that it corresponds to the stage of physical and moral development that the child has attained. During the stage of 'reason of the senses' [*raison sensitive*], before adolescence, children will properly figure things out, engage in quite sophisticated mathematics and natural science (all highly practical and applied), and also in prudential calculations about furthering their own interests, always under the unseen guidance of the tutor. At that stage, any reasoning, whether scientific or moral, which goes beyond those bounds will be false, copied, not the children's own. Children will enter discussions at a level of generality they cannot yet understand, but, being intelligent mimics, and also endowed, since infancy, with the power to enslave the wills of others, unless they are deflected, they will soon use that power to further their ill-channelled *amour-propre*.

When Rousseau uses the terminology of faculty psychology, he calls the faculty of reason a compound of the other faculties, which are derived from the senses. But he does not use that terminology systematically, and elsewhere, as we shall see in a moment, he presents reason less as a compound than as the coordinator of the other faculties. However, throughout the shifting psychological models and the different linguistic forms which mirror them, the thesis that we begin to reason relatively late remains constant.

According to Rousseau, we exercise reason in both scientific and moral practice. It is not easy to find a consistent linguistic form to represent these two domains of reason in his system. The opposition is not one between theoretical and practical reason, since all science in Rousseau's pedagogy is acquired in a practical fashion. Nor is it between a cognitive domain of science and a non-cognitive domain of morality, since there is moral knowledge for Rousseau as clear and objective as scientific knowledge. Perhaps the best we can do is distinguish between moral and non-moral reason, so that moral reason is: 'That reason which leads a man to the knowledge of his duties is not highly compound [*fort composée*]' (Em V.731/382). The modifying adverb [*fort*, highly] allows for some complexity. Figuring out just what one's duty is in complicated situations is itself a complicated business. But Rousseau's thought is that its complexity is within the grasp of anyone who has been properly raised. No further training in advanced reasoning skills is needed.

What picks out moral reason from other reason is that it is, or should be, grounded in the feeling of conscience, which in turn is innate and universal. Hence the importance of 'distinguish[ing] acquired ideas from . . . natural sentiments; for we sense before knowing . . .' (Em IV.599/289–90). Individuals must express that feeling in society, and in so doing they must use reason. Otherwise the critical feeling of conscience is overwhelmed by other more pressing feelings, and it 'degenerates into weakness' (Em IV.547–8/252–3).

So reason is acquired, and it is acquired in stages. First comes the 'reason of the senses'. Only later comes 'intellectual reason':

> Since everything which enters into the human understanding comes there through the senses, man's first reason is a reason of the senses [*une raison sensitive*]; it serves as the basis for intellectual reason. Our first masters of philosophy are our feet, our hands, our eyes. (Em II.370/125)

A few pages later he discusses reason in the context of the thorny problem of the *sensus communis*, or sixth sense:[22]

> it results from the well-regulated use of the other senses and . . . instructs about the nature of things by the conjunction of all their appearances. This sixth sense has consequently no organ. It resides only in the brain and its sensations, purely internal, are called perceptions or ideas. . . . It is the art of comparing them among themselves that is called human reason. . . . Thus what I called reason of the senses or childish reason [*raison sensitive ou puérile*] consists in forming simple ideas by the combination of several

sensations, and what I call intellectual or human reason [*raison intellectuelle ou humaine*] consists in forming complex ideas by the combination of several simple ideas. (Em II.417/157–8)

It is interesting to note that Rousseau does not commit himself to any kind of dualism here. The transition from one stage of reason to the other is couched in rather rough physiological terms, and the brain is referred to as the source of reason at each stage. When Rousseau says that the sixth sense has 'no organ', he means that it has no organ specific to itself, in the way that sight has the eyes and smell the nose. As we observed in Chapter I, Rousseau can best be described as agnostic when it comes to metaphysical questions in the philosophy of mind. To avoid determinism he swings towards dualism. But in psychological discussions like this he is closer to monism.

If all reason is acquired in stages, how do the stages of scientific reason correspond to those of moral reason? In Books II and III of the *Emile*, Rousseau establishes the link between the two kinds of reason through human interests. But the terminology of interests is elusive. Sometimes Rousseau describes human beings as self-interested in the sense that they defend their interests in their own well-being, in all its forms. At other times he talks of the interests people have in matters wholly outside themselves, in things which absorb them, in projects they are drawn to pursue. It is in pursuing interests of the latter kind that our curiosity is aroused. Here Rousseau bids us distinguish the genuine desire to learn 'which is born of a curiosity natural to man concerning all that might interest him [*tout ce qui peut l'intéresser*] closely or distantly' from that which is corrupted by debased *amour-propre*, the desire to be 'esteemed as learned' (Em III. 429/167). When you bring the child towards 'speculative studies' (geometry), you must 'render the problem interesting':

See how we gradually approach moral notions which distinguish good and bad! Up to now we have known no law other than that of necessity. Now we are dealing with what is useful. We shall soon get to what is suitable and good. (ibid.)

But what is the link between curiosity, which leads to an interest in 'speculative studies', and the advent of our awareness of morality? Rousseau does not make the link entirely clear. Burgelin says that Rousseau here points to 'geometry as intermediary' to morality.[23] He finds an analogy with Plato's *Republic*, where geometry played that role in the dialectic, which led through increasing abstraction to insight into the form of the good. But even if Rousseau is aiming for an end point which is similar to Plato's, the route he takes to it is grounded in a different psychological model. In Rousseau's story, the child passes to a higher level through curiosity and 'the innate desire for well-being and the impossibility of wholly fulfilling that desire'. This suggests that curiosity is an irritant, and that, in seeking our well-being, we seek to assuage that irritation. But that would not take us far on the road to morality. Or is it that the desires aroused by curiosity somehow open our eyes to similar desires on the part of others, and the need to show consideration for their desires as well as our own? Or should we follow Bloom's translation and say that a child's interest in geometry develops with curiosity concerning 'all that might have a connection with his interests' [*tout ce qui peut l'intéresser*]? Bloom's translation puts a strain on the verb '*intéresser*', which a native French speaker would not normally understand in this sense. But it does bring out Rousseau's search for continuity through transformation. The term interest [*intérêt, intéresser*], which is so frequent in his vocabulary, carries the unitary sense of concern, and at the same time the opposing senses of preoccupation with self and preoccupation with what is essentially other than self.

Bloom's translation would also tie this passage closely to Rousseau's story of the running race, in which the tutor manipulates the child's greed in order to teach it both intellectual and moral lessons. In this story, the tutor sets up races for other boys, with apparently no concern for his own pupil, who is a greedy child. He awards prizes of cakes to the winners. After a series of these races, the boys begin to cheat, pushing and tripping their opponents. In response, the tutor has them start from different, equidistant, points from the winning post. The pupil starts training, secretly, then enters the race, and wins, at first through trickery, as the tutor fixes the field, later genuinely, against all opposition. Frequently victorious, the pupil becomes generous and shares the prize with his opponents. Then the tutor cheats again, making the distances between the different starting points and the winning post different. Eventually the pupil notices and complains. But the tutor responds that he has no grounds for complaint, since the prizes are in the tutor's gift and entry in the race is voluntary. Finally the tutor allows the pupil to choose his starting point. This leads him in time to estimate distances, and so gain mastery of perspective, by eye. He thereby gains 'a glance almost as sure as a surveyor's chain' (Em II.396/143).

This story conveys many lessons. As a story about moral training, it tells us to apply the correct techniques to the different stages of children's development: elementary stimulus-response, an appeal to greed and self-interest. But at the same time children learn lessons not of simple egotism, since they come to appreciate the pleasures of elementary generosity, as they learn to share the cakes. As a story about scientific training, it tells us that children at this age have a capacity they will never have again to perfect their powers of sense-perception and to master techniques of elementary geometry in practice.

(F)   Reason: the method and the goal. Drawing and geometry

We have seen that in the growth of the child, and of humanity, the 'reason of the senses' precedes 'human reason'. But human reason, the fully developed power of abstraction, deduction and moral judgment, is not devalued by this chronology. The adult human being is destined to acquire this power according to Rousseau's view of science and of the moral-political order, both of which he sees as infused with reason. To be true to Rousseau's thought, we must distinguish between the pedagogy, which addresses children's senses during their formative years, and the objects which the pedagogy allows adults to handle, objects which are ordered in a highly rational system. Geometry and physics are the two key components in children's scientific formation in Rousseau's educational system, and he applies the distinction between the method and the goal of pedagogy to each of them in turn.

Geometry lessons begin in Book II of the *Emile*, in the context of training the senses; first touch, then sight. The deceptiveness of sight makes it particularly valuable in the learning process. Once deceived, we learn to verify one sense against another. The rationale even of drawing lessons is not strictly aesthetic. We teach children to draw to train their sense of sight: 'Since sight is, of all the senses, the one from which the mind's judgment can least easily be separated, much time is needed to learn how to see' (Em II.396/143). Through drawing lessons children are trained in the laws of perspective and proportion, and thereby gain access to nature:

> One could not learn to judge the extension and the size of bodies well without also getting to know their shapes and learning to imitate them; for, at bottom, this imitation depends absolutely only on the laws of perspective, and one can estimate extension by its appearances only if one has some feeling for those laws. (Em II.397/143)

The method is wholly practical, even imitative. Its aim is the in-duction of skills. But that same method leads to a higher level of knowledge, whose objects are general and abstract.

Rousseau advises the same method when the tutor moves on to geometry:

> Make exact figures, combine them, place them one on another, examine their relations. You will find the whole of elementary geometry in moving from observation to observation, without there being any question of definitions or problems or any form of demonstration other than simple superimposition. As for me I do not intend to teach geometry to Emile; it is he who will teach it to me; I will seek the relations, and he will find them, for I will seek them in such a way as to make him find them. For example, instead of using a compass to draw a circle, I shall draw it with a point at the end of a string turning on a pivot. After that, when I want to compare the radii among themselves, Emile will ridicule me and make me understand that the same string, always taut, cannot have drawn unequal distances. (Em II.399/145)

For Rousseau, practice and experimentation come before demonstration in geometry:

> People neglect the exactness of the figures. It is presupposed, and one concentrates on the demonstration. With us, on the contrary, the issue will never be with demonstration. Our most important business will be to draw lines very straight, very exact, very equal. . . . Geometry is for my pupil only the art of using the ruler and compass well. (Em II.400/146)

So the practice is that of the draughtsman or the carpenter. The experimentation is of the same kind: 'We shall sometimes try to foresee the success of the experiment before making it, we shall try to find reasons etc.'. At the end of the learning process Emile will have mastered the axioms, definitions and proofs, although he will not yet be able to order them in a systematic whole: 'We shall argue whether this equality of division ought always to be found in parallelograms, in trapezoids etc.' (ibid.).

We can draw a number of conclusions from Rousseau's advice on geometry teaching. Most importantly, he is not mounting an attack on reason. He advises the tutor to instil the reason of the senses at the age when it is appropriate. But it leads to a mastery of the most abstract principles of geometry. The pupil learns necessary relations. He will mock the tutor for his supposed inability to grasp that 'the *same* string, *always* taut *cannot fail* to draw equal radii'. He debates whether 'equality of division *ought always* to be found . . .' etc. It is also important to note that, while mastery of pure theory is not pursued as an end in itself, and that Rousseau's primary interest is the moral development of the pupil's personality, theoretical reason is a necessary, though not all-embracing, component of that development. Thus at this stage the surveyor rather than the geometer is the model, though the surveyor too needs to grasp the abstract principles of geometry. Both Rousseau's Emile and Plato's slave boy in the *Meno* learn geometry *for themselves*, through skilful orchestration by the instructor. The latter discovers geometrical proofs by recollecting ideas already present innately in him. Through trained practice, Emile discovers proofs by relating himself to the world. He thereby discovers truths about himself, as a learning, practising subject, and at the same time he learns truths about the law-governed world.

(G)   Reason: the method and the goal. Physics

In physics, as in geometry, Rousseau advocates learning by practice, conducted according to a careful sense of timing, which allows children to remain always in control of the material they are handling:

> Let us transform our sensations into ideas, but let us not make a sudden jump from objects of the senses to objects of the intellect [*des objets sensibles aux objets intellectuels*]. It is through the first that we must reach all the others. (Em III.430/168)

Among the distinctions which Rousseau takes off the shelf of the philosophical classics is that between demonstration by analysis and demonstration by synthesis. By analysis we start from what is given in experience, and go *up to* the principles which ground the given; by synthesis we go from axiomatic first principles *down to* the given.[24] In characteristic fashion, Rousseau ignores the metaphysical and logical problems involved in the distinction, but puts it to use in his practice. For the practitioner, faced by the two methods, 'It is not always necessary to choose. Sometimes one can use both resolution and combination in the same researches and guide the child by the method of instruction when he believes he is only analyzing' (Em III.434/171). Later he illustrates the same distinction with the metaphor of the two chains:

> There is a chain of general truths by which all the sciences are connected with common principles out of which they develop successively. This is the method of philosophers . . . There is another entirely different chain by which each particular object attracts another and always shows the one that follows. This order,

which fosters by means of constant curiosity the attention that they all demand, is the one most men follow and, in particular, is the one required for children. (Em III.436/172)

Throughout his pedagogy, in science as in morality, Rousseau's aim is the formation of the autonomous individual. So he dislikes laboratories, in which 'the scientific atmosphere/smell [*l'air scientifique*] kills science' (Em III.441–2/176), and advocates the principle of do-it-yourself, so that children should learn to build their own machines. One learns better from teaching oneself, albeit under supervision. To undergo 'the teaching of another' [*l'enseignement d'autrui*] is 'to submit oneself servilely to authority' (ibid.). Rousseau has an orthodox view that physics is 'the quest for the laws of nature', and his pedagogy does not imply any devaluation of science. Whether or not science should be conceived as a deductive system, deduction (the philosophers' 'chain') becomes an important pedagogical tool:

> without making them go very far in systematic physics, none the less arrange that all their experiments are connected with one another by some sort of deduction, in order that with the aid of this chain they can order them in their minds and recall them when needed . . . (Em III.442–3/176–7).

When we teach children the laws of nature, we must not undermine their intellectual autonomy. They must never find themselves mouthing law-like formulae as explanations of phenomena, when they cannot yet understand those explanations: 'In the quest for the laws of nature, always begin with the phenomena most common and most accessible to the senses, and accustom your pupil to take these phenomena not for reasons but for facts' (ibid.).

(H)   *Physics and morality: tricks with the conjuror*[25]

The teaching of physics (like that of geometry) is harnessed to the teaching of morality, and Rousseau's story of the conjuror is even more curious than that of the running race. Here the pupil demonstrates his knowledge of the principles of magnetism in the fairground, where the conjuror 'magically' draws a toy duck towards him by hiding a magnet in its beak and a piece of metal in some bread. With his newly acquired knowledge the pupil sees through the trick, and proceeds to make a fool of the conjuror by bringing with him his own concealed metal, and replicating the conjuror's 'magic'. The next day the conjuror takes his revenge on the pupil by reversing the polarity: he places metal in the base of the duck and conceals his own child-assistant under the table equipped with a large magnet. The assistant then guides the duck in any direction at the conjuror's command, and frustrates the pupil's attempts to repeat his triumph. The pupil is made to look a fool in public. His discomfiture is compounded when the conjuror later visits him and the tutor in their lodgings and points out the twin moral lessons: that the pupil has been guilty both of displaying corrupt *amour-propre*, showing off in public at the expense of another, and, as a privileged young boy, of having damaged the livelihood of a poor man.[26] The result is that both tutor and pupil are 'much embarrassed' [*très-confus*] (Em III.440/175), but morally instructed.

We must not underestimate the depth of the tutor's deception in this story:

> Each detail of this example is more important than it seems. How many lessons in one. How many mortifying consequences are attached to the first movement of vanity! Young master, spy out this first movement with care. If you know thus how to make humiliation and disgrace arise from it, be sure that a second movement will not come for a long time. 'So much preparation!' you will say. I agree – and all for the sake of making ourselves a compass to take the place of a meridian. (ibid.)

In a handwritten note Rousseau explains that the 'humiliation and disgrace' were devised by the tutor, not by the conjuror. In other words the whole elaborate charade was mounted by the tutor, with the conjuror's complicity. Thus even when the tutor appears to share the pupil's embarrassment and instruction it turns out that he was deceiving him all along. The period of shared games is about to end, but the friendship between tutor and pupil was itself always a construct of the tutor's. Real friendship between the two will be possible only after an intervening stage, that of the 'severity of the master'.[27]

(I) Stoicism: reining in the imagination, closing the gap between desires and reality

Rousseau never underestimates the importance of the imagination, but nor does he value it, in romantic fashion, as a faculty superior to cold reason. Instead he regards it as a powerful psychological drive, dangerous if not kept under tight rein, but essential to the formation of the fully moral adult. To the savage of the *Second Discourse*, who 'lives within himself' (2D 193/66), 'his imagination portrays nothing' (2D 144/28). In the passage from the natural to the social world the imagination is awakened. It allows moral feelings, in particular the sense of justice, to develop. At the same time, in the disordered soul, it can produce a world of chimeras, in which we suffer many times over, plagued by anticipation, anxiety and remorse. 'In short,' in the words of *Rousseau, Judge of Jean-Jacques*, 'such is the empire and influence of the imagination over us that it gives birth not only to the virtues and vices, but to the goods and ills of human life; and it is mainly the manner in which men yield to it that makes them good or bad, happy or unhappy on this earth' (RJJJ 2Dial.815–16/120).[28]

The imagination plays a particularly complex role in the tutor's contrivances to induct Emile successfully into the world of sexuality. The tutor reverses the strategy of the earlier stages of the negative education, when the aim was to postpone the advent of imagination and reflection as long as possible, and now introduces Emile to sexual love by bringing the imaginary before the real: 'There is no true love without enthusiasm and no enthusiasm without an object of perfection, real or chimerical, but always existing in the imagination' (Em V.743/391). What is at stake is the promotion of the right feelings, and they can be stimulated only by an ideal object: 'Everything in love is only illusion, I admit it. But what is real are the sentiments for the truly beautiful with which love animates us and which makes us love' (ibid.).[29]

In Rousseau's mature work the imagination, like *amour-propre*, which it fuels, is morally neutral. In the *Emile*, it is the tutor's task to track its development from infancy and to devise strategies for its control. 'At the beginning of life [in the nursery, as in the Forest] when memory and imagination are still inactive, the child is attentive only to what affects its senses at the moment' (Em I.284/64). As it grows, its imagination, along with its other faculties, becomes active. Rousseau is not entirely consistent concerning the level of that activity. Sometimes he says that the imagination is the initial cause of our passions: 'It is by the imagination alone that the passions are excited' (Letter to the Prince de Wurtemberg, 10 November 1763, CC 18#3017, p. 118).[30] In the *Emile*, his more considered conclusion seems to be that our passions are derived in the first instance from our sensory capacities [*sensibilité*], and that memory and the imagination have a secondary role to play in directing and assigning objects to those passions.[31] Reason and the imagination operate as two contenders for the control of the passions.

In his last works Rousseau treats the imagination in medical terms, describing how it can be 'maddened' [*effarouchée*] (Reveries

I.997/29) and then become 'less inflamed' (Reveries II.1002/35). At that stage it 'intoxicates me less with the madness of revery' (ibid.), a relatively calm reminiscence takes over from the creation of the imagination and the fever subsides.[32]

The unrestrained imagination torments with particular intensity those who have been badly raised in infancy. The key to infant training, for Rousseau, is:

> to accord to children more true freedom and less dominion, to let them do more by themselves and to exact less from others. Thus, accustomed early to limiting their desires to their strength, they will feel little privation of what is not in their power. (Em I.290/ 68)[33]

As children grow, the gap between their strength and their desires increases, fuelled by their growing imagination:

> The real world has its limits; the imaginary world is infinite. Unable to enlarge the one, let us restrict the other, for it is from the difference between the two alone that are born all the pains which make us truly unhappy. (Em II.305/81)

The tutor has surrounded Emile, up to the age of twelve, by a world of artificial necessity, in which the child encounters obstacles which appear not to be willed by others, but rather to be the inevitable outcomes of the child's own behaviour. As a result, 'You will make him patient, steady, resigned, calm, even when he has not got what he wanted, for it is the nature of man to endure patiently the necessity of things but not the ill will of others' (Em II.320/91). The strategy is to instil those stoic traits so deeply in the child's soul that he will retain them through into his adult, moral life, when he will have come to recognize and interact with other human beings as moral agents, endowed with free will like himself. Could the stoic traits survive the passage from childhood to adulthood? Perhaps they could if they were entrenched at a deep, affective level which would remain unchanged even when the adult's rational perception of the nature of its interactions had been transformed.

Maturity, then, is the control, not the annihilation, of the imagination:

> This then is the summary of the whole of human wisdom in the use of the passions: (1) To have a sense of the true relations of man, with respect to the species as well as to the individual. (2) To order all the affections of the soul according to these relations. But

is man the master of ordering his affections according to this or that relation? Without doubt, if he is master of directing his imagination toward this or that object or of giving it this or that habit. (Em IV.501/219)

The tutor continues to arrange the pupil's environment even into adolescence, when the imagination is at its most powerful. His task is still to arrange 'the choice of circumstances in which we put him', but now, instead of constructing a world of artificial necessity, he arranges the array of objects which can excite his imagination. As we shall see below, the lesson of the disastrous marriage of Emile and Sophie may be that the tutor's sense of timing was, at the crucial moment of adolescence, faulty, and that he postponed Emile's release into the 'real' world, where the stage was no longer set, too long, thus leaving him, and his wife, not after all in control of that dangerous drive, the imagination.

(J)   An education for autonomy. Stages of autonomy and authority

We considered the slogan 'prepare from afar the realm of freedom' in Chapter I. We now put it in its context in Book I of the *Emile* and weave it into some other threads of Rousseau's educational theory. He begins: 'The only habit that a child should be allowed is to contract none' (Em I.282/63), a typically provocative comment, since we know that the *Emile* is devoted as much to the inculcation of good habits, as to the prevention of bad ones, picked up from 'the world'.[34] Rousseau continues:

Prepare from afar the reign of his freedom and the use of his forces by leaving natural habit to his body, by putting him in the condition always to be master of himself and in all things to do his will, as soon as he has one. (ibid.)

We have defended Rousseau briefly against the charge that he advocates totalitarian manipulation in his pedagogy. As Emile's education proceeds, Rousseau lays himself ever more open to that charge, as he does in the following sinister passage in Book II:[35]

Take an opposite route with your pupil. Let him always believe that he is the master, and let it always be you who are. There is no subjection so perfect as that which keeps the appearance of freedom. Thus the will itself is made captive. The poor child who knows nothing, who can do nothing, who has no learning, is he not at your mercy? Do you not dispose with respect to him, of

everything which surrounds him? Are you not the master of
affecting him as you please? Are not his labors, his games, his
pleasures, his pains, all in your hands without him knowing it?
. . . It is then that you will be surprised by the subtlety of his
inventions for appropriating all objects he can attain and for truly
enjoying things without the help of opinion . . . (Em II.362–3/
120)

Rousseau can be defended against the charge of totalitarianism only
if his next words are read charitably: 'In leaving him thus master of
his wills you will not be fomenting his caprices. By never doing
anything except what suits him, he will soon do only what he ought
to do.' He admonishes the tutor:

I have to assume that you know the natural developments of the
human heart, that you know how to study man and the
individual, that you know beforehand what will bend your pupil's
will when he confronts all the objects of interest to his age that
you will cause to pass before his eyes. Now, to have the
instruments and to know their use well, is that not to be the
master of an operation? (Em II.364/121)

Rousseau assumes that we can distinguish between caprices and real
freedom. When we are capricious we are at the mercy of 'the world',
which, as we grow up into it, is increasingly one of fashion and fad, in
which we are passive, not active, deprived of the autonomous direction of our own identity, and in which our very identity is a fragmentary set of passing reflections. To form a firm identity requires
discipline, so 'the capriciousness of children is never the work of
nature but of bad discipline'. It is thus to promote the freedom of the
adult that the tutor studies the drives of the child and, through
his knowledge of the 'natural movement of the human heart',
manoeuvres the setting so that the drives will be well directed.

Concealment, guile and stage setting are the techniques deployed
by the tutor. How can they produce a truthful, free, autonomous
adult? What happens to the pupil when he becomes aware of them?
Rousseau signals moments of transition from ignorance to awareness,
but is surprisingly unconcerned about the effect of these revelations
on Emile.

Until the age of twelve (up to the end of Book II), all is simulation. The tutor pretends to be the pupil's friend, his equal, and
conceals his authority over him:[36]

It is his friend, his comrade, it is the companion of his games

81

whom he approaches. He is quite sure on seeing me that he will
not for long remain without entertainment. We never depend on
one another, but we always agree, and with no one else are we so
well off as we are together. (Em II.419/159)

With the episode of the magician, true authority is revealed: 'the
time is approaching when the master's severity must succeed
the comrade's compliance. This change ought to take place gradually' (Em III.440/175). That relationship of inequality between
tutor and pupil will henceforth be recognized by both parties and
will govern their interactions until Emile's marriage. The advent of
sexuality in Book IV seems at first to make Emile immediately into
an adult, and so to free him from his dependence on the tutor's
authority:

> When . . . you have a presentiment of the critical moment,
> instantly abandon your old tone with him for ever. He is still your
> disciple, but he is no longer your pupil. He is your friend, he is a
> man. From now on treat him as such. (Em IV.639/316)

It looks as though the play of authority, friendship and simulation
has finally been played out, and that the tutor and pupil have now
reached a stable relationship of transparency, equality and real
friendship. But nothing is ever so simple in Rousseau's story. In fact,
Book IV inaugurates a phase of true authority, true because it is
recognized and accepted by Emile for what it is:

> Up to now you got nothing from him except by force or ruse.
> Authority and the law of duty were unknown to him. He had to
> be constrained or deceived to make him obey you. But see how
> many new chains you have put around his heart. Reason,
> friendship, gratitude, countless affections speak to him in a tone
> he cannot fail to recognize. (ibid.)

It is notable that this authority relationship is, by the standards of
the *Social Contract*, an impure one, in that it is still deeply rooted in
dépendance personnelle, and in particular in the unreliable personal
emotion of gratitude, which so easily turns into *ressentiment*, and
which Rousseau himself regarded with such suspicion in his own
life. It is perhaps not surprising then that the marriage of Emile
and Sophie was doomed to fail.[37] One might argue that the tutor,
the master of timing, mistimed his final withdrawal from Emile's
life; that in Freudian terms Emile never achieved a fully autonomous superego.[38] By the same token, Sophie, having never

received even the education needed for a (female) savage to live successfully in the cities, falls prey all too swiftly to their corrupt inhabitants.

(K)   Freedom, judgment, knowledge

Some five pages into the 'Profession of Faith of the Savoyard Vicar', Rousseau puts into the Vicar's mouth a rare piece of quite technical philosophy. The Vicar propounds a rough theory of knowledge and philosophy of mind, maintaining that the mind is independent of the feelings, and that it exercises its function of judgment in complete freedom. In this respect, the Vicar is explicitly rejecting the 'sensationism' currently in vogue, and propounded by writers like Quesnay in the *Encyclopédie* and Helvétius in *De l'esprit*. For Quesnay, 'it is sensations themselves that produce judgments. So all our perceptions are just the purely passive operations of a sensory being' [*être sensitif*]. In Helvétius's epigram: '*judging* is never anything but *feeling*' [juger *n'est jamais que* sentir].[39]

In stressing the absolute freedom of judgment, and the independence of the mind from the feelings, the Vicar is returning to Descartes, but as Gouhier has shown, his is an eclectic, unorthodox version, if not travesty, of the method of doubt. Here are Descartes' words: 'since I now wished to devote myself solely to the search for truth, I thought it necessary to . . . reject as if absolutely false everything in which I could imagine the least doubt, in order to see if I was left believing anything that was entirely indubitable.'[40] Now here are the Vicar's:

> taking the love of truth as my whole philosophy, and as my whole method an easy and simple rule that exempts me from the vain subtlety of arguments, I pick up again on the basis of this rule the examination of the knowledge that interests me. I am resolved to accept as evident all knowledge to which in the sincerity of my heart I cannot refuse my consent, to accept as true all that which appears to me to have a necessary connection with this first knowledge, and to leave all the rest in uncertainty without rejecting it or accepting it and without tormenting myself to clarify it if it leads to nothing useful for practice. (Em IV.570/ 269–70)

The differences are as striking as the similarities. Both Descartes and the Vicar seek sure foundations, but they seek them for different purposes. For Descartes the goal is certainty in the sciences. For the Vicar it is peace of mind. Like Descartes, he wants to limit the scope for error, but the limits are those of practice rather than theory. In his words, 'I was to learn to limit my research to what was immediately related to my interest' [*ce qui m'intéressoit immédiatement*] (Em IV.569/269). He will discover his interest by consulting 'the inner light': echo of Descartes, which recurs as the Vicar resolves to admit only 'evident' items of knowledge. But the focus of 'evidence' [*évidence*] has been transformed. Now it relates to 'the sincerity of my heart', not to pure reason. Descartes' *cogito* yields a question: 'But what then am I?', to which the answer is given in two words: '*Res cogitans*', 'a thing that thinks'.[41] He devotes the rest of his *Meditations* to bringing out the content of those two words.

The Vicar in contrast proceeds like this. He poses two questions: (a) 'But who am I?'; (b) 'What right have I to judge things, and what determines my judgments?' In answering them, he at once abandons the method of scepticism: 'I exist and I have senses by which I am affected'. Comparing him with Descartes, we note how naïve the Vicar is, as he immediately reveals the goal of his project, which is to produce a model of the self as an active agent, an independent coordinator of the sensations which it receives: 'Thus my glance must first be turned toward myself in order to know the *instrument* [italics added] I wish to use and how far I can trust its use.' He will seek to answer question (a) by distinguishing two different elements in question (b): (bi): 'Do I have a particular feeling [*sentiment propre*] of my existence?', and (bii) 'Do I feel it [my existence] only through my sensations?' In reaching a negative response to (bii) he will reach a positive one to (bi). Doubt makes a fleeting appearance: 'Here is my first doubt, one which up to now, it is impossible to resolve. For, since I am continually affected by sensations . . . how can I know whether the feeling of *me* is something outside those same sensations, able to be independent of them?' To reach an affirmative answer to that question, he quickly abandons sceptical doubt to distinguish 'inner' sensations from 'outer' causes of sensations, which 'affect me whether I want them to or not', and to proceed directly to the conclusion that 'not only do I exist, but there also exist other beings – the objects of my sensations' (Em IV.571/ 270). Rapidly dismissing disputes between idealists and materialists as meaningless chimeras, the Vicar concludes brusquely: 'All that I sense outside me and that acts on my senses I call matter and all those parts of matter that I conceive to be united in individual beings I call bodies' (ibid.).

With these stumbling steps we have reached the core of the Vicar's epistemology-cum-philosophy of mind: 'Already I am as sure of the universe's existence as of my own. Next I reflect on the objects of my sensations; and, finding in myself the faculty of comparing them, I sense myself endowed with an active force which I did not before know I had.' He continues:

> To perceive is to sense; to compare is to judge. Judging and sensing are not the same thing. By sensation objects are presented to me separated, isolated, such as they are in nature. By comparison I move them, I transpose them, and, so to speak, I superimpose them on one another in order to pronounce on their difference or their likeness and generally on all their relations. According to me, the distinctive faculty of the active or intelligent being is to be able to give a sense to the word *is*. I seek in vain in the purely sensitive being for this intelligent force which superimposes and then pronounces . . . (ibid.)

To understand the connection between sensing and judging, Rousseau reverts to the vocabulary of Malebranche: 'comparative ideas . . . certainly do not belong to the sensations, although my mind produces them only on the *occasion* [italics added] of my sensation' (Em IV.572/271). Furthermore, judging and sensing must be different, for if they were the same, there could be no error, since judgment can err, whereas sensation cannot. Rousseau translates that doctrine of Descartes,[42] into an idiom closer to, but still distinct from, sensationism, arguing that the proper object of judgment is the *relation* between sensations:

> When the two sensations to be compared are perceived . . . their relation is not yet sensed. If the judgment of this relation were only a sensation and came to me solely from the object, my judgments would never deceive me, since it is never false that I sense what I sense. (ibid.)

Finally, asks the Vicar, how could we know that two senses reveal one and the same object if there were 'no communication' between those senses. The rhetorical question supposes that we do know that they reveal one and the same object, so there must be some 'communication' between the senses. Otherwise, we should have 'no way of perceiving the identity of the object'. But since we do, after all, have such a 'way of perceiving identity', there must be some corresponding identity on the side of the perceiver, and it in turn must be a focus of activity: 'this force of my mind which brings together and compares my sensations'. I am not master of controlling all I feel, but I am master of 'examining more or less what I feel' (Em IV.573/272).

The concluding step, like the preceding ones, marks a partial return to Descartes. We have reached a form of dualism in philosophy of mind ('therefore I am not simply a sensitive and passive being, but an active and intelligent being'), and a form of realism in epistemology ('truth is in things and not in the mind which judges them'). But there is still a paradoxical sting in the tail: 'the less of myself I put in the judgments I make, the more sure I am of approaching the truth. Thus my rule of yielding to sentiment more than to reason is confirmed by reason itself' (ibid.).[43]

IV

The *Social Contract*: Principles of Right

(A)   Introduction: the Social Contract, *an uncompleted fragment*

In this and the following two chapters I approach Rousseau's political theory through a detailed reading of the *Social Contract*. The text entitled *Du contract social ou principes du droit politique*, published in 1762, is a fragment. Rousseau says of it that it was an 'extract from a longer work, entitled the *Institutions politiques*, abandoned as soon as it left the pen. It was an enterprise which was anyway beyond my capabilities' (Letter to Moultou, 18 January 1762, CC 10#1641, pp. 41–2). He tells us that he formed the 'first idea' of the *Institutions politiques* when he was diplomatic attaché in Venice in 1743–4, by 'observing the defects of that Republic's highly vaunted constitution' (Conf IX.404/340). Work on it was probably resumed in 1750–1, and its plan was 'digested' in 1754 (Conf VIII.394/331). But he had 'still hardly made any progress on it' by 1756. It was not until 1761 that Rousseau was to produce the first draft of the *Social Contract* (the *Geneva Manuscript*), and by 9 August 1761 he could report to his publisher, Rey: 'I now have a clean copy of my treatise on political right, ready for publication'.[1] If we are to believe the author, then, the gestation period of the *Social Contract* was over twenty years, from the formation of the 'first idea' to the delivery of the manuscript to the publisher.

Rousseau tells us that in the longer work he would have examined international relations (SC III.15.431Fn./194Fn.), and he lays out the contents of this missing section in the brief appendix which is the last chapter of the *Social Contract*: 'the law of nations, commerce, the right of war and conquest, public law, alliances, negotiations, treaties etc.' (SC IV.9.470/224).[2]

Before embarking on the detailed examination of the *Social*

Contract, I list a string of interconnected questions which Rousseau addresses in the course of the text.

(1) How is it possible to overcome the political vices of the *Ancien Régime*, arbitrary rule, inequality and personal dependence, and replace them by the impersonal working of the law, a more equal distribution of wealth and power, and the transformation of the individual into a citizen, dependent on the sovereign people alone?

(2) How can the conditions of a rational consensus be guaranteed?

(3) How can popular sovereignty be realized on a scale larger than the small city state?

(4) How is it possible to devise a particular constitution [*lois politiques*] suitable for a particular people?

(5) How is it possible to inculcate into a people the *moeurs*, the moral ties of republican virtue, which will give it strength and unity?

Rousseau gives the most radical answers to questions (1) and (2), and more conservative ones to (3), (4) and (5). Indeed it is just because the normative demands of the first group of answers are so extreme, so apparently destructive of any established order, that we need such a powerful institutional and moral framework to hold together the new order which Rousseau envisages. In J. S. Mill's words, 'with what a salutary shock did the paradoxes of Rousseau explode in our midst, dislocating a mass of one-sided opinion and forcing its elements to recombine in a better form and with additional ingredients.'[3] We shall see that Rousseau himself both bombs and rebuilds the edifice.

Rousseau's work was rapidly absorbed into the political culture of the French Revolution, and then subjected to the backlash of its liberal critics. Because of its richness, complexity and ambiguity it was exploited for numerous conflicting ideological purposes by different factions at different stages of the Revolution, as they sought to answer question (5), and build what has been called a 'republic of virtue' from Rousseau's materials.[4] As the Terror rose to its height in 1794, the leaders of the Convention sought to fabricate a cult of Nature as an instrument of ideological control over 'the spontaneous disorders and acts of violence', which had been released. In this, the 'ecstatic pantheism' of the 'Profession of Faith of the Savoyard Vicar' was set to music in a cantata, part of the bizarre rites of secularized religion.[5] It had already been decreed in 1791 that the church of Ste Geneviève should be closed for worship and converted into the new Pantheon, which would:

henceforth 'receive the ashes of the great men of French freedom'.
Now in 1794 the Convention decreed that 'the ashes of Jean-
Jacques Rousseau be translated to the Pantheon . . . The entry
into the Pantheon was accompanied by the sound of an organ,
amidst a 'religious reverence', and Cambracérès, the President of
the Convention, pronounced a vibrant discourse: 'Profound
moralist, apostle of freedom and equality, he was the forerunner
who called the nation to the paths of glory and happiness . . . This
day, this apotheosis, this coming together of a whole people, this
triumphal pomp, all this proclaims that the Convention wishes to
render to the philosopher of nature both the debt of the French
and the recognition of humanity'. The ceremony ended with a
Hymn to Jean-Jacques Rousseau . . . of which each group sang one
verse, and all together took up the refrain: 'Oh Rousseau, model
for the wise, Benefactor of humanity, Accept the homage of a
proud, free people, And from within your tomb uphold equality'.[6]

But the same Rousseau, who, in 1794, was variously deified and
converted into an 'apostle of freedom and equality', was seen in
1814, in the aftermath of the Revolution, as the herald of a new and
terrible form of oppression. According to Constant's diagnosis, the
Revolution overthrew the despotism of absolute monarchy, but
replaced it by the despotism of absolute popular sovereignty. The
leaders of the Revolution, he says:

> believed that everything should give way before collective
> authority and that all restriction of individual rights would be
> compensated by participation in the social power . . .

What they failed to recognize, says Constant, is that:

> The social power harmed individual independence in all sorts of
> ways without suppressing the need for it. It was vainly repeated to
> them, following Rousseau, that 'the laws of freedom are a
> thousand times more austere than the yoke of tyranny.'[7]

I shall return to the conflict between the judgments of 1794 and
1814 and face the problem of Rousseau and totalitarianism in Chapter VI (B). In Chapters IV and V I shall focus on the five questions
tabled above, which together constitute the heart of Rousseau's own
concerns in political theory, and which spring from the unresolved
tension between naturalism and deontology identified in Chapter I.

(B)   Right and fact

Rousseau begins the *Social Contract* with a brief foreword apologizing for the fragmentary nature of the work. But the apologetic tone does not last long. The text proper opens with a powerful prologue:

> I want to investigate whether in the civil order there can be any rule of administration which is legitimate and sure, taking men as they are and laws as they can be: in this investigation I shall attempt always to ally what right permits with what interest prescribes, so that justice and utility may not be divided. (SC I. Proem.351/131)

His tone is both personal and authoritative. He bombards the reader with an explosion of antitheses: legitimate/sure, men as they are/ laws as they can be, right permits/interest prescribes, justice/utility. The antitheses proclaim distinctions, but also connections. Rousseau will mark off questions of right from questions of fact, but will also show in outline how it is possible to embody standards of legitimacy in properly constructed institutions, however difficult it may be to do so in practice.[8] So Rousseau's *Social Contract* is not a utopian dream, to be 'relegate[d] . . . to the world of chimeras'.[9] Nor is it a servile justification of the status quo, in the manner of Grotius who would 'always establish right by fact', the method 'most favourable to tyrants' (SC I.1.353/132).

Chapter 1 opens on the same high rhetorical note, with another string of antitheses:

> Man was born free [*L'homme est né libre*], and everywhere he is in chains. One who believes himself the master of others is none the less a greater slave than they. How did this change come about? I do not know. What can make it legitimate? [*Qu'est-ce qui peut le rendre légitime?*] I believe I can answer that question. (SC I.1.351/ 131)

The two phrases left in French are a challenge to the translator. In the first, does Rousseau mean that man *is* or that he *was* born free? And in the second, what is it to make something *legitimate*, and what is it that is to be made legitimate?[10]

In the second problem phrase, Rousseau tells us that a certain change has come about, and it is that *change* that we can 'make legitimate' ['*rendre légitime*']. But to 'make legitimate' is not to 'legitimize' in the sociological sense of providing a justification or legitimation for a particular institution. Rather it is to change that institution so that it becomes (genuinely) legitimate. So Rousseau is calling for the *change*, which has come about he knows not how, to be changed once again, so that a new order can be constructed, which will now be legitimate, and in which the 'chains' of slavery and mastery will be exchanged for the self-legislation of the general will.

Grammatically, the first problem phrase means 'Man was born free', rather than 'Man is born free', and that is the translation I have adopted.[11] The two phrases together then describe a change which has happened to humanity as a whole ['*l'homme*'] and which now needs to be changed again if it is to be made legitimate. The task of the *Social Contract* will be to expound the form and mechanism of that new change.

The contents page of the *Social Contract* gives subheadings to each of the four Books: I, 'In which we investigate how man passes from the state of nature to the civil state, and what the essential conditions of the Pact are'; II, 'In which we discuss legislation'; III, 'In which we discuss political Laws, that is to say the form of Government'; IV, 'In which we continue to discuss political Laws and expound the means of strengthening the constitution of the State'.[12] These subheadings indicate that the focus of Books I and II is right and that of III and IV is fact, but the division is far from watertight. Though it is possible to assign the two axes chapter by chapter, when we come to read them more closely, we shall find that the two axes intersect at many points, and that few chapters are oriented wholly to right or wholly to fact.[13]

Alongside the normative principles of right and the instrumental maxims of politics lie *moeurs*, the morals, customs and opinions (SC II.12.394/164–5) of a people. The theme of the moral health of the body politic, partly depending on and partly contributing to good institutions, runs through the *Social Contract*. We shall return to this theme at Chapter VI (E) below.

(C)   *Nature and convention*

For Rousseau, nature and convention are fundamentally opposed, and the opposition between them must be made absolute before it can be overcome. The *Second Discourse*, the *Emile* and the *Social Contract* are variants on this shared theme. The first stresses the distance between the two, and only gestures towards their reconciliation. The second opens by telling us that their reconciliation is impossible: 'Forced to do battle with either nature or social institutions, we must opt for making a man or a citizen, since it is impossible to make the one and the other at the same time' (Em I.248/39). But by its conclusion Emile has been educated not only to be a successful 'savage made to inhabit [present day, unjust] cities' (Em III.483–4/ 205), but also to be capable of assimilating the lesson of the *Social Contract*,[14] and, armed with that, to transform society from within. But it is the *Social Contract* itself that explores most fully both the opposition and the reconciliation of the natural and the conventional. The 'balance sheet' of SC I.8 describes the 'remarkable change in man', the transformation of the human being who moves from the state of nature to the civil state. Rousseau talks there of *replacing* one set of characteristics by another: 'the voice of duty replaces physical impulse and right replaces appetite'. One 'loses . . . natural freedom' and 'gains . . . civil freedom' (SC I.8.364–5/141–2), and 'in destroying natural equality, the fundamental compact . . . substitutes a moral and legitimate equality for whatever physical inequality nature may have placed between men . . .' (SC I.9.367/144). The Lawgiver performs an extreme, alarming replacement therapy on the people. He must be:

> capable of transforming each individual, who by himself is a perfect and solitary whole, into a part of a larger whole from which this individual receives, in a sense, his life and being, capable of spoiling [*altérer*] [mutilating, *Geneva Manuscript* I.5] man's constitution in order to strengthen it . . . He must in short take away man's own forces in order to give him forces that are foreign to him . . . The more these natural forces are dead and destroyed, and the acquired ones great and lasting, the more the institution too is solid and perfect. (SC II.7.381–2/155)

The present order is defective because in it most people are deprived of freedom, and so of their essential capacity to act as human beings, by the unequal division of power between the rich and mighty and the poor and weak. The result is the world of *dépendance personnelle*, or *dépendance particuliere* (SC II.11.391/162), in which the fate of individuals lies not in their own hands, but in the hands of other individuals.[15] Rousseau maintains that *dépendance personnelle* can be defeated only if it is transformed into an equally total dependence on the body politic as a whole. Then and only then will the natural and the conventional be reconciled. Rousseau asserts this most clearly in the *Emile*, in an explicit commentary on the *Social Contract*:

> There are two sorts of dependence: dependence on things, which is from nature; dependence on men, which is from society. Dependence on things, since it has no morality, is in no way detrimental to freedom and engenders no vices. Dependence on men, since it is without order, engenders all the vices, and, by it,

master and slave are mutually corrupted. If there is any means of remedying this ill in society, it is to substitute law for man and to arm the general wills with a real strength superior to the action of every particular will. If the laws of nations could, like those of nature, have an inflexibility that no human force could ever conquer, dependence on men would then become dependence on things again; in the republic all the advantages of the natural state would be united with those of the civil state, and freedom which keeps man exempt from vices would be joined to morality which raises him to virtue. (Em II.311/85)

The terms 'convention' and 'conventional' [*convention, conventionnel*] have different shades of meaning in Rousseau's writings. In a positive sense, they refer to what is established by a legitimate agreement, in a negative sense to what is established *merely* by agreement, counter to nature. In the *Social Contract* the positive sense becomes dominant, denoting the beneficial effects of a society founded on the legitimate terms of the contract. The *Social Contract* propounds a theory of the radical transformation of natural relations between human beings into a new kind of social relations, ideally those sanctioned by an agreement between free, rational, equal parties.[16]

Rousseau's aim, then, is to construct a legitimate social order in which the nature of human beings will be transformed so that they will once again be able to live integrated lives even within society. In the pages devoted to right, he presents that integration as something to be defined and as something to be aspired to. In those devoted to maxims of politics, he theorizes the conditions under which it could be made a reality:

What makes the constitution of a State truly solid and durable is when the norms [*convenances*] are observed in such a way that natural relations and laws always coincide [*tombent toujours de concert*], on the same points, so that the latter do nothing, so to speak, but assure, accompany and rectify the former. (SC II.11.393/163–4)[17]

In the chapters devoted to maxims of politics, Rousseau investigates what fundamental laws [*lois politiques*] are suited to a particular people, laws which will both correspond to the principles of right, and will also allow that people to flourish.

(D)   *Errors of the predecessors*

Book I of the *Social Contract* is devoted to questions of right. In the critical, polemical chapters SC I.1–5 Rousseau engages with his predecessors briefly but systematically before moving on to expound the core of his own positive normative programme in SC I.6–9. In asserting principles of right, Rousseau propounds definitions, which he substantiates sometimes by rhetoric, sometimes by sketchy arguments. In contrast, when he outlines maxims of politics, his tone is more cautious. These maxims are offered as guidelines rather than precise instructions.

The opening chapter (SC I.1) represents a rich interplay between questions of right and questions of fact. We have already examined its first paragraph, which concludes: 'How did this change come about? I do not know. How can it be made legitimate? I believe I can answer that question' (SC I.1.351/131). The change is the change from freedom in nature to unfreedom in society. In the latter we are bound by 'chains', though except for prisoners and slaves, these are not material chains, but the chains of habitual obedience to superiors. So, in order to answer the question of legitimacy, we must understand the nature of obedience. In this opening chapter Rousseau does not distinguish the factual question 'Why do people obey?' from the normative question 'Why should they obey?'. He considers three possible answers to the composite question: (a) because they are forced to obey; (b) because it is natural for them to obey; (c) because they have agreed to obey.

Answer (b) is the traditional Aristotelian one, that human beings are by nature radically unequal, and by nature those who are weaker in mind and body are suited to obey those who are stronger, and since the relation of command and obedience corresponds to the nature of both parties, neither force nor consent is normally required. Rousseau dismisses this answer in half a sentence in SC I.1. He had already delivered the final blows to that kind of naturalism in the *Second Discourse*, whose aim was to show that neither social inequalities nor relations of obedience based on them were natural.[18] In the *Social Contract*, he gives grounds for dismissing it in SC I.2, 'On the first societies', in which he attacks the idea that political obligation is derived from the obligation of children to obey their parents within 'the most ancient of all societies and the only natural one . . . that of the family' (SC I.2.352/132). Here he takes up Locke's dismissal of Filmer's patriarchalism,[19] and gives the argument his own twist. The main argument is propounded in the first paragraph, where Rousseau reaches the conclusion:

Children remain bound to the father only as long as they need him for self-preservation. As soon as this need ceases, the natural bond dissolves. The children, exempt from the obedience they owed the father, and the father, exempt from the care he owed the children, all return equally to independence. If they continue to remain united, it is no longer naturally but voluntarily, and the family itself is maintained only by convention. (ibid.)

and the second paragraph, in which he grounds the conclusion by linking freedom and self-preservation, two of the natural, pre-social characteristics of human beings:

This common freedom is a consequence of man's nature. His first law is to attend to his own preservation, his first cares are those he owes himself; and as soon as he has reached the age of reason, as he alone is the judge of the proper means of preserving himself, he thus becomes his own master. (ibid.)

Rousseau devotes the rest of the chapter to dismissing Aristotle's view that 'there are slaves by nature', taking up the conclusion of the *Second Discourse* that one can be conditioned into any psychological state, including a slavish one, a state of mind which can be transmitted from generation to generation: 'Every man born in slavery is born for slavery, nothing is more certain. Slaves lose everything in their chains, including the desire to escape them' (SC I.2.353/133).

Answer (a), that obedience is based on force, looks initially like a satisfactory answer to the factual question, why do people obey?, if not to the normative question, why should they? But even at the level of fact, Rousseau argues, (a) is an inadequate answer, because any order based entirely on force, not mitigated by any acceptance that force is justified, must be radically unstable. People who see themselves as only the victims of force will not hesitate to turn the tables on their oppressors if given the opportunity, as Rousseau goes on to show in SC I.3 ('The right of the strongest'). He concludes that, as a matter of fact, the participants in any continuing social order must adopt at least a minimally normative attitude towards obedience, they must *agree* to obey, however grudgingly.[20]

What has been established so far is that there are only three possible grounds of legitimacy, either force or nature or agreement, and since neither force nor nature is acceptable, then, by elimination, legitimacy must be based on agreement, although we know nothing yet about the nature of that agreement. The argument assumes that these three are exhaustive alternatives. It is certainly

95

conceivable that there might be others, but at least they exhaust the range of answers offered by political theorists up to Rousseau's time.

SC I.4 is entitled 'On slavery'. It is addressed not to Aristotle's view that there are slaves by nature, but to the more recent claim by natural lawyers that the contract legitimating the social order could be a 'pact of slavery' or 'pact of submission' between people and rulers.[21] Such a pact, for Rousseau, is unacceptable because it denies two of the essential characteristics of human beings, their drive to self-preservation and their freedom; the former, because the citizens' security is not better secured by an uncontrolled despotism than it is by uncontrolled anarchy; the latter, because 'To renounce one's freedom is to renounce one's status as a man, the rights of humanity, and even its duties' (SC I.4.356/135). In the rest of the chapter, Rousseau demolishes the alleged right of conquest, according to which members of a defeated side would 'agree' to their own enslavement in return for having their lives spared. Rousseau argues that such a 'right' must be invalid. According to his understanding of international relations, war does not take place between individuals, but between states.[22] Individuals, 'as soon as they lay down their arms and surrender, since they cease to be enemies or instruments of the enemy, . . . become simply men once again, and one no longer has a right to their lives' (SC I.4.357/136). More fundamentally, 'the right of conquest . . . has no basis other than the law of the strongest', which has already been shown to be no law at all. Another target of this densely argued chapter is the claim that colonial territories are legitimately subjugated by the right of war.[23]

Rousseau concludes the opening, critical movement of the *Social Contract* at I.5 by arguing, *ad hominem* against Grotius, that the idea that a whole people could enslave itself and 'give itself to a king' (SC I.4.359/137) presupposes that that people already exists. That means that one must 'examine the act by which a people becomes a people', and that act can only be the agreement by which the people unites itself into a people. Why? Because, 'if there were no prior convention, what would become of the obligation for the minority to submit to the choice of the majority?' In short, 'The law of majority voting is itself an established convention, and presupposes unanimity at least once.' With this conclusion, Rousseau is ready to embark on his own model of the legitimate contract.

(E)   *The legitimate contract: free-riders and the 'remarkable change in man'*

Rousseau sets the scene of the social contract at a particular moment in humanity's development, rather than in a timeless eternity. Yet it is a logical, not a historical construction, applicable to the affairs of human beings at any time that they reach that stage:[24]

> I assume men to have reached the point where the obstacles to their self-preservation in the state of nature prevail by their resistance over the forces each individual can use to maintain himself in that state. (SC I.6.360/138)

The 'obstacles' analysed in the historical reconstruction of the *Second Discourse* are initially natural ones, 'barren years, long sharp winters, burning summers', obstacles posed by nature's recalcitrance and parsimony, which led to the enforced socialization of previously unsocialized human beings. Thereafter the obstacles become, increasingly, those produced by human beings themselves, obstacles thrown up as people pursue their natural, and therefore blameless, goal of self-preservation. Within a wrongly ordered society that pursuit turns into a destructive battle between individuals, who find that they can preserve themselves only at the expense of their neighbours.

The parties to the contract are individuals striving to protect their own interests and endowed with a degree of rationality: 'the force and the liberty of each man being the first instruments of his preservation'. A legitimate agreement will be the outcome if and only if each individual engages himself 'without harming himself and without neglecting the care which he owes himself'. The liberal case against Rousseau is that the political order he advocates, based on the terms of the contract laid down in SC I.6, does not guarantee the individual against that harm, and that it therefore lacks the legitimacy Rousseau himself claims for it. We shall consider the liberal critique later.

The three chapters SC I.6, I.7 and I.8 must be read in sequence. None is complete alone. SC I.6 presents the parties to the contract as rational individuals who aim to defend their interests by agreeing to the ground rules of communal action. I.8 presents those same individuals transformed by the process of socialization:

> The passage from the state of nature to the civil state produces a very remarkable change in man, by substituting justice for instinct in his conduct, and giving his actions the morality they previously lacked. Only then, when the voice of duty replaces physical impulse and right replaces appetite, does man, who until then had considered only himself, find that he is forced to act on different principles, and to consult his reason before listening to his inclinations. (SC I.8.364/141)

97

The transformation comes about when the individual 'loses . . . his natural freedom and the unlimited right to all that tempts him and that he can attain', and 'gains . . . civil freedom and property in all that he possesses' (SC I.8.364–5/141–2). Legitimate civil freedom is that which is 'limited by the general will'. To complete the 'balance sheet', to decide whether the individual has gained or lost in the exchange, we therefore need to examine the relation between the individual will and the general will, presented in the pivotal chapter, SC I.7. In SC I.6 Rousseau had already stated that the general will comprises the essence of the contract, which can be 'reduced to the following terms: *Each of us puts his person and all his power in common under the supreme direction of the general will* [*sous la suprême direction de la volonté générale*] *and we receive as a body each member as an indivisible part of the whole*' (SC I.6.361/139). But what is it for the individual to submit to 'the supreme direction of the general will'? Here are the key formulae of SC I.7:

> In fact, each individual can, as a man, have a particular will contrary to or differing from the general will which he has as a Citizen. His particular interest may speak to him quite differently from the common interest . . . he might want to enjoy the rights of the citizen without being ready to fulfil the duties of a subject, an injustice whose spread would cause the ruin of the body politic. In order then that the social compact may not be an empty formula, it tacitly includes the following undertaking, which alone can give force to the others, that whoever refuses to obey the general will shall be compelled to do so by the whole body: which means nothing else than that he will be forced to be free . . . (SC I.7.363–4/140–1)

How are we to understand these notorious words? The most anodyne interpretation runs like this. Driven by *amour de soi*, each individual wants to assert his 'particular interest'. But if *each* individual does that without respecting the 'particular interest' of his neighbour, then *no* individual can have a rational expectation that *his* particular interest will be respected. Hence the importance of Rousseau's words: 'His particular interest may *speak* to him differently from the general interest'. It may thus speak to him. But will it be telling him the truth? The answer to that will depend on the nature of his interests.

Let us consider the free-rider, the person who 'might want to enjoy the rights of the citizen without being ready to fulfil the duties of a subject'. He is served by a bus system in which passengers are required to buy their tickets before boarding the bus, and in which an inspector only rarely checks the tickets. Within an established and more or less law-abiding society, the free-rider's short-term interest tells him not to buy a ticket when he knows there will be no inspector on the bus. His long-term interest tells him both that he needs a bus service and that a bus service cannot survive if free-riding becomes common. But since most people are honest he knows that it will not become common. So, in terms of short-term interest (purely prudential), why should he not fail to pay his fare when possible? Morally, because it is just not fair. But the moral virtue of fairness leaves the free-rider unmoved. To him, his selfish interest will dictate a policy of exploitation of his law-abiding neighbours if he thinks he can escape detection. Hence the need for an enforcement agency to ensure that the long-term interests of all are preserved (here the long-term interest of both the honest and the dishonest in maintaining the bus service) and to ensure that the price of preserving those long-term interests does not fall inequitably on the honest. The honest citizen, in contrast, has undergone the transformation process of SC I.8, so that his particular interest and will, on the one hand, and the general interest and will, on the other, tend to coincide.

Rousseau maintains that the present, unjust society is one which is dominated by free-riders, but in which free-riding is masked by an unjust legal system, enforcing relations of unequal power, and so of *dépendance personnelle*.[25]

In contrast, he envisages that the new, transformed society will be sufficiently egalitarian that relations of *dépendance personnelle* will have disappeared from public life.[26] It is in the context of that transformed society that Rousseau propounds his provocative paradox, according to which to say that the free-rider is constrained 'means nothing else than that he will be forced to be free'. He continues: 'for this is the condition which, by giving each citizen to his country, guarantees him against all personal dependence'.

Thus in the transformed society, the enforcement agency which constrains the free-rider guarantees the honest citizen against personal dependence. Since the honest citizen's interests have been transformed, he acts honestly of his own volition, without need of external enforcement. To defuse the paradox of being 'forced to be free' (and so to make it banal), one could say that in constraining the free-rider we are forcing him, the free-rider, to respect the freedom of his honest neighbour. But only if he, the free-rider, undergoes the transformation of SC I.8, will he see *ex post facto* that he himself was educated by the constraint to engage in the equitable play of non-exploitative social relations, and thus to be 'really' free. Rousseau maintains that most of the citizens of the transformed state will have

99

developed to the point where they recognize that such a play alone is free, that individuals are free if and only if they neither exploit, nor are exploited by, others. They will then experience freedom as reciprocal freedom. According to a distinction Rousseau develops elsewhere, they will have moved beyond independence to freedom:

> We should not confuse independence with freedom. These two things are so different that they are even mutually exclusive. When each one does what pleases him, he often does what displeases others, and it would be wrong to call that a state of freedom. Freedom is not so much the realization of one's will as independence from the will of others, and it does not involve making another's will dependent on one's own. Anyone who is master cannot be free, and to reign is to obey. (LMt 8.841–2)

When these distinctions have been made, the paradox can be defused. As we now understand it, the free-rider has been educated, by constraint, to realize true freedom. In understanding SC I.7 that way, we have anticipated the thesis of SC I.8 that 'the passage from the state of nature to civil society produces a remarkable change in man' (SC I.8.364/141). Liberals object that Rousseau has defused the paradox at the price of a utopian, and sinister, counter-model of transformed human psychology. We shall return to their criticisms later.

Rousseau's 'balance sheet' in SC I.8 tells us that civil society involves duty, right and reason, the state of nature involves physical impulse, appetite and inclinations. In none of those oppositions are we told that the citizen of the ideal society is required to act against his own interests. It is true that in the state of nature, unlike civil society, 'he had considered only himself [*n'avait regardé que lui-même*]' (SC I.8.364/141), but the important word here is 'only'. It is not that he must now *dis*regard his own interests, but that he must now consult the public interest, assured that in so doing he will protect his own. Thus the passage from the natural to the social state involves a passage to a new way of conceiving the relation of the self to others. In a legitimate society, based on the social contract, the individual is once again dependent, but legitimately dependent, because he is dependent on society, not on another individual, and all are equally dependent. The goal of the passage is to transform our moral psychology, in bringing it about that we automatically consult the public interest in our deliberations, while leaving intact the requirement that self-preservation take priority over other demands. Appearing so early in the book, SC I.8 asserts an exposed thesis, unsupported by arguments. It is only later, when the material conditions of legitimacy have been laid out in Book II, that we are given reason to believe that *amour de soi* will indeed be guaranteed by the social order.

(F)   *Interests and rationality*

Both the *Second Discourse* and the *Social Contract* require that the vital interests of individuals be protected. In the Preface to the *Second Discourse*, Rousseau recounts how:

> meditating on the first and simplest operations of the human Soul, I believe I perceive in it two principles anterior to reason, of which one interests us most ardently in our well-being and our self-preservation, and the other inspires in us a natural repugnance to see any sensitive Being perish or suffer, principally those like ourselves . . . (2D 125–6/14–15)

From this he concludes that where the demands of self-protection and of compassion conflict, the demands of the former must prevail over those of the latter:

> so long as [a man] does not resist the inner impulse of compassion, he will never harm another man, or even another sensitive being, except in the legitimate case where his self-preservation is at stake, and he is then obliged to give preference to himself. (ibid.)

In the *Social Contract*, Rousseau develops the idea, already adumbrated in the *Second Discourse*, that our understanding of those interests can itself change within a well-ordered society. The balance sheet of SC I.8 expounds that change of understanding. We have already considered the two sides of the balance sheet, as the duty, right and reason of civil society replace the impulse, appetite and inclinations of the state of nature. We have seen that in the state of nature, the individual 'had considered only himself', whereas in civil society he is 'forced to act upon other principles and to consult his reason before heeding his inclinations' (SC I.8.364/141). We have also seen that, when we change from considering only ourselves to consulting reason, we do not cease to consider our own interests, but rather start to see ourselves as members of a cooperative body, consisting of members whose interests are best served by coordinated actions.

Does SC I.8 also represent a passage from one kind of rationality to another, a move from 'instrumental' to 'expressive' rationality, as

Martin Hollis has suggested?[27] According to Hollis, those guided by instrumental rationality follow moral rules only insofar as that policy promotes their particular interests. Such people will observe 'honour among thieves' because, within a closed group, failure to keep one's word is soon detected and leads to exclusion from the group, which conflicts with one's particular interests. But a society based on the instrumental rationality of 'honour among thieves' will be unstable, because 'where the underlying motive remains personal gain, it cannot be suspended thoroughly enough to stop members of a ring of honour' from cheating when the opportunity presents itself. A stable, just society cannot therefore consist of people motivated only by instrumental rationality. Instead, its members must identify their interests with the public interest. Those thus motivated are guided by expressive, rather than by instrumental, rationality. That means that they express themselves, find their identity, in promoting the common good. This reading of SC I.8 has caught a central theme of the transformation and the balance sheet. Rousseau stresses that human beings undergo a qualitative change as they make the passage, which he describes as a process of increasing identification between the individual and the whole. But one notes that he does not talk about a radical change in types of rationality. Given the sophistication of his terminology, this is unlikely to be a mere oversight. Rather it is because he wants to bring out continuity as well as change. The continuity lies in the requirement that each individual protect his own interests. The change is in the nature of those interests. Transformed individuals come to identify their own interests with the public interest. Untransformed individuals fail to do that. They take advantage of the social order which protects each of them, and then seek a double benefit, that of the general social order, and their own, cheating, free-riding benefit. They thus live both in society and the state of nature.

(G)   Legitimacy and property

Property is an important element in each phase of Rousseau's political thought. In the *Second Discourse* the invention of property in nascent society led to ever increasing inequality between people, an inequality which would be consolidated by laws and political institutions. In that text, Rousseau's comments on the private property system, as it exists in contemporary societies, are entirely negative. But that same institution, which is an instrument of exploitation in unjust societies, can be transformed, in the legitimate society founded on the social contract, into the vehicle of individual autonomy.

But in the *Discourse on Political Economy*, written at the same time as the *Second Discourse*, Rousseau stresses the importance of the property system in holding civil society together and the duty of the sovereign to defend its citizens' property rights:

> It is certain that the right of property is the most sacred of all the rights of citizens, and more important in certain respects than freedom itself, either because it is more closely connected with the preservation of life, or because, since goods are easier to usurp and more difficult to protect than one's person, greater respect should be accorded to what can more easily be stolen, or finally because property is the true foundation [*le vrai fondement*] of civil society and the true guarantee of the citizens' engagements. (3D 263/157)

The same thought is expressed in the *Political Fragments*: 'For since all civil rights are founded on that of property, as soon as the right to property is abolished, no other rights can survive ...' (PolFr III.5.483/22), and in the summary of the *Social Contract* in *Emile* V: 'If sovereign authority is founded on the right of property, this right is the one it ought to protect the most' (Em V.841/461).

Vaughan held that Rousseau shifted from a Lockean, 'liberal' defence of an absolute, irreducible right to private property over to a more 'collectivist' view in the *Social Contract*, in which the property rights of the individual were strictly subordinate to those of the state. That judgment of Vaughan's has been criticized by Derathé on the plausible grounds that Rousseau held consistently to the view that there is no natural right to property (an essential difference from Locke), since property is entirely the outcome of civil society.[28] While it is true that there is no radical break in Rousseau's thought, there may still be some change in emphasis from a phase at which the right to property, albeit a conventional, not a natural, right played a foundational role, to a phase at which it is an important, but not uniquely important item on the total balance sheet. In the first place, the *Social Contract* does not single out the right to private property as the most important right to be defended by the sovereign. The property system is an acquisition of civil society which emerges alongside others in the balance sheet of SC I.8:

> What man loses by the social contract is his natural freedom and an unlimited right to everything that tempts him and that he can get; what he gains is civil freedom and the property right [*la propriété*] in all he possesses. (SC I.8.364/141)

103

Furthermore, Rousseau's focus in the *Social Contract* is on sovereignty and the general will, on the ways in which individuals can participate in the political process. In order for them to do that, the security of their property must be guaranteed. Property is an instrument or vehicle, rather than the essence, of autonomy. But, despite the change of emphasis, SC I.9 is one of the most revolutionary and egalitarian chapters of the *Social Contract*.

We shall examine SC I.9 under three headings: (i) the labour theory of property; (ii) the critique of European claims to colonial property; and (iii) the relation between the sovereign and the individual property owner.

(i) *The labour theory of property*

> Each member of the community gives himself to it at the moment of its formation, just as he currently is – both himself and all his force, which includes the goods he possesses. (SC I.9.365/142)

Here Rousseau expands the compressed clause of the contract of SC I.6: 'the total alienation of each associate, with all his rights, to the whole community . . . *Each of us puts his person and all his power in common under the supreme direction of the general will*' (SC I.6.360–1/138–9). In these words Rousseau does not refer specifically to property, as he had done in the earlier version of the *Geneva Manuscript*, where he wrote: 'Each of us puts his will, his goods, his force, his person in common under the direction of the general will . . .' (GM 290/83). So the opening sentence of SC I.9 picks up what was previously stated explicitly, but was left unsaid in the published version.

In what follows, Rousseau puts radically egalitarian limits on the right to acquire property 'in the absence of legal titles':

> the following conditions are necessary to authorize the right of the first occupant to any land whatsoever. First, that this land not yet be inhabited by anyone. Second, that one occupy only the amount needed to subsist. Third, that one take possession not by vain ceremony, but by labor and cultivation, the only sign of property that one ought to respect in the absence of legal titles. (SC I.9.366/142)

In the *Geneva Manuscript* the third condition is expanded:

> The rights of a man prior to the state of society cannot go any

further, and everything else, being only violence and usurpation contrary to the right of nature, cannot serve as a foundation for social right. Now, when I have no more land than is necessary to maintain myself, and enough hands to cultivate it, if I give some away, there will be less left than I need. (GM 301–2/92)

The 'labour theory of property' is illustrated graphically in the *Emile* (Em II.331/99) with the story of the gardener Robert and the planting of beans and melons.[29] It had been elaborated by Locke, who had argued that 'Whatsoever [someone] removes out of the State that Nature hath provided . . . he hath mixed his Labour with and joyned to it something that is his own, and thereby makes it his Property.' Locke too had enjoined that it must not be so great that it goes to waste, for if it is 'spoiled . . . he took more than his share, and robb'd others.'[30] But Locke had modified the labour theory of property by allowing individuals to own more land than they had mixed their labour with and more than they needed for subsistence, provided both that they did not thereby deprive another of the means of subsistence and that the overall productivity of the land was increased.[31] Rousseau does not explicitly reject Locke's modification. Indeed, insofar as his combination of the sufficiency condition and labour theory of property applies only to the right of first occupant, where there are no legal titles, it would be possible for that combination to be modified by legal titles once they have been introduced in society. But, unlike Locke, he does not discuss the conditions under which such modification would be justified, and he leaves the reader with the impression that the egalitarian restriction on property ownership could well be transposed, unmodified, into society. SC I.9 would then provide a further defence of small-scale land ownership and artisanal production, which Rousseau elsewhere advocated as the economic form best suited to promoting personal and civic virtue.[32]

In the *Geneva Manuscript* Rousseau gives a more explicit defence of the rights of the small-scale producer than he does in the published version of the *Social Contract*, since in the *Manuscript* he not only limits the size of the property that the first occupant may own, but he also makes the positive claim that the individual must have enough land in order to subsist as a self-supporting producer and must not be required to give up property beyond the limits of subsistence:

Now, when I have no more land than is necessary to maintain myself, and enough hands to cultivate it, if I give some away there will be less left than I need. What then can I yield to others without taking away my subsistence, or what agreement could I make with them to give them possession of what does not belong to me? As for the conditions of this agreement, it is very evident that they are illegitimate and null for those who are thereby subjected without qualification to the will of another. (GM. 301/92)

In asserting the negative and positive requirements together Rousseau is defending a specific form of economic production which was under threat and which he strove to restore.[33]

(ii)   Critique of European claims to colonial property

Rousseau holds that European claims to colonial property are illegitimate on three grounds. They trade on a specious notion of the right of the first occupant: 'Will setting foot on a piece of common ground be sufficient to claim on the spot to be its master?' They use force to 'disperse other men'. They infringe the sufficiency condition 'since this act takes away from the remaining men the dwelling place and foods that nature gives them in common' (SC I.9.366/ 142–3).[34]

(iii)   The relation between the sovereign and the individual property owner

The title of SC I.9 '*Du domaine réel*' is hard to translate. 'Real estate' misses two elements in Rousseau's treatment. On the one hand he is concerned with all goods that can be owned, principally land, but other forms of property too. On the other hand, as Derathé points out (OC 3.1450–1), the term '*domaine*' (Latin *dominium*) was already antiquated by 1762, having normally been replaced by '*propriété*' (property). In using '*domaine*', Rousseau is alluding to the distinction between '*domaine éminent*' and '*domaine particulier*' (eminent and private domain), a politically sensitive issue, highlighted in the summary in *Emile* V, but barely surviving, except as an echo, in SC I.9:

What is unique [*singulier*] [admirable, *Geneva Manuscript*] about this alienation is that far from plundering individuals of their goods, by accepting them the community thereby only assures them of legitimate possession, changes usurpation into a true right and use into property. Then, since the possessors are considered as trustees [*dépositaires*] of the public goods, and since their rights are respected by all the members of the State and maintained with all its force against foreigners . . . they have so to

speak acquired all they have given. This paradox is easily
explained by the distinction between the rights of the sovereign
and of the proprietor to the same resource, as will be seen
hereafter. (SC I.9.367/143)

But, at least in the *Social Contract*, the distinction is not developed
'hereafter'. Derathé refers to SC II.4, where Rousseau says that 'each
person alienates through the social compact only that part of his
power, goods and freedom whose use matters to the community' (SC
II.4.373/148), but that does not explain the nature of a system in
which owners of private property are 'considered as trustees of the
public good'.

Just how secure would be the holdings of individuals in such a
system? When he expounds the distinction between eminent domain
and private domain in *Emile* V, Rousseau shows himself more collectivist than some of his predecessors in allowing the state to exercise the right of eminent domain.[35] In the summary, Rousseau says
that he will 'compare the right of property with the right of sovereignty, individual domain with eminent domain', and continues:

> [(a)] If the sovereign authority is founded on the right of property,
> this right is the one it ought to respect most. [(b)] The right of
> property is inviolable and sacred for the sovereign authority as
> long as it remains a particular and individual right. [(c)] But as
> soon as it is considered as common to all the citizens, it is subject
> to the general will, and this will can abolish it. (Em V.841/461)

This dense passage tells us that (a) the overriding rationale of the
social contract is the protection of the private property system, and
(b) within that system private citizens can rely on the sovereign to
protect their property holdings against infringement by other individuals, both domestic and foreign. But (c) the sovereign retains the
right to alter the property system as a whole, through taxation,
nationalization or prohibition of certain types of holdings.

Putting together the three themes of SC I.9, we find a radical,
egalitarian account of property. Rousseau favours the property system of the small-scale, self-supporting producer. He holds that
property claims made by 'advanced' European nations against 'primitive' peoples are illegitimate. He gives the sovereign people an
indefeasible right to regulate the property system as a whole, and to
shift the balance of property ownership from private to public hands
if the public interest so requires.

Rousseau concludes SC I.9 with the final item of the balance
sheet, which reinforces the egalitarian message of the chapter:

I shall end this chapter and this book with a comment that ought to serve as the basis of the whole social system. It is that rather than destroying natural equality, the fundamental compact on the contrary substitutes a moral and legitimate equality for whatever physical inequality nature may have placed between men, and that though they may be unequal in force or in genius, they all become equal by convention and by right. (SC I.9.367/144)

In a final footnote he ties that conclusion to the theory of property and with it makes the egalitarianism even more explicit:

Under bad governments, this equality is only apparent and illusory. It serves only to maintain the poor man in his poverty and the rich man in his usurpation. In fact laws are always useful to those who have possessions and harmful to those who have nothing . . . (ibid.)

In Book II, particularly at SC II.11, Rousseau argues that only when there is a relatively egalitarian distribution of property can a rational consensus emerge. Economic equality is thus a cornerstone of the legitimate political order.

V

The Empire of the Laws: the General Will and Totalitarianism

(A)   The empire of the laws

We return now to the conflicting judgments passed on the *Social Contract* in 1794 and 1814. According to the first, it is a document of liberation, according to the second, it is one of totalitarian enslavement. We now test those judgments in the light of Rousseau's conception of the law, encapsulated in two rhetorical questions and their rhetorical answers:

> [How to] reconcile things that are almost incompatible . . . the empire of the Laws and the power of men? . . . There is no liberty where there are no Laws or where someone is above the Laws . . . A free people obeys, but it does not serve; it has leaders [*chefs*] and not masters. It obeys the Laws, but it obeys only the Laws, and it is by the force of the Laws that it does not obey men . . . Any condition imposed on each by all can be burdensome to no one, and the worst of Laws is worth more than the best master; for every master has preferences, whereas the Law never has any. (LMt 8.838, 842–3)

> How can it be that [men] obey and no one commands, that they serve and have no master, and are all the freer, in fact, because under what appears as subjugation, no one loses any of his freedom except what would harm the freedom of another? These marvels are the work of the law. It is to law alone that men owe justice and freedom. It is this healthy instrument of the will of all that reestablishes, as a matter of legal right [*dans le droit*], the natural equality between men. It is this celestial voice that tells each citizen the precepts of public reason, and teaches him to act according to the maxims of his own

109

judgment and not to be in contradiction with himself. (3D 248–9/146)[1]

The rhetoric of the 'celestial voice' reminds us of the voice of conscience, 'divine instinct, immortal celestial voice, the sure guide for a creature who is ignorant and limited, but intelligent and free, infallible judge of good and bad, sublime emanation of the immortal substance' (Lmor 5.1111).[2] The celestial voices of conscience and of the law command and guide, the one within the individual, the other within the state. Under correct conditions, the guidance of each is infallible. The problem is to specify those conditions.

It is in response to eighteenth-century absolutism that Rousseau puts his faith in law,[3] which would inherit the absolute power of the *Ancien Régime*, but, unlike it, would be general in the formulation and systematic in the application of that power. Furthermore, since the law was to be the expression of the legislative power of a free people, it seemed that it would also guarantee the freedom of the citizens who were its members. Yet this noble ideal evoked the anxiety and hostility of liberal critics such as Benjamin Constant, not only in the distant future, but within a few years of Rousseau's death. The reason is that Rousseau's 'Empire of the Laws' appeared to them no less oppressive than the régime it was designed to replace.

There is no anachronism in bringing a liberal critique to bear on Rousseau's Empire. Rousseau himself was aware that there was a different tradition of resistance to absolutism, that of Locke and his successors. That tradition stressed the division of powers and the independence of the judiciary. He was also aware that he was opposing the absolutism of the *Ancien Régime* with a new absolutism of popular sovereignty, and for that reason he implicitly acknowledges that his sovereign people is all too close to Hobbes's sovereign Leviathan. As we saw in the last chapter, Rousseau was anxious because he could 'see no tolerable middle point between the austerest Hobbism and the most perfect democracy' (Letter to Mirabeau, 26 July 1767, CC3#5991, p. 240). We have followed his desperate attempts to escape from the horns of this dilemma, and to find some form of government which could embody popular sovereignty and yet could avoid the defects of direct democracy. But even if he does manage to do that, Rousseau's liberal critics hold that any form of unlimited popular sovereignty, whatever its form of government, must be totalitarian.

Rousseau's doctrine of popular sovereignty constitutes what Leo Strauss called 'the crisis of modern natural right'.[4] But there are two ways of understanding that crisis. According to Derathé, Rousseau's work represents the culmination of the natural law tradition, and is critical in the benign sense that it could be developed no further: 'We find . . . in Rousseau the traditional distinction [between natural and positive law] admitted by all theorists of natural right. For Rousseau, just as for Cicero or Pufendorf, natural law remains as an authority superior to the state'.[5] According to Masters, on the other hand, the crisis is far deeper. It represents not the highest point of development, but the final disintegration of the natural law tradition. That tradition was founded on a philosophical anthropology, a model of human nature, according to which human beings are endowed with natural tendencies towards sociability and order. A society embodying the principles of natural law fosters those tendencies within a system of positive laws which give them expression.[6] In the Christian version of the tradition, natural law is backed by the authority of God, a benign but implacable sovereign. By the eighteenth century, neither component of the tradition any longer carried general conviction.

Rousseau himself had done much to undermine the first, naturalistic, component in the *Second Discourse*. The religious beliefs underlying the second component were increasingly undermined by the Enlightenment. Masters correctly summarizes Rousseau's dramatic response to the disintegration of the tradition: 'Rousseau substitutes his definition of the nature of law for the traditional natural law', replacing 'the traditional conception of the common good or the common interest' by the 'highly voluntarist' conception of the general will. The result is that the traditional role of natural law as basis for reasoned criticism, through practical reasoning, is displaced by a 'principle of legitimacy [which] is enforced by an unlimited right of revolution'.[7]

In this chapter I do not attempt to define 'totalitarianism'. But I take seriously the view that the *Social Contract* offers only fragile protection against the oppression of the individual, insofar as its core consists in the ideas of *total alienation* and of the *general will*. The former constitutes the key clause of the contract itself. The latter is the outcome of the contract and the vehicle of the exercise of popular sovereignty.

(B) *Total alienation: the contractual basis of absolutism*

Rousseau declares that the principle of total alienation is the key to the contract as a whole: 'These clauses, properly understood, may be reduced to one – the total alienation of each associate, together with all his rights, to the whole community' (SC I.6.360/138). He provides three arguments for this principle. The *first* argument proceeds from *reciprocity*, *equality* and *self-interest*: 'since each one gives his entire self, the condition is equal for everyone, and, since the condition is equal for everyone, no one has an interest in making it burdensome for the others.' (SC I.6.360–1/138). According to this argument, since all members will have alienated exactly the same to the community, namely all their natural liberty, it can be in the interest of member A to limit the (social) liberty of member B only to the extent that A would be willing to have his or her own (social) liberty reciprocally limited by B. A liberal might object that the principle of reciprocity, even when combined with equality and self-interest, will not defend the liberty of individuals in a community with a majority of illiberal, but consistent, citizens, who would be willing to have their own liberties restricted (if they lost their majority), as the price of restricting the liberties of those presently in the minority, to whose views they are opposed.

Nor is the illiberal régime excluded by Rousseau's generality condition, according to which the law must always be general, both in its source and its application, emerging only 'when the entire people enacts something concerning the entire people' (SC II.6.379/ 153), since that condition is designed to exclude only arbitrary enactments benefiting or harming particular named individuals, the fundamental vice of the *Ancien Régime*. It is consistent with the generality condition that 'the law can create several Classes of Citizens, and even designate the qualities determining who has a right to these classes . . .' (ibid.).

The *second* argument is an *all or nothing* argument:

> as the alienation is made without reservation, the union is as perfect as it can be, and no associate has anything further to claim. For if some rights were left to private individuals [*particuliers*], there would be no common superior to judge between them and the public. Each man being his own judge on some point would soon claim to be so on all; the state of nature would subsist and the association would necessarily become tyrannical or ineffectual. (SC I.6.361/138–9)

Here Rousseau claims that anything short of total alienation must lead us back to the state of nature, to either despotism or anarchy. The argument depends on the transition from 'on some point' to 'on all'. But is the transition inevitable? Is it possible to isolate a domain within which 'private individuals' are 'their own judges', and outside which they are not? The natural law tradition inherited from Aristotle held that human beings are naturally sociable. In addition, Aquinas had argued that individuals always preserve a moral autonomy due to their place in God's creation, an autonomy which transcends any political obligations: 'A human being is not subordinate to the political community entirely within his whole self and with all he possesses and therefore it is not required that each of his acts should be well or ill deserving within the political order.'[8]

Traditional liberals, from Constant to Tocqueville, through to J. S. Mill, distanced themselves from the metaphysics, and particularly from the theological underpinnings, of natural law, but continued to work with a philosophical anthropology expressed now in humanistic terms. For them, the sanctity attached to the individual as bearer of an immortal soul was transferred to the individual endowed with autonomy. As in the natural law tradition, the core of the human being 'remains', in Constant's words, 'necessarily, individual and independent, and is rightfully beyond the jurisdiction of society. The scope of sovereignty is always limited and relative.'[9] One's destiny now was to develop one's personal talents, even one's genius. Some versions of traditional liberalism put more stress on the positive ideal of self-cultivation.[10] Others were content to defend the negative condition of that ideal, the absence of external 'interference', 'the right to be let alone'.[11] But all of them presupposed some minimal philosophical anthropology of the natural sociability and the autonomous self-development of the individual.[12] They all also emphasized that popular despotism (Rousseau's position, as they saw it) should not be confused with arbitrary rule. It can involve 'oppression exercised in legal form', as well as 'that exercised through popular frenzies'.[13]

The *third* argument can be called the *nothing lost, everything gained* argument:

> Finally, as each gives himself to all, he gives himself to no one; and since there is no associate over whom one does not acquire the same right one grants him over oneself, one gains the equivalent of everything one loses, and more force to preserve everything one has. (SC I.6.361/139)

This third argument is a gloss on the first argument, from reciprocity. Rousseau now maintains that if the individual's alienation is to everyone, then it is to no one. He anticipates the result of the balance sheet (SC I.8), in holding that individuals are better protected by the power of the sovereign than they ever were by their own efforts in the state of nature.

The general will is the point of intersection between principles of right and maxims of politics. I argue in this chapter that the idea of the general will is not in itself totalitarian, but can be seen as a sophisticated attempt to theorize the nature of an acceptable consensus. But I also hold that, as Rousseau deploys it in the *Social Contract*, in combination with a hostility to political pluralism and a commitment to the absolute alienation of individual rights and to legal voluntarism, the idea offers only fragile protection against totalitarian oppression. I thus continue to take seriously the 'liberal' criticisms of Constant and Tocqueville, which have not yet been definitively rebutted by Rousseau's defenders. I conclude with some reflections, in the two Appendices, on the relevance of the recent discussions of the free-rider and of the prisoner's dilemma to Rousseau's ideas.[14]

(C) Conditions of emergence of the general will: no major inequalities, no factions

Sovereignty and the general will are tied conceptually to one another. When a people exercises its sovereignty it is expressing its general will. Rousseau holds that one cannot, as an individual person, alienate, i.e. abandon or make over to another, one's individual will. Modelling the people on the individual person, and the general will on the individual will, he concludes that the sovereign people cannot alienate its general will: 'sovereignty, being only the exercise of the general will, can never be alienated, and . . . the sovereign, which is only a collective being, can only be represented by itself. Power can perfectly well be transferred, but not will' (SC II.1.368/ 145). Derathé pointed out that Rousseau expressed this idea more clearly in the *Geneva Manuscript*: 'There is in the State a common force which supports it and a general will which directs this force, and the application of the one to the other constitutes sovereignty' (GM 295–6/87). Rousseau develops the analogy between an individual's will and the general will at SC II.2, where he criticizes the ontology of other theories which would make sovereignty into a bundle of powers, condensed and bestowed on a single bearer, the sovereign. Such theories, for Rousseau, can never explain the absolute unity and indivisibility of sovereignty. That can be understood only when we introduce a new ontology of the will which is essentially indivisible and expresses itself in acts of legislation. We replace an ontology of 'parts' by an ontology of 'emanations'.[15]

In theorizing the general will, Rousseau is continuing his project to 'unite what right permits with what interest prescribes' (SC I.Proem.351/131). He maintains that in a well-ordered state that coincidence of right and self-interest is guaranteed by the exercise of the general will:

114

Why is the general will always right, and why do all continually will the happiness of each, if not because there is no one who does not [secretly][16] appropriate this word *each* to himself, and does not think of himself as he votes for all? Which proves that equality of right, and the idea of justice it produces, are derived from the preference each man gives to himself, and consequently from the nature of man . . . (SC II.4.373/148–9)

But the general will can emerge only in a well-ordered state. In a badly-ordered state it is blocked and distorted. So at SC II.3 Rousseau poses the question 'Whether the general will can err', and answers it with a series of antitheses: 'One always wants one's own good, but one does not always see it. One can never corrupt the people, but one can often deceive it, and it is only then that it appears to want what is bad' (SC II.3.371/147). What then makes a well-ordered state? It must be founded on the rational consent given by its citizens to the terms of the social contract (principles), and it must have fundamental laws and institutions corresponding to its needs (maxims). Some maxims are general and apply to any society capable of self-rule. Others are specific to particular societies and vary according to their moral and material circumstances, which in turn are determined by the contingencies of history and geography.

The most general maxim to be observed in any society is that it must fulfil two interlocking political and economic conditions. There must be no factions and there must be no major inequalities of power or wealth between its citizens. This will guarantee that each citizen submit to the law and that none can dominate another by force or by economic coercion. When and only when those conditions are fulfilled can a general will emerge from a process in which each citizen when he votes consults his own interest, and thereby automatically consults the general interest.

Rousseau expresses this idea using different versions of a mathematical metaphor, here in *Considerations on the Government of Poland*:

the law, which is only the expression of the general will, is the result of the combination of all the particular interests which balance one another because of their large number. But since corporate interests [*les interets de corps*] have too great a weight and would disturb the equilibrium, they must not enter the process collectively. Each individual must have his vote, but no collective body of any kind must have one. (GP ch.7.984/42)

and here in the *Social Contract*:

> There is often a great deal of difference between the will of all and
> the general will; the latter considers only the common interest,
> the former considers private interest, and is no more than a sum of
> particular wills: but take away from these same wills the pluses
> and minuses that cancel one another, and the general will remains
> as the sum of the differences. (SC II.3.371/147)

Do the mathematical metaphors explain how the general will
emerges, automatically, procedurally, when decisions are made by
majority vote, once the condition of relative equality is satisfied?
The vocabulary of 'the sum of the differences' is derived from the
calculus, which clearly intrigued the amateur mathematician in
Rousseau.[17] But the calculus provides only the rhetoric, not the
substance, of his position. Rousseau's idea is that the general will
represents a rational consensus, that is a consensus concerning the
common interest. Thus, when three alternatives, left, centre and
right (L, C, R) are presented to the electorate, a well-designed voting
system will seek to identify the largest consensus. So it will favour C
and those parts of L and R which overlap with C when their conflicting extremes are cancelled out.[18] With a sufficiently stable consensus
at the centre, extremists of L and R will not command a majority
alone, and, when factions are excluded, it will be impossible for their
partisans to combine. When the grounds of rational consensus dis-
appear, extreme groups polarize and make tactical alliances to
engineer electoral victory on a particular issue. In that case the
pluses and minuses will not cancel one another out, but will add up
to an artificial majority.[19] In contrast, when the conditions of the
emergence of the general will are satisfied, then there will be no
factions, because the interests of each citizen will be better served by
promoting the common good than by the machinations of factions.
Then the voting system will express what each citizen thinks is best
both for himself and for the community. The interests of individuals
will increasingly coincide and they will gain a clearer understanding
of the means of realizing those interests. In such circumstances
relatively few people will occupy extreme positions simply because
relatively few will have extremely divergent interests. The votes
of those few will cancel one another out, leaving the overlapping
interests of the remainder to be expressed by majority voting.

Rousseau holds that voting must be conducted under strictly
controlled conditions in order to exclude factions, and that when
those conditions are satisfied the 'large number of little differences'
will cancel each other out. As Rousseau understands it, they will
cancel each other out to produce something more substantive than
the morally, epistemologically neutral outcome of the fairly played

game of cards. The phrase 'the general will is always right' condenses two components: the object of the general will on the one hand, and the means for guaranteeing its expression on the other. According to the first component, the general will is right in the sense that it wants the right thing, that is what is in the public interest. According to the second component, the general will is the act of will of the majority when there is equality, there are no factions and there is a suitable voting procedure. Rousseau provides mainly negative arguments for the second component. In distinguishing the will of all from the general will, he highlights the circumstances which hinder the formation of a rational consensus and suggests methods for eliminating those circumstances. When and only when the circumstances are correct will content and procedure automatically coincide.

What is the process whereby the sovereign people reaches correct solutions to legislative questions when it exercises its general will? Rousseau's enigmatic answer lies in the phrase 'One always wants one's own good, but one does not always see it' (SC II.3.371/147). In one respect Rousseau is an arch-rationalist concerning moral psychology. Each of us seeks what is good for us, or what we think is good for us. In a bad environment, our perception of that good becomes distorted, so that a gap opens up between our real and apparent good, even though the will is not corrupted in the process. In moving from the educational theory of the *Emile* to the political theory of the *Social Contract*, Rousseau is transposing a thesis concerning the moral psychology of the individual to the level of social choice. At both levels, well-ordered environments, which have been arranged by the tutor and by the Lawgiver respectively, present choosers with appropriate objects of choice. In a badly-ordered society, in contrast, the search by each of us to realize our own good leads to conflict.

Thus Rousseau concludes SC II.6 with a final string of antitheses as he strives to bring knowledge and will together:

> Particular individuals [*les particuliers*] see the good they reject; the public wants the good it cannot see. All are equally in need of guides. The former must be obliged to make their wills conform to their reason. The latter must be taught to know what it wants. Then public enlightenment results in the union of understanding and will in the social body . . . (SC II.6.380/154)

Elsewhere Rousseau resorts to more concrete metaphors to explain the perniciousness of factions. Here the metaphor is mechanical:

> since corporate interests have an excessive weight, they would

destroy the equilibrium, and should therefore not enter into deliberations as collectivities. Each individual should have his own voice. No corporate body of any kind should have one. (GP ch.7.984/42)

But, as we have already seen, the heart of his explanation lies in the connection between freedom and equality:

> If one seeks for precisely what constitutes the greatest good of all, which ought to be the end of every system of legislation, one will find that it reduces itself to two main objects, *freedom* and *equality* – freedom, because all particular dependence is so much force taken away from the body of the state, and equality because freedom cannot exist without it . . . With regard to equality, this word must not be understood to mean that degrees of power and wealth should be absolutely the same; but that power shall never be great enough for violence, and shall always be exercised by virtue of rank and law . . . (SC II.11.391–2/162)

These sentences embody an important intersection between principles of right and maxims of politics. In them we can distinguish an organicist metaphor, according to which the general will is the result of aggregating particular wills, derives its strength from them, and is weakened when they are alienated by *dépendance particulière*. But a more serious political theory can be isolated from that metaphor, according to which: (1) all factions are the result of an unequal distribution of economic and political power; and (2) all factions necessarily obstruct the emergence of a rational political consensus. At SC IV.1 Rousseau gives a graphic account of the degenerate state, in which inequality reigns and individuals sell their votes for money [*à prix d'argent*] (SC IV.1.438/199). But his insight goes beyond that specific example, to all relations of major inequality, holding between classes, as well as between individuals. In any society, Rousseau argues, these two maxims must be satisfied if the general will, or rational consensus, is to be exercised.

(D)   No factions: Rousseau's anxiety concerning pluralism

Rousseau is sometimes tempted to go beyond the relatively abstract conditions outlined above, and to maintain that there can be no legitimate *political* organization representing the aspirations of a particular section of the people within a relatively egalitarian order. This does not mean that he would exclude all sub-groups from the legitimate order. Indeed, in other texts he highlights the importance of such groups in fostering the moral health of society as a whole: 'Every political society is composed of other smaller societies of different sorts, each of which has its interests and its maxims, . . . [and] whose various relationships, when they are well observed, provide real knowledge of morals' (3D 245–6/143–4).[20] But however important such 'smaller societies' may be, the abstract model of the *Social Contract* leaves little space for diverse *group* interests, or their political expression. The only interest which it is legitimate to express is the interest of the individual, insofar as that interest conforms to, or at least does not conflict with, the general interest. Elsewhere, particularly in his applied work, *Considerations on the Government of Poland*, he is less dogmatic, allowing for the existence of different corporate groups with different interests which would be legitimately expressed in the political arena.

After discussing maxims of politics in some detail in Book III, Rousseau returns to the general will in Book IV, whose opening chapter bears the optimistic title 'That the general will is indestructible'. He begins by expanding the definition of the general will started in Book II: 'As long as several men together consider themselves to be a single body, they have only a single will, which relates to their common preservation and general welfare' (SC IV.1.437/ 198). That happy situation is found when 'all the mechanisms of the State are vigorous and simple, its maxims are clear and luminous, it has no tangled contradictory interests; the common good is clearly apparent everywhere, and requires only good sense to be perceived'. Such a simple life is lived by 'groups of peasants . . . deciding affairs of State under an oak tree'. In those circumstances there is little deception and there are few complex rules. Rousseau's sympathy is for the small group, where such a life can flourish. Elsewhere in the *Social Contract* he returns repeatedly to the problem of transposing the ideal model to large-scale societies. In SC IV.1 he describes the stages in which the general will fragments as 'the social tie begins to slacken, and the State to grow weak'. At that stage, private interests start to make themselves felt and small societies to influence the larger one'. Then the gap between the will of all and the general will, announced as a possibility at SC II.3, becomes a reality, so that, through the influence of factions, majority voting no longer realizes common interests:

Finally, when the State, close to its ruin, continues to subsist only in an illusory and ineffectual form; when the social bond is broken in all hearts; when the basest interest brazenly adopts the sacred name of the public good, then the general will becomes mute . . . (SC IV.1.438/198)

119

But though it has been silenced, it does not 'follow from this that the general will is annihilated or corrupted' (SC IV.1.438/199). It remains, says Rousseau, 'constant, incorruptible and pure, but it is subordinated to other wills which prevail over it'. When the general will is thus 'subordinated', free-riders come into their own. A gap begins to appear between general and particular, between public and private, between open and secret. Free-riders are not revolutionaries:

> Each person, detaching his interest from the common interest, sees perfectly well that he cannot completely separate himself from it; but his share of the public misfortune seems like nothing to him compared to the exclusive good which he claims that he is getting. With the exception of this private good, he wants the general good in his own interest just as vigorously as anyone else. (ibid.)

Rousseau concludes IV.1 with a rapid restriction of popular sovereignty:[21]

> I could make many reflections here about the simple right to vote in every act of sovereignty – a right that nothing can take away from the Citizens; and on the right to give an opinion, to make proposals, to analyse, to discuss, which the Government is always very careful to allow only to its members. But this important subject would require a separate treatise, and I cannot say everything in this one. (SC IV.1.438–9/199)

The restriction, as Derathé points out, corresponds to the constitution of Geneva. Rousseau had already stated in the Dedication to the *Second Discourse* (2D 114/6) that he was not advocating direct democracy, and that the People were not to propose laws, only to vote on them. Nonetheless, this hurried passage is another reminder of the fragmentary nature of the *Social Contract*.

(E)   *Voting procedures to guarantee the emergence of the general will*

Rousseau concludes his presentation of the general will at SC IV.2 with some comments on voting, which provides an index of the degree of consensus in the state:

> The more harmony there is in the assemblies, that is, the closer opinions come to obtaining unanimous support, the more dominant as well is the general will. But long debates, dissensions

and tumult indicate the ascendence of private interests and the decline of the State. (SC IV.2.439/199)

Near unanimity is thus a sign of the moral 'health of the body politic'. But also, 'At the other extreme unanimity returns . . . when the citizens, fallen into servitude, no longer have either freedom or will' (SC IV.2.439/200). Although unanimity is desirable, it is essential only for the social contract itself. Thereafter, 'the vote of the majority always obligates all the others'. But is majority rule compatible with individual freedom? 'How can the opponents be free yet subject to laws to which they have not consented?' Rousseau replies that 'the question is badly put. The Citizen consents to all the laws, even to those passed in spite of him . . .' This response simply explains the rules of fair play, and carries no metaphysical charge. But Rousseau's next move goes far beyond it:

> When a law is proposed in the assembly of the People, what they are being asked is not precisely whether they approve or reject the proposal, but whether it does or does not conform to the general will, which is their will. Each one, in giving his vote, states his opinion on that point; and the declaration of the general will is drawn from the counting of the votes. Therefore when the opinion contrary to mine prevails, that proves nothing except that I was mistaken, and that what I thought to be the general will was not. (SC IV.2.440–1/200–1)

This notorious passage suggests that each voter is caught in a circle, having to calculate what every other voter will do before he casts his own vote. We can escape this paradox only if we distinguish three components which Rousseau condenses, namely (1) will, (2) interest and (3) opinion. Thus, according to the distinction made in Book II, 'one always wants one's good [(1)], but one does not always see it [(3)]', (SC II.3.371/147). This means that one always wants what is, or what appears to be, in one's interest (2). But one's opinion about how to realize one's will, how to serve one's interest (3) is often mistaken. When Rousseau now tells us in Book IV that the voter should replace question (a) 'Do I approve or disapprove of this motion?' by question (b) 'Is this motion in accordance with the general will?', he is saying that question (b) has priority. I am asked to decide first whether the motion will promote the common interest. Assuming that the conditions of the emergence of the general will are satisfied, I can answer that question by consulting my own will, which automatically promotes my own interest, and under these ideal conditions, my own interest automatically coincides with the common interest. The answer to (a) then flows automatically from the answer to (b). When I find myself in the minority, 'I was mistaken'. In what sense? Always assuming that the conditions of the ideal society are realized, only in sense (3). I was wrong in my opinion about what would realize the common, and therefore my own, interest.

(F) Legal voluntarism

For Rousseau, the general will is the foundation of legitimacy. It embodies political legitimacy in virtue of its source, the sovereign people, and in virtue of the rigorous conditions which must be satisfied if it is to emerge. For this reason it is important to dismantle any obstacles to its expression. The government, as the people's *commissaire,* cannot *represent* the will of the people, but can only carry it out. Within Rousseau's system, while there is an established corpus of rules, the 'political laws' (or constitution), devised by the Lawgiver, there is no role for an autonomous body which would interpret the constitution and set limits to the bounds of the general will. Rousseau expresses this thesis most clearly at SC II.12:

> The laws which regulate this relation [of the sovereign to the state] bear the name of political laws, and are also called fundamental laws, not without some reason if these laws are wise. For if there is in each state only one good way of ordering it, the people that has found it should hold fast to it; but if the established order is bad, why should one accept as fundamental laws that prevent it from being good? Besides, in any case, a people is always the master to change its laws, even the best ones; for if it chooses to do itself harm, who has the right to prevent it from doing so? (SC II.12.393–4/164)

He puts it more succinctly at SC III.11: 'It is not through laws that the State subsists, it is through the legislative power. Yesterday's law is not binding today, but tacit consent is presumed from silence.' (SC .III.11.424/188–9). Concerning the establishment of the rights of citizens, Rousseau is more ambivalent. The fundamental political task is to ensure that the necessary conditions for the emergence of the general will are satisfied. Once that is done, then the rest can be left to procedural regularity. Yet his work is impregnated with the terminology of natural rights. Does this mean that he might allow the individual to retain certain natural rights *against* the general will? In a number of passages, he points to a distinction between the public and the private domains which might allow for such a liberal reading, as here in the *Social Contract*:

> But, besides the public person, we have to consider the private persons who compose it, and whose life and freedom are naturally independent of it. It is a matter, then, of making a clear distinction between the respective rights of the Citizens and the Sovereign, and between the duties that the former have to fulfil as subjects, and the natural right which they should enjoy in their quality as men.
>
> It is agreed that each person alienates through the social compact, only that part of his power, goods and freedom whose use is important to the community; but it must also be agreed that the Sovereign alone is judge of what is important. (SC II.4.373/148)

Here Rousseau first draws the traditional liberal distinctions between the public and the private, and restricts legitimate state control to the former. But he then makes the distinction operationally empty by entrusting to the sovereign judgment of what is or is not of public 'importance'.

In the *Geneva Manuscript*, Rousseau omits the concluding sentence. The result is a clean liberal assertion of reserved natural rights, independent of public recognition:

> Everything consists in making a clear distinction between the rights which the sovereign has over the Citizen and those which it must respect in them; and the duties which they have to fulfil insofar as they are subjects from the natural right they should enjoy insofar as they are men. It is certain that each person alienates through the social compact only that part of his natural faculties, goods and freedom whose possession is important to society. (GM 306/95)

The programmatic summary of SC I.6 in *Emile*, Book V, is particularly elusive:

> Given that there is no common power superior to the two contracting parties (the individual on the one side, and the public on the other) to adjudicate on disputes between them, we shall examine whether each of them remains entitled to break the contract if it pleases him, that is to renounce his own commitment to it as soon as he feels he has been wronged. (Em V.840/461)

123

Burgelin notes that this passage 'leaves the door open' to the individual's withdrawal. But Rousseau offers the possibility in the form of a tendentious rhetorical question. He suggests two possible conditions under which his opponent might hold that the citizen would be justified in withdrawing: (1) 'if it pleases him'; and (2) 'as soon as he feels he has been wronged'. The first would trivialize the grounds, allowing individuals to withdraw 'any time they felt like it'; the second would subjectivize them. No place would be left for an objective judgment on whether or not his rights were infringed.[22]

Finally Rousseau addresses the relation between public and private in the *Letters from the Mountain*: 'it is no more permissible to violate natural laws by the social contract than it is to violate positive laws by contracts between particular individuals' (LMt 6.807). This passage asserts a premiss: the social contract is not entitled to infringe natural laws. From that premiss we could proceed as follows:

(1) If the function of the social contract is to realize natural laws, and if the function of natural laws is to give expression to natural rights (understood as non-defeasible individual liberties), then the social contract is not entitled to infringe natural rights.
(2) If the general will is the product of the social contract, and if its decisions are determined by the terms of the social contract, then the general will is not entitled to infringe natural rights.

In the form in which Rousseau asserts it here, the premiss is purely normative. It states what the social contract is not permitted to do. But more often he asserts the premiss as a combination of prescription and description: a prescription on the one hand of what the social contract is not entitled to demand, and on the other hand a factual, descriptive statement, that individuals cannot be harmed by a corporate body to which they have committed themselves, along with all others, on terms of exact equality of mutual total alienation of natural liberty. Putting that statement of fact together with the natural law prescription that individuals have a right not to harm themselves, it then becomes rational for them to commit themselves to the terms of the social contract, with the assurance that their fundamental natural right, of self-preservation, will be guaranteed. The question remains whether reciprocity and equality of alienation in themselves guarantee anything beyond reciprocity and equality in the distribution of whatever are the objectives of the general will, and whether the general will in turn, when governed by the stringent conditions laid down by Rousseau, can will only liberal objectives. Liberals answer no to that question, on the grounds that, even when the conditions are satisfied, the formal terms of the contract will not exclude an illiberal regime, since they do not ensure the sanctity of personal freedom.

To respond to the liberal criticism, we must return to Rousseau's account of civil freedom, the freedom that citizens exercise within society. 'To renounce one's freedom is to renounce one's status as a man [*qualité d'homme*], the rights of humanity, and even its duties', he tells us at SC I.4.356/135. True civil freedom means freedom from two kinds of constraint. One must be master of oneself, free from external constraint by another individual. But one must also be free from internal constraint, from the need to enslave another:

> Freedom is not so much the realization of one's will as independence from the will of others, and it does not involve making another's will dependent on one's own. Anyone who is master cannot be free, and to reign is to obey. (LMt 8.843)

Rousseau would persuade us that citizens will attain both external and internal freedom within the framework of the new order. Applying the lessons of the morality of the senses, Rousseau holds that the new citizens will be placed within a new motivational field. He had argued in the *Second Discourse* that the drive to dominate stems from anxiety caused by insecurity, and that insecurity in turn is caused by major inequalities of wealth and power. Only if we accept this explanatory story will we be convinced that through the total alienation of our natural rights we shall indeed guarantee our civil freedom. For when our motivational field is altered in the way Rousseau holds it will be, then the self-interest of no individual or group will depend on the oppression of another individual or group. Thus the combination of reciprocity, equality and self-interest will after all prevent members of the new order from behaving in an illiberal fashion, but only on the assumption that the transformation envisaged by Rousseau takes place. In predicting that transformation he commits himself to an exposed and vulnerable position, and one which is only minimally sketched in the *Social Contract*. Its credibility depends on the anthropology and psychology elaborated elsewhere.

Appendix I   Internal and external sanctions: the voice of conscience and the free-rider

The passage from the state of nature to civil society is one of radical change, but change of what? The answer must lie in the environment, which will be transformed to allow the feelings of self-preservation and compassion, which remain unchanged from the state of nature into civil society, to be re-channelled into non-exploitative, non-destructive directions. Civil society introduces reason, but reason must *re*-establish (*rétablir*) rules which are already founded in the feelings. Conscience must now intervene to mediate feeling through reason.

If conscience is innate and universal, what then is the source of our moral ills? Rousseau invites us to consider two possibilities.

The first possibility is the most catastrophic. It is that an evil environment, dominated by false opinions, could corrupt [*altére*] conscience: 'Opinion changes everything, it depraves nature, it corrupts conscience . . .' (FM 225). But could the very feeling which founds conscience be destroyed? Rousseau addresses that question in *Rousseau, Judge of Jean-Jacques*, where, finding himself the victim of conspiracy, his mood swings between despair and utopian hope. In the latter mood he looks beyond the present age which the dominant 'cruel doctrines' have rendered 'as despicable as it is unhappy':

> Those innate sentiments which nature has engraved in all hearts, to console man in his misery and encourage him to virtue, can be stifled in individuals, but they are quickly reborn in future generations, and they will always bring man back to his primal dispositions [*ses dispositions primitives*], just as the seed of a grafted tree always reproduces the wild stock . . . The voice of conscience can no more be stifled in the human heart than the voice of reason in the understanding, and the lack of moral sensibility [*l'insensibilité morale*] is as unnatural as madness. (RJJJ 3 Dial.972/ 242)

While conscience can be 'stifled in individuals', it cannot be 'stifled in the human heart'. Here, as elsewhere, the sentiment is innate and universal, but according to the morality of the senses, it is only within a correctly ordered environment, economic, political, intellectual and spiritual, that the sentiment will both flourish and be directed towards appropriate objects.

It is that thought which leads to the second possibility, which is less extreme. In civil society, our 'natural repugnance at seeing any other sensible being . . . suffer pain or death' must be strictly channelled. Otherwise it is mere squeamishness and sentimentality, or else it leads to unfairness and favouritism. In political theory, Rousseau is more interested in the latter outcome. The natural feeling, to be transformed into the social principle of justice, must be denatured, universalized. How does the transformation come about? It is part of our nature that we want to favour ourselves and those close to us, and to spare them suffering. Yet justice demands the equitable treatment of all:

> It is a beautiful and sublime precept to do unto others as we would have done unto ourselves. But is it not evident that, far from serving as the foundation of justice, it itself needs a justification? For what clear and solid reason have I, being myself, for behaving according to the will I would have if I were someone else? It is also clear that this precept is subject to a thousand exceptions which have never been explained except by sophistry. Would not a judge who condemns a criminal wish to be pardoned if he were a criminal himself? (GM 329/113)

Furthermore the judge's duty is to harm the criminal: 'there are a thousand cases where it is an act of justice to do harm to one's neighbour'. Yet Rousseau wants to avoid the radical opposition between feeling and principle that Kant would espouse. For him there is a continuity as well as an opposition between the natural and the social. The function of reason in society is to 're-establish on other foundations' what feeling established in nature. The continuity is realized only if we approximate to the ideal identification between individual and society: 'This is the wise man's first interest after his private interest, for each is part of his species and not of another individual'. In identification, we come to extend our feeling of identity, and thereby generate moral feelings:

> The less the object of our care is immediately involved with us, the less the illusion of particular interest is to be feared. The more one generalizes this interest, the more it becomes equitable, and the love of mankind is nothing other than the love of justice . . . let us never tolerate in [Emile] a blind preference founded solely on consideration of persons or on unjust bias. And why would he hurt one to serve another? It is of little importance to him who gets a greater share of happiness provided that it contributes to the greatest happiness of all. This is the wise man's first interest after his private interest, for each is part of his species and not of another individual. (Em IV.547–8/252–3)

Only through this process of extension of the feelings, yielding a sense of identification with society, and then with humanity, do the natural drives of *amour de soi* and pity found a society which is both cohesive and equitable:

> To prevent pity degenerating into weakness, it must, therefore, be

generalized and extended to the whole of mankind. Then one yields to it only insofar as it accords with justice, because of all the virtues justice is the one that contributes most to the common good of men. For the sake of reason, for the sake of our love of ourselves, we must have pity for our species still more than for our neighbor, and pity for the wicked is a very great cruelty to men. (ibid.)[23]

Because, even in the ideal order, the human beings who compose it are not perfect, and the identification between individuals and society is also not perfect, legal sanctions remain as the legitimate counter to the free-rider:

Whatever is good and in accordance with order is so by the nature of things, independently of human conventions. All justice comes from God; He alone is its source; but if we knew how to receive it from on high, we should need neither government nor laws. Doubtless there is a universal justice emanating from reason alone; but to be acknowledged among us, this justice must be reciprocal. Considering things from a human point of view [A considérer humainement les choses], the laws of justice are ineffectual among men for want of a natural sanction. They merely benefit the wicked man and harm the just, when the latter observes them towards everyone while nobody observes them towards him. Therefore there must be conventions and laws to combine rights with duties and to bring justice back to its object. (SC II.6.378/ 152)

In the *Emile*, Rousseau explains the necessity of legal sanctions in the same way, in terms of the free-rider:

Even the sentiment of doing unto others as we would have them do unto us has no true foundation other than conscience and sentiment; for where is the precise reason for me, being myself, to act as if I were another, especially when I am morally certain of never finding myself in the same situation? And who will guarantee me that in very faithfully following this maxim I will get others to follow it similarly with me? The wicked man gets advantage from the just man's probity and his own injustice. He is delighted that everyone, with the exception of himself, be just. This agreement, whatever may be said about it, is not very advantageous for good men. (Em IV.523.Fn./235.Fn.)

But he then goes on to contrast the free-rider to the just citizen. The

128

latter, unlike the former, comes to identify himself with social norms. His *amour de soi*, educated and extended, makes him do his duty without constraint:

> But when the force of an expansive soul makes me identify myself with my neighbour, and I feel my own self, so to speak, in him, then it is in order not to suffer myself that I want him not to suffer. I am interested in him out of love for myself, and the reason for the precept is in nature itself which inspires in me the desire for my own well-being in whatever place I feel myself to exist. From this I conclude that it is not true that the precepts of natural law are founded on reason alone. They have a base more solid and sure. Love of men derived from love of self is the principle of human justice . . . (ibid.)

Legal sanctions impose force. Assuming the ideal order, the threat of force needs to be addressed only to those citizens whose sentiments have been improperly formed, and who fail to find their own good in the public good:

> Laws, you will say, although they obligate conscience, nevertheless also use constraint with grown men. I admit it, but what are these men if not children spoiled by education? This is precisely what must be prevented. Use force with children, and reason with men. Such is the natural order. The wise man does not need laws. (Em II.319/91)

Can these 'spoiled children' be changed by the imposition of force? Of course not. For that reason Rousseau in the *Social Contract* puts so much stress on *moeurs*, the moral-cultural condition of the people, and gives such a key role first to the Lawgiver, and then to the Censors, in forming those *moeurs*, and in devising and regulating the framework within which they can flourish.

Appendix II   Interests, free-riders and the general will

Rousseau's concept of the general will has divided social choice theorists. For those most critical of Rousseau, if the general will is to emerge as Rousseau would have it, society must be bound together by a degree of consensus which is either inconceivable, or, if conceivable, then a dangerous option which should be avoided.[24] Kenneth Arrow, for instance, understands the general will like this:

> [E]ach individual has two orderings, one which governs him in

129

his everyday actions and one which would be relevant under some ideal conditions and which is in some sense truer than the first ordering. It is the latter which is considered relevant to social choice, and it is assumed that there is complete unanimity with regard to the truer individual ordering. . .

. . . Voting, from this point of view, is not a device whereby each individual expresses his personal interests, but rather where each individual gives his opinion of the general will.[25]

Against Arrow, Runciman and Sen have argued that Rousseau is not committed to the thesis of 'two orderings', that he:

does not require us to impute to each person more than a single set of orderings, ... [since] each person has . . . a single and consistent aim. The conflict between the will of all and the general will arises not because the individual must be required to change his preference orderings, but because of the difference between the outcome of individual strategy and of enforced collusion.[26]

How are we to adjudicate between Arrow's two orderings and Runciman and Sen's single ordering? The answer depends on the nature of the interests that individuals recognize as their own. Since those interests undergo a transformation between SC I.7 and SC I.8, so too does the psychology of ordering our preferences when we are required to make political decisions. In that sense, then, Runciman and Sen's single ordering would apply directly to a well-ordered society. Arrow's two orderings on the other hand would apply to a relatively ill-ordered one, in which there are still many free-riders who 'wish to enjoy the rights of the citizen without wanting to fulfil the duties of a subject' (SC I.7.363/141), and in which virtuous citizens striving to realize the public interest amidst less than optimal circumstances must experience a gap between the particular and the general in their will and interests when they come to make social choices.[27]

Appendix III   'Conventions' and 'contracts'

In the *Second Discourse*, Rousseau talks of the first steps whereby:

men could imperceptibly acquire some crude idea of mutual engagements and of the advantages of fulfilling them, but only insofar as present and perceptible interest would require; for foresight meant nothing to them, and far from being concerned about a distant future, they did not even think about the next day. Was it a matter of catching a Deer, everyone clearly felt that for this purpose he ought faithfully to keep his post; but if a hare happened to pass within reach of one of them, there can be no doubt that he pursued it without scruple, and that having obtained his prey, he cared very little about having caused his Companions to miss theirs. (2D 166–7/45)

Raymond Boudon accurately formalized the deer hunt as follows, the figures standing for positive units of advantage:

		AGENT 2	
		Cooperation	Defection
	Cooperation	3,3	0,2
AGENT 1			
	Defection	2,0	2,2

He commented:

'the structure of interaction illustrated by the hunting expedition is close to [that] . . . in the prisoner's dilemma. One classic way out for agents who have fallen into this trap is to accept freely the constraint which will oblige them to cooperate. Of course constraint, whether public or private, is not the only possible way out of the prisoner's dilemma. Loyalty is another, but it is unlikely to be found in all situations.'

He was right to see that, when the participants are unreliable, the 'trap' can be sprung only by an agent of 'enforced collusion'. But Boudon was wrong to call the deer hunt a prisoner's dilemma.[28] In the prisoner's dilemma, if I defect and you keep faith, then I gain more than I would have done if we had both kept faith. In that way the prisoner's dilemma illustrates the thinking of the free-rider. The free-rider *does* gain more for himself provided the honest remain honest. In the case of the prisoners, it is only when *both* defect that *both* suffer. Similarly in the case of the bus service, it is only when a sufficiently large number fail to pay their fares that all, including the free-riders, suffer, since the bus company cannot absorb such losses.

Rather than a prisoner's dilemma, the deer hunt is an 'assurance game'. Rousseau tells us that the deer hunt fails because the hunters are irrational, 'perfect strangers to foresight', and they are also unreliable, failing to 'abide faithfully by [their] post'. But assuming that all the hunters are equally unreliable, then even if all were rational, each would still have to decide whether to abide by or to

131

abandon his post. In that situation, driven by a rational estimate of the unreliability of the others, any of whom might equally be confronted by an available hare, he would be driven to make the rational, but less than optimal decision, that he should abandon his post and pursue the hare. The problem of the deer hunt, like that of the prisoner's dilemma, can be solved by an agent of 'enforced collusion'.

We can understand the contrast between Rousseau's *Social Contract* and his deer hunt by means of David Lewis's distinction between a 'social contract' and a 'convention'. In both cases, the participants engage in a reasoning process concerning their interests, which leads them to an agreement in order to achieve certain goals. But their reasoning and their perception of their interests is different in the two cases. Lewis defines 'convention' and 'social contract' thus:

In a 'convention',

- each agent prefers general conformity
- to conformity by all but himself,
- ignoring his preferences regarding states of general nonconformity.

In a 'social contract',

- each agent prefers general conformity
- to a certain state of general nonconformity,
- ignoring his preferences regarding conformity by all but himself.

According to this distinction, the agreement of the deer hunters is a Lewis convention. In it, we have a potential defector who is instrumentally irrational in defecting, relative to the gains of universal conformity. He must therefore be prevented from being instrumentally irrational. For him, the agreement of SC I.6 is a Lewis social contract. In it, we have a potential defector who is instrumentally rational when he alone defects, though this would cease to be so if all defected. He must therefore be prevented from being instrumentally rational at the expense of his neighbours.

In the light of Lewis's distinction, we can understand that Rousseau is aiming to transform SC I.6 from a Lewis social contract into a Lewis convention. He bids the legislator change the circumstances which surround us, by removing inequality and factions. He will thereby change the nature of our interests, not by denying us our interest in our self-preservation, but by altering our perception of the self, so that we preserve it not by exploiting our neighbours, but by identifying with them.[29]

VI

The *Social Contract*: Maxims of Politics

In this chapter I focus on the 'naturalist' strand in Rousseau's political thought, addressing some often ignored passages in Parts III and IV of the *Social Contract*. In them Rousseau theorizes the ways in which the principles of right can be realized by different types of government, according to the material conditions of a particular people in a particular historical and geographical context. If we fail to take those passages seriously, we risk a serious misreading of the *Social Contract*, since without them it becomes what Rousseau said it was not, namely another utopia, inapplicable in practice.[1]

(A)   The people

The general will is the will of the people. Rousseau's image of the people is ambivalent, and he swings between extremes of optimism and pessimism about its capacities. He is painting a picture of a people which does not yet exist, or which no longer exists except in small, isolated communities. Rousseau holds that when the people consists of free, equal, informed citizens, who are provided with an effective institutional framework for making decisions, then there will be no serious conflicts of interests and the only disagreements will be about the best methods of reaching agreed substantive goals. But, as things are, individuals are mystified and misled, in 'chains' that are spiritual as well as political, constantly lacking the conditions which would make a genuine consensus possible.

Rousseau begins his examination of the people at SC II.8,9,10. Some commentators have dismissed these chapters as irrelevant to his central purpose of establishing the grounds of legitimacy. But such a dismissal ignores half of Rousseau's political theory, in which he seeks a political order that is 'sure' as well as 'legitimate'.[2] The empirical data Rousseau adduces are speculative and interlaced with pessimistic rhetorical declamations concerning timing and lost opportunities. The Lawgiver *'institutes'* his people (SC II.7.381/155), gives it institutions and educates it, an *'instituteur'* being a teacher as well as a founder. Like Emile's tutor, he must be a master of timing. Once a people has passed the climactic moment for legislation, and has become both cowed and hardened by tyranny, it will have acquired habits of servility which can rarely be shaken off. Shifting metaphors now to medicine, Rousseau suggests that a revolution may produce amnesia, so that a people can forget those old habits, and start again from scratch. But such events are rare. In most cases one should heed the ominous warning: 'Free peoples, remember this maxim; Freedom can be acquired, but it can never be recovered' (SC II.8.385/158). Rousseau had difficulty in developing the metaphors. On the one hand, 'Peoples, like men, are docile only in their youth, they become incorrigible as they grow older' (SC II.8.385/157). On the other hand,

> There is for Nations, as for men, a time of maturity which one needs to await before one submits them to laws. But it is not always easy to recognize the maturity of a people, and if it is anticipated, the work is ruined'. (SC II.8.386/158)

He tried to resolve the conflict in a compromise formula: 'Youth is not childhood. There is for nations, as for men, a time of youth, or, if you like, of maturity which must be awaited . . .'[3] The truth is that beneath his metaphors Rousseau does not have a detailed theory of timing for peoples comparable to the psychological theory of the individual's development in the *Emile*. He has in mind certain exemplary mistakes, in particular that of Peter the Great of Russia, who with 'the genius of an imitator . . . saw that his people was barbarous, but did not see that it was not ripe for political order [*police*] . . .' (ibid.). At the same time, he also has a model of the ideal configuration of 'a people suitable for legislation' (SC II.10.390/162). But between the two there is only speculation and metaphor.

Once a people has been 'instituted', provided with basic laws and a form of government, a demographic test, which we shall examine in a moment, will reveal whether or not it is flourishing with those institutions. Since the people as a whole is sovereign, the smaller the population, the larger is the share in sovereign power of each individual citizen, and vice versa. That at least appears to be the meaning of the sentence: 'The more the social bond stretches, the looser it becomes and in general a small state is proportionally stronger than a large one' (SC II.9.386/159).[4] Rousseau makes frequent criticisms of big states. They are morally and politically weak because their members are too numerous and too heterogeneous: 'the people has less affection for its chiefs which it never sees, for its native land [*patrie*] which is in its eyes like the world, and for its fellow citizens, most of whom are strangers to it' (SC II.9.387/159). At the same time, 'the State ought to procure a sufficient basis to be solid . . . [since] the weak risk being rapidly swallowed up, and none can hope to preserve itself except by establishing a kind of equilibrium with all the others' (SC II.9.388/160).

A people is at its best size when it is small enough that its citizens feel the ties of shared membership, but big enough that it can survive in the international arena. There should be a correspondence between sizes of population and of territory so that there is enough land to sustain the inhabitants, and as many inhabitants as can be supported by the land. Then there will be neither famine nor territorial expansion driven by the need for *Lebensraum*.

Rousseau is now ready to answer the question: 'What people then is suitable for legislation?' (SC II.10.390/162). The conditions are severe. It is one 'already linked by some union of origin, interest or agreement; has not yet born the real yoke of laws; has no well rooted customs or superstitions'. It must be strong enough to resist invasion either alone or in alliance with others, but small enough that 'each member can be known to all, and where it is not necessary to impose on any man a greater burden than a man can bear'. This condition may mean that at least a minimal level of prosperity is necessary, otherwise the people's survival might depend on subject labour. Rousseau does add that it should be 'neither rich nor poor, and can be self-sufficient'. In terms of international relations, it is a people 'which does not depend on other peoples, and on which no other people depends'. It has been noted that Rousseau's views on this last condition were in flux, and that in the *Political Fragments* he seems to have preferred a dominant position for his people, rather than one of equal coexistence.[5]

(B) *'Institutional systems'*

Book II concludes with two chapters on 'The various systems of legislation' (SC II.11) and 'Classification of laws' (SC II.12). In SC II.11 Rousseau specifies the two conditions which guarantee a legitimate consensus, relative equality and the absence of factions. These he calls the 'general objects of all good institutions' (SC II.11.392/163).[6] They in turn:

must be modified in each country according to the relationships which arise as much from the local situation as from the character of the inhabitants, and it is on the basis of those relationships that one must assign to each people a particular institutional system [*un système particulier d'institution*] which should be the best, not perhaps in itself, but for the State for which it is destined. (ibid.)

An 'institutional system' includes geographical, demographic and economic factors, as well as legal and political ones. The wise Lawgiver takes all of these into account when he 'institutes' a people by giving them the appropriate 'political laws', so that 'natural relationships and the laws always agree on the same points' (SC II.11.393/163–4).

Rousseau concludes Book II with a taxonomy of four types of law, specified by the 'relation' each type establishes between the legislator and the subject of legislation (SC II.12.393–4/164–5). (1) There are 'political laws', the fundamental constitution of the state, devised for it by the Lawgiver, relating 'the whole body to itself', as the sovereign lays down the rules of its own conduct. Since the people is absolutely sovereign, it 'is always master to change its laws – even the best laws' (SC II.12.394/164). (2) There are 'civil laws', which determine the relation 'of the members to each other and to the entire body'. These would seem to order contractual and family relations. The aim of these laws is that 'each Citizen should be in perfect independence from all the others, and in excessive dependence on the City'. They would thus contribute to the final demise of feudal ties.[7] (3) There are criminal laws, which cover 'the relation of disobedience and penalty'. (4) Finally, 'the most important of all' is the law of 'customs, morals [*moeurs*] and . . . opinion'. As we know from the morality of the senses, this inner element of the social consensus is not an independent variable, but is itself partly dependent on the social environment, constituted by the first three types of law.

(C)   'The form of government'

In the maxims of Books III and IV Rousseau explores how far it is possible to realize the normative principles of right, which require that the sovereign people express its general will in legislation, and that its sovereignty be absolute, indivisible and inalienable. In these investigations he engages in applied political theory, which may appear to the modern reader to be of little empirical interest and also to be irrelevant to the central normative concerns of the *Social Contract*. Yet it is clear that for Rousseau they are of great importance, since without them he will be unable to respond to the charge that the book embodies a mere utopia, a 'world of chimeras'. As we noted above, Rousseau aims to show that a state can be constructed to satisfy both terms of the Proem, being both 'legitimate and sure'. We shall consider Rousseau's investigations of 'the form of government' under four headings: (i) the theoretical basis of the maxims expressed in ratios (SC III.1–2); (ii) an examination of the forms of government suited to countries of different sizes (SC III.3–8); (iii) an examination of the ways in which these different forms of government degenerate and perish, and of measures that can be taken to prevent or postpone those tendencies (SC III.9–14); (iv) development of the doctrine of the subordination of the government to the sovereign people (SC III.15–18).[8]

(i)   Theoretical basis (SC III.1–2)

Rousseau begins his presentation ominously: 'I warn the reader that this chapter should be read carefully, and that I do not know the art of being clear for those who are not willing to be attentive' (SC III.1.395/166). But Rousseau's mathematical formulations are a challenge to even the most attentive reader. Masters has both identified the key sentences in Rousseau's text and transformed them into intelligible equations.[9] With his help we can unravel the knots of normative and descriptive threads in passages where Rousseau speaks both of relations which should hold ideally, and of relations which must hold in fact in particular circumstances.

Before moving on to those complexities, Rousseau begins with a simple, dualistic model to explain action: 'When I walk towards an object, it is necessary first that I want to go to it; and secondly that my feet carry me there' (SC III.1.395/166). By analogy, to bring about social action, a will, the general will, must activate organs to execute that will. These two elements are termed 'legislative power', directed to general objects, and 'executive power', directed to particular objects. They are exercised by, and only by, the sovereign people and the government respectively. The government is not to be 'confounded with the sovereign, of which it is only the minister' (SC III.1.396/166). Rousseau warns against the usurpation of sovereign power by the government, as is practised by most régimes of the time. It is equally wrong for the sovereign people to usurp the government's executive power and address itself to particular persons, instead of to classes of persons, who are the proper subject of laws. But that danger is specific to direct democracy and so is rarely encountered.

Following Masters, we distinguish four ratios (R1, R2, R3 and

R4) in III.1 and III.2. R1 expresses the sovereign's relationship to the state, that is to the people as subjects. Rousseau says that it:

> can be represented by the extremes of a continuous proportion, of which the proportional mean [*la moyenne proportionnelle*] is the Government. The Government receives from the Sovereign the orders which it gives to the people; and in order for the State to be in good equilibrium, once adjustments are made,[10] the product or power of the Government, taken by itself, must be equal to the product or power of the citizens, who are sovereigns on the one hand and subjects on the other. (SC III.1.396/167)

In Masters's gloss, 'a continuous proportion is a geometric progression such that $A/B = B/C \ldots$', and B is the 'proportional mean'.[11] In this case, the government is the 'proportional mean'. So, if we substitute S (sovereign), G (government), P (people as subject), we obtain the ratio:

$$[R1] \quad \frac{S}{G} = \frac{G}{P}$$

R1 is transformed by the following simple steps, multiplying through by P:

$$\frac{S \times P}{G} = G$$

$$\therefore \; S \times P = G^2$$

$$\therefore \; G = \sqrt{S \times P}$$

But Rousseau tells us that 'one of the extremes, namely the people as subject, is fixed and represented by unity' (SC III.1.398/168), so:

$$P = 1$$

$$\therefore \; G = \sqrt{S}$$

This is the conclusion for which Rousseau is driving. He foresees that critics will mock his schoolboy mathematics:

> If, in ridiculing this system, it was said that in order to find this proportional mean and form the body of the Government, it is

only necessary, according to me, to calculate the square root of the number of people [as sovereign], I would reply . . . that if I momentarily borrow the vocabulary of geometry in order to express myself in fewer words, I am nevertheless not unaware that geometrical precision does not exist in moral quantities. (ibid.)

But the mocking comment is correct. Rousseau's response means only that there is a margin of error 'in moral quantities'. So, to calculate the 'product or power' of the government needed to control a citizen body of a given size, one must take into account factors other than numbers of magistrates and citizens. These would include, presumably, the government's technical resources and imponderables such as the citizens' *moeurs*. But with those provisos, the formula $G = \sqrt{S}$ does indeed represent the conclusion of R1. It means that a large population is to be administered by a relatively small number of magistrates, a small one by a relatively large number. So if 1,000,000 citizens require 1,000 magistrates, 10,000 citizens require 100 magistrates.

Where R1 represented a ratio simply between numbers of magistrates and numbers of citizens, R2 and R3 introduce the idea of the strength or force of government and of sovereign:

Now the less relationship there is between private wills and the general will, that is between the morals and the laws, the more repressive force must increase. Thus in order for the Government to be good, it ought to be relatively stronger in proportion as the people is more numerous. (SC III.1.397/168)

This yields the ratio:

$$[R2] \quad \frac{Ga}{Pa} = \frac{Gb}{Pb}$$

where G represents strength of government and P represents size of population. Thus the larger the population, the stronger must be the government, and vice versa. Rousseau continues:

On the other hand, as the enlargement of the State gives those entrusted with the public authority more temptations and means to abuse their power, the more force the Government must have to restrain the people, the more the Sovereign must have in turn to restrain the Government. (SC III.1.398/168)

This yields the ratio:

$$[R3] \quad \frac{Sa}{Ga} = \frac{Sb}{Gb}$$

where S represents the strength of the sovereign and G represents the strength of the government. Thus the stronger the government, the stronger must be the sovereign, whose agent the government is, and vice versa.

According to R2, a larger population requires a stronger government to administer it. According to R3 a stronger government requires a stronger sovereign to control it. Putting R2 and R3 together, we infer that a larger population requires a stronger sovereign. But Rousseau has already established, as a matter of fact, that the larger the population the weaker is the sovereign people, and vice versa: 'there is a *maximum* of force in every body politic which it cannot exceed and of which it often falls short by growing larger . . . in general a small state is proportionately stronger than a large one' (SC II.9.386–7/159). The requirements, in short, conflict with the fact.

The fourth ratio ties R1 to R2 and R3. It relates the number of magistrates (the size of government) to the strength of government: 'the more of [its] . . . force the government uses on its own members, the less is left for acting on the entire people' (SC III.2.400/170). From this it follows that 'the more numerous the Magistrates, the weaker the Government'. So the strength of the government is in inverse proportion to its size. This yields the ratio:

$$[R4] \quad \frac{Ga}{Ma} = \frac{Gb}{Mb}$$

where G represents the strength of the government and M represents the number of the magistrates. Putting R4 together with R2 we see that the size of the government must be in inverse proportion to the size of the population (SC III.3.403–4/173).

The ratios explain why Rousseau is pessimistic about the possibility of maintaining popular sovereignty. A population 'naturally' grows in size; as population grows, its government becomes smaller and stronger; as the government becomes stronger, the sovereign people needs to become stronger in order to control its government; but a large people is 'naturally' relatively weaker than a small people. If we are to believe his critical comments on the Government of Geneva in the *Letters from the Mountain*, his pessimism is even deeper, since he seems to think that the tendency of governments to condense in size and so increase their power relative to the sovereign people is a universal one, and is independent of demographic factors:

> The principle which constitutes the different forms of Government consists in the number of members which compose it. The smaller this number is, the more force the Government has; the larger it is, the feebler the Government is; and as sovereignty always tends to slacken, so the Government always tends to become stronger. (LMt 6.808)

Rousseau rarely keeps factual and normative questions wholly separate. Thus in SC III.1, he expounds the first three ratios as matters of fact, expressing tendencies and functional requirements, and then returns to the purely normative level to define the dissolution of the body politic, which would occur:[12]

> If it finally came about that the Prince had a private will more active than that of the Sovereign, and that he used some of the public force at his discretion to obey that private will, so that there were so to speak two sovereigns – one de jure, the other de facto – at that moment the social union would vanish and the body politic would dissolve. (SC III.1.399/169)

He concludes the whole discussion of the ratios with a clear distinction between the two levels, saying 'I refer here only to the relative force of the Government, and not to its rectitude. For on the contrary the more numerous the body of magistrates, the closer the corporate will is to the general will' (SC III.2.402/171–2).

(ii)   *Forms of government suited to countries of different sizes (SC III.3–8)*

Rousseau propounds an austere three-fold taxonomy of possible forms of government, determined by the proportion of the people to whom the Sovereign can 'entrust the Government' [*commettre le dépôt du Gouvernement*]. If it entrusts it 'to the entire people or to the majority of people . . .', then it is democracy. If it restricts it in 'the hands of a smaller number', then it is aristocracy. If it 'concentrate[s] the whole Government in the hands of a single magistrate', then it is 'Monarchy or royal Government'. He mitigates the austerity by conceding that 'all these forms admit of different degrees . . . Even Royalty admits some division'. By application of the ratios, 'it follows that in general Democratic government is suited to small

States, Aristocratic to medium-sized ones, and Monarchical to large ones' (SC III.3.403–4/173).

According to the principles of right established in Book II, all three can be legitimate forms of 'republican government':

> I . . . call every State ruled by laws a Republic, whatever the form of administration may be, for then alone the public interest governs and the commonwealth really exists [*la chose publique est quelque chose*]. Every legitimate Government is republican.

He explains the word 'republican' in a footnote:

> By this word I do not mean only an Aristocracy or a Democracy, but in general any government guided by the general will, which is the law. In order to be legitimate, the Government must not be confounded with the Sovereign, but must be its minister. Then monarchy itself is a republic. (SC II.6.379–80/153)

A legitimate government is here defined as any government which is subordinate to the general will of the sovereign people, and he takes pains to emphasize that that is the principle of republican government in general, not of democratic government in particular.[13] It is not surprising that Rousseau's critics immediately recognized that it made the *Social Contract* subversive of virtually all contemporary régimes, since it made all governments provisional, dependent on the people's endorsement. Here is the verdict of a contemporary critic:

> An essential defect of the whole *Social Contract* is that it places sovereignty in the body politic, so that even when the government is monarchical, the community still does not allow it to be sovereign, since the king is and can be only the magistrate and executor of the people's wills. This means that the *Social Contract* does not, fundamentally, recognize monarchy or aristocracy, but only democracy.[14]

In Rousseau's model of democratic government in the *Social Contract*, all, or most, of the citizens participate in the administration of the government personally, as magistrates. If practicable at all, democratic government is beset by its own specific problems. It is a condition of legitimacy that legislative sovereignty and executive government be kept separate. But if the members of both branches are identical, how can the separation be effected? One solution suggested is to 'share government functions between several tribunals, which leads to a greater authority for those [tribunals] with fewest numbers' (SC III.4.404–5/173). Thus within the democratic form of government, if it is to remain legitimate, there is a tendency to dilute its absolute egalitarianism and to allow government power to condense around restricted groups.

Four difficult conditions must be fulfilled if democratic government is to flourish. (1) The community must be small, so that the whole people can assemble and each citizen can be known by the others. (2) They must have a simple way of life, so that there is no complex business to discuss. (3) There must be relative equality of rank and fortune. (4) There must be little or no luxury, since it 'corrupts both rich and poor'. The third condition must be satisfied in all legitimate states, and both second and fourth are a recurring theme of much of Rousseau's work, from the *First Discourse* to the *Second Discourse* to the *Emile*. In short, Rousseau is describing a people in good moral health, possessing good *moeurs*, and thus building into the conditions of democracy a positive model of the ideal community, consisting of elements which are desirable in themselves. The hardest problem is posed by the first condition. Is it possible to have a direct participatory democracy in anything larger than a small city state? Indeed is it possible to have popular sovereignty, no matter what its form of government, on a large scale? Rousseau will respond to that question at III.13 and further in Book IV. Even if it is practicable, democratic government as defined by Rousseau is beset by instability, 'subject to civil wars and internal agitations' (SC III.4.405/174). Difficult to realize and unstable when realized, perhaps democratic government is a utopian dream: 'If there were a people of Gods, they would govern themselves democratically. So perfect a Government is unsuited to men' (SC III.4.406/174).

Given his pessimism about the feasibility of democratic government, it is not surprising that Rousseau is relatively enthusiastic about what he calls aristocracy. He distinguishes three kinds of aristocracy, natural, or government by elders, elective and hereditary. 'The first is suited only to simple peoples. The third is the worst of all Governments. The second is the best; it is Aristocracy properly so-called' (SC III.5.406/175). Elective aristocracy has certain advantages over democracy. It has 'two very different moral persons, that is the Government and the Sovereign', and so keeps separate functions which democracy wrongly conflates (SC III.5.406/174). It is more efficient because it allows for the choice of the best magistrates. 'In a word, it is the best and most natural order that the wisest govern the multitude, when one is sure that they will govern it for its profit, and not for their own' (SC III.5.407/175). There is a risk that elective aristocracy may become effectively

143

hereditary, as elected magistrates accumulate power and wealth and transmit them to their children. There is also the risk that the corporate interest of the magistrates as a body may interfere with the exercise of their duty, which is the execution of the sovereign's general will.

In his summary of the *Social Contract* in the sixth *Letter from the Mountain* Rousseau heads off a misreading of this chapter: 'One must remember here that the constitution of the State and of the Government are two very distinct things and that I have not confused them. The best of Governments is the aristocratic; the worst of Sovereignties is the aristocratic' (LMt 6.808–9).[15]

It is notable that Rousseau's judgment on monarchy at SC III.6 is entirely negative, after he had so explicitly stated at SC II.6 that monarchy was a possible form of legitimate, republican government (SC II.6.380/153). Now he makes a clear contrast. 'Republics,' he says, 'pursue their goals by means of policies which are more consistent and therefore better followed', whereas 'each revolution in a royal ministry causes one in the State' (SC III.6.412/179). The implication is that, however it may be in theory, in practice a monarchy can never come up to the standards of republican government. In monarchy the 'moral and collective power' of government is 'united in the hands of a natural person, a real man who has the right to dispose of it according to the laws' (SC III.6.408/176). A monarchy is by nature inconsistent and it demands virtues in the person of the reigning monarch which no single individual is likely to possess.

Monarchy, as we know from the ratios, is the form of government best suited to administering large states:

> everything responds to the same moving force, all the springs of the machine are in the same hands; everything moves towards the same goal; there are no opposing movements that are mutually destructive; and there is no constitution imaginable in which a lesser effort produces a greater action. Archimedes sitting tranquilly on the shore and effortlessly pulling a huge Vessel over the waves is my image of a skilful monarch governing his vast States from his study, and setting everything in motion while appearing immobile himself. (ibid.)

But however effectively a monarchy may exercise control, it does so with the least attention to the general will or to public happiness.

Rousseau draws up no formal balance sheet on the three forms of government. He would prefer an elected aristocracy based on merit, but sees the seeds of its corruption as meritocracy gives way to plutocracy. In the *Social Contract*, he leaves the reasons for his pessimism shrouded in elementary mathematics, but in later years he would despair of finding any order that would be both stable and legitimate:

> In my old ideas, this was the great problem of politics, which I compare to squaring the circle in geometry . . . : *to find a form of Government which puts the law above man.*
>
> If this form can be found, then let us seek it and try to establish it . . . If unfortunately [it] cannot be found, and I admit openly that I think that it cannot, my view is that we should pass to the other extreme, and all at once put man as far above the law as he can be: I should like the despot to be God. In a word, I can see no tolerable middle point between the austerest Hobbism and the most perfect democracy; for the conflict between men and laws, which introduces into the State a continual civil war, is the worst of all political states.
>
> But despots like Caligula, Nero, Tiberius! . . . I roll on the ground, and I groan at being a man. (Letter to Mirabeau, 26 July 1767, CC 33#5991, p. 240)

After briefly dismissing the category of 'mixed governments' at III.7, Rousseau returns to the descriptive mode at SC III.8, 'That not every form of government is suited to every country'. Here he begins with some speculations on climate in the style of Montesquieu: 'Freedom, not being the fruit of every climate is not within the reach of all peoples'. He continues:

> In all the Governments of the world, the public person consumes, yet produces nothing. What then is the source of the substance it consumes? The labor of its members. It is the excess of private individuals that produces what is necessary for the public. It follows from this that the civil state can subsist only so long as the product of men's labor exceeds their needs. (SC III.8.414/181)[16]

Rousseau uses this chapter, which is perhaps the most speculative in the *Social Contract*, to give a sketchy economic grounding to his view that a free polity flourishes best in conditions of moderation, where there is neither starvation and penury nor luxury and excess: 'Places where surplus of products over labor is moderate are suited to free peoples' (SC III.8.416/182). Assuming a rough correlation between warm climate and fertility, Rousseau hedges his climatic speculations with qualifications, since one should 'always distinguish between general laws and the particular causes which can modify their effect', but, very generally, 'the effect of climate makes despotism suited to hot countries, barbarism to cold countries, and a good polity to intermediate regions'. True to the morality of the senses ('the wise man's *materialism*'), Rousseau is attracted by the idea of grounding the human sciences in the natural ones. But nowhere does he seriously develop that project.

(iii)   Good government, degeneration, conservation (SC III.9–14)

The chapter 'On the signs of good government' (SC III.9) is equally naturalistic. There is in fact only:

> one sign so simple that we would be in bad faith if we did not agree on it. What is the end of the political association? It is the preservation and prosperity of its members. And what is the surest sign that they are preserved and prospering? It is their number and population. (SC III.9.419–20/185)

With this simple demographic test, Rousseau seeks again to provoke:

> All other things being equal, the Government under which . . . the Citizens populate and multiply the most is infallibly the best. One under which a people grows smaller and dwindles away is the worst. Calculators, it is up to you now. Count, measure, compare. (ibid.)

Rousseau was much preoccupied by demographic questions. A falling birth rate, the outcome of bad government and bad *moeurs* threaten the security of the state. The 'demographic imperative' to maintain the population runs through his thinking about women in *Emile* V. The test may be over-simple, and in the modern world threatened by population explosion, may appear naïve. But it is not absurd to think that the negative correlation, between bad government and a dramatically falling birth rate, does hold.

In the following chapters, concerned with degeneration and conservation (III.10–14), Rousseau alternates between the descriptive mode of maxims and the normative mode of principles. His pessimism is conveyed by the title of SC III.10.421/186: 'On the abuse of the government and its tendency to degenerate'. His favoured metaphor of the spring [*ressort*] of the machine is suited to the pessimistic tone. Every spring weakens in time. Every mechanical watch, even a Swiss one, has a finite life. The opening words of the chapter set the tone:

> Just as the private will acts incessantly against the general will, so

the Government makes a continual effort against Sovereignty. The greater this effort becomes, the more the constitution deteriorates . . . it must happen sooner or later that the Prince finally oppresses the Sovereign and breaks the social treaty. That is the inherent and inevitable vice which, from the emergence of the body politic, tends without respite to destroy it, just as old age and death destroy the body of a man. (ibid.)

The tendency is inevitable, 'it must happen' [*il doit arriver*], and the tendency is to deteriorate [*s'altere*], not just to change.[17]

Rousseau distinguishes 'two ways in which a Government degenerates'. One is when the Government contracts [*se reserre*]. The other is when the State dissolves [*se dissout*].

A government contracts when its membership passes from a greater number to a smaller, as democracy to aristocracy, aristocracy to monarchy. Contraction, says Rousseau, is the 'natural tendency' [*inclinaison naturelle*] of governments, and he adduces the history of Rome to illustrate the phenomenon. He claims that the opposite tendency, from fewer to more members, is impossible, but he gives no evidence for that 'doctrinaire' conclusion.[18] What causes a government to contract? 'In fact a government never changes its form except when its worn-out spring leaves it too feeble to be able to preserve its own form' (SC III.10.422/187). It seems that the government as a whole has a spring whose function is to hold it in its allotted, uncontracted form, and that when its spring wears out the government implodes.

The spring metaphor is then cashed out, as Rousseau distinguishes two cases of dissolution of the state (ibid.). The first case is that of usurpation from the centre, when 'the Prince [i.e. the governing body as a whole] no longer administers the State according to the laws and usurps sovereign power'. The second is that of usurpation from the periphery, when 'members of the Government separately usurp power which they should exercise as a body'. Tucked away in the middle of this apparently descriptive chapter is a powerful normative conclusion, that 'the instant the Government usurps sovereignty, the social pact is broken and all the ordinary citizens, returning by right to their natural freedom, are forced but not obliged to obey' (SC III.10.422–3/187).

In SC III.11 ('On the dissolution of the body politic') Rousseau takes up his most fatalistic, elegiac note: 'Such is the natural and inevitable tendency of the best constituted Governments. If Sparta and Rome perished, what State can hope to endure for ever?' (SC III.11.424/188). He returns now to the organic metaphor, as the mortality of the body politic mirrors that of the human body. But once again the descriptive model-building is inseparable from normative principles of right: 'The principle of political life lies in the Sovereign authority. The legislative power is the heart of the State; the executive power is its brain, giving movement to all its parts' (ibid.). With the idea of 'legislative power' Rousseau develops a legal voluntarism, in which the will operates with inertia, so that one act of will remains in force until replaced by another act of will:

> It is not through laws that the State subsists, it is through the legislative power. Yesterday's law does not obligate today, but tacit consent is presumed from silence, and the Sovereign is assumed to confirm constantly the laws it does not repeal while having the power to do so. Everything the sovereign has once declared it wants, unless it revoked the declaration. (SC III.11.424/188–9)

Rousseau heads off the objection that this legal voluntarism would involve constant change, as one act of popular will succeeds another, arguing that a strong will is consistent, not vacillating, and that veneration for old laws is a sign that the present will is strong.

Chapters 12, 13, 14 ('How sovereign authority is maintained') also combine principles and maxims: 'The Sovereign, having no other force than the legislative power, acts only by laws, and since laws are only authentic acts of the general will, the Sovereign can act only when the people is assembled' (SC III.12.425/189). The conclusion of this argument is the sticking point of the *Social Contract*: 'The people assembled, it will be said. What a chimera!' (ibid.). And if it is but a chimera, then the whole of Rousseau's political philosophy is but a utopian dream. He will devote much of the rest of Books III and IV to showing that popular sovereignty, based on the assembled people, is a real possibility, not a utopian dream. He will find exemplars of it in Roman history, as well as in more recent times: 'It is a chimera today, but this was not the case two thousand years ago. Have men changed their nature? . . . Let us consider what can be done on the basis of what has been done' (SC III.12.425/189). He concludes the chapter with the general rule: 'From the existent to the possible the inference seems to me to be good' (SC III.12.426/ 190). By that he must mean that 'from the fact that something has existed in the past to the possibility that it could exist again in the future the inference seems to me to be good'. Re-phrased like that, the inference is weaker, since circumstances may have changed so much that what was a reality in the past may now be impossible. With uncharacteristic optimism, Rousseau does not raise that objection, envisaging that present circumstances can themselves be changed: 'The limits of the possible in moral matters are less narrow than we think. It is our weaknesses, our vices, our prejudices that shrink them' (SC III.12.425/189).

To prevent popular sovereignty from descending into mob-rule, the assemblies of the people must be legitimate, held on due dates or at other times 'called by magistrates appointed for that purpose' (SC III.13.426/190).

But, even if that danger can be averted, the central problem of popular sovereignty remains to be solved. Members of small groups can participate regularly and directly in the political process. But small groups are vulnerable in a world of large, powerful states. Rousseau's provisional response at SC III.13 is that small city states can, together, be strong enough to resist large ones if they form leagues. Examples are drawn from ancient Greece, Holland and Switzerland. Alternatively, if a large state becomes necessary, direct participation could be maintained if the seat of government were circulated. Returning to the problem at the end of SC III.15, Rousseau says:

> All things considered, I do not see that it is henceforth possible for the Sovereign to preserve the exercise of its rights among us unless the City is very small. But if it is very small, will it be subjugated? No. I shall show later how it is possible to combine the external power of a great People with the ease of regulation and good order of a small State. (SC III.15.431/194)

But there he breaks off his examination of the topic with a footnote in which he apologizes for his failure to complete his work with a treatment of 'external relations' and 'confederations', which would have been contained in the *Institutions Politiques*. All these answers are sketchy and insufficient. In Book IV he will look to the institutions of republican Rome to provide a model which combines popular sovereignty with military power. In Book III he concludes his comments on maintaining popular sovereignty with the normative principle that 'the instant the People is legitimately assembled as a Sovereign body, all jurisdiction of the Government ceases, executive power is suspended . . .' (SC III.14.427/191). This leads to the final normative section of Book III.

(iv)   Subordination of the government to the sovereign (SC III.15–18)

Rousseau begins this part with a criticism of degenerate, rich societies, whose members prefer private to public life, pay mercenaries to defend them and appoint 'deputies' to 'represent' them. The last of these corrupt practices conflicts with the principle derived from the social contract that:

> sovereignty cannot be represented for the same reason that it cannot be alienated. It consists essentially in the general will and the will cannot be represented . . . The deputies of the people, therefore, are not nor can they be its representatives; they are merely its agents. (SC III.15.429/192)[19]

After further criticism of the idea of representation, Rousseau ends the chapter on an unusual note of realism about ancient Greece, recognizing that there popular sovereignty was based on slavery, and responding to the interjection:

> What! Freedom can be maintained only with the support of slavery? Perhaps. The two extremes meet . . . There are some unfortunate situations where one cannot preserve one's freedom except at the expense of others, and the Citizen can be perfectly free if the slave is completely enslaved. (SC III.15.431/193)

But the ancient option is not open to the moderns, as Rousseau himself has shown in rejecting slavery in Book I.

In SC III.16 ('That the institution of government is not a contract'), Rousseau returns to attack the view that a legitimate order could be founded on a 'pact of submission' between people and rulers,[20] a view which he had already rejected at SC II.1, and which he now shows to be incompatible with the doctrine of the subordination of government to sovereign. In SC III.17 ('On the institution of government') Rousseau addresses another problem of the internal logic of the contract. The sovereign people, having formed itself into a people through the social contract, and now instructed by the Lawgiver, enacts a law that there shall be magistrates, to be appointed in the particular fashion of its 'form of government'. That law of appointment, like all laws, is general. But the appointment is a particular act, therefore an act of government. Yet it takes place before there is any government. How is that possible? Only, says Rousseau, if the same individuals who constitute the people 'change their relation' and become the first provisional government of the new state, and thereby entitled to nominate the members of the first full government.

Rousseau applies the principle that 'the election of leaders is a function of government, not of sovereignty' (SC IV.3.442/202, 'On elections') to the procedures for selecting magistrates in the three forms of government, once they are instituted. There he concludes that election by lot is appropriate for a democracy, by voting for an aristocracy. A monarchical government has no place for elections of any kind: 'Since the Monarch is by right the sole Prince and unique Magistrate, the choice of his lieutenants is his alone' (SC IV.3.443/ 203).

In the last chapter of Book III (SC III.18, 'The means of preventing usurpation of the government'), Rousseau applies the conclusion of SC III.17 to enforce the principle of the subordination of government to sovereign:

> the act which institutes the Government is not a contract but a Law . . . the holders [*dépositaires*] of the executive power are not the masters but the officers of the people, which can establish and depose them when it pleases. (SC III.18.434/196)

Robert Tronchin, the Procurator General of Geneva, cited two passages from this chapter as grounds for condemning the *Social Contract*:[21]

> when it happens that the People institutes a hereditary
> Government . . . this is not an engagement [*un engagement*] that it
> undertakes. It is a provisional form it gives to the administration
> until it wishes to organize things differently . . . These assemblies
> [of the sovereign people] whose only object is the maintenance
> of the social treaty, should always be opened by two
> propositions that can never be omitted and that are voted on
> separately:
> The first: *Does it please the Sovereign to preserve the present form of*
> *Government.*
> The second: *Does it please the People to leave the administration in the*
> *hands of those who are currently responsible for it.* (SC III.18.434–6/
> 196–7)

Rousseau's legal voluntarism had already established the general principle that there is no decision of the sovereign people, even the social contract itself, which cannot be revoked. SC III.18 applies that voluntarism to the daily working of popular sovereignty. Caution is necessary:

> It is true that these changes are always dangerous, and that the
> established Government must never be touched until it becomes
> incompatible with the public good. But this circumspection is a
> maxim of politics and not a rule of right . . . It is also true that . . .
> it is impossible to be too careful about observing all the requisite

formalities, in order to distinguish a regular, legitimate act from a seditious tumult. (SC III.18.435/196)

But, given those provisos, there must, in principle, be no obstruction to the expression of the general will.

(D)   Maxims drawn from history: the inference from the existent to the possible

The structure of Book IV of the *Social Contract* is peculiar. It begins with two chapters on the general will and a chapter on the selection of magistrates. There then follow four chapters on the institutions of republican Rome, the first of which (SC IV.4, 'On the Roman *comitia*') is one of the longest in the whole work. It terminates with another long chapter, 'On civil religion' (SC IV.8) and a brief envoi (SC IV.9). Commentators have not been kind to Rousseau's historical excursus. Derathé is particularly dismissive:

> this essay in four chapters on primitive Roman institutions has only a distant connection with the 'principles of political right' and they are of hardly any interest to the reader. In fact, Rousseau simply had to fill out this fourth book, even if that involved a digression, so that he could insert the chapter on civil religion which . . . was written at the last moment.[22]

It is true that neither the classical scholar nor the general reader will learn much about Roman history from these chapters. But they still form an important component in Rousseau's case that the *Social Contract* is not a utopian dream. In them he attempts to substantiate the rule that 'From the existent to the possible the inference seems to me to be good', in particular that popular sovereignty did once flourish in the Roman republic, which was 'a large State, and the city of Rome a large city . . . One could imagine the difficulties of calling frequent assemblies of the immense population of that capital and its environs. Yet few weeks went by in which the Roman people was not assembled, and even several times' (SC III.12.425/189). Rousseau wishes to show that his principles of right can be realized on a larger scale than the tiny city state, and republican Rome is the test case for that demonstration.

The greatness of the Romans, according to Rousseau, was founded on two things, their *moeurs* and their political institutions, in particular the organs of government known as the *comitia*. Rousseau praises:

the early Romans' taste for country life . . . [which] they derived
. . . from the wise founder who combined rustic and military
labors with freedom, and so to speak, relegated to the town arts,
crafts, intrigue, fortune and slavery . . . The simple and
hardworking life of village People was preferred to the idle and
lax life of the Bourgeois in Rome. (SC IV.4.445–6/204)

He goes on to talk of 'the simple *moeurs* of the early Romans, their
disinterestedness, their taste for agriculture, their disdain for
commerce and the desire for profit' (SC IV.4.448/206–7). In
Rousseau's idealized image of the early Romans, a bucolic way of
life, desirable in itself, survived transposition into a metropolis,
where it was artificially fostered by institutions favouring rural over
urban 'tribes'. On that basis, popular sovereignty continued to be
exercised through the *comitia*, by which 'the Roman people was
truly sovereign by right and fact' (SC IV.4.449/207). The long and
mainly valueless presentation of detail leads up to that conclusion,
important not for the light it sheds on Roman history, but for the
strategic role it plays in Rousseau's claim that the *Social Contract*
is more than a utopian model of political right, more than a
chimera.

In *Rousseau, Judge of Jean-Jacques*, responding to critics who
accused the *Social Contract* of being a subversive text, Rousseau
writes:

He [Rousseau] had worked for his homeland and for little states
constituted like it. If his doctrine could be of some utility to
others, it was in changing the objects of their esteem and perhaps
thus slowing down their decadence . . . But . . . the bad faith of
men of letters and the foolishness of *amour-propre* which persuades
everyone that they are always the focus of attention when they
aren't even being thought of made the large nations apply to
themselves what had been intended only for small republics . . .
(RJJJ 3Dial.935/213)

According to this, the *Social Contract* was aimed only at 'little
states', and was not applicable to 'the large nations'. In one respect
that response does indeed represent Rousseau's strategy in the *Social
Contract*, where, at SC II.10, he poses the question: 'What people,
then, is suited for legislation?' (SC II.10.390/162) and answers that
we should seek a small one, uncorrupted by the vices endemic
in large modern states. At no point in the *Social Contract* does
Rousseau say that a large, corrupt modern state could ever again be
'suited to legislation'. His understanding of timing is pessimistic.

In general, he holds that the moment of institution for modern states has already passed, never to be regained. For them it may simply be too late. With a gloomy fatalism, Rousseau suggests that it is now impossible to make France legitimate. Republican Rome then constitutes a critical counter-model, a model of a state which once existed and which remained legitimate, even after it had become large, having started out with good institutions and *moeurs* when it was small, and having maintained its initial form through the process of growth. If that reading of Rousseau's self-defence is correct, then he is being honest when he says that in the *Social Contract* 'he had worked for little States', since they alone could benefit from being properly 'instituted'. France would then be subjected to a critique in the light of the counter-model, but that critique would not bring with it any proposal for radical change, since France would have already passed the point where it could undergo such a change. Rousseau continues his self-defence like this:

> people stubbornly insisted on seeing a promoter of upheavals and disturbances in the one man in the world who maintains the truest respect for the laws and national constitutions, and who has the greatest aversion to revolutions and conspirators of every kind . . . (RJJJ 3Dial.935/213)

The idea that Rousseau had 'the truest respect for the laws' of contemporary France stretches belief a little, since they manifestly failed to express the general will, and systematically confused the functions of sovereignty and government.[23] If Rousseau 'respected' those laws, it was only in the minimal sense that he obeyed them.

Roman institutions, like all others, were doomed to degenerate. The *comitia*, the key institution of popular sovereignty, became the vehicle of popular usurpation:

> The Laws and the election of the leaders were not the only points submitted to the judgment of the *comitia*: once the Roman people had usurped the most important functions of the Government, one can say that the fate of Europe was decided in its assemblies. (SC IV.4.449–50/208)

Popular usurpation was reinforced by the office of the tribune of the people, which 'degenerates into tyranny when it usurps the executive power, of which it is only the moderator, and when it wants to dispense laws, which it should only protect' (SC IV.5.454/211).[24]

The last two chapters on Roman institutions concern the offices of dictatorship (SC IV.6) and censorship (SC IV.7). Rousseau approves of both, so long as they are properly exercised. A dictator was properly appointed only in emergencies, 'in . . . rare and manifest cases' when public safety demanded that 'responsibility for it be placed in the worthiest hands'. 'The general will is not in doubt . . . the suspension of legislative authority does not abolish it' (SC IV.6.456/ 212–13). Though the censorship was also a Roman institution, the chapter devoted to it differs from the previous ones since Rousseau abandons the role of amateur historian and uses it as an excuse once again to 'speak as a moralist'.[25]

(E)   Moeurs: *laws 'engraved in the hearts of the citizens'*

At SC II.12 Rousseau had classified morals as a type of law:

> the most important of all . . . not engraved on marble or bronze, but in the hearts of the citizens; which is the genuine constitution of the State; which gains fresh force each day; which, when other laws age or die out, revives or replaces them, preserves a people in the spirit of its institution, and imperceptibly substitutes the force of habit for that of authority. I am speaking of morals [*moeurs*], customs, and above all of opinion – a part of laws unknown to our political thinkers, but on which the success of all the others depends. (SC II.12.394/164–5)

If a people has good *moeurs*, according to Rousseau, it is united by a moral consensus, by shared 'opinions' about good and bad, and those opinions are largely correct. This moral consensus underlies a political consensus, expressed in the general will. Good *moeurs* are, like good institutions, instrumentally valuable because only in a people of good *moeurs* can principles of right be realized. But they are also valuable in themselves. The way of life of a relatively small, homogeneous community, requiring few and simple laws, and riven by few conflicts of interests, is for Rousseau self-evidently desirable. It corresponds to the requirements of individual psychology, as well as to those of political legitimacy.[26] The same image of *moeurs* infuses the chapters on the general will at SC IV.1. Can such *moeurs* be transposed beyond the small group in which individuals naturally identify their own interests with the community's? Rousseau is generally pessimistic, holding that consensus disintegrates as the state grows in size. When he praises patriotism and criticizes cosmopolitanism it is because the *patrie* and not the cosmos provides a real moral context of personal interaction and reinforcement.[27]

We saw above that the Lawgiver stands for the process which transforms each human being 'into a part of a larger whole, from which this individual receives, in a sense, his life and being . . .' (SC II.7.381–2/155). The process involves the construction of 'political laws' and other institutions suited to the particular people of which this individual is a member. When these are in place, the Lawgiver will be able to reach his real target, within the hearts of individuals, who:

> must have more palpable motives to give them the first habit of acting rightly. These motives are rewards that are well chosen and even better distributed – without which far from honoring virtue, they only excite hypocrisy and nourish greed. This choice and this distribution are the masterpiece of the Lawgiver. (PolFr IV.9.494/ 30)[28]

When a people has good *moeurs*, individuals will be generally well motivated, and so less in need of the deterrent power of the law: 'A bad tutor knows only how to give whippings; a bad minister knows only how to hang people or put them in prison' (ibid.). The Lawgiver's concern will be transmitted to the sovereign people itself: 'Ancient history is full of proofs of the attention paid by the People to the *moeurs* of private individuals [*des particuliers*], and that attention itself was its most palpable penalty or reward' (PolFr IV.14.496/31).

The complex picture of *moeurs* at SC IV.7 develops elements already sketched at SC II.12. According to this, the moral behaviour of a people, as of an individual, is the outcome of will and opinion. One wants certain things and one judges that those things are worth wanting:

> There is no use in distinguishing between the *moeurs* of a nation and the objects of its esteem, for all of those things spring from the same principle and are necessarily intermingled. Among all the peoples of the world, it is not nature, but opinion that determines the choice of their pleasures. (SC IV.7.458/214–15)

The task of the Censors is to act on our behaviour by influencing our opinions: 'Reform men's opinions and their *moeurs* will purify themselves'. But even though our moral behaviour is ruled by opinion, not by nature, we can still have mistaken, and therefore also correct, moral opinions:

> One always likes what is beautiful or what one finds to be so, but

it is this judgment that may be mistaken . . . The office of Censor maintains *moeurs* by preventing opinions from becoming corrupt; by preserving their rectitude through wise application; sometimes even by determining them when they are still uncertain. (SC IV.7.459/215)

The Censors represent the point of intersection between law and morals, between outer and inner regulation: 'Although the law does not regulate *moeurs*, it is legislation that gives birth to them' (ibid.). Rousseau does not elaborate on the distinction between 'the law' and 'legislation'. But later in the chapter he reiterates his view, already expressed in the *Letter to d'Alembert*, that he is not advocating penal sanctions to regulate public opinion, which 'is not subject to restraint'. Instead, he is giving the Censors power to strengthen and even anticipate public opinion, which itself is the outcome of the fundamental laws (legislation) of their people. In slightly more modern terminology, the censors would not be concerned to criminalize particular forms of sexual behaviour, but rather to draft family law, concerning divorce, child support, etc., which through the tax system would motivate people to favour one kind of personal life over others. They would thus inherit the Lawgiver's task of arranging the motivational field so as to make virtuous behaviour more desirable.

(F) Cosmopolitanism and 'the little platoon'

Rousseau holds that we learn civic virtues within the closely integrated confines of a well-ordered *patrie*. In Burke's famous phrase, 'To be attached to the subdivision, to love the little platoon we belong to in society, is the first principle (the germ as it were) of public affections'.[29] We are familiar with Rousseau's devotion to an idealized model of the ancient city state, uncorrupted by high culture and luxury.[30] The schoolroom of republicanism is 'the little platoon'. From that basic insight Rousseau never deviates. But how far can we leave that schoolroom behind? To that question his answers are more ambivalent. As we have seen, a central problem of the *Social Contract* is whether the model of the *polis* can be realized on a larger scale.

Rousseau passes negative judgments and, more rarely, positive ones on cosmopolitanism. But both judgments stem from the naturalism of the morality of the senses, and reflect Rousseau's changing views of the moral capacities of individuals and peoples. Those capacities stem from feelings, and feelings are in turn determined by environments. Crucial here is the feeling of identification. There are two outer limits to the capacity of an individual to identify with others, as it were zero and infinity. The model of those who naturally experience no identity of interests with others, Hobbesian individuals, can be constructed in theory, but is a model which, according to Rousseau, does not correspond to reality, since compassion is one of the natural qualities of our species. In the real world then the narrowest degree of identification, nearest to the 'natural' end of the spectrum, is the feeling of identification within the family. It is there that we experience the feelings idealized by Rousseau in the description of the 'Youth of the World' in the *Second Discourse*:

> the habit of living together gave rise to the sweetest feelings known to men, conjugal love and Paternal love. Each family became a little society all the better united because mutual affection and freedom were its only bonds. (2D 168/46)

Although the 'Youth of the World' is a long way from the pure state of nature, the family, being united first of all by biological ties, is closer to nature than any more developed social forms. In the family we encounter the world, both as parents and as children, through identification. Rousseau's thoughts here need to be expounded carefully. For though the family gives us our first, indispensable experience of identification, it is not to be taken as the model of society as a whole. Patriarchalism in particular must be false since political obligation cannot be based on parents' love and care for their children or on children's feelings of gratitude towards their parents. Those 'natural' feelings would be misleading if they were transposed directly to civil society:

> Although the functions of the Father of a Family and of the Prince should be directed toward the same goal, the paths they take are so different, their duties and rights are so dissimilar, that one cannot confuse them without forming the most erroneous ideas about the principles of society . . . Indeed, while nature's voice is the best advice a Father can heed to fulfill his duties, for the Magistrate it is a false guide, working continuously to separate him from his people . . . (GM 300/91)[31]

We must take with us from nature to society the feeling of identification with others which we have learnt within the family, yet once we have made the transition, we must learn to distance ourselves, particularly when we hold office, from those very feelings of family loyalty. Here we are at the middle point between the family, at one extreme, and humanity, at the other, as citizens of a *patrie*. What then is the *patrie*? The word is linked, etymologically, to *pater*, the natural parent. But at the same time it is constituted by non-natural ties:

> It is neither the walls nor the men which make the *patrie*: it is the laws, the *moeurs*, the customs, the Government, the constitution, the way of being that results from all that. The *patrie* is [exists] in the relations of the State to its members; when those relations change or are annihilated, the *patrie* vanishes. (Letter to Col. Pictet, 1 March 1764, CC 19#3162, p. 190)[32]

Rousseau's model of the legitimate *patrie* is thus complex. Its citizens are tied to it by a love learnt in the family. Indeed it embodies both parents in one, in that the *patrie* ('father'-land) also 'shows itself as the common mother of the citizens' (3D 258/153). Identification will take place when citizens come to recognize that their particular interests coincide with those of the *patrie*. And that will happen when the *patrie* is governed justly by laws emanating from the citizens themselves. The morality of the senses would then be embodied in the *patrie* like this: 'If the citizens derive from it everything that can give value to their own existence – wise laws, simple morals, necessities, peace, freedom, and the esteem of other peoples – their zeal for such a tender mother will be kindled.' (PolFr XI.2.536/58). Adult citizens will come to identify themselves with the *patrie* to the point where they will sacrifice themselves for its defence: 'They will know no other true life than that which it provides, no true happiness except to use their life to serve it. And they will include among its benefits the honor of shedding their blood to defend it if necessary' (ibid.). Political virtue in turn is defined as a pure identification between the aspirations of citizen and *patrie*: 'according to the definition I have given of virtue, love of the fatherland necessarily leads to it, since we willingly want what is wanted by those we love.' (PolFr XI.3.536/59).[33] In Rousseau's epigrammatic definition: 'virtue is only this conformity between the particular will and the general will' (3D252/149).

From this perspective the legitimate *patrie* is the environment within which one can best live an integrated life at the political level. The *patrie* is immediate in that it focuses the love and loyalty of individuals who identify their private with their public interests. But it is universal in that it is the bearer of the universal values of freedom and equality. Within a well-ordered *patrie*, families flourish, providing the primary lessons in love and identification. At the same time it embodies the public space within which citizens live a republican life, identifying themselves with the whole through political participation. The particular *patrie* constitutes a particular environment, a geography, climate, history and culture, encountered and transformed by its citizens. Rousseau recognizes that political virtue is both created and reinforced by this immediate environment. His hostility to cosmopolitanism is based on the naturalistic assumption that 'the feeling of humanity seems to evaporate and become feeble as it extends over the whole earth' (3D 254/151). But it is reinforced by his characteristic bitterness about the hypocrisy of the *bien-pensants*:

> those supposed Cosmopolitans who, justifying their love of the *patrie* by means of their love of the human race, boast of loving everyone in order to have the right to love no one. (GM 287/81)

> Distrust those cosmopolitans who, in their books, seek to find far away those duties which they disdain to fulfil around them. A philosopher loves the Tartars in order to be excused from loving his neighbour. (Em I.249/39)[34]

But the closure is not absolute. The drive to extend compassion and to identify with people beyond one's immediate circle appears to be a natural one. In the 'Profession of Faith', the Savoyard Vicar describes a process in which *amour de soi* expands through imagination to make us identify with others. That in turn is mediated by reason to produce the sense of justice, which becomes increasingly comprehensive until 'compassion for our species [becomes] more than compassion for our neighbour' (Em IV.547–8/252–3). Even 'cosmopolitan', so often a term of abuse, can take a positive charge, as it does, surprisingly, in the *Second Discourse* at the point where Rousseau describes international law. At that level, he says, since the parties are too distantly related to feel any immediate identification with one another, the most we can hope for are 'some tacit conventions'. These would serve:

> to make intercourse possible and to take the place of natural commiseration which, losing between one Society and another nearly all the force it had between one man and another, no longer dwells in any but a few great Cosmopolitan souls, who surmount the imaginary barriers that separate Peoples and who, following the example of the sovereign Being who created them, include the whole human race in their benevolence. (2D 178/54)

Rousseau thus recognizes a dynamic within the feeling of identification, but lacks confidence in its power. As things are, he suggests, most individuals, apart from the 'great Cosmopolitan souls', are united by shared feelings of identification within families and in the few well-ordered *patries*. But at the level of the *patrie* those feelings are more than gut loyalty to blood and soil, since they are mediated by recognition of the normative demands of just, self-imposed laws. Just as in the well-ordered *patrie* individuals might transcend loyalty to family without betraying their family, so too, in a better world, groups of individuals might come to experience ties of fraternity which would transcend those of the *patrie* without being forced to betray their *patrie*. In such a world, cosmopolitanism could be more than a hypocritical excuse for failure to perform one's immediate duties. Rousseau is pessimistic about the possibility of extending ties of fraternity so far, and for that reason he gives cosmopolitanism its predominantly negative charge. But his morality of the senses allows for the possibility, however remote, that the *'grande ville du monde'* could eventually be realized.

VII

Amour-propre

We have already glimpsed the importance of *amour-propre* in the *Second Discourse* and the *Emile*. In this chapter, I subject that elusive idea to a systematic examination. I begin obliquely, by comparing Rousseau to Hobbes:

> in the nature of man we find three principall causes of quarrell. First, Competition; Secondly, Diffidence; Thirdly, Glory. The first, maketh men invade for Gain; the second, for Safety; and the third, for Reputation. The first use Violence, to make themselves Masters of other mens persons, wives, children, and cattell; the second, to defend them; the third, for trifles, as a word, a smile, a different opinion, and any other signe of undervalue, either direct in their Persons, or by reflection in their Kindred, their Friends, their Nation, their Profession, or their Name. (Hobbes, *Leviathan*, Chapter 13)

Those driven by Hobbes's third cause, reputation, resemble those driven by a certain kind of *amour-propre* in Rousseau. But Rousseau distances himself from Hobbes in two respects. First he rejects the Hobbesian premiss that the three 'causes of quarrell' derive from 'the nature of man'. For Rousseau all three are in different ways the result of disordered social conditions. The *Second Discourse* provides the causal story of their genesis. Second, he assigns to *amour-propre* a pivotal role in the formation of humanity, of the individual and of the citizen. The outcome of that formation, whether for good or for evil, depends on the correct channelling of *amour-propre*. At this level *amour-propre* is morally neutral. It is the vehicle of socialization, which takes place through the play of recognition, interaction and meaning, at all levels, from politics to love and sexuality.[1] But

162

Rousseau's work alternates between extremes of pessimism and optimism about the possibility of realizing the conditions of the morality of the senses. Those extremes are reflected in the negative and positive moments in his thought about *amour-propre*.

(A)   *The genesis of* amour-propre

In the *Second Discourse* humanity develops in a series of leaps or revolutions. Each stage of this development is marked by a change in the degree and kind both of social inequality and of *amour-propre*. Let us recapitulate the stages. The pure state of nature, in which isolated individuals barely interacted, was interrupted by climatic changes, 'barren years, long and sharp winters, scorching summers . . .' (2D 165/44). In response came the invention of fire, elementary technology and elementary cooperation (the deer hunt) and the beginnings of *amour-propre*:

> This repeated application of things different from himself, and different from one another, must naturally have engendered in the human mind perceptions of certain relations between them. Those relations which we denote by the terms great, small, strong, weak, swift, slow, fearful, bold . . . must have at length produced in him some kind of reflection . . . (ibid.)

As a result of hunting animals, 'the first time he looked into himself, he felt the first stirring of pride' (ibid.).

Changes in housing and technology, the move from caves to huts and the invention of stone tools, inaugurated 'a first revolution' (2D 167/46), which brought humanity from elementary cooperation to 'the youth of the world' (2D 171/48). It marked the origin of settled families, rudimentary property and morality. In this framework *amour-propre* began to grow, for only now, within settled, permanent relationships could individuals begin to engage in the mutual play of recognition and reflection, to respond to one another, to expect responses and to find those expectations confirmed or rebutted. It is here, in the huts of 'the youth of the world', that Rousseau locates the origin of the purest form of *amour-propre*, 'the sweetest feelings ever known to human beings, conjugal and parental love'. There 'each family became a little society' (2D 168/46). But comparison and emulation were also present in *amour-propre* from the start. Their seeds were already sown in the hunt, as the hunter compared himself to his prey. Rousseau traces their growth in 'the youth of the world', as life became more sedentary and 'permanent neighbourhood . . . produce[d] in time some connection between different families' (2D

169/47). The key to the change lay in the interaction between fortuitous, external factors and the repertoire of feelings present within each human being, dormant, but ready to be activated:

> Young people of different sexes, living in neighboring Huts; the transient commerce [*commerce passager*] demanded by nature soon leads to another kind no less sweet and more permanent through mutual frequentation. (ibid.)

Love was an essential component of *amour-propre*, but no longer the almost animal immediacy of 'conjugal and parental' love. It now played a liberating but dangerous role in bringing human beings further into society:

> People grow accustomed to consider different objects and to make comparisons, imperceptibly they acquire ideas of merit and beauty which produce feelings of preference . . . A tender and sweet feeling insinuates itself into the soul, and at the least obstacle turned becomes an impetuous fury: jealousy awakens with love; Discord triumphs, and the gentlest of the passions receives sacrifices of human blood. (ibid.)

Rousseau describes the ensuing steps with urgency. Social 'contacts spread and bonds are tightened'. Leisure brought singing and dancing: 'Each one began to look at the others, and to want to be looked at himself; and public esteem [*l'estime publique*] had a value' (ibid.). Rousseau still treats *amour-propre* neutrally, descriptively, as the key to socialization, seeing every society, legitimate and illegitimate alike, as held together by ties of 'consideration', its members motivated by 'public esteem'. But in the historical reconstruction of the *Second Discourse*, *amour-propre* developed simultaneously with dangerous forms of inequality, yielding 'vanity and contempt . . . shame and envy; and the fermentation caused by these new leavens finally produced combinations fatal to happiness and innocence' (2D 169–70/47). Although Rousseau does not integrate the two stories, the story in which previously unimportant natural inequalities are made important by the advent of sexual rivalry,[2] and the story in which growing economic inequalities lead to destructive competition, he sees the two stories leading to the same outcome, an unstable situation in which all the components of Hobbes's third cause of 'quarrell' are ready to be activated:

> any voluntary wrong became an outrage because, along with the harm which resulted from the injury, the offended man saw in it

164

contempt for his person which was often more insupportable than the harm itself. (2D 170/48)

Yet, with all its defects, 'the youth of the world' was 'the least subject to revolutions, and the best for man' (2D 171/48). Within it a properly ordered *amour-propre* could lead to social integration rather than the Hobbesian state of war:

> though men had come to have less endurance/patience, and their natural compassion had already suffered some deterioration, this period of the development of the human faculties, keeping a just mean between the indolence of the primitive state and the petulant activity of our *amour-propre*, must have been the happiest and most durable of epochs. (ibid.)

The 'youth of the world' gave way to 'nascent society' through the second 'great revolution', the 'fatal accident' of the discoveries of metallurgy and arable farming. With these discoveries, elementary property relations were solidified into a property system, enforced by a legal system and fostering a constant increase in social inequality. But even here the fate of humanity was still in the balance, *amour-propre* remaining a force for both good and evil: 'Behold then all our faculties developed, memory and imagination in play, *amour-propre* interested, reason rendered active, and the mind having almost reached the limit of which it is capable' (2D 174/51). With hindsight we see the balance tip in the direction of evil, as *amour-propre* is converted definitively into a play of deception and enslavement:

> for one's own advantage, it was necessary to appear to be other than what one in fact was. To be and to seem to be became two altogether different things; and from this distinction came conspicuous ostentation, deceptive cunning and all the vices that follow from them . . . behold man, due to a multitude of new needs, subjected, so to speak, to all of Nature and especially to his fellows, whose slave he becomes in a sense, even in becoming their master. (2D 174–5/51–2)

Rousseau gives a decisive verdict on the cause of this downturn: 'All these evils are the first effects of property and the inseparable consequence of nascent inequality' (2D 175/52). So the unequal distribution, first of talents, then of property, converted positive *amour-propre* into its negative mirror image, pretence, hypocrisy and personal dependence. The causal story is unambiguous. It runs from the cause, inequality, to the effect, moral depravity. Without inequality, *amour-propre* could have flourished as a positive integrating force, and it can still flourish in that way wherever inequality can be banished from our social interactions³. When nascent society has descended into the state of war, from which it has up to now been retrieved only by the specious contract holding together modern despotic society, *amour-propre* is reduced to its lowest point. Individuals have lost all autonomy and self-reliance, but have gained no social integration in return. Instead they live hollow lives of hypocrisy, deception and dependence on the unstable opinions of other equally worthless individuals: 'the Savage lives within himself; the sociable man, always outside of himself, knows how to live only in the opinion of others; it is, so to speak, from their judgment alone that he derives the feeling of his own existence' (2D 193/66).

(B)   Amour-propre *as the key to socialization: the* Emile

The *Second Discourse* was a history of the slow advent, followed by the fast and dangerous development, of *amour-propre* in the human race. The *Emile* traces the same story within the individual, and outlines ways of steering its development into healthy channels. A dominant task of Emile's tutor is the negative one of depriving his pupil of most of the stimuli of a conventional upbringing. The passage from Book III to Book IV of the *Emile* (from utility to morality) is marked by the 'arousal' of *amour-propre*. Up to that point:

> [Emile] considers himself without regard to others and finds it good that others do not think of him. He demands nothing of anyone and believes he owes nothing to anyone. He is alone in human society; he counts on himself alone . . . *Amour-propre*, the first and most natural of all the passions, is still hardly aroused in him. (Em III.488/208)

Amour-propre is 'the first and most natural of all the passions' in the sense that the baby is subject to it from the first moment of social interaction, with parents and nurses. Rousseau describes its premature 'arousal' like this:

> A child cries at birth; the first part of his childhood is spent crying. At one time we bustle about, we caress him in order to pacify him; at another we threaten him, we strike him in order to make him keep quiet. Either we do what pleases him, or we exact from him what pleases us. Either we submit to his whims, or we submit him to ours. No middle ground; he must give orders or

166

receive them. Thus his first ideas are of domination and servitude. Before knowing how to speak, he commands; before being able to act, he obeys. (Em I.261/48)

What is 'natural' is the drive, present in infancy, to preserve oneself and to assert one's claim to survival in the face of opposition, whether real or imagined. That drive turns into a damaging play of manipulation, of 'domination and servitude', at the earliest possible moment, unless adults prevent it from doing so, by negative education. So, to repeat, the aim is to postpone, not to exclude, *amour-propre*. An adult individual untouched by *amour-propre* would not be fully human, would not be 'an integral part of his species' (Em IV.501/220).

There is no ready-made definition of *amour-propre* to be extracted from Rousseau's texts. It is the central theme of Book IV of the *Emile*, but Rousseau's approach to it is allusive and oblique. There is a teasing suggestion that the reader already knows just what it is, while the author figures and re-figures it from one context to the next. Here are two formulations:

Since my Emile has until now looked only at himself, the first glance he casts on his fellows leads him to compare himself with them. And the first sentiment aroused in him by this comparison is the desire to be in the first position. This is the point where *amour de soi* turns into [*se change en*] *amour-propre* and where begin to arise all the passions which depend on this one. (Em IV.523/235)

Remember that as soon as *amour-propre* has developed, the relative *I* is constantly in play, and the young man never observes others without returning to himself and comparing himself with them. The issue then is to know in what rank among his fellows he will put himself after having examined them. (Em IV.534/243)

These passages contain no criticism of *amour-propre*. According to them, one is driven by *amour-propre* to relate oneself to others, and to establish 'the relative *I*'. Someone untouched by *amour-propre* 'considers himself without regard to others'. As one compares oneself, one wants both to establish one's rank-ordering, and to excel in that ordering. Competition, properly orchestrated, is healthy, enforces one's positive sense of oneself, as one realizes one's capacities through interaction with others:

Although his desire to please does not leave him absolutely

167

indifferent to the opinion of others, he will concern himself with their opinion only insofar as it relates immediately to his person, and he will not worry about arbitrary evaluations whose only law is fashion or prejudice. He will have the pride [*orgueil*] to want to do everything he does well, even to do it better than another. He will want to be the swiftest at running, the strongest at wrestling, the most competent at working, the most adroit at games of skill. But he will hardly seek advantages which are not clear in themselves and which need to be established by another's judgment, such as being more intelligent than someone else, talking better, being more learned, etc.; still less will he seek those advantages which are not at all connected with one's person, such as being of nobler birth, being esteemed richer, more influential, or more respected, or making an impression by greater pomp. (Em IV.670–1/339)

The healthy person, then, will 'want to do everything well'. Competition, the desire to 'do it better than another', confirms that primary want. The tutor's task is to orchestrate the conditions of competition to ensure two things. First, he must prevent the pupil from mistaking superiority due to chance ('nobler birth' etc.) for superiority due to his own skill or effort:

> *Amour-propre* is a useful but dangerous instrument. Often it wounds the hand making use of it and rarely does good without evil. Emile, in considering his rank in the human species and seeing himself so happily placed there, will be tempted to honor his reason for the work of yours and to attribute his happiness to his own merit. (Em IV.536–7/244–5)

Second, he must ensure that his pupil interacts with others who are worthy of his interaction, who will recognize in him what is worthy of recognition. At first he suggests that this will put the pupil beyond the judgment of others, but in the next paragraph he modifies that suggestion:

> He loves men because they are his fellows, but he will especially love those who resemble him most because he will feel that he is good; and since he judges this resemblance by agreement in moral taste, he will be quite gratified to be approved in everything connected with good character. He will not precisely say to himself, 'I rejoice because they approve of me,' but rather, 'I rejoice because they approve of what I have done that is good. I rejoice that the people who honor me do themselves honor. So

168

long as they judge so soundly, it will be a fine thing to obtain their esteem.' (Em IV.671/339)

Although it is not named here, this is the clearest specification of the positive role of *amour-propre* in the *Emile*. *Amour-propre* is now connected with reflection. One must find oneself in the eyes of others, but those others must yield a true reflection of oneself.

It is through the imagination that children first step outside themselves. The imagination unlocks the door opening on to the social world, which is in turn a moral world:

So long as his sensibility remains limited to his own individuality [*son individu*], there is nothing moral in his actions. It is only when it begins to extend outside of himself that it takes on, first, the sentiments and, then, the notions of good and evil which truly constitute him as a man and an integral part of his species [*partie intégrante de son espéce*]. (Em IV.501/219–220)

Imagination then illuminates our *amour-propre*, makes each one of us identify with others, see others as themselves endowed with their own *amour-propre*, entitled to the same respect as our own. Through the imagination we can put ourselves in the place of the *amour-propre* of others, and this imaginative move is the source of our sense of justice:

Let us extend *amour-propre* to other beings. We shall transform it into a virtue, and there is no man's heart in which this virtue does not have its root. The less the object of our care is immediately involved with us, the less the illusion of particular interest is to be feared. The more one generalizes this interest, the more it becomes equitable, and the love of mankind is nothing other than the love of justice. (Em IV.547/252)

This, then, is the dominant image of *amour-propre* in Book IV of the *Emile*. It is morally neutral. *Amour-propre* is neither praised nor condemned, though the dangers inherent within it are indicated. It is presented as the key to socialization which may be channelled in good or evil directions. But beyond these passages, both within the same book and elsewhere, terminological and conceptual problems abound.

A notoriously difficult passage is the following:

Let us set down as an incontestable maxim that the first movements of nature are always right. There is no original perversity in the human heart. There is not a single vice to be found in it of which it cannot be said how and whence it entered. The sole passion natural to man is [(i)] *amour de soi* or *amour-propre* taken in an extended sense. [(ii)] This *amour-propre* in itself or relative to us is good and useful; and since [(iii)] it has no necessary relation to others, [(iv)] it is in this respect naturally neutral. It becomes good or bad only by the application made of it and the relations given to it. (Em II.322/92)

The first sentence of the passage reiterates the opening of Book I, and its concluding words are familiar from our previous analysis: *amour-propre* is morally neutral in itself, and takes on its moral character from its application. But the middle of the passage offers a change in terminology which is hard to interpret. Here (i) Rousseau considers as synonymous '*amour de soi*' and '*amour-propre* taken in an extended sense' [*pris dans un sens étendu*]. He holds (ii) that *amour-propre* 'in itself or relative to us' [*en soi ou rélativement à nous*] is good and useful; (iii) that *amour-propre* as defined in (ii) 'has no necessary relation to others' [*point de raport nécessaire à autrui*]; and so (iv) that 'in this respect' *amour-propre* is 'naturally neutral' [*naturellement indifférent*]. The passage raises at least three problems. First, how can we square (i) with the numerous passages in which Rousseau contrasts *amour de soi* with *amour-propre*, seeing the latter as a perversion or degenerate form of the former? We shall return to the story of degeneration at (E) below. But even if that story is accepted, terminological and conceptual problems will remain. In particular, how can *amour-propre* be both 'good and useful' in itself (ii) and also be 'naturally neutral' (iv), since the latter must mean 'neither good nor evil' in itself? Again, the answer can only be that the individual's drive to maintain itself, the drive of self-preservation and self-assertion, is 'good and useful' for the individual concerned, but that when the individual is placed in society, that same drive is neutral, in the sense that its realization may be good or evil, both for the individual itself, and for others, and that the outcome depends on two interacting factors: the education of the individual and the social order in which that individual lives. Again, how can *amour-propre* be said to have 'no necessary relation to others' (iii), when elsewhere it is characterized as an essentially relational property?

Later we shall examine how *amour-propre* develops in the individual at adolescence, as Emile encounters sexuality and so makes the transition to the social, moral world of adulthood. It is one of Rousseau's most challenging claims that only those who have experienced passionate love and have learnt to harness its power are moral beings in the full sense. Only they have become utterly

170

engaged in the play of mutual mirroring in which each seeks recognition in the eyes of the other: 'Love must be reciprocal. To be loved one has to make oneself lovable. To be preferred, one has to make oneself more lovable than another, more lovable than every other, at least in the eyes of the beloved object.' (Em IV.493–4/214). Why does Rousseau conclude that reciprocal love between the sexes is all but impossible? We shall return to that question in Chapter VIII. For the moment, we simply note that Rousseau's ambivalent attitude to love and sexuality mirrors his underlying ambivalence about the role of *amour-propre* in all our interactions.

(C) Amour-propre: *positive pole*

There is one context in which Rousseau's comments on *amour-propre* are consistently positive, that of patriotism. In the political fragments devoted to 'honour and virtue', Rousseau writes:

> What is the source of the Lacedaemonians' virtue if not to be considered virtuous? . . . There lies a source of interest more certain and less dangerous than wealth, for the glory of having acted well is not subject to the same disadvantages as that of being rich and it gives a far more intense satisfaction to those who have learnt to savour it. How then are we to arouse men to virtue? We must teach them to find it beautiful and to esteem those who practise it. A very considerable advantage for a State thus constituted is that in it those with bad intentions have no power to carry out their evil plans, and that vice cannot make any kind of fortune. (PolFr V.1.501/35)

> The task is to arouse the desire for virtue and to facilitate the means of attracting through virtue the same admiration that today is attracted only through wealth. (PolFr V.2.502/36)

> It is therefore certain that it is less in ourselves than in the opinion of others that we seek our own happiness . . . if the best among us ceased for a moment to feel that they were being looked at, neither their happiness nor their virtue would survive . . . All want to be admired. That is the secret and final goal of men's actions. There are just different means to it. Now the choice of those means depends on the skill of the Lawgiver . . . (PolFr V.3.502–3/36)

The first of these passages from the *Political Fragments* tells us that in uncorrupted societies virtue is rewarded by 'glory'. If we put that together with the second, we see that the desire to be admired is not in itself bad. What is important is to replace admiration of riches by admiration of virtue. Underlying the love of riches in corrupt societies is the love of distinction, but that can be re-channelled into love of virtue, provided that virtue attracts the response presently given to riches. The third passage reiterates that idea in a slightly cynical tone, and makes it the Lawgiver's task to organize the re-channelling. In the *Discourse on Political Economy*, Rousseau succinctly combines *amour-propre* and virtue in patriotism:

> It is certain that the greatest miracles of virtue have been produced by love of country. This sweet and intense feeling, which combines the force of *amour-propre* with all the beauty of virtue, gives virtue its energy without disfiguring it and makes it the most heroic of all the passions. (3D 255/151)

Amour-propre plays an equally important positive role in the *Considerations on the Government of Poland*. The most important task of public education is to inculcate patriotism in the hearts of free citizens who are to be: 'accustomed from an early moment to rules, to equality, to fraternity, to competitions, to living with the eyes of their fellow-citizens upon them, and to seeking public approbation' (GP ch.4.968/22). Such healthy *amour-propre* will flourish in small communities 'because all their citizens know each other and keep an eye on each other' [*s'entreregardent*] (GP ch.5.970/25). In keeping with the morality of the senses, people will be motivated by an appeal to their interests, but in the small, egalitarian society envisaged those interests will be transformed, so that moral incentives, channelled through *amour-propre*, will replace financial ones. Social mobility will depend on constant public scrutiny, so that:

> every citizen shall feel the eyes of his fellow-countrymen upon him every moment of the day; . . . no man shall move upward and win success except by public approbation . . . every post and employment shall be filled in accordance with the nation's wishes . . .everyone shall depend so much on public esteem [*l'estime publique*], that without it one will not be able to do, acquire or attain anything. (GP ch.12.1019/87)

The point at which Rousseau endorses *amour-propre* as providing the moral glue that holds the legitimate state order together is also the point at which liberal critics feel most uneasy about the totalitarian features of this utterly transparent social order.[4]

(D)   Amour-propre: *negative pole*

We have noted the one occasion on which Rousseau called *amour de soi* 'amour-propre taken in an extended sense'. We now turn to the negative pole of *amour-propre*, in which he contrasts the two and characterizes *amour-propre* as the degenerate form of *amour de soi*. Here is the stark contrast in note XV to the *Second Discourse*:

> One must not confuse *amour-propre* with *amour de soi-même*, two passions very different in their nature and in their effects. *Amour de soi-même* is a natural feeling which makes every animal look to its own conservation and which, in man, when guided by reason and modified by pity, produces humanity and virtue. *Amour-propre* is only a relative feeling, artificial and born in Society, which makes each individual attach more importance to himself than to any other. It inspires in men all the evils which they do to one another, and it is the real source of honour. (2D note XV 219–220/91)

Rousseau makes the same contrast in Book IV of the *Emile*:

> *Amour de soi*, which regards only ourselves, is contented when our true needs are satisfied. But *amour-propre*, which makes comparisons, is never content and never could be, because this sentiment, preferring ourselves to others, also demands others to prefer us to themselves, which is impossible. This is how the gentle and affectionate passions are born of *amour de soi*, and how the hateful and irascible passions are born of *amour-propre*. Thus what makes man essentially good is to have few needs and to compare himself little to others; what makes him essentially wicked is to have many needs and to depend much on opinion. (Em IV.493/213–14)

These passages convey two thoughts. The first is continuous with the neutral pole of *amour-propre*. It criticizes only an unfair, non-reciprocal *amour-propre*, which would prevent one individual from considering the *amour-propre* of another, from 'extending' one's *amour-propre* to make it the key to an equitable interaction between equal subjects. The bearer of such *amour-propre* demands the impossible, that is a world in which the *amour-propre* of all but himself is ignored. The second thought goes beyond that neutral position. The note to the *Second Discourse* suggests that autonomy is to be attained by, and only by, a retreat from society to a world of radical self-sufficiency. The *Emile* passage does not go so far. It is more nuanced. Goodness comes from the absence of needs and comparisons and of

173

dependence on opinion. The neutral model stressed not the absence of those things, but their quality. To depend on opinion in the sense of passing fashions would indeed be to surrender one's autonomy. But to find one's identity in the mutual play of considered judgments would be an ideal to be striven for. Yet Rousseau was repeatedly drawn to the model of withdrawal. The *Second Discourse* concluded with the favourable judgment on 'the Savage [who] lives within himself', contrasted to 'sociable man, who lives always outside of himself' (2D 193/66).

The same theme runs through the *First Discourse*, where it underpins Rousseau's claim that morals are corrupted by culture, by the cultivation of the sciences and the arts: that this is a historical fact and that it stems systematically from the nature of culture as a social form. The *First Discourse* begins and ends with a contrast between inner and outer. It opens with the injunction that one should 'go back inside oneself to study man, to know his nature, his duties and his goal' (1D 6/4), and concludes with the challenge: 'What use is it to seek our happiness in the opinion of others if we can find it within ourselves?' (1D 30/22). The polemic in between presents the world of culture as a world of hypocrisy, inhabited by 'happy slaves . . .[with] the appearance of all the virtues without the possession of any' (1D 7/5), in which 'one no longer dares to appear as one is' (1D 8/6). How close is the link between these vices and culture? In his 'Last Response' to Objections to the *First Discourse*, Rousseau concedes that culture is not a necessary and sufficient condition of the emergence of the vices, since ignorance is neutral, being compatible with, though not necessarily accompanied by, virtue. Culture, in contrast, is not similarly neutral. It is a historical law that 'the beautiful time, the time of virtue for each People was that of its ignorance; and to the extent that it has become learned, Artistic and Philosophical, it has lost its morals and its decency' (1D 76/113). When we go back to the *First Discourse* itself, we find that the link is established through *amour-propre*, taken in its most negative sense. Nonetheless, through the denunciatory rhetoric, a shadow positive role for *amour-propre* can still be discerned. Consider people of culture who:

> smile contemptuously at these old-fashioned words like
> Fatherland and Religion and consecrate all their talents and
> philosophy to destroying and vilifying all that men hold sacred.
> Not that they basically hate either virtue or our dogmas; they are
> enemies of public opinion, and to bring them back to the foot of
> our altars, it would be enough to exile them among atheists. Oh
> frenzy for distinction, of what are you not capable? (1D 19/14)

174

This passage allows for, indeed it entails, an important positive role for healthy public opinion, embodying 'all that men hold sacred'. Rousseau's target here is the deranged 'frenzy for distinction', the urge to be different for its own sake, not for the sake of excellence. Rousseau returns repeatedly to criticize artists and writers for seeking applause. But his target is the social order in which applause is given to the wrong people for the wrong reasons:

> What is the origin of all these abuses, unless it be that fatal inequality introduced among men by the distinction of talents and the vilification of virtue? . . . The wise man [*le sage*] does not pursue riches, but he is by no means insensible to glory, and when he sees it so ill distributed, his virtue, which might have been animated by a little emulation and turned to the advantage of society, languishes and peters out in poverty and obscurity. (1D 25–6/18–19)

Here emulation, which lies at the heart of *amour-propre*, is clearly neutral. Whether competition is good or evil depends on the nature of the rewards. Those are established by public opinion, whether or not pronounced by a legislator. The end point of the *Discourse* is a distinction between the world of real science and the world of culture. The former should be inhabited by geniuses, in isolation from the world of public opinion:

> Let scholars of the first rank [*les savants du premier ordre*] find an honourable refuge [*honorables aziles*] in their [royal] courts. Let them there enjoy the only reward worthy of them, that of contributing, by their influence, to the happiness of the Peoples to whom they will have taught wisdom. It is only then that we shall see what virtue, science and authority can do, when animated by a noble emulation and working in concert towards the felicity of the human race. (1D 30/22)

Within the scientific community emulation again plays a key role, properly controlled within the context of pure research, whose products would be usefully applied.

(E)   *From positive to negative: the mechanism of degeneration*

We have still to address the problem posed by Hobbes. Must our natural drive to interact with our fellows lead to vice and unhappiness because, as Hobbes thought, all interactions are zero-sum, the advantage of one being attained only at the price of the disadvantage of the other? Such is Rousseau's thought when he stresses the negative pole of *amour-propre*, particularly in his last works, those of the 'retreat from society':

> Kindly recall the distinction . . . between *amour de soi-même* and *amour-propre*, and the way in which each of them acts upon the human heart. Positive sensibility stems immediately from *amour de soi*. It is quite natural that someone who loves himself should seek to extend his being and his enjoyment and to appropriate for himself what he feels to be good for him by attaching it to himself. This is a pure matter of feeling, and reflection does not enter into it at all. But as soon as this absolute love degenerates into the comparative feeling of *amour-propre* [*en amour-propre et comparatif*], then it produces negative sensibility, because as soon as we acquire the habit of measuring ourselves with others and of going outside ourselves in order to assign ourselves the first and best position, it is impossible to avoid aversion for all that surpasses us, all that humiliates us, all that confines us, all that by being something prevents us from being everything. *Amour-propre* is always irritated or discontented because it would like every other human being to prefer us above all others, including himself, which is impossible . . . A feeling of inferiority to one person poisons one's feeling of superiority to a thousand others. (RJJJ 2Dial.805–6/112–13)

The terminology of *amour-propre* as the degenerate form of *amour de soi* is inconsistent with that of Em II.322/92, where *amour de soi* is described as '*amour-propre* taken in an extended sense', but it is consistent with Em IV (523–4/235), where Rousseau writes that '*amour de soi* turns into [*se change en*] *amour-propre*'. In that latter passage he proceeds to explain the change from the one to the other thus:

> But to decide whether among these passions the dominant ones in his character will be humane and gentle or cruel and malignant, whether they will be passions of beneficence and commiseration or of envy and covetousness, we must know what position he will feel he has among men, and what kinds of obstacles he may believe he has to overcome to reach the position he wants to occupy. (Em IV.523–4/235)

Where the Second Dialogue is Hobbesian, suggesting that destructive, zero-sum interactions are the only expression of *amour-propre*, this last passage from the *Emile* is closer to the morality of the senses, Rousseau's own naturalistic, but non-deterministic, approach to moral psychology. It bids us look for the particular circumstances which will channel *amour-propre* in a positive or negative direction. The circumstances are the obstacles, encountered by agents as they seek to maintain and assert their identities in the social world. These obstacles are mediated through the imagination which yields true or false beliefs to the agent. The model of degeneration through the encounter of obstacles is present in *Rousseau, Judge of Jean-Jacques:*

> The primary passions, which all tend directly to our happiness, focus us only on objects which relate to that happiness. Their guiding principle is just *amour de soi* and they are all essentially loving and sweet. But when they are turned away from their object by obstacles, they become more concerned with the obstacle, so as to avoid it, than with the object, so as to obtain it. They then change their nature and become angry and hate-filled. That is how *amour de soi*, which is a good and absolute feeling, becomes [*devient*] *amour-propre*, which is a relative feeling, by which we compare ourselves. *Amour-propre* is a feeling which demands preferences, and the enjoyment of that feeling is purely negative. It seeks its satisfaction, not in our own well-being, but only in the ills of others. (RJJJ 1Dial.669/9)

The *Reveries* represent the purest moment of retreat and the purest condemnation of *amour-propre*, contrasted as before with *amour de soi*, but with no place left for the righting of social circumstances:

> I was never much given to *amour-propre*, but in the world this artificial passion has been exacerbated in me, particularly when I was a writer . . . At first it rebelled against injustice, but in the end it came to treat it with contempt. Falling back on my own soul, severing the links which make it so demanding, and giving up all ideas of comparison or precedence, it was content that I be good in my own eyes. And so becoming once again *amour de moi même* it returned to the order of nature and freed me from the yoke of opinion. From this time on I recovered my peace of mind and something akin to happiness. Whatever our situation it is only *amour-propre* that can make us constantly unhappy. When it is silent and we can listen to the voice of reason, this can finally console us for all the misfortunes which it was not in our power to avoid. (Reveries VIII.1079–80/129)

The Rousseau of the *Reveries* was one who had concluded that he 'was never properly fitted to civil society' (Reveries VI.1059/103).

(F) Amour-propre, *self-esteem, pride and vanity*

The opposition between *amour-propre* and *amour de soi* shifts, as we have seen, following the shifts from the positive to the negative poles of socialization. But in other contexts Rousseau sets *amour-propre* off against other terms, here, in the *Reveries*, against self-esteem:

> Self-esteem [*l'estime de soi-même*] is the strongest motive force in proud souls [*des âmes fiéres*]. *Amour-propre*, generator of illusions, disguises itself and passes itself off for that esteem, but when its fraud is finally uncovered and *amour-propre* can no longer hide itself, after that it is no longer to be feared, and although it may be hard to destroy, it can easily be mastered. (Reveries VIII.1079/ 129)

Great and small souls are contrasted in Book IV of the *Emile*, but here as bearers of two forms of *amour-propre*, itself a transformation of *amour de soi*:

> Extend these ideas and you will see where our *amour-propre* gets the form we believe natural to it, and how *amour de soi*, ceasing to be an absolute sentiment, becomes pride [*orgueil*] in great souls, vanity in small ones, and feeds itself constantly in all at the expense of their neighbors. (Em IV.494/215)

The same contrast between pride and vanity occurs in the context of patriotic virtues in the *Project for a Constitution for Corsica*:

> That opinion which puts a great price on frivolous objects produces vanity; but that which bears on objects great and beautiful in themselves produces pride. One can therefore make a people proud or vain according to the choice of objects upon which it directs its judgments. Pride is more natural than vanity, since it consists in valuing oneself [*s'estimer*] by reference to really valuable [*estimables*] objects; whereas vanity, giving a price to what is worthless, is the work of prejudices which are generated slowly. (PCC 937–8/326)

Esteem, which is a 'relative' feeling, is given a positive charge here, as it was in the Preface to *Narcisse*, where Rousseau had attacked 'the taste for philosophy' because it 'loosens all the bonds of esteem and benevolence which attach men to society' (PN 967/192). But none of these oppositions is tied to a fixed terminological distinction. On

178

the same page of the Preface to *Narcisse* Rousseau also denounces pride and *amour-propre* in the same breath.

(G)   *Towards an anarchic egalitarianism?*

Judith Shklar attributes to Rousseau the view that:

> the well-governed society was so free from *amour-propre* that the conditions of natural equality were totally restored. Not even moral differences are given public recognition . . . To deny the public relevance of moral inequality, to refuse any public recognition to the difference between good and bad is indeed the ultimate step in egalitarianism. In a mood of furious anger and self-deception Rousseau was driven to accept anarchy.[5]

Her source appears to be the following passage from the Preface to *Narcisse*:

> In a well-constituted State all the citizens are so very equal that none can be preferred to the others as being the most learned or even the cleverest, but at most as being the best: even this last distinction is often dangerous, for it creates deceivers and hypocrites. (PN 965/191)

But though Rousseau is anxious here about the dangers inherent in public distinction, he is not recommending moral anarchy. Indeed he goes on to attack 'the taste for letters, for philosophy and for the fine arts' which 'destroys the love of our primary duties and of true glory':

> Once talents have taken over the honours due to virtue, everyone wants to be agreeable rather than good. Thence arises another inconsistency, that we reward people for qualities which do not depend on them: for we are born with our talents, our virtues alone are acquired. (PN 966/191)

The implication is clear. In the well-ordered state, virtues, rather than talents, are honoured. The contrast in the Preface is more absolute than the nuanced model of *Emile* IV, which would allow a legitimate role for pride in, and recognition of, one's natural talents as well as one's virtues. But it does not commit Rousseau to an anarchic egalitarianism.

VIII

Men and Women

The body is the point of intersection between the natural and the social aspects of the human being. Rousseau maintains that it is through sexuality that we enter the moral world, yet, as a physical drive, sexuality is never fully transformed by social control. The key to socialization thus remains partly in the hands of nature. Critics have highlighted the provocations and 'paradoxes' that mark Rousseau's dealings with women, both in his writings and in his personal relationships. Mary Wollstonecraft, the most acute and devastating critic of Rousseau on this topic, said that he 'was accustomed to make reason give way to his desire for singularity, and truth to a favourite paradox.'[1] In this chapter, I shall respond to the charges of the critics, not by denying them, but by showing that the 'paradoxes' have deeper roots in Rousseau's thought than the mere 'desire for singularity'.

In denouncing modern culture in the *First Discourse* of 1751, Rousseau makes surprisingly few comments on women. In one extended footnote (1D 21/15) he talks neutrally of 'the advance of women' [*l'ascendant des femmes*].[2] With no apparent sarcasm, he advocates giving 'a better . . . education to that half of the human race which governs the other', holding that 'men will always be what is pleasing to women'. He continues, apparently seriously, to say that 'Plato's reflections' [on equal education for women of the Guardian class in *Republic* V] 'deserve to be better developed by a writer worthy of following such a master'. Since Plato's view of women's education was so unusual in the ancient world, we can only assume that Rousseau was making a feminist statement in approving of it, even while refusing to expound it personally himself. In the last of the Replies to Objections to the *First Discourse*, he advocates strictly separate lives for men and women, a theme to which he would return repeatedly later: 'Man and woman are made to love each other and unite. But beyond that legitimate union, all commerce of love between them is a dreadful source of disorders in society and morals' (1D 75Fn/113Fn). But separation does not in itself entail inequality, and at this stage in his writing Rousseau is advocating the former, not the latter.

According to the *Second Discourse* (1755), although there are 'natural' physiological and psychological differences between individuals and sets of individuals, these gain significance only when they are recognized and rewarded in society. In the conclusion to the *Second Discourse*, it will be remembered, Rousseau argued that 'moral', i.e. socially sanctioned, inequalities were legitimate only where they corresponded to 'physical' inequalities, that is to natural inequalities of talent. In that text he gives every reason to think that women are naturally the equals of men, and, since they are, then they should also be their social equals.

However, in many other texts, culminating in the *Emile*, Book V, Rousseau propounds a theory of the essential difference between the two sexes, and advocates a political programme which would not only reinforce that difference, but would embody it in relations of radical inequality. We shall consider three different versions of that programme, as it is propounded in the *Third Discourse* (1755), in the *Letter to d'Alembert* (1758) and finally in the *Emile* (1762). In direct contrast to Plato, Rousseau will be found to advocate entirely different forms of education for Sophie and for Emile, on the traditional natural law grounds that the two sexes essentially perform contrasting functions, and that the woman's function is 'entirely dependent on maternity', a physical dependence which would be transformed, in the ideal social order, into a moral duty.[3]

(A)   An anthropology of identity: the Second Discourse

We start with men and women in the Forest, Rousseau's Garden of Eden, the pure state of nature, where men and women have not yet been touched by society and have developed neither reason nor morality, but are already endowed with the feelings of self-preservation and compassion. But if the latter are universal and independent of all socialization, then surely the mother's feeling of care for her child will be equally universal. Will it not then be possible to reconstruct upon Rousseau's own basis of *feeling* the natural law view that the family is the essential link between the natural and the social? Rousseau addresses this challenge obliquely, in response to the view that communication, and in particular language, has a 'natural' origin within the family. To this he replies that the family itself is not 'natural', and he sketches a critique of any doctrine of 'natural' relations between mother and child, let alone between mother and father. His predecessors, he claims:

> always see the family gathered in the same habitation and its members maintaining among themselves a union as intimate and permanent as among us, where so many common interests unite them. Instead, in the primitive state, having neither Houses nor Huts, nor property of any kind, everyone took up his lodging by chance and often for only one night. Males and females united fortuitously, depending on encounter, occasion and desire, without speech being a very necessary interpreter of the things they had to say to each other; they left each other with the same ease. The mother nursed her Children at first for her own need [*pour son propre besoin*]; then, habit having endeared them to her, she nourished them afterwards for their need. As soon as they had the strength to seek their food, they did not delay in leaving the Mother herself . . . (2D 146–7/30)

The central thesis of the *Second Discourse* is that all social forms are radically contingent, that none is founded in nature. In applying that thesis to the family, he claims that not only particular forms of kinship structure, but any forms at all, come about simply in response to needs, to the 'spur of necessity'. The family is the test case for this radical thesis. If he can 'denature' the family, the most 'natural' of social forms, he should have little difficulty with other 'higher' forms. It is for this reason that, in one of the longest and most elaborate notes to the *Second Discourse*, Rousseau criticizes Locke's view that the institutions of marriage and the family are natural because they are rooted in needs, in that human children need long-term care from their parents, and their mother needs long-term protection by the father of her children. Rousseau uses the charge of circularity which is his standard weapon against the natural law tradition:

> Locke's reasoning . . . falls apart, and all the Dialectic of this Philosopher has not saved him from the error committed by Hobbes and others. They had to explain a fact of the state of Nature, that is to say of a state where men lived isolated, and where a given man had no motive for living near another given man . . . and they did not think of carrying themselves back beyond the Centuries of Society, that is to say of those times when men always had a reason to live near one another, and when a

given man often has a reason for living beside a given man or a given woman. (2D noteXII.218/90)

Locke's claim was that:

> the Male and Female in Mankind are tyed to a longer conjunction than other Creatures . . . because the Female is capable of conceiving, and *de facto* is commonly with Child again, and Brings forth too a new Birth long before the former is out of dependancy for support on his Parents help, and able to shift for himself, and has all the assistance is due to him from his Parents: whereby the Father, who is bound to take care of those he hath begot, is under an Obligation to continue in Conjugal Society with the same Woman longer than other Creatures, whose Young being able to subsist of themselves, before the time of Procreation returns again, the Conjugal bond dissolves of itself . . .[4]

Rousseau brings three arguments against Locke. These arguments are empirical, but hypothetical. He sketches how things must have been, or at least are likely to have been, in the pure state of nature. There, he argues, (1) speedily repeated pregnancy is unlikely in the absence of institutionalized marriage; (2) before the 'abuse' of reproductive faculties in society, women could conceive and bear children later in life; (3) before children were 'softened' in society, they were able to 'shift for themselves' at a younger age. Putting these three arguments together, Rousseau concludes that in the state of nature a mother could look after a child adequately on her own, and would need to devote less time to that task. There would therefore be no *natural* function for the father to provide continuing support for mother or child. Before the biological sex drive has been socialized, while it has not yet become love, the man does not connect the sexual act with procreation:

> Why will he help her to raise a Child he does not even know belongs to him, and whose birth he neither planned nor foresaw? . . . His appetite satisfied, the man no longer needs a given woman, nor the woman a given man. The man has not the least concern nor perhaps the least idea of the consequences of his action. (2D note XII 217/89)

Following the guiding thread of the *Second Discourse*, Rousseau is seeking to make a rational reconstruction of a model of zero social relations, in this case a model of sexual encounter unsupported by education or by expectations stemming from a social structure, however minimal. Adolescent schoolboys would be its semi-socialized representatives. Where memory is short and there is no social context within which one can form preferences, another partner will, for both sexes, be as good as the last for purely animal satisfaction. For women, Rousseau's conclusion is particularly liberating. Outside society, continuing passion and need are both absent:

> if, in the state of Nature, the woman no longer feels the passion of love after the conception of the child, then the obstacle to her Society with the man thereby becomes much greater still, since she then no longer needs either the man who impregnated her or any other. (2D note XII 218/90)[5]

As he approaches the end of Part I of the *Second Discourse*, Rousseau momentarily abandons the chronological narrative to 'distinguish between the moral and the Physical in the feeling of love' (2D 157/38). As he draws up the balance sheet, the physical elements shrink almost to vanishing point. In the pure state of nature complete indifference reigns: 'The Physical is that general desire which inclines one sex to unite with the other. The moral is that which determines this desire and fixes it exclusively on a single object . . .' (ibid.) The male lacks the resources of discrimination and memory with which to make enduring comparisons between women, so that 'any woman is [equally] good for him'. Rousseau's picture of the pure state of nature indicates that exactly the same argument applies to the female. Nothing suggests any asymmetry between the sexes. The passage to civil society, from the physical to the moral, is the passage to comparisons and preferences, 'founded on certain notions of merit and beauty'. In this context, for the first time, Rousseau's sexism emerges. 'The moral element of love,' he says, is an 'artificial feeling, born of the usage of society, and extolled with much skill and care by women in order to establish their empire and to make dominant the sex that ought to obey' (2D 158/38–9). Voltaire's marginal comment, 'Why?',[6] is unanswerable in the context of the pure state of nature. The passage to society is also marked by the development of imagination, which gives rise to jealousy, aggression and disputes between suitors. None of the latter are based in nature, since there is a rough balance of numbers between the sexes, and the human female, unlike other mammals, is permanently in season. The outcome of socializing love in a bad social order is catastrophic, equivalent on the personal plane to the Hobbesian state of war on the political. Only with society does sexual passion become 'an ardent impetuous one . . . a terrible passion which braves all dangers, overcomes all obstacles, and which, in

184

its fury, seems fitted to destroy the human Race it is destined to preserve' (2D 157/38).

Sexuality makes its next appearance in the *Second Discourse* at the stage of the Youth of the World, after men and women have moved into their first permanent homes, the 'huts'. The negative and positive effects of the first step to society are evenly balanced. On the one side come 'quarrels and combats' between families seeking the best places of residence, on the other come 'the first developments of the heart . . . the habit of living together gave rise to the sweetest sentiments known to men: conjugal love and paternal love' (2D 167–8/46). It is only now, for the first time, that the *difference* between the sexes becomes significant. Its development is slow; it is contingent on the circumstances of a changed lifestyle, and is not rooted in nature:

> it was then that the first difference *was established* in the way of life of the two Sexes, which until this time had had but one. Women *became* more sedentary and *grew accustomed* to tend the Hut and the Children, while the man went off to seek their common subsistence. (2D 168/46, italics added)

The passage from the physical to the moral element of sexuality, anticipated at the end of Part I, is now set in its historical context, as 'everything begins to change its appearance' (2D 169/47). The transition from a nomadic to a settled way of life produces 'some link [*liaison*] between families', and that 'link' finds sexual expression:

> Young people of different sexes living in neighboring Huts; the transient commerce demanded by Nature soon leads to another kind no less sweet and more permanent through mutual frequentation . . . People grow accustomed to consider different objects and to make comparisons; imperceptibly they acquire ideas of merit and beauty which produce feelings of preference. (2D 169/47)

As we discovered in Chapter VII, *amour-propre* develops as society becomes more complex. The inequalities between people, unimportant in the pure state of nature, take on a new significance and are reinforced as social contacts increase, and as more stable social relations develop. Along with all other aspects of life, as sexuality is socialized, it becomes increasingly dominated by *amour-propre*. But this transformation of sexuality can take a healthy or an unhealthy turn. *Dépendance personnelle* may become either one-way obsession or mutual love:

By dint of seeing one another, they can no longer do without
seeing one another again. A tender and gentle sentiment is
gradually introduced into the soul and at the least obstacle
becomes an impetuous fury. Jealousy awakens with love; Discord
triumphs and the gentlest of all passions receives sacrifices of
human blood. (ibid.)

So the point at which *amour-propre* develops is the point at which
sexuality becomes socialized. It is the point where people come to
fix, to institutionalize, by convention the place of singing and dancing, the place of sexual encounter: 'People grew accustomed to
assembling in front of the Huts or around a large Tree: song and
dance, true children of love and leisure, became the amusement, or
rather the occupation of idle and assembled men and women' (ibid.).
Only in that public, social forum could *amour-propre* flower:

> Each one began to look at the others and to want to be looked at
> himself, and public esteem had a value. The one who sang or
> danced best, the handsomest, the strongest, the most adroit, or
> the most eloquent came to be the most highly considered; and
> that was the first step toward inequality and, at the same time,
> toward vice. From these first preferences were born on the one
> hand vanity and contempt, on the other shame and envy; and the
> fermentation caused by these new leavens eventually produced
> compounds fatal to happiness and to innocence. (2D 169–70/47)

According to the story of the origin of sexuality in the *Second Discourse*, social inequality between the sexes is not grounded in nature.
If it can be justified, its justification must be found in the 'remarkable change in man' (and presumably in woman) brought about by
socialization. The story of that change is told in the texts we shall
now examine.

(B)   A politics of difference: the Third Discourse

In the *Discourse on Political Economy* (1755), Rousseau begins by distinguishing '*general, or political, economy*' from '*domestic, or private,
economy*', and explains that he will be addressing only the former (3D
241/140). That distinction leads into a brief but important discussion of the family. He dismisses the patriarchal idea that the political order of the state could be modelled on the domestic order of the
family, since the two 'differ too much in size to be capable of being
administered in the same way' (ibid.). The family, even within a
developed social order, maintains a closer link with nature than does

the state. The father's rule over the family is based on natural feelings, whereas 'political authority . . . can be founded only on conventions, and the magistrate can command the others only by virtue of the laws' (ibid.). We shall return to the distinction between nature and convention later. What concerns us here is Rousseau's judgment on domestic economy that 'for several reasons derived from the nature of the thing, the father should command in the family.' (3D 242/141). The four reasons he adduces are very different in character.

First, authority should not be equally divided between husband and wife because 'it is necessary that the government should be one.' (ibid.)

Second, Rousseau alleges the physiological 'reasons' that the woman has periods of inaction during pregnancy, and (provocatively) that

> the husband should oversee his wife's conduct, because it is important to him to be assured that the children he is forced to recognize and nourish do not belong to anyone other than himself. The wife, who has no such thing to fear, does not have the same right over her husband. (ibid.)

Third, Rousseau produces an argument of reciprocal obligation between father and children who 'should obey their father, at first through necessity, later through gratitude. After having their needs met by him for half their lives, they should devote the other half to attending to his needs'. (3D 242–3/141)

Fourth, '. . . domestic servants . . . too owe him their services in return for the livelihood he gives them, unless they break the bargain when it no longer suits them.' (2D 243/141).

Each of the four reasons is problematic. In the first, there is an interesting asymmetry between the domestic and political spheres. In politics it is the sovereign, the unitary sovereign people, that must be one, not the government, since the latter is composed of numerous government agents. Why, one might ask, should the sovereign parental power in the family not have as its two agents the mother and the father? Within the second, Rousseau was undoubtedly more interested in the second component, the husband's fear that his wife's children might not be his own, and he was to return to that theme in later works.[7] Neither component provides a substantial ground for the subordination of wife to husband within the domestic economy. In the third, Rousseau gives a good argument that there are reciprocal obligations between parents and children, but no argument that the children have a greater obligation to their father than to their mother. In the fourth he is addressing the relations of obligation which hold within an extended household, with some residual feudal trappings, but no longer any unbreakable bonds of serfdom. The head of such a household would normally have been a man, but Rousseau was well aware that there were many exceptions to the rule,[8] a rule which itself can hardly be said to be 'derived from the nature of the thing'.

In short, the politics of difference sketched in the *Third Discourse* is based on the flimsiest of arguments. Rousseau expands some of those arguments in subsequent texts, but he does not greatly improve them.

(C)   A *culture of difference: the* Letter to d'Alembert

In the *Letter to d'Alembert* of 1758, Rousseau criticizes the proposal to establish a theatre in Geneva. In the course of it he attacks many aspects of contemporary culture, including the role of women. We turn our attention now to that polemic, which is conducted on a high rhetorical note of challenge, of confrontation with received ideas. It contains certain novel elements and others already sketched in the *Third Discourse*, and later developed in the *Emile*.

(i)   *The law of nature*

It is 'according to the law of nature', says Rousseau, that women resist men's sexual advances, and that 'men can conquer that resistance only at the expense of their own freedom' (Ld'A 43/47). Also based in nature are the double standards applied to promiscuity and unfaithfulness in men and women:

> 'Why', they ask, 'should what is not shameful for a man be so for a woman? Why should one of the sexes make a crime out of what the other believes is permitted for itself?' As if the consequences were the same on the two sides! As if all the austere duties of the woman were not derived from the single fact that a child ought to have a father. (Ld'A 77/85)

Rousseau develops this argument in more detail in the *Emile*, and we shall consider it later. Here he continues:

> Even if these important considerations were lacking to me, we would . . . still have the same response . . . Nature wanted it so; it is a crime to stifle its voice; [(1)] the man can be audacious, such is his destiny; there must be one who declares. [(2)] But every women without chastity is guilty and depraved;

188

because she tramples under foot a feeling natural to her sex.
(Ld'A 78/85)

Rousseau's rhetorical flourish masks a slippery argument. (1) looks like a plausible premiss, a claim that intercourse, and so reproduction, requires a male capable of performing, that is 'one who declares'. But (2) has little connection with (1). From the fact that the man must be, physiologically, active it does not follow either that he is entitled to be promiscuous, or that the woman should not be. One would need a more elaborate argument to reach that 'social' conclusion from some 'natural' premiss.[9]

(ii) Separation or exclusion

Rousseau is convinced that both men and women benefit from a way of life in which each sex has its own sphere of activity, strictly separated from the other, that each sex has suffered as the barriers between them have broken down in the modern world. That idea carries no explicit inegalitarian implications, and many feminists have advocated the construction, or reconstruction, of a space which would belong more exclusively to women. But in the present order of things, when women are separated within a male-dominated society, they find themselves excluded from power, assigned to roles which are in fact inferior and which they have not chosen for themselves.

Thus Rousseau, in calling for separate spheres, suggests that men will debase [avilir] their own sex if they even seek the advice of women, since in doing so they will allow women some access to the public domain (Ld'A 44/47). Women, he holds, achieve their full potential when separated from men and confined to the domestic world: 'there are no good moeurs for women outside a withdrawn and domestic life . . . the peaceful care of family and home are their lot . . . the dignity of their sex consists in modesty . . .' (Ld'A 75–6/82–3) Rousseau finds examples of that way of life in the ancient world and, surprisingly, in England, the modern embodiment of Sparta, where 'the two sexes like to live apart', and where both sexes, 'withdrawn more into themselves, give themselves less to frivolous imitations' (Ld'A 74–5/81–2). While moral benefit might be derived from contact between the sexes if a 'lovable and virtuous woman . . . moves a [man's] sensitive heart and bears it towards the good', even that faint ray of hope is extinguished by a waspish rhetorical question: 'But where is that heavenly object hidden?'

(iii)   Variations on the theme of women's modesty in seven movements

For Rousseau, modesty [*pudeur*] is the essential virtue of women. But is it founded in nature or culture? In an extraordinary passage of the *Letter to d'Alembert* (Ld'A 78–82/85–90) he runs that question through seven movements.

First, he examines a list of observed physical and psychological differences between the sexes, and asks, rhetorically, 'is it not nature' that established them? His answer is that women 'had to be strong enough to succumb only when they want to and weak enough always to have an excuse for submitting' (Ld'A 79/86).

Second, passing 'from reasoning to experience' (that is to a conclusion derived from comparative ethnography), Rousseau argues:

(i)   If (a) modesty were 'a prejudice of society and education', then (b) 'modesty should increase in places where more care is taken over education and where social laws are ceaselessly refined; it should be weaker wherever man has stayed closer to the primitive state'(ibid.)

(ii)ʾ   But (b) is false.

(iii) Therefore (a) is false. (Applying modus tollens to (i) and (ii)).

Rousseau holds that (b) is false because the correlation goes in the opposite direction, since the less refinement a society has, the more modest are its women. This sketchy ethnography is familiar from the *First Discourse*. It owes more to Rousseau's disapproval of the loose morals of contemporary French noblewomen than to empirical study of real 'primitive' societies.

The third and fourth movements stand in counterpoint to one another. In the third, he holds that any comparison with lower animals is irrelevant because:

> Man is not a dog or a wolf . . . It is only necessary in his species to
> establish the first relations of society to give his feelings a
> morality unknown to beasts. The animals have a heart and
> passions; but the holy image of the decent and the fair enters only
> the heart of man. (Ld'A 79/86–7)

In the fourth, in contrast, he allows that some creatures other than humans do exemplify modesty. Pigeons for instance show 'Nature's innocence' (Ld'A 80/87).

Fifth, even if modesty were not natural to women, he poses the rhetorical question: 'would it be any the less true that in society their lot ought to be a domestic and retired life and they should be

190

raised in principles appropriate to it?' This leads to the heart of Rousseau's argument that even if timidity, chastity and modesty are social inventions, it is still important for society that women should acquire these qualities, since a society without good family values is a bad society: 'A home whose mistress is absent is like a body without a soul . . .' (Ld'A 80/87–8).

In the sixth, Rousseau takes a rapid glance at comparative ethnology. He agrees that other societies have other institutions, some allowing the promiscuous mingling of men and women, but finds in ancient Greece and republican Rome the classic model of domestic separation (Ld'A 81/88–9).

The seventh, and final, movement is a fanciful historical reconstruction of the source of our present ills. 'All is changed', intones Rousseau, as the barbarian invasions brought women as camp-followers. The old classical order was destroyed by 'the licentiousness of the camps combined with the natural coldness of the northern climates, which makes reserve less necessary . . .' (Ld'A 82/89–90).

It is hard to make a more rational reconstruction of this extraordinary flow of thoughts. Only the fifth movement displays some kind of argument, but it does so at the cost of straining the link between the natural and the social almost to breaking point.

(D) A psychology of difference: the Emile

The tutor has postponed the advent of Emile's sexuality as long as possible. But at a given moment in his adolescence Emile finally encounters someone of the opposite sex. The tutor engineers that encounter whereby Emile will make his final step into the social world: 'As soon as man has need of a companion, he is no longer an isolated being. His heart is no longer alone. All his relations with his species, all the affections of his soul are born with this one . . .' (Em IV.493/214). Rousseau assigns a key role to love and sexuality in the socialization of the individual, but he is profoundly ambivalent in his attitudes towards them. This mirrors his underlying ambivalence about the role of *amour-propre* in all our interactions. But in treating sexuality, Rousseau swings with more than usual violence between optimism and pessimism. On balance his verdict is finally pessimistic about the possibility of an egalitarian, non-exploitative outcome of the battle of the sexes:

Love must be reciprocal. To be loved one has to make oneself lovable. To be preferred, one has to make oneself more lovable than another, more lovable than every other, at least in the eyes of

191

the beloved object. This is the source of the first glances at one's fellows . . . of the first comparisons with them . . . of emulation, rivalries and jealousy . . . With love and friendship are born dissensions, enmity and hate. From the bosom of so many diverse passions I see opinion raising an unshakable throne, and stupid mortals, subjected to its empire, basing their own existence on the judgments of others. (Em IV.494/214–15)

Why should that be? Rousseau gives no simple answer. I follow those who seek a solution in these lines which Rousseau deleted from an earlier draft:

If you ask me how it is possible that the morality of human life should be generated by a purely physical revolution, I shall reply that I have no idea. I am basing myself throughout on experience and do not seek to give an explanation of these facts. I do not know how the seminal spirits [esprits seminaux] can be related to the affections of the soul, nor how our sexual development relates to our feeling of good and evil. I simply observe that these relations exist. My reasoning is not aimed to explain them, but to put them to good use.[10]

Rousseau professes complete ignorance of the mechanism which connects the advent of sexuality to that of morality. Sexuality spans nature and culture, our physical being and our moral being. Sexual needs receive physical satisfaction, but differ from the physical needs of hunger and thirst. When the latter are not satisfied, we die, whereas celibates survive, often prosper. Thus the three sources of needs which Rousseau distinguishes are survival, sensuality and opinion (PolFr X.1.529/53–4), and he assigns 'the union of the sexes' to the second. At the same time, our sexuality, as soon as it advances from the ideal-typical abstraction of chance encounter in 'the forest', engages us in the play of *amour-propre*, in which we project and find our identities by interacting with others. In most of our dealings, this play involves domination and subordination. The goal of the morality of the senses is to reconstruct the conditions of our lives so that, at least in our political and economic interactions, they might be transformed into a play of freedom, equality and reciprocity. Yet our sexual relations remain brutally resistant to that transformation. Why is that? Rousseau does not tell us, for he never theorized an answer, but he leaves us clues. Intense sexual relations are so unstable just because they span the two worlds which cannot peacefully coexist, the natural and the social:

When man once encroaches on the care which nature takes of him, she then abandons her work and leaves everything to human art. Those same plants which flourish in the wasteland die in our gardens when we neglect them. An animal, once it is domesticated, loses its instincts along with its liberty, and does not ever regain them when once more released. It is the same with our species; we can no longer do without the institutions which produce our miseries. Natural man has disappeared, never to return, and the one who is furthest from his natural state is he whom art has most neglected, for his only education is a worldly one, the worst which one can receive. (FM 57)

Rousseau applies that thought epigrammatically to the political world: 'men become unhappy and wicked in becoming sociable, . . . the laws of justice and equality mean nothing to those who live both in the freedom of the state of nature and subject to the needs of the social state . . .' (GM 288/81–2). But in that context he is hopeful about the outcome: 'far from thinking that there is neither virtue nor happiness for us and that heaven has abandoned us without resources to the depravation of the species, let us attempt to draw from the ill itself the remedy that should cure it' (ibid.). But in affairs of the heart we cannot hope to find *le remède dans le mal*. In *Julie, ou la Nouvelle Héloïse,* Julie speaks for Rousseau when she judges that such love is 'accompanied by a constant disquiet caused by jealousy or by privation . . . There is no passion which produces such strong illusions in us as love' (JNH III.20.372/306). For her, sexual passion is the enemy of order and reason: 'disordered affections corrupt [our] judgment as well as [our] will' (JNH III.18.358/295). As reported by St Preux, Julie 'claims that everything that depends on the senses and is not necessary to life alters its nature as soon as it becomes a habit, that it ceases to be a pleasure as soon as it becomes a need' (JNH V.2.541/443). In sexual passion, physical drives are mediated through the imagination, which transforms love into jealousy, sets up 'inexplicable contradictions' in the feelings of the lover, who becomes 'at once submissive and bold, impetuous and shy' (JNH I.10.53/43).

(E) An education for difference: 'Sophie, ou de la femme'

We have reached the last act of the play of youth, but we are not yet at its dénouement. It is not good that man should be alone. Emile is a man; we have promised him a companion, we must give her to him. (Em V.692/357)

193

Rousseau opens Book V of the *Emile* on a note of high rhetoric. It heralds the final passage from childhood to the adult world, from nature to society. Its concluding flourish marks a clear departure from the egalitarianism of the *Second Discourse*. The first four books of the *Emile* have addressed the education of a boy, who has been guarded against premature contact with members of the opposite sex. Now that Sophie makes her belated appearance, it is not in her own right, but as 'a companion' [*une compagne*], to be 'given' to Emile. Throughout the dialectic of Book V she will maintain the subordinate role which Rousseau has assigned to her here.

But the sexual inegalitarianism of *Emile* V is complex, and there are points at which the feminist reader can extract '*le remède dans le mal*'. The theme of the interplay of identity and difference is no less dominant here than it is in the *Second Discourse*, and here as before, it is identity that takes first place:

> In everything not connected with sex, woman is man. She has the same organs, the same needs, the same faculties. The machine is constructed in the same way; its parts are the same; the one functions as does the other; the form is similar; and in whatever respect one considers them, the difference between them is only one of more or less. (Em V.692/357)

But now comes the crucial change: 'In everything connected with sex, woman and man are in every respect related and in every respect different.'[11] There had been no hint of this move in the *Second Discourse*. There, any differences that might be 'connected with sex' [*tient au séxe*] were minimal. And in the next sentence Rousseau betrays the fact that he lacks empirical evidence for founding important differences in biology:

> By comparative anatomy and even by simple inspection one finds general differences between them which do not appear to be connected with sex. They are nevertheless connected with sex by links which we are not in a position to perceive. We do not know how far these links may extend. All that we do know is that everything men and women have in common comes from the species, everything different from the sex. (Em V.693/358)

What we have here is a principle for assigning identity and difference to a source. Neither the empirical marks of identity and difference nor their normative implications have yet been propounded. In terms of biology, men and women are neither unequal nor identical:

how vain are the disputes as to whether one of the two sexes is superior or whether they are equal – as though each in fulfilling nature's ends in accordance to its own particular purpose were thereby less perfect than if it resembled the other more! In what they have in common they are equal. Where they differ they are not comparable. (ibid.)

The 'relations and differences' between men and women must, says Rousseau, 'have an influence on morality' [*inflüer sur le moral*]. By this he means that they will entail normative imperatives imposing contrasting duties on men and women in the social state. Rousseau locates three differences within and around the sex act itself.

At the purely physiological level, in order for the sex act to be consummated, Rousseau holds, the two parties must have different drives. The man must (a) be 'active and strong', and (b) both 'want and be able' to perform. The woman must (c) 'put up little resistance', and (d) be 'passive and weak'. But a moment's reflection shows that this distribution of drives is odd. While (a), (b) and (c) can be said to be naturally, biologically required for consummation, which in turn is required by the 'biological imperative' to reproduce the species, (d) is rather different. Rousseau might have said that the imperative would be satisfied even if the woman were 'passive and weak' in sexual intercourse, so long as the man were not. But he goes further. He suggests, without quite saying it, that women are *required* by the imperative to be 'passive and weak', and that suggestion is evidently false.[12] In making that suggestion, in slipping from (c) 'put up little resistance' to (d) 'be passive and weak', Rousseau has deprived women of activity and power in the sex act, and thereby assigned to them a certain 'moral' duty which extends beyond it.

Then, Rousseau proceeds:

this principle once established, it follows that the woman is created to please the man; if the man has to please her in his turn, it is by a less direct necessity, his merit lies in his power, and he pleases by the very fact that he is strong. This is not the law of love, I agree, but it is the law of nature, prior to love itself. (ibid.)

On a first reading, the speculative biology of this passage seems implausible. In other species the males engage in elaborate courtship behaviour apparently to please the females, so why should men not do the same for women? But Rousseau's argument is still driven by the demographic imperative. In brief, the male must be sufficiently 'pleased', that is aroused, by the female to achieve erection, penetration and ejaculation, to which the female must simply submit. In

195

that sense it is 'not the law of love ... but ... the law of nature', since the latter requires only performance of the act which reproduces the species.

Assuming that we accept this implication of the demographic imperative, it is still not clear how the natural differences are to 'influence' the moral ones. How far does the notion of 'influence' support the next step of the argument? 'If the woman is created to please and to be subjugated, she must make herself agreeable to the man instead of provoking him (ibid.).' What is it for a natural difference to 'influence' a moral one? In this context, a natural difference is displayed in the sex act, while a moral difference is a settled disposition of character. Rousseau then wants to suggest that 'subjugation' in the sex act, understood in the elementary biological sense discussed above, should 'influence' or give rise to a permanent relationship of 'subjugation' between husband and wife. But understood in that light, the connection between the physical and the moral is tenuous.

The fear of women's power to enslave men runs through all of Rousseau's story. A woman may be virtuous, in which case she will be endowed with 'the modesty and the shame with which nature armed the weak in order to enslave [*asservir*] the strong' (ibid.). Alternatively she may be wanton, in which case the result is even worse, 'especially in hot countries, where more women are born than men. [There] men would be tyrannized by women, would end up as their victims, and would see themselves dragged to their death without being able to defend themselves' (Em V.694/359). If tyranny is to be feared and detested in private life as much as it is in politics, then Rousseau must be right to fear women's supposed tendency to tyrannize men. Of course the two cases may be wholly different. There may be nothing in common between being 'enslaved' by a virtuous woman and being 'tyrannized' by a vicious one. The former, within an intimate, egalitarian sexual relationship, might correspond to the ideal of the citizen for whom 'obedience to the law which he has prescribed to himself is freedom' (SC I.8.365/142). The latter, instead, would be locked into a disordered sexual play of obsession and exploitation. But the clear insight into the contrast between two kinds of relationship is obscured by the suggestion that sexual tyranny can be exercised only by women over men. Throughout his analysis of the dynamics of sexual passion, Rousseau swings from moment to moment from acute, realistic insights to expressions of the most irrational fear of women.[13]

Yet this is not the final step in the dialectic of sexuality through nature to society. In the final step Rousseau turns the tables on the relation of strength and weakness, domination and subjugation.

'Here then is the third consequence of the constitution of the sexes',
he says:

> it is that the stronger is always master in appearance, but in fact is
> dependent on the weaker. This is due not to a frivolous practice of
> gallantry or to the proud generosity of a protector, but to an
> invariable law of nature which gives women more ability to excite
> desires than men to satisfy them. This causes the latter, whether
> he likes it or not, to depend on the former's wish and constrains
> him to seek to please her in turn, *so that she will consent to let him be
> the stronger*. (Em V.695–6/359–60, italics added)

Mary Wollstonecraft quotes this passage, and adds a brief footnote of
her own to the last (italicized) phrase: 'Perfect nonsense!'.[14] Most
of her criticisms of *Emile* V are unanswerable, but this judgment
may be too hasty, for this passage could be read as providing a sharp
insight into the dynamics of our sexual dealings. At the heart of the
play of love, the natural difference between men and women, their
relative strength and weakness itself becomes a token in the game. It
gains value only if it is freely granted, otherwise it constitutes rape,
which is 'not only the most brutal of all acts, but the one most
contrary to its end . . .'. How can this sophisticated understanding of
sexual love, as a perilous play of physiological and socially negoti-
ated tokens, coexist with the crudely inegalitarian picture of the
social relations between men and women? I shall return to that
question at the end. Even on this page of the *Emile* Rousseau proceeds in the remainder of the paragraph to ruin the point he has just
made. Mary Wollstonecraft mercilessly quotes his next words:

> Then what is sweetest for man in his victory is the doubt whether
> it is weakness which yields to strength or the will which
> surrenders. And the woman's usual ruse is always to leave this
> doubt between her and him. In this the spirit of women
> corresponds perfectly to their constitution. Far from blushing at
> their weakness, they make it their glory. Their tender muscles are
> without resistance. They pretend to be unable to lift the lightest
> burdens. They would be ashamed to be strong. Why is that? It is
> not only to appear delicate; it is due to a shrewder precaution.
> They prepare in advance excuses and the right to be weak in case
> of need. (Em V.696/360)

Rousseau claims that women's essential function is child-bearing,
and he argues, not unreasonably, that, given a fifty per cent infant
mortality rate, each woman will need to produce an average of four

children in order to sustain the population (Em V.699Fn./362 Fn).[15] This in itself would not justify the unequal treatment of women in society. The passage to that inegalitarianism runs through the family, which Rousseau had claimed in the *Second Discourse* to be a wholly social construct, but which he now endows with features which bring it closer to nature:

> When woman complains . . . about unjust man-made inequality, she is wrong. This inequality is not a human institution – or, at least, it is the work not of prejudice but of reason. It is up to the sex that nature has charged with the bearing of children to be responsible for them to the other sex. Doubtless it is not permitted to anyone to violate his faith, and every unfaithful husband who deprives his wife of the only reward of the austere duties of her sex is an unjust and barbarous man. But the unfaithful woman does more; she dissolves the family and breaks all the bonds of nature. (Em V.697/361)

Given his own insights in the *Second Discourse*, Rousseau's arguments here are confused. Insofar as the family is a creation of society, not of nature, then even if the woman, by committing adultery, 'dissolves the family', she does not thereby 'break all the bonds of nature', only the bonds of society, albeit the fundamental ones. Rousseau is right to hold that adultery introduces distrust and contempt, makes the family into 'a society of secret enemies', but he holds that the woman is guiltier than the man in this respect because of the possible effects of her betrayal:

> If there is a frightful condition in the world it is that of an unhappy father who, lacking confidence in his wife, does not dare to yield to the sweetest sentiments of his heart, who wonders, when embracing his child, whether he is embracing another's, the token of his dishonor, the plunderer of his own children's property. (Em V.698/361)

All this rings true, but true of a highly developed society, governed by a legal code and a system of property mediated through the family.

Those conclusions were based on a distribution of natural faculties between the sexes, in which:

> The Supreme Being . . . while giving man inclinations without limit, . . . gives him at the same time the law which regulates them, in order that he may be free and in command of himself.

While abandoning man to immoderate passions, He joins reason to these passions in order to govern them. While abandoning woman to unlimited desires, He joins modesty to those desires in order to constrain them. (Em V.695/359)

True to the ideal of complementarity, Rousseau holds that those faculties, 'taken together . . . balance out' (Em V.701/363). The distribution owes something to the tradition, and something to Rousseau's own idiosyncratic views about psychology.

In stark contrast to the *Second Discourse*, Rousseau derives women's alleged timidity from their need to be protected during pregnancy. Most importantly, Rousseau holds that women in society should be absolutely dependent on the opinion of others, whereas men should form that opinion. And that dependence is natural: 'By the very law of nature women are at the mercy of men's judgments' (Em V.702/364). Why should that be? Rousseau links women's dependence to his view of adultery: 'It is important . . . not only that a woman be faithful, but that she be judged to be faithful by her husband, by those near her, by everyone' (Em V.698/361). But that in itself is not enough. Women must be marked by some deeper incapacity to form autonomous moral codes. Yet even that formula must be made more precise.

Rousseau paints a grotesque picture of the passivity of women. One must educate girls into women by teaching them to subordinate themselves to men:

To please them, to be useful to them, to make themselves loved and honored by them, to raise them when young, to look after them when grown, to advise them, to console them, to make their lives agreeable and sweet: those are women's duties in every age, and they must be taught them from childhood on. (Em V.703/365)

From there Rousseau proceeds to advocate a return to the ways of ancient Sparta, in which women lived public lives before marriage, but thereafter were shut up in their houses, 'as nature and reason prescribe' (Em V.704–5/366).

But Rousseau's version of 'complementarity' is unstable. Women's 'natural' passivity, which was supposed to found their social subordination to 'active' men, also makes women 'naturally' superior to men in an important part of their moral dealings:

In social relations I note that generally the politeness of men is more obliging and that of women more caressing. This difference

199

does not come from education; it is natural. Man appears to make more of an effort to serve you and woman to please you. It follows from this that whatever the character of women may be, their politeness is less false than ours; women's politeness is simply an extension of their primary instinct. But when a man feigns to prefer my interest to his own, no matter what protestations he may make to cover the lie, I am quite sure that he is telling one. (Em V.719/376)

Rousseau arrives at this conclusion obliquely, as he considers the education of boys and girls and their different 'timings', in particular girls' precocity in learning to talk. Throughout his writings Rousseau systematically praises truthfulness and transparency, and condemns deceptiveness as the characteristic evil of the modern world. He here attributes honesty to women as part of their 'natural' goodness, if not acquired virtue. Women are thus by nature good, whereas men must struggle to become so. This opposition between men and women mirrors the underlying tension at the heart of Rousseau's thought about ethics and moral psychology which was identified in Chapter I, that between the naturalism of the morality of the senses and the deontology of virtue understood as an irreducible 'state of war'. The ideal of the former is an integrated order in which individuals are reconciled with society, with God, with themselves. In the latter, battle honours are won by those who subordinate their passions to the control of duty. In terms of the morality of the senses, women must be rated superior to men, but in terms of the austere deontology, they appear inferior precisely because they are less tempted by vice, and so are also less tested. The instability of Rousseau's verdict on women in *Emile* V thus mirrors the instability of the ethical theories implicit in his work from the start.

(F)   The natural and the social

How then are we to explain the contrast between what Rousseau says about women in the *Second Discourse* and what he says about them in most of his other texts?

Throughout his work Rousseau is concerned with the opposition between nature and convention. He holds that the opposition must be absolute, but that its terms can be reconciled in the ideal social order, where human beings live according to those conventions which alone allow them to regain their essential freedom and equality, vulnerable in the state of nature, but now translated into the autonomy of moral agents and the civic equality of citizens, both defended by the force of the law. The political programme, as we have seen, carries the risk of totalitarianism, but it is egalitarian insofar as it distributes freedom equally to all citizens. According to Rousseau's vision, what we lose in leaving the state of nature we recuperate in society through a radical transformation of human nature. But when he applies that vision to the relations between men and women, the dénouement is anything but egalitarian.

In other words, Rousseau envisages a radical denaturation in which the individual becomes a fraction of the whole, a numerator of the social denominator. But in politics that transformation is seen as *restoring* a certain autonomy which had been lost in a despotic social order. It replaces *dépendance personnelle* by dependence on the whole. That dependence in turn is legitimate only in a context of radical equality between citizens. But in relations between men and women no such *restoration* takes place. The reason is that in the personal relationship between a man and a woman the move from personal to universal dependence cannot be total. And in the resulting mix between personal and universal dependence, the allocation of dependence between the two partners is asymmetrical. Both are (personally) dependent on the love and esteem of the other partner. Each must please the other, but the woman must please and obey, whereas the man must please and command. Each is also (universally) dependent on public opinion, but each is differently related to that public opinion. Women earn public approval entirely for their private conduct, for their reputation for fidelity to their husbands, whereas men compete for civic glory. At the same time, women are the passive recipients of public opinion, whereas men help shape it. So men engage in the play of autonomous citizens, seeking and offering recognition in the public forum. In that forum women are only seekers. If equality is restored at the most intimate moment of their dealings, in the sexual play of strength and 'permitted strength', it is an equality that is strictly confined within the walls of the seraglio. One might doubt whether equality could continue to flourish there, within a public sexual order which is little short of despotism.[16]

IX

Language

(A)   The search for origins in history and psychology

Rousseau addresses the origin of language as a historical problem, the problem of how humanity came to acquire language, in two texts, briefly in the *Second Discourse* of 1755, and at greater length in the *Essay on the Origin of Languages*, published posthumously and probably completed by 1761.[1] He also addresses it as a psychological problem, the problem of how the individual child comes to learn a language, in the *Emile*.

Like most of his contemporaries, Rousseau seeks a naturalistic explanation of origins, though at one point, as we shall see, he is driven by the difficulty of the problem to entertain the possibility, with tongue not wholly in cheek, that language might after all have a divine origin. Rousseau approaches language in an eclectic fashion. Nowhere, even in the *Essay*, does he elaborate a technical 'theory of language'. He is concerned with language, as he is with other human institutions, in order to teach moral lessons, to trace a story of degeneration and possible salvation. At the same time he is engaged in continuous debate and polemic with the self-styled experts. Yet language is of central importance for Rousseau. It is the vehicle of truth and falsity, of transparency and deception, and of every form of *amour-propre*. It is thus the key to all our social interactions.

So, although he is, almost always, a naturalist in his approach to language, Rousseau still reserves a privileged place for human beings as language-users. In the opening words of the *Essay*: 'Speech differentiates man among the animals . . .' (EOL ch.1.375/240). He holds that non-human animals do indeed communicate, but they do so at a sub-linguistic level.

The search for the origin of languages is a search for absolute

202

beginnings. Rousseau asserts that 'since speech is the first social institution, it owes its form to natural causes alone' (ibid.). The causes are natural, but they produce language only when they are brought to bear upon human beings. Here then is the absolute beginning of language, as told in the *Second Discourse*:

> Man's first language, the most universal, most energetic and only language he needed before it was necessary to persuade assembled men, is the cry of Nature. Since that cry was torn from him only by a sort of instinct on urgent occasions, to implore for help in great dangers or relief in violent ills, it was not of much use in the ordinary course of life, where more moderate feelings prevail. When men's ideas began to extend themselves and multiply, and closer communication was established among them, they sought more numerous signs and a more extensive language; they multiplied the inflections of the voice and added gestures which are by their Nature more expressive, and less dependent for their meaning on prior determination. (2D 148/31)

On this account, the very first step towards human language is entirely natural. It is 'the cry of nature', the instinctive expression of need or warning, no different from that emitted by animals in the same circumstances. These cries and gestures constitute a 'proto-language', a form of communication which is sub-linguistic, but which can lead to language proper.

In Chapters 1 and 2 of the *Essay* Rousseau takes a somewhat more complicated route from the same naturalistic starting point. There he suggests that there are only 'two ways to act on the senses of another . . . the language of gesture and that of the voice', both of which are 'equally natural, although the former is easier and depends less on convention' (EOL ch.1.375/240). At the same time, there are two possible causes for the invention of language of any kind, on the one hand 'the desire or [on the other hand] the need to communicate one's feelings and one's thoughts' to one's neighbour, as soon as that person 'was recognized by another as a feeling, thinking Being similar to oneself' (ibid.). Rousseau concludes that 'needs dictated the first gestures, passions dragged out the first utterances [*voix*]' (EOL ch.2.380/245). Assuming that the passions referred to here correspond to 'desire' in the previous citation, then it is desire or passions, as opposed to needs, that take us beyond gesture to utterance. If there is not a direct inconsistency between the two texts here, there is certainly a tension. The *Second Discourse* had stated that the first 'cries', minimal utterances, expressed needs and warnings, whereas the *Essay* claims that their 'first needs served to separate men, not to bring them together'. Rousseau's argument for this aphorism is confused. The thought that 'the origin of languages is not due to men's first needs; it would be absurd for the cause of their separation to give rise to the means to unite them' (EOL ch.2.380/245) hardly bears on the question of language, since even if the needs caused by natural scarcities drove groups of people apart in search of subsistence, yet within any group those same needs would drive individuals together and be a spur to communication.

Rousseau is attempting to explain how it is that human beings, like other animals, start with a proto-language, an elementary form of communication embodied in cries and gestures, which are more or less instinctive and driven by needs, but how they, and they alone, take the crucial next step, to language proper.

For Rousseau the passage to language proper comes with the passage to *interactive passions*, which are specifically human. Human beings are linked to other animals, since like them they experience *pitié*, the 'innate repugnance at seeing a fellow creature suffer'. But other animals lack imagination, which is the vehicle to interaction and, eventually, to *amour-propre*. In the *Essay*, the passage to language proper is addressed in Chapter 9 ('The formation of the southern languages'), the longest and most elaborate chapter in the book. Rousseau devotes most of it to recapitulating the phase of the 'Youth of the World' of the *Second Discourse* (2D 167ff/45ff). There he had told the story of a period of elementary, family-based society, where 'the habit of living together engendered the sweetest feelings known to man, conjugal and Parental love', where 'each family became a little society' (ibid. 168/46). In the previous phase ('nascent man'), communication had been at the level of proto-language, 'inarticulate cries, many gestures, some imitative noises' (2D 167/45). Now and only now did language proper develop, along with social interaction and *amour-propre*, and 'the first developments of the heart' (2D 168/46). Here, in Chapter 9 of the *Essay*, he tells the story of the growth of 'southern' languages into 'domestic languages, not languages of peoples'. Here the first languages were 'the daughters of pleasure, not of need' (EOL ch.9.407/272), produced by 'agreeable passions', not by 'ardent passions' which expressed 'pressing needs'. In the future lies another world of needs, the fully socialized world driven by impersonal economic requirements. In that world, languages will turn into 'institutions'. Rousseau presents us with three aspects of a three-stage sequence: three stages of social interaction, at which we are linked first by natural needs, then by pleasures, and finally by social needs; three stages of determination and freedom, at which we are first determined by nature, then we engage in free play, and finally we are determined by society; three linguistic stages, first cries and gestures, then the expressive language of free agents, and finally language as institution, acting as a constraining framework. Within the *Second Discourse*, Rousseau gives little theoretical space to emancipatory political institutions, and equally little space to linguistic structures or 'institutions' which could be the vehicle for communication between free, equal individuals.

The historical story of the *Second Discourse* corresponds to the psychological one of *Emile* I and II:

> All our languages are the works of art. Whether there was a language natural and common to all men has long been a subject of research. Doubtless there is such a language, and it is the one children speak before knowing how to speak. This language is not articulate, but it is accented, sonorous, intelligible . . . [Nurses] understand everything their nurslings say; they respond to them; they have quite consistent dialogues with them; and although they pronounce words, these words are perfectly useless; it is not the sense of the word that children understand, but the accent which accompanies it. To the language of the voice is joined that of gesture, no less energetic . . . (Em I.285–6/65)

All the components of the historical proto-languages are here. They have the same cause, the communication of physical needs; they have the same form, inarticulate sounds and gestures; and the progress from proto-language to full language is also the same:

> The first tears of children are prayers. If one is not careful, they will soon become orders. Children begin by getting themselves assisted; they end by getting themselves served. Thus from their own weakness, which is in the first place the source of the feeling of their dependence, is subsequently born the idea of empire and domination. But since this idea is excited less by their needs than by our services, at this point moral effects whose immediate cause is not in nature begin to make their appearance; and one sees already why it is important from the earliest age to disentangle the secret intention which dictates the gesture or the scream [*démêler l'intention secrette qui dicte le geste ou le cri*]. (Em I.287/66)

In the psychological story, as in the historical one, we start with a physical creature, driven by physical needs, interacting minimally with other human beings. But that creature has the capacity for free action and, most important, the capacity to develop language in order to realize its intentions. According to the *Emile*, Book I, the mastery of language is a crucial moment in the emergence of *amour-propre*, which itself comes from the interaction of free wills. 'Empire' is the domination of one free will by another. It is born when the 'gesture or cry' turns into a *sign*. The child emits a sign with some degree of intention, both to establish its domination and to be recognized as a free dominator of another free will. The intention is 'secret'. It needs to be 'disentangled', or decoded. Its message is not fully transparent to the adult who receives it or to the child who emits it. On this psychological model, one can act intentionally without being wholly conscious of the content of one's intention.

For Rousseau, intentional action has a history. It emerges from a naturalistic, reactive origin. We start with a deterministic system of physical needs and their physical communication. As we encounter other human beings, that system develops into one of free intentions and interactions. Rousseau's naturalism is not the reductionist naturalism of La Mettrie's *L'homme machine*, which was monistic, materialistic and deterministic. La Mettrie had held that it was a reasonable (or at least an entertaining) hypothesis that animals could be taught to speak, since 'neither language, nor reason, nor any other ability traditionally considered distinctly human set man apart from the animals'. In the human machine language is 'simply a mechanical or automatic correlation between brain and the vocal cords'.[2] Rousseau's account of language formed part of his general campaign against this materialist mechanism. Against the materialists, Rousseau maintains that human beings alone have the potential for free, intentional action, and thus for full language. Like Descartes, Rousseau holds that human beings differ qualitatively from animals in their capacity to generate and use a fully developed language, the latter being defined, minimally, as a set of 'articulated' and arbitrary signs, to which ideas can be attached. Like Descartes, Rousseau holds that the incapacity of animals in this respect stems not from their physical limitations, but from the fact that humans, unlike other animals, are free and perfectible. But, true to his naturalism, Rousseau is particularly interested in the process in which the system of free, intentional action develops out of the deterministic system of physical needs. He holds that the transition from the one to the other is the outcome of contingent factors, which, in the case of any particular individual, might or might not be realized.

As the child grows, it advances from the stage of being passive recipient of sensations to that of being active judge and coordinator of ideas:

> Before the age of reason the child does not receive ideas but only images . . . images are no more than absolute pictures of sensible objects . . . whereas ideas, as notions of objects, are determined by

relations. An image can be alone in the mind which represents it to itself; whereas every idea presupposes others. When we imagine, we do nothing but see; when we conceive, we compare. Our sensations are purely passive, whereas all our perceptions or ideas arise from an active principle which judges. (Em II.344/ 107)[3]

Rousseau is sketching a move from passive reception to active engagement with our environment. That progress is particularly important for language.

(B)   From passive to active: linearity and 'l'arbitraire du signe'

Rousseau learnt most of his lessons in linguistic theory from Condillac. From him he adopted two theses, that of the 'linearity of speech', and that of the arbitrariness of the linguistic sign. According to the first thesis, when we acquire full mastery of language, we no longer simply communicate our instantaneous reactions to our environment, but use 'articulated' signs. Condillac wrote: 'if a thought has no succession in the mind, it does have succession in discourse, where it is decomposed into as many parts as the ideas it contains.' This represents an important step from passivity to activity: 'As this happens, we can observe what we do in thinking, we can render account of it to ourselves; we can consequently learn to conduct our reflection. Thinking becomes an art, and it is the art of speaking.'[4]

For Rousseau, the move to articulate sounds is important. He is interested in it first as a development in phonetics, particularly as it related to music. But he sees that it had implications for semantics too. According to Rousseau the inarticulate language 'would have few adverbs and abstract words . . . instead of arguments it would have pithy sayings; it would persuade without convincing, and depict without demonstrating' (EOL ch.4.383/248).

The second thesis adopted from Condillac is that of the arbitrariness of the linguistic sign, according to which, when we acquire language proper, we move from 'natural' to 'conventional' signs.[5]

Condillac had distinguished (1) accidental signs, (2) natural signs, and (3) signs by institution. In using both (1) and (2), the speaker is more or less passive. With (1), 'the exercise of one's imagination is not yet in one's power', and 'natural cries' (2) are merely the passive 'consequences' of one's perceptions. As soon as we move into the active mode, we have reached (3). It is there, for Condillac, as for Descartes, that we find a crucial point at which human beings differ from animals. The former, unlike the latter, are able to articulate their thoughts in language and to attach arbitrary

207

signs to ideas. This ability is due to a qualitative difference of mind, not to mere physical differences between the species.[6]

Rousseau takes over from Condillac almost casually both the thesis of the 'linearity' of language and the thesis of the arbitrariness of the linguistic sign. He does not clearly distinguish the one thesis from the other, and he uses them both for his own purposes. In the *Second Discourse*, Part I, he describes the move from the proto-language of gestures to the language of:

> articulations of the voice which, without having the same relation to certain ideas, are better suited to represent all ideas as instituted signs [*signes institués*]; a substitution which cannot have been made except by common consent, and in a way rather difficult to practice for men whose crude organs had as yet had no training, and even more difficult to conceive of in itself, since that unanimous agreement must have had a motive, and since speech seems to have been highly necessary in order to establish the use of speech (2D 148/31).

In Part II he talks of a universal proto-language, comprising 'inarticulate cries, many gestures and a few imitative noises', and the move to language proper, and at the same time the fragmentation of the proto-language, with 'the addition to it, in every Region, of a few articulated and conventional sounds, the institution of which is . . . not too easy to explain' (2D 167/45). We shall return to that difficulty shortly.

In the *Second Discourse* version, Rousseau is in fact more interested in the role of 'instituted signs' in the acquisition of general ideas than he is in their arbitrariness. Condillac had maintained that general terms would be needed 'early' [*de bonne heure*] to represent general ideas.[7] For Rousseau, in contrast, it is the slow pace of all development that is important. Like Condillac, he holds that we started with a language of unwieldy specificity, in which each object received a particular name, the first oak being called A, the second B, etc. 'The inconvenience [*l'embarras*] of all that nomenclature could not be removed easily.' In order to arrive at general terms, we needed 'to know the properties and the differences' of things, to make 'observations' and 'definitions', to engage in 'natural history and metaphysics' (2D 149/32). It is not clear that language and theory must have developed in tandem in quite the way Rousseau imagines. Condillac's common sense view is that general *terms* are needed 'early', and are used in all our day-to-day transactions, prior to scientific or metaphysical abstraction. Abstraction develops late in human history, and so too does a corresponding abstract terminology. But that does not show that general terms as such would develop later than terms standing for particulars.

(C)   The origin of languages: two dilemmas

For all his concern with problems of origins, Rousseau raises and leaves unsolved two dilemmas concerning the origin of languages. Both dilemmas arise from posing the question: 'Which came first?' In the first dilemma, we ask: 'Which came first, language or social relations?', and in the second dilemma: 'Which came first, language or thought?'

(i)   The first dilemma: language and social relations

Rousseau presents the first dilemma like this:

> The first [difficulty] which presents itself is to imagine how [languages] could have become necessary; for, since Men had no interaction with one another and no need of any, one cannot conceive either the necessity or the possibility of that invention if it were not indispensable. (2D 146/30)

Rousseau shows his customary respect for 'M. l'Abbé de Condillac' here. The Abbé's researches illuminated the *'embarras'* of the origin of languages, but they were insufficiently radical. Condillac had hypothesized that language originated after the Flood of the Old Testament in the first family formed when two wandering children of opposite sex came together.[8] Rousseau objects that, on this hypothesis, the existence of language presupposes the existence of the family, as the most elementary form of socialization, an assumption which he criticizes at length in the *Second Discourse*. Rousseau demands the extreme assumption that human beings have 'no relationships [*nulle correspondance*] with one another and no need of any'. Some pages later Rousseau appears to admit that the dilemma has defeated him, and that he is tempted to resort, against the guiding naturalism of the *Second Discourse*, to divine intervention:

> convinced of the almost proven impossibility that Languages could have arisen and been established by purely human means, I leave to anyone who wishes to undertake it the discussion of this difficult Problem: which was the more necessary, an already united Society for the institution of Languages, or already invented Languages for the establishment of Society? (2D 151/33)

The author of the *Encyclopédie* entry *'Langue'* (Nicolas Beauzée) is brutally critical:

> The philosopher of Geneva has correctly seen that inequality of conditions was a necessary consequence of the establishment of society; that the establishment of society and the institution of language presupposed each other, it being a difficult problem to decide which of the two was the more important necessary condition of the other. So why did he not take several steps further? Having seen and demonstrated that, if we assume the hypothesis of savage man, languages are impossible, why did he not reach the same conclusion concerning society? Why did he not then abandon the hypothesis entirely as equally incapable of explaining the one as the other? . . .

Instead, Beauzée concludes,

> It is . . . God himself who was not content simply to give the first individuals of the human race the precious ability to speak, but who at once activated that ability fully by immediately inspiring in those individuals the desire and the skill to devise the necessary words and phrases for the needs of nascent society.[9]

The feebleness of Beauzée's conclusion only highlights the radicalism of Rousseau's own investigations. Rather than admit defeat, Rousseau might have taken up the distinction between proto-language and full language which is the guiding theme of his account of origins. Thus Rousseau criticizes Condillac for failing adequately to resolve 'the difficulties which he presented himself on the origin of instituted signs' (2D 146/29). Rousseau could have gone some way towards their resolution if he had made explicit what is already implicit in his naturalist story. The gap between 'natural' cries and gestures, on the one hand, and 'instituted', conventional signs, on the other, would be filled by the interaction of contingent, natural events, impinging on human beings, in their natural state of isolation, self-preservation, compassion, freedom and perfectibility.

(ii)   *The second dilemma: language and thought*

Rousseau calls the second dilemma a 'new difficulty, even worse than the preceding one':

> if Men needed speech in order to learn how to think, they needed even more to know how to think in order to find the art of speech

. . . even if it were understood how the sounds of the voice were taken as the conventional interpreters of our ideas, it would still leave open the question of what could have been the interpreters of that convention for ideas which have no sensible object and which could not therefore be pointed to by gesture or by voice . . . (2D 147/30)

Again Rousseau seems to abandon the dilemma, holding that it is beyond his powers to solve it: 'it is scarcely possible to frame tenable conjectures about the origin of this Art of communicating one's thoughts and of establishing exchanges between Minds' (2D 147–8/ 30–1). But as with the first dilemma, Rousseau's own naturalism has given the clue to its solution. As Beauzée had suggested, the answer may be that speech and thought develop simultaneously, but, counter to Beauzée, there is no need to invoke divine intervention to explain that fact. Rousseau suggests that we learn our first words indexically, as the speaker emits a particular sound in the presence of the object referred to, while pointing to it. Is there circularity here? Must the learner already have grasped the rules of the 'indexical game' before being able to play it, and if so, how can one grasp those rules unless one has already mastered language? The circle can be broken only if the game as a whole is played within a context that is not wholly linguistic. The *Emile* shows how the pupil learns by practice, by interacting with the teacher. The interactions involve words, but other things too: facial expressions, reactions of encouragement and disapproval, giving rewards and punishments. So the use of indexicals, of gestures and pointing in language teaching might be less mysterious than it seemed at first. The next stage, that of linguistic 'convention[s] for ideas which have no sensible object and which could not therefore be pointed to by gesture or by voice', would also be mastered by practice, and Rousseau devotes much of the *Emile* to detailed descriptions of the practices appropriate to different ages, as the child acquires increasingly abstract ideas and the corresponding abstract terminology together.

(D) 'Le génie des langues'

Rousseau follows Condillac in emphasizing the importance of '*le génie des langues*',[10] the idea that 'each language expresses the character of the people that speaks it'. For Condillac this does not involve a linguistic determinism, in which a people would be imprisoned by its language, but rather a linguistic 'familiarization', so that individuals are 'accustomed to conceive things in the same manner as they were expressed in the language which they had learnt from birth'.

Rousseau steers Condillac's theme in his own characteristic direction, and tells an informal story of interaction between language and environment. Particular languages emerged, according to the *Second Discourse*, when natural disasters (the formation of islands, ravines, etc.) forced particular groups of people to live together and separately from other groups. Thereafter each group would 'form a common idiom' (2D 168–9/47), and specific tongues came to express different cultures. The more sophisticated and specialized techniques of agriculture and industry required more elaborate vocabularies.

In the *Emile*, Rousseau holds that young children should not be taught foreign languages for this reason:

> People will be surprised that I number the study of languages among the useless parts of education. But remember that I am speaking here only of studies appropriate to the early years . . . I agree that if the study of languages were only the study of words – that is to say of the figures or the sounds which express them – it could be suitable for children. But in changing the signs, languages also modify the ideas which these signs represent. Minds are formed by languages; the thoughts take on the color of the idioms. Only reason is common; in each language the mind has its particular form. This is a difference which might very well be a part of the cause or of the effect of national characters; and what appears to confirm this conjecture is that in all the nations of the world language follows the vicissitudes of morals and is preserved or degenerates as they do. (Em II.346/108–9)

Apart from prodigies, Rousseau tells us, no child under 12 years of age has ever really learnt two languages. This contention sounds empirically implausible, but what lies behind it? Rousseau applies the idea of the '*génie des langues*', to pedagogy. His view is that in learning a language we are learning more than just words, we are also learning the ideas those words express. The words in turn do not passively mirror the ideas, but react upon them and mould them. From this perspective, if you try to make small children bilingual, you will impoverish rather than enrich them. Given the organic link between language and culture, children, unable to master several cultures at once, will use one language instrumentally, and inappropriately, to express ideas whose proper home is another language. Rousseau holds that it is important for you to learn another language as an adult in order properly to understand your own, but that is possible only when you have mastered comparison, a skill which the child has not yet acquired.[11]

From the perspective of the *'génie des langues'*, particular languages are particularly adapted to express the cultures of particular peoples. In the *Essay*, Rousseau gives that expressivism his own particular historical twist. Chapters 9 and 10 are supposed to address the differences between the languages of the south and those of the north, understood in geographical terms. But it emerges in Chapter 11 ('Reflections on these differences') that modern European languages are a mixture of southern and northern elements, between the 'lively, sonorous, accented, eloquent and often obscure' languages of the south, and the 'muted, crude, articulated, shrill, monotone and clear' languages of the north. Those western languages in turn are contrasted with Arabic and Persian, designated 'oriental languages'. In the West, Rousseau now tells us, we have a 'private language of men who give each other mutual aid', a language which is better written than spoken. In contrast, oriental languages are primarily spoken languages, suited to eloquence and the arousal of enthusiasm. This fleeting opposition between West and East mirrors an opposition closer to the heart of Rousseau's concern, that between ancient and modern languages and the cultures they express. Thus in Chapter 12 ('The origin of music') Rousseau describes the ancient world, where 'verse, song and the word' still retained their 'common origin', where poetry still prevailed over prose, and passions over reason. The melodious language of the ancient Greeks exhibited the 'prodigious effects of poetry and eloquence'. Rousseau devotes the next six chapters of the *Essay* to music and its deterioration. Despite its title ('How music has deteriorated'), Chapter 19 marks a return to the history of language. There Rousseau sketches the transformation of the ancient Greek world with the arrival of reasoning and 'perfected grammar'. This destroyed the 'living, passionate tone of the language'. Sophists and philosophers displaced poets and musicians, and language came to 'convince and not to move' (EOL ch.19.425/290–1).

(E)   *The development of language*

Both the *Essay* and the *Second Discourse* address origins, but they are equally concerned with the subsequent development of human institutions. The story of origin is at the same time a story of how we come to be where we are now, and how we might escape from our present predicament. We have already embarked on the story of development in relating the first moments of language in both history and psychology. We have seen how human beings progress from a proto-language to a full language as their innate capacities interact with their natural and social environments.

Our linguistic capacities develop along with our other psychological and physical capacities. Three aspects of our development are important: (1) To a greater or lesser extent passion gives way to reason; (2) from being passive recipients, we come to engage actively with our environment; (3) we move from imagination to perception. Imagination yields particular impressions, but with perception we construct general ideas. Rousseau applies these aspects specifically to language in Chapter 3 of the *Essay* ('That the first language must have been figurative'), linking the psychological transition from passion to reason to the linguistic transition from 'figurative language' (the language of metaphor) to 'proper (literal) meaning' [*le sens propre*].[12] To the common-sense objector who asks 'how an expression can be figurative before it has a proper (literal) meaning, since the figure consists solely in the transposing of meaning' (EOL ch.3.381/ 246), Rousseau explains that in language the figurative is prior to the literal because the 'illusory image offered by the passions shows itself first'; the language which 'responds' to that illusory image is therefore the 'first invented': 'It then became metaphorical when the enlightened mind, recognizing its first mistake, came to use expressions of that first language only when moved by the same passions as had produced it' (EOL ch3.382/247). The explanation in terms of error, popular at the time, looks fanciful. But the more general thought, that the very distinction between the metaphorical and the literal, is a relatively sophisticated one, is correct. So too is the suggestion that people came to value the literal more highly than the metaphorical only in a particular context, when poetry, myth and rhetoric came into competition with science and logic as general explanatory frameworks.[13] Rousseau is not making the implausible claim that metaphorical language would or should be absolutely surpassed. He is putting his own view into the mouth of St Preux, who protests to Julie: 'However little warmth one has in one's spirit, one needs metaphors and figurative expressions in order to make oneself understood ... I maintain that only a geometer and a fool can speak in non-figurative language' (JNH II.16.241/198). Rousseau envisages that new linguistic forms will emerge, corresponding to the new world, yet to be born: a new oratory for the new political order, a new language of the heart for the transformed private world. His own richly figurative language can be read as an anticipation of these new languages, and as part of the revolutionary transformation which is already in train.

A crucial moment in the development of language was the invention of writing. Here is Rousseau's verdict on its effect:

Writing, which appears to fix [*fixer*] language, is precisely what changes it for the worse [*l'altére*]; it changes not its words but its genius [*pas les mots mais le génie*]; it substitutes precision for expressiveness [*l'exactitude à l'expression*]. One conveys one's feelings in speaking, and one's ideas in writing. (EOL ch.5.388/253)

As with other human institutions, so with language; Rousseau's nostalgia for the 'primitive' is precisely balanced by his respect for inevitable historical progress:

> In proportion as needs increase, as dealings grow more involved, as enlightenment spreads, the character of language changes; it becomes more precise and less passionate; it substitutes ideas for feelings; it no longer speaks to the heart but to the reason . . . language becomes more exact and clear, but more sluggish, subdued and cold. This progress seems entirely natural to me. (EOL ch.5.384/249)

Rousseau traces the development of writing from picture writing (hieroglyphs, as in ancient Mexico and Egypt), to 'conventional characters', each of which stands for a word (as Rousseau understands Chinese characters), to alphabetic writing. The second stage 'already involves a twofold convention', in that the word stands for the idea and the character stands for the word. Convention means agreement, and agreement means exercise of freedom. In that sense the invention of writing constitutes progress. The use of conventional characters is possible 'only once the language is fully formed and an entire people is united by shared Laws'. At the same time it can enslave the spirit: 'In writing one is compelled to use every word in conformity with common usage [*l'acception commune*]' (EOL ch.5.388/253). Is there any way in which the language can be turned again into an instrument of liberation, and cease to be an instrument of our enslavement to received custom and political despots? Rousseau sketches two answers to that question, two dénouements to the historical story he has recounted.

(F) Language and liberation: two dénouements

(i) The first dénouement: forward to a new eloquence

We have seen that language had already begun its process of rationalization in ancient Greece. From the time of the sophists, it served 'to convince and not to move'. Like many of Rousseau's oppositions, this one conveys a loss, even if it is a necessary loss. In the conclusion to the *Essay* (EOL ch.20, 'The relation of languages to governments'), he returns to the theme of eloquence, which had already emerged in the historical sketches of the ancient world. Rousseau now transposes that theme to the present day. Eloquence now becomes the form of discourse which could go beyond the opposition between 'convince' and 'move', between reason and passion. That new eloquence would be ideally suited to the new political order yet to be elaborated in the *Social Contract*. In this context Rousseau now gives his own politically charged turn to the expressive idea of the *'génie des langues'*:

> Languages are naturally formed according to men's needs; they change and are transformed as those same needs change. In ancient times, when persuasion served in lieu of public force, eloquence was necessary. Of what use would it be today, when public force replaces persuasion? It requires neither art nor figures of speech to say *such is my pleasure*. (EOL ch.20.428/293–4)

In the *Emile*, Rousseau makes the same comments on the ancient and the modern world, and the different role of eloquence in each, but there he advocates something closer to a step back to a more primitive form of language, the 'language of signs':

> One of the mistakes of our age is to use reason in too unadorned a form [*trop nüe*], as if men were nothing but mind. In neglecting the language of signs which speak to the imagination, we have lost the most energetic form of language. The impression of the word is always weak, and one speaks to the heart far better through the eyes than through the ears . . . Reason alone is not active. It sometimes restrains, it arouses rarely, and it has never done anything great. Always to reason is the mania of small minds. Strong souls have quite another language. It is with this language that one persuades and makes others act. I observe that in the modern age men no longer have a hold on one another except by force or by self-interest; the ancients by contrast acted much more by persuasion and by the affections of the soul because they did not neglect the language of signs. (Em IV.645/321)

In the *Essay*, too, there is an interaction between languages and political institutions: 'Some languages are conducive to liberty; namely the sonorous, rhythmic, harmonious languages in which speech can be made out from far away. Ours are made for the buzz in the Sultan's Council Chamber' (EOL ch.20.428/294). But in the last sentence of the book Rousseau writes: *'To describe and to give examples of the extent to which the character, the morals and the interests of a people influence its Language would provide matter for a rather philosophical inquiry* (EOL ch.20.429/295, italicized by Rousseau), and abandons further pursuit of that inquiry. The chapter simply hints that a new eloquence, favourable to liberty, might yet emerge. Citizens of the new order would use persuasion to win over an audience in the public forum. They would address themselves to their fellow citizens, as members of the sovereign people, properly assembled. They would move their fellow citizens by appealing to their hearts, and convince them by appealing to their reason. In thus combining passion and reason, action and cognition, the new eloquence would overcome the oppositions present in previous linguistic forms, and would become the vehicle of the general will. It could operate only within perfected social conditions, but it would itself contribute to the realization of those conditions.[14]

In his criticism of the theatrical profession in the *Letter to d'Alembert* (1758) Rousseau contrasts the actor with the orator, for fear they be thought similar:

> The orator and the preacher, it could be said, make use of their persons, as does the actor. The difference is, however, very great. When the orator appears in public, it is to speak, and not to show himself off; he represents only himself; he fills only his own role, speaks only in his own name, says, or ought to say, only what he thinks; the man and the role being the same, he is in his place; he is in the situation of any citizen who fulfils the functions of his estate. (Ld'A 74/80–1)

The two requirements, that he 'represents only himself', and that 'he is in the situation of any citizen . . .', embody the ideal bearer of the general will, free of factions and thus of *dépendance personnelle*, and united with the sovereign people of which he forms part, and thus interchangeable with any other citizen. Leading citizens of a well-ordered society will be skilled orators, since oratory is the form of public discourse whose goal is to discern and formulate the general will.

(ii)   The second dénouement: inward to direct communication between initiates

In both the education of the child and the historical development of languages, direct communication by cry and gesture is soon surpassed. Yet in his late work Rousseau yearns to recover the immediacy and transparency of that proto-language. In *Rousseau, Judge of*

Jean-Jacques and the *Reveries* he has become pessimistic about the possibility of founding a new egalitarian political order, of overcoming corrupt, manipulative *amour-propre*, and of transforming human beings so that they would no longer exploit one another in the public domain. His remaining hope is that the decent person may retreat from society, communicate with nature and with a few uncorrupted individuals, those possessing an *âme sensible*, the 'initiates' of the *Dialogues*, who speak a secret language:

> the initiate soon distinguishes between his brother, and one who simply adopts his accent without really being one, and this distinction can also be felt in writing. The inhabitants of the enchanted world generally write few books, and do not arrange their lives to do so. Writing is never a profession for them. (RJJJ 1Dial.672/12)

For those possessing an *âme sensible,* 'the weighty succession of discourse is insupportable; they are frustrated by its slow pace . . .' For them, 'what they feel must come into the open and penetrate from one heart to another without the cold agency of words [*le froid ministere de la parole*]' (RJJJ 2Dial.862/157). To the '*gens d'esprit*', people with 'a lively wit and a frozen heart', in contrast, 'ideas present themselves to them in pre-arranged phrases [*en phrases tout arrangées*]' (ibid.).[15] We have already examined the idea that language is the agent of linear reasoning, that it 'decomposes instantaneously given images into a succession. . . .' The theme of the linearity of languages, propounded by Condillac and Diderot, was already well established. Rousseau shows his originality in introducing the dialectical twist, in recuperating the instantaneous proto-language in the romantic image of direct communication. In the *Dialogues*, that direct communication, which he had earlier presented as merely sub-linguistic, now re-emerges as *beyond* normal language, rather than beneath it. Earlier, in his most puritan mood (the *Letter to d'Alembert*) Rousseau had denounced the 'language of love'. To be true, that language must be created for the loved one alone. Once it is public, it becomes a 'dreary jargon'. Those 'who use it,' he challenges, 'do they not use it equally for all women?':

> In the way that I conceive of this terrible passion, its perplexity, its frenzies, its palpitations, its transports, its burning expressions, its even more energetic silence, its inexpressible looks which their timidity renders reckless and which give evidence of desire through fear, it seems to me that, after a language so vehement, if the lover only once brought himself to say, 'I love

you', the beloved, outraged, would say to him, 'you do not love me any more', and would never see him again in her life. (Ld'A 95–6/104)

Like the language of the initiates, the language of love does not need the 'cold intermediary of words [*la froide entremise de la parole*]' (JNH V.3.560/459), and it becomes corrupt and false as soon as that agency intervenes. The second dénouement condenses all the negative features of the progress of language which Rousseau had identified in the *Second Discourse* and the *Essay*. Languages had become rigid, cliché-ridden, cold and, worst of all, vehicles for deception and domination. In the first dénouement, Rousseau had envisaged that the new oratory might constitute some kind of *remède dans le mal*. But in the second he abandons the search and retreats definitively within.

(G)   *Rousseau's position in the history of linguistics*

Taken separately, none of the elements of Rousseau's theory of language is original. He tells a story of development, from the natural to the conventional sign, from instinctive reaction to free active communication, from figurative to literal, from passionate to rational, from poetic to prosaic, from spoken to written language. This story was the common currency of the linguistic theory of the time, fully developed by Condillac, much of it going back to the 'Cartesian linguistics' of Port Royal.[16] The story of '*le génie des langues*' concerning the specificity of particular languages and the ways in which they interact with and express the cultures of their speakers was also in circulation, and expounded in some detail by Condillac. Many authors were engaged in the search for the origin of language, for which they were hoping to find a naturalistic, non-theological explanation.

Rousseau shows his originality in the way in which he combines the familiar elements. He brings to bear his own intense awareness of the passage of time and of the irreversible changes which all our institutions have undergone. He infuses all the elements with a new rhetorical charge, with a poignancy, with a nostalgia for a world of transparent, immediate communication now lost for ever. He sketches a vision of a new order of things, with its own new form of discourse, but eventually backs away from that vision as an unrealizable utopia. When Rousseau muses on the origin and development of languages, his mind is always on the moral and political implications of his story.

Rousseau's approach to language is 'romantic' in many respects,

219

but it cannot be aligned with any simplistic oppositions in intellectual history. Rousseau stresses the expressive power of language in his version of the '*génie des langues*', and in his account of the connection between language and the passions and of the importance of metaphor. But he does not want to overthrow 'Cartesian linguistics'. He does not reject the thesis of the arbitrariness of the linguistic sign or the central denotatory function of language. Instead Rousseau, the eclectic autodidact, gathers the elements he needs for his own particular purposes. True to the rationalism of Descartes, he defends human freedom against La Mettrie's monistic, determinist materialism, and holds that it is in virtue of that freedom that human beings alone are capable of acquiring language. But at the same time he is a naturalist in search of the trigger mechanisms in the environment which alone activate the specifically human potential within individuals. The two dénouements represent two alternative outcomes inscribed as possibilities within the historical story.[17]

X

Religion and Politics

(A)   Introduction. Social Contract *IV.8 'On civil religion'*

'No chapter of the *Social Contract* aroused so many polemics and protests in the eighteenth century as the one on civil religion.'[1] Civil religion represents the point at which the coercive power of the state is entitled to limit the range not only of the practices, but also of the beliefs, of its citizens. It is the point of extreme tension between libertarianism and totalitarianism in Rousseau's political theory, the point at which the Empire of the Laws reaches its outer limit, at the inner workings of our hearts. Wherever Rousseau fixes the point, he incurs the wrath of the religious authorities on the one hand, and their *Encyclopédiste* enemies on the other. Rousseau is drawn by his unconventional, deeply-held, pietistic Christian faith to advocate a simple religion of devotion and good works, and by his experience of monopoly religions in both Geneva and France to advocate tolerance and oppose the 'establishment of religion'. But he understands that some kind of shared religion is essential to provide ideological cohesion and counter the centrifugal forces of the individualist modern order. Derathé notes that:

> Rousseau wrote the chapter on the back of the chapter on the Lawgiver, and that is because it constitutes the natural complement to that chapter. Rousseau ends the chapter on the Lawgiver by raising the problem of the relations between religion and politics. Civil religion provides a solution to that problem. In formulating 'a purely civil profession of faith', Rousseau is really proposing to reinforce the authority of the laws with that of religion.[2]

221

We now turn to consider SC IV.8 in detail. The chapter is complex. The differences between the first version (the *Geneva Manuscript*) and the published version are considerable, not so much in content, but in the arrangement of the content. Rousseau evidently had difficulty in deciding how to order the three quite separate movements that make up the chapter. We shall examine the published version, in which the movements are ordered thus: first a historical sketch; then an abstract typology; finally a normative programme. We shall note striking variations in the *Geneva Manuscript* in passing.

(B)   *Historical sketch*

The *Geneva Manuscript* begins with an overview of the theme of the chapter, which bridges the speculative history and the normative programme. 'As soon as men live in society,' says Rousseau, 'they need a Religion to keep them there. No people has ever survived or will survive without religion . . .' The 'need' for religion is not spiritual, but practical. Without religion, a people would soon be destroyed: 'In any state which can require its members to sacrifice their lives, any person who does not believe in the after-life is either a coward or a madman . . .' (GM 336/117)

'Primitive' religion, for Rousseau, was a polytheism practised by small societies relatively isolated from one another: 'From the very fact that God was set over every political society, it followed that there were as many gods as peoples . . . National divisions . . . led to polytheism, and this in turn gave rise to theological and civil intolerance' (SC IV.8.460/216). Rousseau's history is not an innocent one. He uses the historical narrative in order to contrast the relationship between religion and the state as it is in modern times and as it was in the past. Thus 'primitive' intolerance is different from modern intolerance, so that 'in paganism, where each society had its worship and its tutelary deities, there were no wars of Religion' (ibid.). Indeed, in the *Geneva Manuscript*, Rousseau even talks of the 'mutual tolerance' at the heart of 'pagan superstition' (GM 338/119). Rousseau removes that latter comment from the published version, and with it an apparent contradiction. But if we bear in mind the contrast between the ancient and the modern, we can understand Rousseau's train of thought like this. Ancient peoples were aggressive towards neighbouring peoples. Since religious identity and political identity were more or less fused, 'political war was also theological war' (SC IV.8.460/216) and 'since the obligation to change one's religion was the law of the vanquished, one had first to be victorious before one talked about

222

[conversion]' (SC IV.8.461/217). In that sense the pagans of old were intolerant. But at the same time they observed a 'mutual tolerance' (GM 338/119), since, unlike modern crusaders, they did not go to war in order to convert the infidel. Such an idea makes no sense until the arrival of monotheist religions with ambitions of universal conversion. Instead, among polytheistic pagans, the defeated recognized the conquerors' gods as part of the panoply of their power.

The unification imposed by the Roman Empire put an end to the diversity of polytheism within its borders, and 'paganism throughout the known world finally came to one and the same religion'. The moment of Christianity was at hand:

> It was in these circumstances that Jesus came to establish on earth a Spiritual kingdom, which, by separating the theological from the political system, made the state no longer one, and caused the internal divisions which have never ceased to trouble Christian peoples. (SC IV.8.462/217)

The historical sketch has been an elaborate reconstruction, mounted in the manner of the *Second Discourse*, to lead up to this point. Rousseau announces it by raising the rhetorical tone in denouncing 'this double power and conflict of jurisdiction [which] have made all good polity impossible in Christian States; and men have never succeeded in finding out whether they were bound to obey the master or the priest' (SC IV.8.462/218). Only one Christian writer, 'the philosopher Hobbes, has seen the evil and the remedy' (SC IV.8.463/218).

(C)   Abstract typology

The typology is distilled from the history:

> Considered in relation to society, which is either general or particular, religion can be divided into two kinds, namely the Religion of man and that of the Citizen. The former, without Temples, altars or rites, limited to the purely internal worship of the Supreme God and to the eternal duties of morality, is the pure and simple Religion of the Gospel, or true Theism. The latter, inscribed within a single country, gives it its Gods, its own tutelary Patrons. It has its dogmas, its rites and its external form of worship prescribed by the laws; outside the single Nation that follows it, everything is considered infidel, foreign, barbarous; it extends the duties and rights of man only as far as its altars. (SC IV.8.464/219)

223

The religion of the citizen is here indistinguishable from the poly-theistic cults described in the historical sketch. The religion of man, in contrast, is an ideal type, supposedly extracted from the Gospel, a combination of monotheism and moral duty. Rousseau continues:

> There is a third, more bizarre, type of Religion which, by giving men two legislative systems, two chiefs, two homelands, subjects them to contradictory duties, prevents them from being at the same time pious men and Citizens. Such is the Religion of the Lamas, such is that of the Japanese, such is Roman Christianity. One might call this the Religion of the Priest. It results in a kind of mixed, unsociable code [*droit*] which has no name. (SC IV.8.464/219)

He dismisses it in a sentence: 'The third is evidently bad, so it is a waste of time to amuse oneself in demonstrating it' (ibid.). But this is misleading, since we know from the historical sketch that it has been dominant throughout the Christian era, down to Rousseau's own time, and it is a principal target of his polemic in the chapter.

Rousseau then outlines the positive and negative features of the two main types. From this it emerges that each is the precise inverse of the other. The religion of the citizen:

> is good in that it unites divine worship with love of the laws, and in making the homeland the object of citizens' adoration, it teaches them that to serve the State is to serve its tutelary God . . . But it is bad in that, being founded on error and lies, it deceives men, makes them credulous and superstitious, and drowns true worship of the divinity in vain ceremonial. It is bad too when it becomes exclusive and tyrannical and makes a people bloody and intolerant . . . (SC IV.8.464–5/219–20)

Through the religion of man, in contrast, 'that holy, sublime true religion, men, the children of the same God, recognize each other universally as brothers, and the society which unites them is not dissolved even at death'. Its disadvantage is that it:

> having no particular relation to the body politic, leaves the laws with only their intrinsic force without making any addition to it; and so one of the great bonds which can unite a particular society remains without effect. Even worse, far from attaching the hearts of the Citizens to the State, it detaches them from all earthly things: I know of nothing more contrary to the social spirit. (SC IV.8.465/220)

This last phrase aroused a furore of protests.[3] In his letter to Usteri, Rousseau distinguishes 'the great society, human society in general, [which] is founded on humanity, on universal beneficence':

I say, and I have always said, that Christianity is favourable to it. But particular societies, political civil societies, have an entirely different principle. They are purely human institutions. Christianity therefore detaches us from them, as it does from all that is merely earthly. It is only human vices that render our institutions necessary, and only human passions that conserve them. (Letter to Usteri, 18 July 1763, CC 17#2825, p. 63)[4]

In all its aspects, Christianity is of negative value politically. The virtue of charity leads to quietism, the acceptance of tyranny and oppression, which it regards as sent by God to punish his wicked children. Christianity instils stoicism, not martial ardour in troops, who 'know how to die, rather than how to conquer'. In short, says Rousseau:

I am mistaken when I speak of a Christian Republic; these two words are mutually exclusive. Christianity preaches only servitude and dependence. Its spirit is so favourable to tyranny that tyranny always profits from it. True Christians are made to be slaves. They know it and are hardly worried by it. This short life is of too little value in their eyes. (SC IV.8.467/221)

We can now summarize the positive and negative features of the two types. The religion of man is founded on theological truth, and so yields accurate knowledge about God. It inspires benevolence towards the universal community and indifference towards the particular. The religion of the citizen, being founded on theological error, is mistaken about the real nature of God. Failing to recognize a universal community, it inspires in its believers a hostility towards members of other particular communities and limitless loyalty to their own particular community. 'Considered in relation to society' (SC IV.8.464/219), given that there are only particular societies, and no real universal community, on earth, the religion of the citizen is superior to the religion of man in instilling the ideological cohesion needed to ensure that citizens will respect the laws and enthusiastically defend their native land against external aggression. The problem is that the model of the religion of the citizen is derived, historically, from a social order that is passed. Citizens of a modern state are unwilling to believe the particular mythologies which held 'primitive' communities together. The modern order is stamped by the universalist claims made by the monotheistic religions on the one hand, and by the sciences on the other.

(D)   Normative programme

'But setting political considerations aside, let us return to right' (SC IV.8.467/222), says Rousseau, as he introduces his normative programme for religion. As he does frequently in the *Social Contract*, Rousseau here separates questions of fact from questions of right. The former bear on, but are secondary to, the latter. First he specifies the extent of the sovereign's power over the citizens' religious practices and beliefs:

> The right that the social pact gives the Sovereign over the subjects does not overstep . . . the limits of public utility. Subjects are therefore answerable to the Sovereign for their opinions only insofar as those opinions are of importance to the community. (SC IV.8.467–8/222)

But just which opinions are 'of importance to the community'? Rousseau explains that 'every citizen should have a religion which makes him love his duties', whereas 'the dogmas of that religion are of no concern to the state or its members, except where they relate to morality and to the duties which the adherent is expected to fulfil towards his neighbours' (SC IV.468/222). But the dividing line between what is, and what is not, the sovereign's concern, is still vague. So Rousseau proceeds:

> There is therefore a purely civil profession of faith, whose articles are for the Sovereign to establish, not exactly as dogmas of Religion, but as feelings of sociability, without which it is impossible to be a good Citizen or a faithful subject. Without being able to oblige anyone to believe them, the Sovereign can banish from the State those who do not believe them. He can banish the unbeliever not for being impious, but for being unsociable, for being incapable of sincerely loving the laws and justice, incapable of sacrificing his life to duty, if it should be necessary. If someone who, after publicly acknowledging these same dogmas, conducts himself as though he did not believe them, he should be punished by death; he has committed the greatest of crimes, he has lied before the laws. The dogmas of the civil Religion must be simple and few in number, enunciated with precision, without explanations or commentaries. [(1)] The existence of a powerful, intelligent, beneficent, foresighted,

providential Divinity, [(2)] the life to come, [(3)] the happiness of the just, [(4)] the punishment of the wicked, [(5)] the sanctity of the Social Contract and of the Laws; these are the positive dogmas. As to the negative dogmas, I limit them to a single one, namely [(6)] intolerance: it belongs with the cults we have excluded. (SC IV.8.468–9/222–3)

Dogmas (1)–(4) are an abstract of the minimal deist theology propounded by the Savoyard Vicar, while (5) endows the legitimate political order with a continuing sanctity inherited from the Foundation Myth of the Lawgiver. The one negative dogma (6) imposes a strong exclusion clause: 'whoever dares say "Outside the Church there is no salvation"' must be chased from the State, so long as the State is not the Church, and the Prince is not the Pontiff (SC IV.8.469/223–4).

In his discussion of the Lawgiver, Rousseau had said: 'We should not conclude that among us politics and religion have a common object, even though in the origin of nations the one is the instrument of the other' (SC II.7.384/157). In the 'Purely civil profession of faith', Rousseau is seeking a form of religion of the citizen suitable for the modern order. It is to have the same integrative role as its pagan predecessor, but it will have been passed through the purifying filter of minimal Christianity to remove the barbarous pagan elements. In its old style, the religion of the citizen had a rich, particular content. But in its new style it is no less abstract than the religion of man. Indeed the dogmas (1)–(4) of the new style religion of the citizen are identical with those of the religion of man. The religion of man is transformed into the religion of the (modern) citizen by the simple addition of (5). Rousseau's citizen is thus expected to adhere to a doctrine which combines universalist deism with deference to the constitution of one's own particular country.

It is now time to press Rousseau harder on the limits of tolerance. Rousseau sketches two different grounds on which a doctrine might be held to be intolerable. Each of these grounds throws up its own problems.

(E) The problem of toleration

(i) Intolerance of the intolerant

The first and simplest limit of tolerance is that we should not tolerate the intolerant. Most liberals hold to some version of this. The more libertarian they are, the more they will give the benefit of the doubt to their intolerant opponents.[5] Rousseau poses the limit close to the inner world of individuals' views. Those who dare 'say "Outside the Church there is no salvation" must be chased from the State', even if they do not attempt to impose that view on others, let alone persecute them for failing to hold it. We might object that simply to hold that intolerant view in theology, or even to utter it, cannot in itself jeopardize public safety, unless it is thought that one cannot consistently hold the view without trying to impose it. In the *Letter to de Beaumont* Rousseau argues that the sovereign has more or less absolute power to order the external forms of religious practice within the state, and is entitled to 'prevent a foreign cult from being introduced into the country' (LdeB 978). But that power is limited by historical facts, so that 'it is unjust and barbarous to destroy religions by violence once they are established and tolerated in a country'. In particular, the Protestant religion, 'once it had been passed down from parents to children, became part of the French Nation'. In a subsequent letter Rousseau explains that passage in the following terms:

> I distinguished those cults in which essential religion is found from those in which it is not. The former are good, the latter bad; I said that. One is only obliged to conform to the particular religion of the state, indeed one is only permitted to follow it, when essential religion is found in it, as it is found for example in the various Christian communions, in Mahommedanism and in Judaism. But in Paganism it was quite different. Since it is very evident that essential religion is not found there, the Apostles were permitted to preach against paganism, even amongst the pagans, even despite their opposition. (Letter to M. Antoine Audoyer, 28 May 1763, CC 16#2730, pp. 261–2)[6]

But Rousseau is hardly giving a close exegesis of his own words in the *Letter to de Beaumont*. There he had asserted that a sect has the right to exist in a state once it has become an organic part of it. He does not discuss the content of the beliefs of its adherents, but he suggests, as he does in SC IV.8, that all religions are to be tolerated if they are themselves tolerant, and forbidden if they are not. In his commentary to Audoyer, however, he sets a quite different limit on the range of tolerable religions. Referring now to the theological content of the religions, he holds that it is legitimate for a sovereign to impose the forms of any one of the three 'essential', monotheistic Religions of the Book, since their content is, presumably, held to be at least minimally rational. It is equally legitimate for the sovereign to forbid pagan, non-rational religions, presumably on grounds of their internal irrationality. But it can be seen at once that the two limits do not coincide. Two of the great monotheistic religions, Christianity and Islam, have been historically the most intolerant, whereas pagan religions, as Rousseau noted in the *Geneva Manuscript*, tended to be 'mutually tolerant'.

Rousseau thus asserts a relatively clear limit of tolerance: only intolerant religions cannot be tolerated. That limit does not refer to the theological content or dogmas of the religions, except to those relating to tolerance. But at the same time he wishes to exclude systems of belief which fall below a level of rationality roughly equivalent to his own minimal deism. But exclusion of the intolerant entails exclusion of the irrational only if irrationality leads inevitably to intolerance. But does it? As we have already seen, Rousseau sometimes thought that it does, but sometimes recognized that it does not. For that reason, the single negative dogma of the purely civil profession of faith is less simple than it seems at first.

(ii)   Opinions of importance to the community

The principle that one should not tolerate the intolerant is a particular application of the more general principle enunciated in SC IV.8 that 'subjects are answerable to the sovereign for their opinions only insofar as those opinions are of importance to the community'. That phrase delimits the range of opinions which the sovereign is entitled to control, the range that affects the well-being of the public, as well as that of the individual who holds the opinion. This distinction is familiar in the liberal tradition, where J. S. Mill enshrined it in his *Essay on Liberty* in the distinction between self-regarding and other-regarding actions.[7] Rousseau and Mill differ not because they formulate different principles, but because they draw a different demarcation line between what is and what is not 'of importance to the community'. Most importantly, Rousseau holds that belief in all the six dogmas of the purely civil profession of faith is of such importance. The dogmas include the purely political dogma of 'the sanctity of the Social Contract and of the Laws', and the 'negative dogma', that of intolerance. But they also include the four purely theological dogmas considered above. In SC IV.8 Rousseau provides no independent theological arguments for those dogmas, but simply presupposes the view that one cannot 'be virtuous without religion' (Ld'A 89Fn./97 Fn.). Rousseau explains the political implications of that view in the *Letter to de Beaumont*:

> Why should one man have the right to inspect the beliefs of another and the state the right to inspect the beliefs of the citizens? It is because one assumes that mens' beliefs determine

their morality, and that their conduct in this life depends on the ideas that they have of the life to come. If that is not so, why does it matter whether they believe or merely pretend to believe? The outward appearance of religion would then serve only to dispense them from having a real one.

In society everyone has the right to be informed whether his neighbour believes himself obliged to be just, and the Sovereign has the right to examine the grounds on which each person founds that obligation. In addition, the national forms [of worship] must be observed; I have insisted strongly on that point. But in passing judgment on questions which do not concern morality, have no influence on actions and do not lead to lawbreaking, each person is his own master, and no-one has either the right or the interest to prescribe to others how they should think. (LdeB 973)

In the *Letter*, Rousseau is defending his work against the *Mandement* imposed on it by the French Catholic hierarchy, and it contains some powerful arguments for theological tolerance. It is therefore striking that it also contains this unambiguous assertion that the sovereign is entitled to proscribe atheism, even when it is a purely private belief.

Each time Rousseau tries to disentangle what is from what is not 'of importance to the community' in citizens' religious beliefs, he raises more problems than he solves. Here, for instance, in the first *Letter from the Mountain* he tells us that 'the wise Lawgiver' should:

first . . . establish a purely civil religion, in which he will include all the fundamental dogmas of every good religion which are really useful to society, whether universal or particular, and omit all those which may be important to faith, but which have no bearing on our earthly good, which is the sole object of legislation. [(1)] For how could the mystery of the Trinity, for example, contribute to the good constitution of the state? [(2)] How will its members be better citizens if they have rejected the merit of good works? [(3)] And what effect does the dogma of original sin have on the cohesion of civil society? (LMt 1.705)

But the rhetorical questions are tendentious. The details of the doctrine of the Trinity may indeed be distant from practical behaviour. But Rousseau himself has argued that the doctrine of original sin is morally dangerous, and the reader of Weber's *Protestant Ethic* might be persuaded that belief in justification through works is a spur to an industrious life. So neither (2) nor (3) is intrinsically 'self-regarding'. And that is confirmed by Rousseau's own rhetoric. He suggests at one and the same time that the dogmas are irrelevant to practical life, and that belief in those dogmas is politically damaging.

Even if it is finally possible to draw the line between beliefs which are, and beliefs which are not, 'of importance to the community', a deeper problem still remains. For, according to Rousseau, to believe or not to believe that something is the case, to give or withhold our belief, is not within our power. He repeats that view many times:

> Men have heads which are organized in such diverse ways that they cannot all be equally affected by the same arguments, particularly in matters of faith. What appears to one person to be evidently true does not appear even probable to the next. All may sometimes agree on the same things, but rarely for the same reasons. And that shows . . . how little sense the[ir] dispute had in the first place. It is as absurd as trying to force someone else to see things through our own eyes. (LMt 3.727)

> I believe in God as firmly as I believe any other truth, because believing and not believing are the things which depend least on me . . .
> . . . I am indignant, as you are, when each person's faith is not left in the most perfect liberty, and when someone dares to inspect the internal workings of consciousnesses into which one cannot penetrate [*ose controller l'intérieur des consciences où il ne sçauroit pénétrer*]; as though it depended on us whether we believed or did not believe in areas where proof has no place, and where one has never been able to subject reason to authority. So do the Kings of this world have some right of inspection in the world to come? Do they have the right to torture their subjects here below, in order to force them to go to Paradise? No; every human government is limited by its nature to civil duties . . . (LV 1070, 1072)

How can we square the philosophical thought that we are not responsible for our beliefs, since we cannot be responsible for what does not depend on us, with the political view that we can be held accountable for certain theological beliefs, particularly the beliefs that God exists and that there is an afterlife in which rewards and punishments will be allotted for our conduct in this life? So strong is the claim that we are responsible for those beliefs, and so heinous is the crime of holding the wrong beliefs, that we can even be put to death for that crime.

A first response might be that some 'beliefs' are morally intolerable, e.g. the 'belief' that torturing babies is fun. But it is intolerable

231

because it is a *component* of intolerable acts. Such a 'belief' is evidently different from a 'belief' that a moral obligation is founded on an entirely human duty (roughly Kant's view), and needs no divine sanction to back it.

Rousseau's own response might be that the two thoughts are at least formally consistent. The Sovereign in SC IV.8 'cannot oblige anyone to believe these [articles]' (SC IV.8.468/222–3), and cannot therefore 'penetrate into the interior of consciousnesses'. But he can control, rigorously, external conduct, including conduct that betrays lack of real inward belief in the essential dogmas. That solution is Jesuitical, however, since it gives the unbeliever a choice between exile on the one hand, or a life of hypocrisy on the other. The latter alternative is particularly unattractive, since it results in the death penalty if one is found out.

Rousseau's solution is bizarre, not only because he deems us to be punishable for holding beliefs for which we are not responsible, but also because he himself was uncertain about the punishment of the wicked in the afterlife, one of the four theological dogmas which we are required to believe. If we return to the arguments for the existence of God through 'seeing as', we might conclude that one could be brainwashed to see the world as something different from what one saw it as before. From that perspective, one person might manipulate another's consciousness. But Rousseau never uses that form of argument in that way, and never hints that one would seek to alter another's Gestalt by force. But even if one succeeded in doing that, the belief one produced in the other person would be even less within that person's control.

So it is natural that Rousseau himself comments in an author's footnote to *Julie, ou la Nouvelle Héloïse*:

> no true believer could be intolerant or a persecutor. If I were a magistrate, and the law prescribed the death penalty for atheists, I should begin by seeing to it that anyone who came and denounced another for that crime should be burnt. (JNH V.5.589/482)

But this tells us only that Rousseau is merciful, not that he is consistent.

(iii)   Doubts about the value of tolerance

We have tracked the shifting frontiers of tolerance, as Rousseau draws and redraws them. Those frontiers do not defend a 'liberal' heartland within which the burden of proof is always on those who advocate restricting freedom of thought. Rousseau is too well aware that ideology, in particular religious ideology, plays a constitutive role in the formation of a sovereign people capable of legislating for itself and defending itself against external aggression. From that perspective, the sovereign has a *prima facie* duty to ensure the people's ideological unity, as well as its military strength.[8] But in most of his writing Rousseau asserts no less strongly than his *Encyclopédiste* opponents that fanaticism is a danger to the modern state:

> Charity is not murderous. Love of one's neighbours does not lead us to massacre them. Thus zeal for the salvation of men is never the cause of persecutions; it is *amour-propre* and pride which causes them. The less reasonable the religion, the more one seeks to establish it by force . . . Intolerance and illogicality have the same source. You must ceaselessly intimidate and frighten people. If you let them reason for a moment, you are lost. (LdeB 971)

But against the *Encyclopédistes*, Rousseau holds that fanaticism may finally have less dangerous effects on society than atheism. He makes this unexpected turn in the extraordinary footnote to the 'Profession of Faith':

> Bayle has proved very well that fanaticism is more pernicious than atheism, and this is incontestable. But what he does not take care to say, and which is no less true, is that fanaticism, though sanguinary and cruel, is nevertheless a grand and strong passion which elevates the heart of man, makes him despise death, and gives him a prodigious energy that need only be better directed to produce the most sublime virtues. On the other hand, irreligion – and the reasoning and philosophic spirit in general – causes attachment to life, makes souls effeminate and degraded, concentrates all the passions in the baseness of private interest, in the abjectness of the human *I*, and thus quietly saps the true foundations of every society. For what private interests have in common is so slight that it will never outweigh what sets them in opposition.
>
> If atheism does not cause the spilling of men's blood, it is less from love of peace than from indifference to the good. Whatever may be going on can be of little importance for the allegedly wise man, provided that he can remain at rest in his study. His principles do not cause men to be killed, but they prevent them from being born by destroying the morals which cause them to multiply, by detaching them from their species, by reducing all their affections to a secret egoism as deadly to population as to

virtue . . .Thus fanaticism, although more deadly in its
immediate effects than what is today called the philosophic spirit,
is much less so in its consequences. (Em IV.632–3Fn./312 Fn.)

It is not clear how seriously we should take this outburst. We have
already noted Rousseau's concern that modern mores, from abortion
to the prevalence of wet-nurses, were undermining the population.
Many of his reactionary attitudes towards women were driven by the
'demographic imperative' to keep up the birth rate and produce
healthy children. This apocalyptic passage targets atheists for being
necessarily selfish, unwilling to strive for their fellow human beings,
or even to reproduce them. In contrast to this image of moral decay,
the image of the healthy, if barbarous, fanatic is relatively attractive.
But he is not *salonfähig*, and he gains admission only in a footnote.
There he stands, more as a brutal contrast to the degeneracy of
modern society than as a model of the citizen of the society to come.

Negative Theology: Revealed Religion Criticized

(A) Rousseau's religiosity

Rousseau's religiosity has not endeared him to his critics. Indeed it is the one element in his life and thought that has united them in their hostility, Catholics, Protestants, believers, sceptics, agnostics and atheists.

Throughout the many and often conflicting reconstructions Rousseau makes of his own life, the preoccupation with religion is a constant theme. The most poignant of those reconstructions is the Third Walk of the *Reveries*. There Rousseau meditates on elements at the heart of the Christian faith, the shortness of our lives and 'learning how to die' (Reveries III.1012/48). Combining imagination and memory, he portrays his childhood thus:

> Born into a family in which morals and piety [*sic*] reigned, and brought up affectionately by a minister full of virtue and religion, I had received from my earliest years principles and maxims – prejudices, some might say – which have never entirely deserted me. (Reveries III.1013/49)

He glosses over the 1740s and early 1750s, his *Encyclopédiste* period,[1] when he was closest to the *philosophes* in his naturalistic approach to mankind and society. Religion plays little or no part in the explanatory story of the *Second Discourse,* which marks the high point of this phase of his thought. In it he tells a story of determination by chance, and sees the world we inhabit as the outcome of contingent processes, from which divine providence is markedly absent.[2]

In the Third Walk, Rousseau logs the imagined dramatic moment when he turned against the religious programme of the *philosophes*, the point of decision to 'fix once and for all my opinions and principles and to remain for the rest of my life as I found I should be, having thought well about them' (Reveries III.1016/53).[3] He then came to see them as fanatical defenders of an unprovable dogma, centred on mechanistic determinism, working in complicity with established power to deprive the poor of their last vestige of comfort in an uncaring world. In propounding his own idiosyncratic theology, Rousseau attempts to reverse each of these elements. In so doing he antagonizes both sides of the great ideological divide, particularly since he never tires of identifying his religious and anti-religious opponents as equally bigoted:

> This mutual hatred [between Jesuits and *philosophes*] was at bottom a power-struggle like that between Carthage and Rome. Those two bodies, both imperious, both intolerant, were consequently incompatible, since the fundamental system of each was to rule despotically. (RJJJ 3Dial.967/239)[4]

Rousseau counters to them the 'true defenders of theism, of tolerance, or of morality' (ibid.). The same thought, that the *esprit fort* (free thinker) and the *philosophe* are as fanatical as their opponents, is present as early as the *First Discourse* (1D 3/3). Rousseau can no longer stomach the *légèreté* of style and brutish mechanism of content characteristic of those who 'studied the workings of the universe, as they might have studied some machine they had come across, out of sheer curiosity' (Reveries III.1012/48–9). Against them he will call for an attitude of awe and wonder at the spectacle of a divinely ordered purposeful universe. Surprisingly, for those raised on the Enlightenment (and, later, Marxist) critique of religion, Rousseau sees atheism as 'the philosophy of the fortunate of the age' [*la philosophie des heureux du siécle*], (RJJJ 1Dial.727/52) for two reasons. On the one hand, to remove the fear of punishment after death is to remove the last restraint on the rich and the powerful. He had held that view as long ago as the *Letter to d'Alembert* (1758), where he wrote: 'I don't mean . . . that one can be virtuous without religion; I held that erroneous opinion for a long time, but I have been well and truly disabused of it' (Ld'A 89/97). On the other hand, it deprives the weak and exploited of any hope that they may attain some degree of happiness in the hereafter.[5]

In short, Rousseau's religiosity comes from his critical reaction to the ideological forces of his time, the established Christian churches on the one side, and the entrenched powers of materialistic intellectuals on the other. Against the former he uses negative arguments to mount a radical sceptical critique of the dogmas of revealed religion. Against the latter he displays a deep hatred of atheism, materialism and determinism, and advocates a simple theism based on a belief in divine order, individual free will and a personal encounter with a beneficent, sustaining, consoling deity. Here his strategy is more complex and contains a combination of negative and positive arguments.

In the 'Profession of Faith of the Savoyard Vicar' (Em IV.565–635/266–313), Rousseau gives the most sustained expression of those two strands in his thought. It falls into two halves. The first part contains a positive theology, in which the Vicar propounds and defends a minimal natural religion (Em IV.565–606/266–94); in the second, negative, part he criticizes the dogmas of revealed religion (Em IV.606–35/294–313).[6] Voltaire reacted predictably to the 'Profession of Faith'. He approved of the second part, of which he said 'the pages against Christianity are some of the boldest that anyone has ever written'.[7] At the same time he damned the first part with comments like 'what sophistry', 'puerile declamation', 'contradiction', 'extravagant absurdity'.[8]

In what follows, I shall reverse Rousseau's order of presentation, and devote this chapter to Part II of the 'Profession of Faith', the critique of the doctrines of revealed religion, and examine Part I, Rousseau's own version of natural religion, in Chapter XII.

(B)   Rousseau and the Vicar

Modern scholars have followed Masson in holding that the first draft of the 'Profession of Faith', dating from 1757,

> corresponded more closely to Jean-Jacques' deepest feelings. In it, the Vicar appealed to only two masters, the spectacle of nature and the voice of conscience, without subtle discussions or technical philosophy. The dissertations which he later inserted on sensation, judgment, substance, matter and movement were absent from it.[9]

It seems that the 'technical' passages were the subsequent additions, in which Rousseau tried his best to 'straighten things out, once and for all' with the purely intellectual arguments of the *philosophes*.

The positive theology is asserted in three 'Articles of Faith', which are asserted dogmatically and then defended in arguments. Some of these are rationalistic, *ad hominem* engagements with Rousseau's atheistic opponents. Others are less technical expressions of belief based on feelings and transformed perceptions of the world (Em IV.574–94/272–86). In a transitional passage between the first, 'positive', part and the second, 'negative', part of the 'Profession of Faith', the Vicar links theology to morality in a discussion of reason and conscience (Em IV.594–606/286–94).

Although Rousseau puts the 'Profession of Faith' in the mouth of a fictional character, he makes it clear in the *Letter to de Beaumont* that it represents his own views, describing it as 'the best and most useful writing to appear in the age in which I published it'. Indeed he declares that it is the direct expression of his own religious principles:

> I shall state my Religion, because I have one, and I shall state it loudly, because I have the courage to state it . . . Monseigneur, I am a Christian, and sincerely a Christian, according to the doctrine of the Gospels. I am a Christian, not as a disciple of Priests, but as a disciple of Jesus Christ. (LdeB 960)

(C)   The critique of revelation: scripture and interpretation

How is the rational person to attain knowledge of God? One route is to discard books altogether. In the words of the Vicar,

> I . . . closed all the books. There is only one book open to all eyes, that of nature. It is in that great and sublime book that I learn to serve and adore its divine author. No one can be excused for not reading it, for it speaks to all men in a language which is intelligible to all minds.' (Em IV.624–5/306–7).

If we follow the Vicar's reflections, that route will yield the proofs of the existence of God and of the immortality of the soul, and knowledge of God's essential properties. To be a deist is to remain reading the book of nature, which yields such minimal proofs and knowledge. But Rousseau claims to be more than that: 'I am a Christian, not as a disciple of Priests, but as a disciple of Jesus Christ' (LdeB 960). The deist can reach God on a desert island, and come to know, love and serve him, having encountered no one, and having no knowledge of 'what happened in ancient times in a certain corner of the world'. But the Christian claims some specific knowledge beyond that available to all rational people of good will, that is the knowledge of Christ. That is true even of the radical Protestant that Rousseau claims to be, who has by-passed priests and sought direct access to Christ's teaching, needing no human intermediaries to interpret that teaching to him. Once he takes that step beyond the desert island, beyond mere rational religion, he faces the problem that the only way to discover Christ's teaching is through the

Gospels, which are held to deliver first-hand testimony of his message. Protestant believers still encounter one intermediary between themselves and God, the sacred texts, which they themselves must now interpret, individually and directly, without the aid of clergy. Rousseau is wary of the toils of language and often yearns for a moment of direct transparent insight which will by-pass it:

> Our languages are the work of men, and men are limited. Our languages are the work of men, and men are liars. Just as there is no truth so clearly enunciated that one cannot quibble with it, so there is no lie so gross that one cannot support it with some false reasoning . . . (LdeB 971–2)

But there is, in the end, no escape from the need to interpret. How else can we demonstrate the limitations and lies of our opponents? Now Rousseau wants to maintain the absolute autonomy of each interpreter. In his radical Protestantism, there is no place for the authorized interpreter:

> When the Reformers separated themselves from the Roman Church, they accused it of error; and, to correct that error at its source, they gave Scripture another meaning from that which the Church had given it. They were asked on what authority they were thus departing from received doctrine. They replied that it was on their own authority and that of reason. They said that concerning salvation the meaning of the Bible was intelligible and clear to all men, and so everyone was a competent judge of doctrine and could interpret the Bible, which is the rule of salvation, according to his particular mind [*selon son esprit particulier*]; that everyone was in agreement about essential things, and those things about which they might disagree were inessential. Thus the individual's mind [*l'esprit particulier*] was established as the sole interpreter of Scripture; thus the authority of the Church was rejected; thus each person was granted his own jurisdiction over doctrine. Those were the two fundamental points of the Reformation: to recognize the Bible as the rule of one's belief, and to admit no other interpreter of the meaning of the Bible apart from oneself. (LMt 2.712)

These 'two fundamental points' coexist uneasily. The second says that, as an interpreter, one should rely on oneself and on reason. But before one becomes an interpreter, one must accept that there is a privileged text to interpret, one must 'recognize the Bible as the source of one's belief'. But how does that act of recognition come about? Through reason or through revelation? True to his cautious rationalism, Rousseau, speaking through the Vicar, is agnostic about the claim that the Gospels embody revealed truth: 'There are so many reasons for and against that I neither admit it nor reject it, since I don't know how to make up my mind. I reject only the obligation to recognize revelation, since such an alleged obligation is incompatible with God's justice . . .' (Em IV.625/307). On the positive side, 'I admit . . . that the majesty of the Gospel astonishes me, the sanctity of the Gospel speaks to my heart'. The story of the life of Jesus recounted there contrasts so strikingly with that of the life of Socrates, that the one, but not the other, seems marked by the divine stamp, even though Rousseau remains agnostic on the question of whether Christ himself was divine or simply an exemplary human being inspired by God. But on the negative side, the Gospels relate many incredible things which are incompatible with revealed truth (Em IV.627/308).

'What should we do in the midst of all these contradictions?' asks the Vicar. 'We should always be modest and circumspect . . . respect in silence that which we can neither reject nor understand, and be humble before the great Being who alone knows the truth' (ibid.). Burgelin comments on this sentence: 'Here is the unexpected reversal which has so often shocked readers. The Vicar now adheres to a book which claims to be revealed truth, having previously accepted no book apart from the book of nature . . .' But, as Burgelin observes, it is not a complete reversal. Even if the Vicar admits the possibility of revealed truth, it is a revelation filtered through reason and conscience, leaving 'a residue, what is essential. The Gospel is revealed truth when it receives the approval of our conscience, when the person and teaching of Jesus speak to us'.[10]

In Rousseau's idiosyncratic theology, revealed truth speaks to the heart of the individual, directly, and it is the individual, using conscience and reason, who recognizes it in any particular text. We can follow the convolutions of Rousseau's thought in this debate with de Beaumont:

> *However, the Author believes {in the authenticity of the Gospel} only in consequence of human testimonies.* [De Beaumont's words in italics.] You are wrong, Monseigneur; I recognize [its authenticity] in consequence of the Gospel itself and the sublimity I see in it, without further testimony. I do not need anyone to affirm to me that the Gospel exists when I am holding it. *But there are always men who report to him what other men have reported to them.* Not at all; no one reports to me that the Gospel exists; I see it with my own eyes, and even if the whole Universe maintained to me that it does

not exist, I should know perfectly well that the whole universe is lying, or is mistaken. *But how many men stand between God and him?* There is not one. The Gospel is the document [*la pièce*] which decides the matter, and that document is in my hands. In whatever manner it arrived there, and whatever Author wrote it, I recognize the divine spirit in it: that is as immediate as it can be; there are no men between that proof and me; and in the sense in which there were any [intermediaries], historical questions concerning this Holy Book [*l'historique de ce Saint Livre*], its authors, the time when it was written, etc. are part of the critical discussion, in which the moral proof is admissible. (LdeB 994)

Rousseau's response to de Beaumont can be understood best in the light of his view of miracles, discussed below. Rousseau agrees that we are informed that miracles have taken place by human beings who wrote down their testimony in books. Reason tells us that we are justified in doubting that testimony, because miracles, by definition, flout the laws of nature, and we know from reason that the laws of nature are not flouted. At this point, therefore, we are right to engage in a sifting process, involving scholarly examination of 'historical questions concerning this Holy Book', and to attribute divine revelation only to the bits of Scripture which conform to reason and morality:

Doctrine coming from God ought to bear the sacred character of the divinity. Not only should it clarify for us the confused ideas which reasoning draws in our mind, but it should also propound a form of worship, a morality and maxims that are suitable to the attributes with which alone we conceive His essence. (Em IV.613/ 299)

(D)   No original sin

In the eyes of the church, Catholic and Protestant alike, the denial of original sin constituted Rousseau's worst error in theology. In the words of de Beaumont:

The author of the *Emile* proposes an educational plan which, far from being in accordance with Christianity, is not even suited to forming citizens of men . . . ' Let us pose,' says Rousseau, 'as an indisputable maxim, that the first movements of nature are right; there is no original perversity in the human heart.' This language is at complete variance with the doctrine of Holy Scripture and of the Church concerning the revolution which has come about in

our nature . . . Yes, my dear children, there exists within us a
striking mixture of the high and the low, of the desire for the
truth and the taste for error, of the inclination for virtue and the
tendency for vice . . . an astonishing contrast: and revelation
discloses to us the source of that contrast in the deplorable Fall of
our first father.[11]

Far from disputing this charge, Rousseau repeatedly accepts it. The
Emile opens with the words: 'Everything is good as it leaves the
hands of the Author of things; everything degenerates in the hands
of man' (Em I.245/37). In his summary of its contents, Rousseau
says that that denial of original sin is the *Leitmotiv* of the whole book,
which is 'simply a treatise on the original goodness of man, destined
to show how vice and error, strangers to his constitution, are introduced to it from outside and corrupt it imperceptibly' (RJJJ
3Dial.934/213).

Rousseau brings a series of arguments against the doctrine. First,
he says, it explains less than his own naturalistic account of human
degeneration does: 'We are, you say, sinners because of the sin of our
first father. But why was our first father himself a sinner?'(LdeB
939) He expands that rhetorical question into two further ones:
'Why should the same reason by which you will explain his sin be
not [equally] applicable to his descendants without reference to original sin? And why should we impute an injustice to God, by making ourselves sinners, liable to punishment for the vice acquired at
birth, whereas our first father was a sinner and punished, without
it?' (ibid.). From that he concludes that 'Original sin explains everything except its principle, and it is that principle that needs to be
explained':

You can only see man in the hands of the Devil, whereas I see how
he fell into his hands; according to you, the cause of evil is our
corrupted nature, but that very corruption is an evil for which we
need to find the cause. Man was [originally] created good; I
believe we both agree on that. But you say that he is wicked
because he has been wicked [in the past]. Whereas I show how he
has [become] wicked. In your opinion, which of us is more
successful in reaching the basic principle [we seek]? (LdeB 940)

Rousseau claims that the doctrine is doubly inconsistent. As an
explanation, it is not needed to explain the sin of Adam, whereas it is
needed to explain the sin of his descendants, yet there is no difference in the phenomenon to be explained, human sin. It also involves
a moral or legal inconsistency, since, according to it, God punishes

arbitrarily, allotting the same punishment to the first sinner, who had no excuse, and to all later sinners, who have at least the *prima facie* excuse that, having inherited sin, their freedom of choice was more limited than Adam's. If these charges of inconsistency are relatively trivial, it is because they are simply components of the central and most important charge, that, if the doctrine were true, then God would be guilty not only of procedural injustice, but of grave substantive injustice, in punishing one person for a crime committed by another. For believers in original sin 'would prefer to make God unjust and to punish the innocent for their father's sin, rather than to renounce their barbarous dogma' (Em IV.624/306).

Finally, the doctrine of original sin is morally debilitating, since it allows us to shift the responsibility for our wickedness from ourselves to God. Rousseau's own naturalism, in contrast, has more explanatory power, is more honest and more conducive to self-improvement:

> If, even in the state of abasement which we are in during this life, all our first inclinations are legitimate, and if all our vices come to us from ourselves, why do we complain of being subjugated by them? Why do we reproach the Author of things for the evils we do to ourselves and for the enemies we arm against ourselves? (Em IV.604/292–3)

But if there is no original sin and human beings are entirely responsible for their own 'abasement', we must then explain the mechanism of that 'abasement' in human terms. Burgelin poses the problem thus:

> The 'state of abasement' is our union with our body. Once that is recognized, the doctrine of the *Emile* remains true: our fallen nature remains good at first. We are not naturally corrupted. But how do our vices come from us ourselves? Who is this *us*? Is it collective or singular? In what follows Rousseau seems to hesitate between the two interpretations. Man [*l'homme*] is spoilt by men [*les hommes*], whose 'first corruption comes from their will', and that would imply some kind of radical evil, in the Kantian sense. But there is a less extreme position, which is that our downfall comes from our weakness: 'I have always the power to will, but not always the force to exercise it' (Em IV.586). And this weakness in turn comes from our socialization and our education.[12]

At one end of the spectrum, the Vicar explains vice as the victory of the body, enslaved by passions, over the soul, endowed with free will:

> I always have the power to will, I do not always have the force to execute. When I abandon myself to temptations, I act according to the impulsion of external objects. When I reproach myself for this weakness, I listen only to my will. I am enslaved because of my vices and free because of my remorse. The sentiment of my freedom is effaced in me only when I become depraved and finally prevent the voice of the soul from being raised against the law of the body. (Em IV.586/280)

This end of the spectrum is that of Kantian duty, the realm of virtue which is always 'a state of war'. At the other end of the spectrum is the naturalism of the morality of the senses. Here Rousseau explains that changes in the psychology of human beings are brought about by changes in their institutions. The source of their downfall lies in 'the contradictions of the social system . . . *man* is naturally good and . . . it is by these institutions alone that *men* become wicked' (LMa 1135–6/575, italics added). At both ends of the spectrum individual human beings are free, their choices are not governed by deterministic laws. At the Kantian end, Rousseau focuses on the individual and on the struggle between two conflicting drives within the individual. At the naturalistic end, he focuses on the social environments within which the individual makes every choice. As at the Kantian end, individuals do not lose their free will, but the range of objects of choice expands and contracts in different natural and social environments. That is Rousseau's naturalist, gradualist version of the Fall:

> Men are wicked; sad and continual experience spares the need for proof. However man is naturally good; I believe I have demonstrated it. What then can have depraved him to this extent, if not the changes that have befallen his constitution, the progress he has made and the knowledge he has acquired? (2D, note IX, 202/74)

Though the basic elements of human nature remain the same, the drive to self-preservation becomes ever more anti-social and exploitative, as it is channelled through increasingly inegalitarian social relations. Rousseau rejects original sin at both Kantian and naturalistic poles. At the Kantian pole he remains closer to traditional Christianity in seeing the Fall as the victory of the body over the spirit, whereas at the naturalistic pole he stresses the interaction between individuals and their societies and their natural environments. At both poles, human free will is an absolute datum and the 'Fall' from human goodness is explained in wholly human terms, without reference to God.

In short, de Beaumont is right in holding that Rousseau's 'educational plan' is not 'in accordance with Christianity', but fails to substantiate his second charge that it is 'not even suited to forming citizens of men'.[13] To do that, one would need a more powerful armoury than a dogmatic reassertion of the traditional doctrine of the Fall.

(E)   No personal providence

Like the general will, providence, for Rousseau, operates at the level of the whole, the universal, the universe, not at the level of the individual. Rousseau expounds this view in his *Letter to Voltaire*, a response to the latter's *Poems on the Lisbon Disaster and on Natural Law* (1756), in which Voltaire saw in the Lisbon earthquake further proof that pessimism, not optimism, is the rational attitude to adopt to the fate of the world, a view which he would later expound in his satirical masterpiece, *Candide*. In one of his rare jokes, Rousseau writes that he was 'struck by the sight of this poor man [Voltaire] prostrated, so to speak, by riches and glory for constantly declaiming bitterly against the miseries of this life and always finding that all was bad' (Conf IX.429/360). It was then that Rousseau

> formed the crazy project of bringing him back to his senses and proving that all was well. Voltaire, while always appearing to believe in God, has always only really believed in the Devil, since his so-called God is just a malefactor who, according to him, takes pleasure only in harming us. (ibid.)

In his *Letter to Voltaire*, Rousseau holds that evils of two sorts befall human beings, moral and physical. The source of moral evils is 'man, free, perfected, and therefore corrupted': a rapid summary of Rousseau's naturalist version of the Fall. Physical evils, on the other hand, are inevitable, since human beings have a dual nature, spiritual and material, and matter is subject to destruction. But even physical evils are often the result of human activity. In the case of the earthquake, 'nature didn't assemble 20,000 inhabitants in six or seven storey blocks'.

The argument here is hardly at a high level. Rousseau becomes more serious later in the Letter, as he attacks Diderot's indeterminacy thesis, considered above, and as he transforms the unrealistic

245

slogan that 'all is well' [*tout est bien*] into his own thesis that 'the whole is well' [*le tout est bien*]. He mounts this thesis with a crude instrumentalism of whole and parts, in which the good of the 'system' as a whole takes precedence over its parts:

> No doubt this material universe should not be dearer to its Author than a single thinking or feeling being. But the system of this universe which produces, conserves and perpetuates all the thinking and feeling beings must be dearer to him than one of those beings. Despite his goodness, or rather because of his very goodness, he can therefore sacrifice something of the happiness of individuals for the conservation of the whole. (LV 1067)

He proceeds with a little speculative science fiction:

> I believe and I hope that I am worth more in the eyes of God than the surface of a planet. But if the planets are inhabited, as they probably are, why should I be worth more in his eyes than all the inhabitants of Saturn? . . . for God the conservation of the universe seems to have a morality which is multiplied by the number of inhabited worlds. (ibid.)

Rousseau's theodicy hinges on 'the addition of an article', so that 'instead of *all is well* [*tout est bien*], it would perhaps be better to say *the whole is good* [*le tout est bien*] . . .' (LV 1068). This allows Rousseau to distance himself from the mockery of optimism of Voltaire's *Candide*, in which Panglosse absurdly repeats 'all is well', despite mounting evidence to the contrary. In this context, Rousseau's God is modelled on his political sovereign, ruling impersonally through the Empire of the Laws:

> We should believe that the *particular events* [italics added] have no significance in the eyes of the Master of the universe, that his Providence is only universal, that he is content to conserve genera and species, without worrying himself about how each individual passes his short life. (LV 1069)

Rousseau maintains his optimism against Voltaire by attributing to God two separate functions. His first function is to maximize the good of the whole, from a distance, indifferent to the fate of individual human beings. His second function is to judge, reward and punish individuals in the afterlife. These two functions are not strictly incompatible. But they do represent different perspectives on the personal involvement of God in the affairs of mortals. Reflecting on the analogy between divine and political rule, one might be surprised to find God operating as sovereign legislator, concerned only with the universal, when performing his first function, but as judge and enforcement agent, addressing the minutiae of particular merit and guilt, in performing his second function.

(F)   No miracles. Prayer as rational communication, not entreaty

Like Rousseau's sovereign, Rousseau's God presides over a rationally ordered domain. Rousseau thinks it unlikely that God should make piecemeal dispensations from the laws of nature so that particular miracles can take place, or that he should respond to particular entreaties from those who pray to him.

Rousseau offers a classic rationalist argument against miracles in the third *Letter from the Mountain*. He begins with a definition: 'A miracle is an immediate act of divine power in a particular event, an observable change in the order of nature, a real and visible exception to nature's laws' (LMt 3.736). Given that definition, Rousseau poses two questions: 'First, can God perform miracles? that is, can he depart from the laws which he has established?' The answer to that question is clearly 'yes', since if God is omnipotent, it is within his power to follow or depart from his own rules. 'Second, does God want to perform miracles?' To this question, Rousseau begins with an impatient expression of agnosticism: 'This question is entirely irrelevant to our concerns. It does not affect the glory of God, whose plans we cannot fathom.' He then becomes more openly sceptical: 'I'll go further: if it could make any difference to our faith . . . the greatest ideas we could have of divine wisdom and majesty would tend to a negative reply, counteracted only by human pride.' The question then amounts to one concerning the credibility of testimony: 'When a mortal person comes along and declares obstinately that he has seen a miracle, he puts an end to further questions. You must simply judge whether you believe his word! There are thousands of claimants whom I should not believe.' But even if we accept as accurate the report of the observed event:

> Allowing that the facts have been established with all possible certainty, we must then distinguish what the senses can affirm from what reason can conclude from the testimony of the senses. Since a miracle is an exception to the laws of nature, we must know those laws in order to judge it, and in order to judge it surely, we must know them all. For a single law which one did not know could, in certain cases unknown to the onlookers, change the effect of the laws that one did know. So someone who

pronounces that such and such an act is a miracle is claiming to know all the laws of nature and to know that this act is an exception to them. But who is the mortal who knows all the laws of nature? Newton never boasted of knowing them all. A wise man who has witnessed an unheard of event can testify that he has seen that event and that people are entitled to believe him. But no wise man on earth will ever affirm that a particular event, however astonishing it may be, is a miracle, for how could he know it? (LMt 3.738)

In short, 'miracles are . . . proofs for simple people, for whom the laws of nature form a very narrow circle around them' (LMt 3.742–3). In this context, Rousseau's belief in the powers of science is limitless:

The constant discoveries which are being made about the laws of nature . . . the past, present and future progress of human industry; the different limits which peoples lay down to the extent of possibilities, according to their greater or lesser enlightenment, all of this proves to us that we cannot know what those limits are. Yet for a miracle to be a real one, it must exceed those limits. Whether there are or are not miracles, the wise man cannot know whether any event that might take place is or is not one. (LMt 3.744)

Rousseau's scepticism about miracles runs deep. On the one hand he feels that it is incompatible with God's dignity that he should interfere with his own law-governed universe, as though he were an arbitrary sovereign. On the other hand, since it is not logically impossible that an omnipotent God should break his own laws, and that miracles could therefore take place, it would still be impossible for a finite mind to know, rather than surmise, that a particular anomaly would not yet be fitted into a broader explanatory pattern, as an instance of a more fully formulated law.

Given his views on providence and miracles, Rousseau's attitude to prayer is not wholly surprising. The Vicar says:

I practice sublime contemplation. I meditate on the order of the universe, not in order to explain it by vain systems but to admire it constantly, to worship the wise Author who makes himself felt in it. I converse with Him; I fill all my faculties with his divine essence; I am moved by His benefactions; I bless Him for his gifts. But I do not pray to Him. What would I ask of Him? That He change the course of things for me, that He perform miracles in my favor. I who ought to love, above all, the order established by His wisdom and maintained by His providence, would I want this order to be disturbed for me? (Em IV.605/293)

Superstitious people, when they pray, entreat God to interfere with his order for their own particular purposes, just as subjects of an arbitrary despot entreat their superior to waive his rules for their particular advantage. Rousseau in contrast engages with God in 'conversation', not with an equal, but with a rational, omnipotent sovereign, who ordains rational laws, and in whose legislative power rational subjects can freely participate, by identifying their individual selves with God's sovereign, rational will.

XII

Positive Theology: Natural Religion Defended

We turn now to Rousseau's own positive theology, his eccentric version of minimal theism, infused by the personal commitment of a pietistic protestant Christian. The three articles of faith of the Savoyard Vicar will be our principal source, but we shall also make use of other texts, including letters and *Julie, ou la Nouvelle Héloïse*. Even though Rousseau does present his own positive views here, he still does so in his characteristic elusive style, critically, defensively, *ad hominem*, and often concealed behind a *persona ficta*.

(A)   Article I: 'A will moves the universe'

The opening pages of the 'Profession of Faith' (Em IV.565–73/266–72) contain the Vicar's fictional autobiography, followed by the philosophy of mind which we examined at the end of Chapter II. Building on the latter, the Vicar proceeds directly into metaphysical and theological reflections:

> Having, so to speak, made certain of myself, I begin to look outside of myself, and I consider myself with a sort of shudder, cast out and lost in this vast universe, as if drowned in the immensity of beings, without knowing anything about what they are either in themselves or in relation to me. I study them, I observe them, and the first object which presents itself to me for comparison with them is myself. (Em IV.573/272)

From this he argues against the view that the universe as a whole is 'a great animal which moves of itself' (Em IV.575/273). Focusing on himself, and then extrapolating, he finds in the material universe 'none of that freedom which appears in the spontaneous movement

250

of man and animals'. He adds the premiss that 'every movement that is not produced by another can come only from a spontaneous act'. And from that he derives his first 'dogma', or article of faith, that 'a will moves the universe and animates nature' (Em IV.576/273). This is a rough argument, but it is an argument. The Vicar admits that dualism is obscure, but responds that materialism yields an unresolved dilemma in response to the question whether motion is essential to matter. If it is, then matter cannot be at rest, which is absurd, so materialism is false. If it is not, then motion must come from something other than matter, so the universe contains a non-material substance, so materialism is false.

The Vicar seems not to be confident that this dilemma will settle the argument with scientists working with more sophisticated notions of force and fields. He now dismisses as meaningless 'those vague words *universal force* and *necessary motion*', but that suggests that he has not yet shown the absurdity of the first horn of the dilemma, according to which motion is essential to matter. For him, as for Descartes, 'motion is nothing other than the idea of transport from one place to another', in other words, a mere accident of matter. His second attempt to refute the idea of necessary motion is more detailed but more obscure than his first. He poses a new dilemma:

Does all the matter in a body have a uniform motion, or does each atom have its own movement? According to the former idea, the whole universe ought to form a solid and indivisible mass. According to the latter, it ought to form only a scattered and incoherent fluid without it ever being possible for two atoms to join. (Em IV.577/274)

The Vicar holds that the idea of essential motion is incoherent. As he understands it, if a body, macro or micro, has essential motion, then it is tracked in one and only one direction, whether that tracking operates by final or efficient cause. He seems to accept from Descartes that there is no vacuum, but to reject Descartes' mechanics of motion through vortices. From that arises the first horn of the dilemma. The second horn arises from taking atomism seriously, while rejecting, as 'jargon of metaphysics', any theory of fields or forces which would explain the way in which atoms hang together to form macro bodies. Once one reaches even this level of detail, it is clear that Rousseau takes the scientific arguments seriously, even though materialist scientists would not be alarmed by the rough-hewn dilemmas which are claimed to face them.

251

(B)   Article II: 'Matter moved according to certain laws shows me an
intelligence'. Rousseau vs. Diderot

The Vicar makes the transition from the first to the second Article
thus: 'If moved matter shows me a will, matter moved according to
certain laws shows me an intelligence' (Em IV.578/275). Thus the
Vicar embarks on his version of the traditional argument from
design, one which preoccupied Rousseau and to which he returned
many times, both in his published work and in his correspondence.
He proceeds negatively via a critique of the argument, popularized
by Diderot, that order could be the outcome of disorder, that the
ordered universe could emerge from the random interactions of
pieces of matter. Rousseau had been attracted by a form of that
argument in the *Second Discourse*, in which he made repeated use of
the vocabulary of determination by chance: 'the fortuitous concur-
rence of many extraneous causes' [*le concours fortuit de plusieurs causes
étrangeres*]', 'the different accidents' [*différens hazards*], 'the surprising
power of very trivial causes' (2D 162/42).[1] The same vocabulary is
present in the *Essay on the Origin of Languages*, Chapter 9[2]: 'Human
associations are to a great extent the result of accidents of nature;
floods . . . overflowing seas, volcanic eruptions, earthquakes . . .'
(EOL ch.9.402/267–8). But the *Essay* departs from the naturalism of
the *Second Discourse* in one particular, the hypothesis introduced not
entirely without seriousness, that 'He who wanted men to be sociable touched the axis of the globe with his finger and inclined it
relative to the axis of the universe' (EOL ch.9.401/266).[3] The different climates and seasons of the different latitudes of the earth are
caused by the tilt of the earth's axis relative to the sun. That was
common knowledge in the eighteenth century. But did that tilt take
place at a moment in history? That question divided *Encyclopédistes*
from religious believers. Amongst the former, Buffon answered 'no',
holding that the earth has always been so tilted.[4] Rousseau in contrast answers 'yes', albeit ironically, and in this respect takes his
distance from his erstwhile friends in the *Encyclopédie*, and departs for
once from his scepticism about miracles.[5]

But his concession to religious orthodoxy is minimal. The image
of the touch of God's finger suggests that divine intervention is only
momentary. The tilt of the earth's axis causes extremes of climate in
different zones. That, along with particular geographical disasters,
concentrates populations in favourable environments. Thereafter, all
subsequent miseries of humanity are explained in naturalistic terms,
as human beings, with their limited intellectual and moral
resources, mishandle the arts and sciences, become embroiled in the
play of exploitation and degenerate *amour-propre*, as they respond

without much foresight to the contingent problems posed by nature.[6] Yet the introduction of God, even in this hypothetical, light-hearted passage, points to a change of emphasis.[7]

Let us begin by distinguishing two different interpretations of the idea of determination by chance, expressed in the vocabulary of 'many small causes'. On the first, weak, interpretation, the micro causes are so small that it is impossible to determine the causal chain determining a given macro event; it is not just contingently impossible, but necessarily impossible, for a finite investigator, even though it would be possible for an infinite investigator, *a fortiori* it would be possible for the infinite creator of the causal chain, God. On the second, strong, interpretation, there is a radical indeterminacy at the heart of the universe; this would mean that certain events or classes of events occur at random; they are radically undetermined in the eyes of finite and infinite investigator alike. This appears to be Diderot's position in *Pensée philosophique* no.21:

I open the notebooks of a celebrated professor, and I read: 'Atheists, I'll grant you that movement is essential to matter. But what do you infer from this? That the world is the result of the random throw of atoms? You might as well tell me that Homer's *Iliad* or Voltaire's *Henriade* is the result of the random throw of letters.' Now I should be wary about granting the atheist this argument, since he could exploit the analogy to his advantage. For, according to the laws of probability, the atheist will reply, one should not be surprised by the occurrence of any possible event, and in throwing dice the unlikeliness of an outcome is counterbalanced by the number of throws. If I correctly calculate the odds, I can figure how many times I shall have to throw a thousand dice in order to get a thousand sixes. Imagine that someone proposed to generate the *Iliad* by chance, by throwing down a finite number of letters. Whatever that number of letters were, there would be some finite number of throws on which I could make a winning bet concerning a successful outcome. And my win would be infinitely certain if I were given an infinite number of throws. You will agree with me, he will continue, that matter has existed for all eternity and that movement is essential to it. Since you have granted me that, I shall respond by granting you that the world is without limits; that there is an infinite number of atoms; and that this astonishing order holds universally. Given these reciprocal admissions, it does not follow that the possibility of generating the universe by chance is very small. It follows rather that, if the number of throws is infinite, then the unlikeliness of the outcome is more than sufficiently counterbalanced by the number of the throws. Now, since matter has been in motion from all eternity, and since there may well be an infinite number of admirable arrangements in the infinite total of possible combinations, the supposition that is repugnant to reason is that one of those admirable arrangements should never have been realized in the infinite series of arrangements which have succeeded one another. Therefore our minds should be more astonished by the supposed duration of chaos than by the real birth of the [ordered] universe.[8]

As we have seen, Rousseau's reaction to the idea of determination by chance shifts. While he never clearly distinguishes the two interpretations, it is evident that in the *Second Discourse* he is attracted by at least the weak interpretation, whether or not he would also have accepted the strong. After his return to religion, he explicitly rejects the strong interpretation and asserts that the universe is an ordered, determinate whole. He infers from its orderliness that its order is to be explained teleologically, that it is the outcome of God's rational ordering. La Mettrie rapidly identified that false inference, as we shall see in a moment.

In the *Essay on the Origin of Languages* Rousseau's thought is in transition. Radical contingency is asserted alongside divine intervention. By 1756, in the *Letter to Voltaire on Optimism*, Rousseau is arguing against indeterminism, holding that 'apparent irregularities' in nature 'undoubtedly come from certain laws of which we are ignorant and which nature follows as faithfully as it does those which we know', and that 'the strangest curve [*la courbe la plus bizarre*] . . . is as regular to the eyes of nature as is the perfect circle to ours' (LV 1064–6). For every event there *is* a cause, for every apparently chaotic phenomenon there *is* an underlying patterned schema. Rousseau simply rejects a distinction between events which have effects and events which have no effects. For him all events have effects, but 'the smallness of the causes often renders their examination ridiculous'. Equally unthinkable is the idea of 'events without cause; which is repugnant to all philosophy'. Rousseau now attributes the difficulty of determining or predicting causal connections to our limited powers of observation, as finite investigators. The *combination* of many micro causes can produce a macro event: 'several almost imperceptible effects [*sic*] unite to produce a considerable event', and though the dust raised by the carriage on the road does not affect the progress of the carriage, yet, 'since there is nothing unconnected to the universe [*rien d'étranger à l'univers*], everything which happens in it necessarily has an effect on the universe itself.'

In a fragment of the letter to Voltaire,[9] Rousseau makes an explicit criticism of Diderot's *Pensée philosophique* no.21, which he calls 'the work . . . which has struck me most forcefully in all my life' (LV 1071). Rousseau's first criticism is that Diderot's argument depends on the assumption that:

> movement is necessary [to matter] something which no one in this dispute has ever emphasized strongly enough for my liking; as far as I am concerned, I state that I do not know of any response containing the slightest bit of common sense which would verify or falsify the hypothesis. But I do know that one should deny as a falsehood what one cannot know, namely that movement is essential to matter. (ibid.)

In reaction to Diderot's hypothesis, Rousseau reasserts his faith in order and teleology, but refuses to engage in further rationalistic discussion of the question. Since the question is not soluble by reason, it is best to admit agnosticism. The truly rational thing to do at this point is, paradoxically, to abandon reason and retreat to feeling.

> But the difference between these two opposed positions is that while both seem to me to be equally plausible, I am persuaded only by the second. As to the first, if you come and tell me that the *Henriade* was composed by throwing down letters at random, I will deny it without consideration. (ibid.)

Why will he deny it? The explanation is not entirely clear: 'I feel that there is a point where, for me, the moral impossibilities yield a physical certainty' (ibid.). It would appear to mean that it is 'morally', i.e. psychologically, impossible for him to believe so implausible a thesis, and, in the absence of a decisive proof, it is reasonable to conclude that its falsity is 'physically' certain, i.e. that the real world was certainly not the outcome of random movements.

Rousseau approaches the terms of Diderot's argument again for a moment, but only to abandon them:

> You can talk in vain about the eternity of time, for I have never passed through it; of the infinite number of throws, for I have never counted them; and my incredulity, however unphilosophical it may be, will still triumph over the demonstration itself. (ibid.)

He recognizes that this move will not satisfy his opponents. But he suggests that we have here reached a question posed within the scientific debate which science itself is incapable of answering, and that it is therefore rational (or at least not irrational) to move to another level of 'proof', the 'proof from feeling' [*preuve de sentiment*]:

> I do not deny that what I call a *proof from feeling* will be called *prejudice* by my opponents. I do not propose this stubbornness of belief as a model. But, with a perhaps unparallelled good faith, I present it as an invincible disposition of my soul, which nothing will ever be able to overcome. (ibid.)

Rousseau's second criticism is the more specific one, that determination by chance cannot explain the origin of living matter ('the generation of organized bodies') and the connected question of the 'perpetuation of germs'. These problems, which Rousseau says (rightly in 1756) had not been explained by materialism, were arousing passionate debate within the scientific and generally cultivated community of the time, and were to concern Diderot in particular some years later.[10] But Rousseau adds little to that debate in his rapid comments here.

Rousseau returns to the *Pensée philosophique* no.21 several times.[11] In the longer version of the same argument, in the 'Profession of Faith', Rousseau addresses the two themes of Diderot's thought, the explicit theme of the emergence of order out of chance, and the inexplicit theme of the emergence of the organic out of the inorganic:

> They can talk to me all they want about combination and chance. Of what use is it to you to reduce me to silence if you cannot lead me to persuasion, and how can you take away from me the involuntary sentiment that always gives you the lie in spite of myself? If organized bodies were combined fortuitously in countless ways before taking on constant forms, if at the outset there were formed stomachs without mouths, feet without heads, hands without arms, imperfect organs of every kind which have perished for want of being able to preserve themselves, why do none of these unformed attempts strike our glance any longer, why did nature finally prescribe laws to itself to which it was not subjected at the outset? I should not, I agree, be surprised that a thing happens, if it is possible and the difficulty of its occurrence is compensated for by the number of throws of the dice. Nevertheless if someone were to come to me and say that print thrown at random had produced the *Aeneid* all in order, I would not deign to take a step to verify the lie. 'You forget,' I shall be told, 'the number of throws.' But how many of those throws must

I assume in order to make the combination credible? As for me, seeing only a single throw, I can give odds of infinity to one that what it produced is not the result of chance. Consider also that combination and chance will never result in anything but products of the same nature as the elements that are combined; that organization and life will not result from a throw of atoms; and that a chemist combining mixtures will not make them feel in his crucible. (Em IV.579/275–6)

Now Rousseau evidently dislikes both determinism by chance and the iron determinism of d'Holbach, La Mettrie and later Laplace. Both make God redundant. Iron determinism is incompatible with human freedom, understood as the expression of an autonomous will, while determination by chance leaves only a vestigial role for the will to play. Determination by chance was the scientific theory currently at the centre of scientific, and general cultivated, debate. But determination by chance, at least in the strong version distinguished above, and iron determinism represent incompatible theses. Rousseau does not address the latter until Article III of the 'Profession of Faith'. At this point, in concentrating exclusively on determination by chance, he leaves it open for the iron determinist to make the obvious objection, which La Mettrie does make in *L'homme machine*: 'in destroying chance, we do not thereby prove the existence of a supreme Being, since there could be something which was neither chance nor God, I mean Nature.'[12] As La Mettrie observes, *tertium datur*: for him, and for d'Holbach, the world is ordered deterministically by a nexus of efficient causes, and by efficient causes alone, even if some of those causes escape the finite investigator.

The importance of the Vicar's second article of faith is now clear. Rousseau sees Diderot's idea of determination by chance as the most serious contender for the ground previously occupied by the argument from design. In order to reconstitute that argument, Rousseau must first refute *Pensée philosophique* no.21. But even if he succeeds in doing that, he still leaves the ground open to the iron determinists. In retrospect, in the light of modern physics and mathematics, the determinists' reoccupation of that space looks less secure. This does not mean that the argument from design is any more secure now than it was then. But it does mean that the stand-off between Rousseau and his opponents on this issue is not resolved. Serious scientists are prepared to treat the argument from design with respect, and for reasons not so different from those adduced by Rousseau.

The argument of Article II is very cautious. The Vicar finds a harmony in the universe, even though he does not know 'why the universe exists'. He is like the man who sees 'a watch opened for the first time' and says:

> I do not know what . . . the whole is good for, but I do see that each piece is made for the others; I admire the workman in the details of the work; and I am quite sure that these wheels are moving in harmony only for a common end which it is impossible for me to perceive. (Em IV.578/275)

At the conclusion of the article he maintains that the world is governed by a powerful and wise will, but dismisses further speculation about whether it is created or eternal, those questions being 'useless to [his] conduct and superior to [his] reason' (Em IV.580–1/276–7).[13]

(C) Article III: 'Man is . . . free in his actions and as such is animated by an immaterial substance'

When the Vicar argues for the immortality of the soul, he uses first an argument from feeling, then an argument from reason, and the two follow one another without a break. Here is the argument from feeling:

> If the soul is immaterial, it can survive the body; and if it survives the body, providence is justified. If I had no proof of the immateriality of the soul other than the triumph of the wicked and the oppression of the just in this world, that alone would prevent me from doubting it. So shocking a dissonance in the universal harmony would make me seek to resolve it. I would say to myself, 'Everything does not end with life for us; everything returns to order at death.' (Em IV.590/283)

But the proof from feeling, even if we accept its premisses, leads to no very precise conclusions about the afterlife. The Vicar's reflections continue: 'I believe that the soul survives the body long enough for the maintenance of order. Who knows whether that is long enough for it to last for ever?' (ibid.). In Burgelin's words, the proof 'implies survival, but not exactly immortality'.[14] For it requires only that wrongs should be righted after death, not that they should be righted by eternal punishment.

Rousseau is uncertain about the whole question of recompense in the afterlife. When he focuses on the political significance of religion, he seems to maintain a simple, even primitive, belief in heaven and hell.

At the very end of Part II of the 'Profession of Faith', in a lengthy footnote, he introduces the image of Poul-Serrho:

> The Mohammedans say . . . that after the examination which will follow the universal resurrection, all the bodies will pass over a bridge called Poul-Serrho which crosses over the eternal fire . . . it is here that the separation of the good from the wicked will be made . . .
>
> Should I believe that the idea of this bridge, which corrects so many iniquities, never prevents any? If one took this idea away from the Persians by persuading them that there is no Poul-Serrho or any place like it where the oppressed wreak vengeance on their tyrants after death, is it not clear that this would put the latter very much at their ease and would deliver them from the care of placating these unfortunates? . . . Philosopher, your moral laws are very fine, but I beg you to show me their sanction. Stop beating around the bush for a moment, and tell me plainly what you put in the place of Poul-Serrho. (Em IV.634.Fn/313.Fn)

Atheism, Rousseau holds, is the 'convenient philosophy of the fortunate and rich who make their paradise in this world'. It both deprives their victims of 'hope and consolation' (RJJJ 2Dial.971/241) and 'delivers tyrants from the only brake suited to restrain them' (JNH V.5.592/485). Rousseau returns often to the thought that fear of hell is the only brake on the passions of the mighty and wicked, some of whom maintain vestiges of religious faith, undergo torments of fear on their deathbeds, and may even make tardy repentance. Occasionally other villains have witnessed these 'final moments of their accomplices', which have 'often served as a brake for the imposters' (RJJJ 3Dial.968/239). But that happens rarely, since a conspiracy of secrecy prevents such scenes from acting as effective deterrents. Atheism then is not only a 'desolating' system, but a dangerous one, which reinforces a régime of violence, inequality and oppression.

The prospect of Poul-Serrho is important even for the normal moral agent, not rich, powerful and vicious, but weak-willed and more or less egotistical, who will always be fallible once they are in possession of Gyges' ring. Without the internalized fear of the all-seeing eye of God, such people will succumb to temptation when there is no fear of discovery here on earth. Morality, in short, requires religion as its ultimate sanction: 'I do not mean . . . that one can be virtuous without religion; I held that erroneous opinion for a long time, but now I am only too disabused' (Ld'A 89/97Fn). So Rousseau does not introduce religion in his educational programme until

Book IV of the *Emile*, when his pupil has reached the stage of moral behaviour, when he finally understands 'what is proper and good'. With religion:

> How many new means we have for speaking to his heart! It is only then that he finds his true interest in being good far from the sight of men and without being forced by the laws, in maintaining justice between God and himself, and in fulfilling his duty even at the expense of his life, and in carrying virtue in his heart. He does this not only for the love of order, to which each of us always prefers love of self, but for the love of the Author of his being – a love which is compounded with that same love of self – and finally for the enjoyment of that durable happiness which the repose of a good conscience and the contemplation of this Supreme Being promise him in the other life after he has spent this one well. Abandon this, and I no longer see anything but injustice, hypocrisy and lying among men. Private interest, which in case of conflict necessarily prevails over everything, teaches everyone to adorn vice with the mask of virtue. Let all other men do what is good for me at their expense; let everything be related to me alone; let all mankind, if need be, die in suffering and poverty to spare me a moment of pain or hunger. This is the inner language of every unbeliever who reasons. Yes, I shall maintain it all my life. Whoever speaks otherwise although he has said in his heart, 'There is no God', is nothing but a liar or a fool. (Em IV.636–7/314–15)

This last epigram is repeated in slightly different forms in many passages. Rousseau says, for instance: 'Take away eternal justice and the prolongation of my being after this life, and I see in virtue nothing but a madness to which one gives a beautiful name' (Letter to Carondelet, 4 March 1764, CC 19#3166, p. 199), and 'If the divinity does not exist, it is only the wicked man who reasons, and the good man is nothing but a fool' (Em IV.602/291).

But when reflecting on the soul in a more personal vein, Rousseau, both in his own voice and in that of the Vicar, is far less dogmatic. On rewards, the Vicar comments: 'I don't say that the good will be rewarded; for what good can an excellent being attain other than to exist according to its nature?' (Em IV.591/284). Rousseau also refuses to commit himself to any doctrine of eternal punishment. He is most sceptical in his *Letter to Voltaire*: 'I have the good fortune to believe [in the immortality of the soul], even though I know that reason can doubt it, . . . [but] in the eternity of punishments, neither you nor I nor anyone who thinks well of God will ever believe' (LV 1070). He makes the Vicar sound slightly more agnostic:

> And don't . . . ask me if the torments of the wicked will be eternal; I don't know, and I don't have the vain curiosity to clarify useless questions. What difference does it make to me what will become of the wicked? I take little interest in their fate. However I have difficulty in believing that they are condemned to endless torments. If supreme justice does take vengeance, it does so beginning in this life . . . It is in your insatiable hearts, eaten away by envy, avarice and ambition, that the avenging passions punish your heinous crimes in the bosom of your false prosperity. What need is there to look for hell in the other life? It begins in this one in the hearts of the wicked. (Em IV.591–2/284)

But in 'naturalizing' the doctrine with the rhetorical question: 'What need is there for hell in the other life?', he has taken us a long way from the bridge of Poul-Serrho. For, at that stage of the proof from feeling, the wicked and powerful are utterly corrupted by their worldly prosperity. As a result they are enslaved to their passions, which in turn bring with them all the torments of 'envy, avarice and ambition'. But those very passions, far from acting as a deterrent to the wicked, merely spur them on to worse excesses. In that state of corruption, the only possible deterrent lies beyond the grave. So the Vicar's hypothetical hell on earth cannot perform the role demanded by the proof.

Madame de Warens, Rousseau relates in the *Confessions*, adopted a compromise position, which he describes with ironic indulgence:[15]

> What was bizarre was that, although she did not believe in Hell, she did not fail to believe in Purgatory. This came from her not knowing what to do with the souls of the wicked, since she could not either damn them or put them with the good until they had become such; and one must admit that the wicked are always very vexing both in this world and in the other. (Conf VI.229/192)

In Maman's compromise position, the prospect of a finite period in Purgatory might perhaps deter the wicked. But in traditional theology only those who had committed venial sins went to Purgatory, to undergo a limited term of punishment before admission to Paradise. Maman's Purgatory seems to admit those who have committed the most grievous mortal sins. We do not know whether they too were ultimately destined for Paradise or for extinction. In either case, Maman's Purgatory might be insufficiently fearful to deter the truly wicked. Neither she, nor the Vicar, nor Rousseau himself give further answers.

The Vicar adds a more traditional argument from reason for the immortality, rather than mere survival, of the soul, and comments that, though he may be only half persuaded by the proof from feeling, the 'question is no longer a difficulty for me as soon as I have acknowledged two substances'. Rousseau follows Descartes in his dualism, but where Descartes held that God had established a happy harmony between mind and body, Rousseau holds that 'they are of such different natures, they were in a violent condition during their union'. The two substances are characterized in roughly Cartesian fashion. Mind is 'the active and living substance': matter is 'the passive and dead substance'. Also presupposed, but not stated, is the Cartesian assumption that mind is indivisible, matter divisible. That leads to the rapid conclusion:

> whereas I can conceive how the body wears out and is destroyed by the division of its parts, I cannot conceive of a similar destruction of the thinking being; and, not imagining how it can die, I presume that it does not die. (Em IV.590/283)

But even here reason does not have the last word: 'Since this presumption consoles me and contains nothing unreasonable, why would I be afraid of yielding to it?'

(D) Religion and morality

According to Rousseau's theodicy:

> It is the abuse of our faculties which makes us unhappy and wicked. Our sorrows, our cares and our sufferings come to us from ourselves. Moral evil is incontestably our own work, and physical evil would be nothing without our vices, which made us sense it. (Em IV.587/281)

Once again rejecting Voltaire's pessimism in *Candide*, Rousseau declaims: 'Take away our fatal progress, take away our errors and our vices, take away the work of man, and everything is good' (Em IV.588/282).

At this point one might expect that Rousseau would explain our unhappiness and wickedness according to the morality of the senses, as the outcome of bad environments, whether social, political or educational. But in fact he appears to abandon the morality of the senses here, putting into the Vicar's mouth a more traditional religious explanation based on a substantial dualism of body and soul. What we must do is make 'good use of reason, that is reason illuminated by the light of conscience'.[16] But conscience, we are now told, is the voice of the soul, the passions are the voice of the body, and those two voices can easily contradict one another (Em IV.594/ 286). From the point of view of the morality of the senses, even these deep contradictions would be explicable by reference to the environment. They would be caused by bad socialization, and corrected by its improvement. Nothing within human nature would be wholly beyond such modification. Certainly the bodily passions would have no 'natural' propensity to evil.

Before going further, we need to reflect on Rousseau's understanding of conscience. According to him, it is a feeling of a very particular kind. On the one hand it is innate and prior to reason. On the other hand it is infused with a moral content. Hence, the Vicar maintains, we must:

> distinguish our acquired ideas from our natural feelings; for we sense before knowing, and since we do not learn to want what is good for us and to flee what is bad for us but rather get this will from nature, by that very fact love of the good and hatred of the bad are as natural as the love of ourselves. The acts of the conscience are not judgments but feelings. Although all our ideas come to us from outside, the feelings evaluating them are within us, and it is by them alone that we know the compatibility or incompatibility between us and the things we ought to seek or flee. (Em IV.599/289–90)

He proceeds to found conscience on that distinction:

> To exist, for us, is to sense; our sensibility is incontestably anterior to our intelligence, and we had sentiments before ideas. Whatever the cause of our being, it has provided for our preservation by giving us sentiments suitable for our nature, and it could not be denied that these, at least, are innate. These sentiments, as far as the individual is concerned, are the love of self, the fear of pain, the horror of death, the desire of well-being. But if, as cannot be doubted, man is by his nature sociable, or at least made to become so, he can be so only by means of other innate sentiments relative to his species; for if we consider only physical need, it ought certainly to disperse men instead of bringing them together. It is from the moral system formed by this double relation to oneself and to one's fellows that the impulse of conscience is born. (Em IV.600/290)

263

Rousseau transposed the above formulation directly from the *Lettres morales* of 1757 (OC 4.1109) to the *Emile*, but in the *Emile* the following sentences are added:

> To know the good is not to love it [*conoitre le bien, ce n'est pas l'aimer*]; man does not have innate knowledge of it [*l'homme n'en a pas la conoissance innée*], but as soon as his reason makes him know it, his conscience leads him to love it. It is this sentiment which is innate. (Em IV.600/290)

Conscience, according to Rousseau, is a feeling innate in every human being, which carries its bearer towards what presents itself to that bearer as its good. But reason has to identify what that good is. Only through education do we learn to discriminate between real and apparent goods as they are presented to us. This reading puts a strain on the phrase 'To know the good is not to love it'. If that reading were correct, it would have been more natural if Rousseau had written the inverse: 'To love the good is not to know it', in the sense that one always loves what appears to one to be good, although one does not always know what one's real good is. But Rousseau's intention is simply to mark off knowing from loving, to assert the familiar view that reason unmotivated by feeling is powerless, passive, neutral, usable for good or ill. It is at best the instrument of well-ordered sentiment. If sentiment is well ordered, then its drive towards the real good is incorrigible: 'as soon as his reason makes him know it, his conscience leads him to love it'.

At times Rousseau seems to attribute a more active role to reason, as here, in the *Reveries*, where he tells of his rejection of the:

> quibbles and metaphysical subtleties [of the philosophers], which have no weight beside the fundamental principles adopted by my reason, confirmed by my heart, and which all bear the seal of inner approval [*assentiment intérieur*] given in the silence of the passions. (Reveries III.1018/55–6)

Reason is mentioned first as the faculty which 'adopts' the principles. But the material of those principles, amongst which it must discriminate, is furnished by the sentiments. As Rousseau writes a few pages later:

> Can I put an enlightened trust in appearances which lack all solidity in the eyes of my contemporaries and would seem illusory to me if my reason were not supported by my heart? (Reveries III.1020/58)

Conscience, then, is natural and innate. So why is it ignored? 'Well, this is because it speaks to us in nature's language, which everything has made us forget' (Em IV.601/291). Rousseau generally explains this forgetting in terms of the divided self, and the Vicar speaks directly for his creator when he portrays himself thus:

> Constantly caught up in the combat between my natural feelings which spoke for the common interest, and my reason which related everything to me, I would have drifted all my life in this continual alternation – doing the bad, loving the good, always in contradiction with myself – if new lights had not illuminated my heart, and if the truth, which settled my opinions, had not also made my conduct certain and put me in agreement with myself. (Em IV.602/291)

In other contexts, this inner conflict might find secular resolution. Here, because it is supposed to be generated by the necessarily contradictory demands of body and soul, religion must apparently intervene. It alone allows individuals to order and integrate the warring elements within themselves, both by providing consolation and hope, and by giving them a vision of the totality of which they form a part. It is to that vision that we now turn.

(E)   Religion, order and 'seeing as'

For Rousseau, the order of things is completed by religion. Without it, we are confronted at worst by chaos, at best by a provisional, contingent order, which emerges from disorder, only to return to it.

In a more than usually confused passage, the Vicar condenses goodness, justice, order and power and bestows them on God:

> the supremely great Being, because He is supremely powerful, ought also to be supremely just. Otherwise he would contradict Himself; for the love of order which produces order is called *goodness*, and the love of order which preserves order is called *justice*. (Em IV.589/282)

On the basis of this rough-hewn definition of the perfections of God, he proceeds to assert the moral necessity of the individual's survival after death. When he returns to the attributes of God a few pages later, he follows traditional theology in holding that a single term, like goodness or justice, can apply to both an infinite and a finite being, yet means something radically different in the two contexts. Compared with St Thomas, the Vicar's use of this device is amateurish:[17]

God is good; nothing is more manifest. But goodness in man is
the love of his fellows, and the goodness of God is the love of order
. . . man's justice is to give each what belongs to him, and God's
justice is to ask from each for an account of what He gave them.
(Em IV.593–4/285)

The God of order, as Rousseau argued against Voltaire on providence, occupies himself with the totality of things, even if that
totality can be maintained only at a cost to the individual: 'Despite
his goodness, or rather because of his very goodness, he can . . .
sacrifice something of the happiness of individuals for the conservation of the whole' (LV 1067).

In the Vicar's theology, God's concern for order on earth has its
brutal side. On the question of how, if at all, God is concerned to *re-*
order things in the afterlife, the Vicar is, as we have seen, undecided.
At times he looks only for a realm of peace and reconciliation: 'I
aspire to the moment when, delivered from the shackles of the body,
I shall be *me* without contradiction or division and shall need only
myself in order to be happy' (Em IV.604–5/293).

This kind of order is the keynote of Julie's minimalist theology in
Julie, ou la Nouvelle Héloïse. After her dramatic religious experience in
church, in which she was 'ravished by a change so great, so sudden
and so unexpected' (JNH III.18.355/293), Julie admonishes her
erstwhile lover St Preux:

> Adore the Eternal Being, my worthy and wise friend: [(1)] with
> one breath you will destroy those phantoms of reason which are
> but empty appearances and which flee like shadows before the
> immutable truth. [(2)] Nothing exists except through him who
> is, [(3)] It is he who gives a foundation to virtue and a price to this
> short life employed to please him. It is he who ceaselessly cries out
> to the guilty that their crimes have been seen, and he who informs
> the forgotten just person: 'Your virtues have a witness.' [(4)] It is
> he, it is his unalterable substance, which is the true model for the
> perfections of which we all carry an image within ourselves. (JNH
> III.18.358/295)

Several strands of Rousseau's own religious vision are condensed in
this exclamation. In the dramatic image of (1), 'phantoms of reason'
are opposed to 'the immutable truth'. This is not the voice of a pure
mystic who would bid us abandon reason and seek truth in a realm
inaccessible to it. The 'phantoms' are generated by reasoning [*raisonnement*], trivial logic-chopping harnessed to a dogmatic *parti-pris*.[18]

The epigram of (2) rapidly summarizes the Vicar's first two

Articles of Faith, the arguments for a Creator and for a Sustainer of the Universe. Applying the idea of the general will to theology, Rousseau denies that God has any interest in ordering the minutiae of the Universe. So, if Julie's thought that 'nothing exists except through him who is' represents Rousseau's, then it must be taken to apply to the Universe as a whole, not to its particular workings. (3) and (4) bring us from 'the starry heavens above' to 'the moral world within', and so to the heart of Rousseau's thought. (3) is the familiar argument from consolation and deterrence which so outraged Voltaire and Russell.[19] (4) is expressed in the terminology of aesthetics, the language of exemplars and models. Julie identifies the Form of the Good with the Form of the Beautiful. She seeks to embody that form in an integrated, well-ordered life. A good education makes one 'an integral part of the species'. A good society transforms one from 'a stupid and limited animal . . . [into] an intelligent being and a man'. Only through religion does one become fully part of an ordered universe.

Rousseau is thus driven by a longing to complete the programme of the morality of the senses, to reach a point where contradictions present within each of us may be overcome without the sacrifice of freedom. In his most original writings about religion, he expresses that aspiration through the vocabulary of 'seeing as'. Here, for example, in *Julie, ou la Nouvelle Héloïse*, St Preux, writes of his beloved and devout Julie and her atheist husband, Wolmar:

> Imagine Julie out for a walk with her husband; one of them admiring, in the rich and brilliant apparel displayed by the earth, the work and gifts of the Author of the universe; the other seeing in the whole thing just a chance combination of elements linked together only by a blind force . . . [*l'autre ne voyant en tout cela qu'une combinaison fortuite où rien n'est lié que par une force aveugle*]. (JNH V.5.591/484)

The distance between believer and unbeliever lies in what they see *in* the same phenomena, what they see the same phenomena *as*. The sight arouses different feelings in the two observers, admiration in Julie, clinical analysis in Wolmar. The world presents itself to Julie holistically, as a unitary whole, and aesthetically, as personified, wearing 'rich and brilliant apparel'. At the same time it presents itself religiously, as 'the work and gifts of the Author of the universe'. In each of these aspects the world presents itself differently to her husband. For him, as for Diderot, it has no essential unity, no rational pattern, but is 'just a chance combination of elements linked together only by a blind force'. Husband and wife are divided by two different ways of seeing the world. Between them there is no communication. Neither can make the Gestalt switch to see the world as the other sees it. To do that one would have to abandon one's whole way of being in the world.[20]

In the 'Allegorical fragment on revelation', Rousseau describes, from within, how such a switch might be made. The 'indiscreet philosopher' (himself):

> finally tired of floating amidst so much dispute between doubt and error, discouraged by finding his mind torn between unproved systems and unanswered objections, was ready to give up those deep but frivolous meditations which tended to inspire in him more pride than knowledge, when suddenly a ray of light came to strike his mind and to unveil to him those sublime truths which man cannot know on his own, and which reason serves only to confirm, not to discover. (OC 4.1047)

The change does not come about through an act of will, from within, but by a revelation, from without:

> A new universe offered itself, so to speak, to his contemplation; he perceived the invisible chain that links all beings to each other, he saw a powerful hand extended over everything that exists, the sanctuary of nature was opened to his understanding as it is to heavenly intelligences, and all the most sublime ideas that we attach to this word *God* presented themselves to his mind . . . The course of the Heavens, the magnificence of the stars, the earth's apparel, the order of Beings [*la succession des Etres*], the relations of harmony and utility [*rapports de convenance et d'utilité*] which he noticed between them, the mysteries of organization and of thought, in a word, the play of the whole machine [*le jeu de la machine entiére*] all became something which it was possible to conceive of as the work of a powerful Being [*possible à concevoir comme l'ouvrage d'un Etre puissant*], the director of all things . . . (ibid.)

This is not the narrative of a religious crank who claims to have had visions of God or the saints in person. What is revealed to him by the ray of light is simply what is revealed to Julie, the world *as* an ordered whole. He did not see some new particular object or person. The 'course of the heavens' was there already. When '[a] new universe offered itself, so to speak, to his contemplation', it was a moment when he 'saw', 'noticed', 'perceived' phenomena in a new way, as a harmonious whole. Finally, 'the play of the whole machine all became possible to conceive as the work of a powerful Being'. The description of the psychological transformation is convincing. Some readers will recognize some of the states as their own. Some may follow the 'indiscreet philosopher' through different stages of seeing the universe as an integrated whole, but may still balk at the final stage, which Rousseau offers in only the most tentative terms. It is now 'possible to conceive' the universe as 'the work of a powerful Being'. The ray of light does not compel assent.

Appendix   Rousseau and Kant

I conclude with a brief comparison between Rousseau's and Kant's versions of the proof from feeling. Burgelin comments that Rousseau 'sees in the existence of God the absolute condition of the moral life and of freedom of choice', and holds that his approach is 'the inverse of Kant's'.[21] By that, Burgelin seems to suggest that, for Kant, morality and freedom would be the conditions of the existence of God. But it is not clear that Kant does 'invert' Rousseau in quite that way. In his *Critique of Practical Reason*, Kant reaches his moral theology by an indirect route, starting from the premiss that we act as moral agents, and then seeking the conditions for the possibility of that moral action. Those conditions, called 'postulates of pure practical reason' are the immortality of the soul, the existence of God and 'freedom affirmatively regarded'.[22] Such a postulate is defined as 'a theoretical proposition which is not as such demonstrable, but which is an inseparable corollary of an a priori unconditionally valid practical law'.[23] Leaving aside the third, non-theological, postulate, we glance briefly at Kant's arguments for the first two.

In support of the first postulate, Kant holds that we are bound to strive for the goal of holiness, 'complete fitness of the will to the moral law', which 'our knowledge of ourselves' shows to be unattainable by mortals: 'only endless progress from lower to higher stages of moral perfection is possible to a rational but finite being'.[24] Since the attainment of the goal is 'necessary' for our existence as moral beings, then, if the goal is impossible, it follows that our existence as moral beings is impossible. But our existence as moral beings is possible. Therefore the attainment of the goal too is possible. But it is not possible in this finite existence. Therefore it is possible beyond it. Thus the goal is attainable only in the immortality of the soul.

Kant argues for the existence of God in similar fashion:

[T]here is not the slightest ground in the moral law for a necessary connection between the morality and proportionate happiness of a being which belongs to the world as one of its parts and is thus dependent on it . . . Nevertheless, in the practical task of pure reason, i.e. in the necessary endeavor after the highest good, such a connection is postulated as necessary: we *should* seek to further the highest good (which therefore must be at least possible). Therefore also the existence is postulated of a cause of the whole of nature, itself distinct from nature, which contains the ground of the exact coincidence of happiness with morality.[25]

Kant concludes that it is 'morally necessary to assume the existence of God', but that 'this moral necessity is subjective, i.e. a need, and not objective, i.e. duty itself'.[26] In an interesting move in the argument Kant goes from the premiss that if we are obliged to attempt to attain the highest good, then that attainment must be possible, to the conclusion that we must postulate the existence of a being which makes that attainment not only possible but actual.

It is axiomatic for Kant that we should still be absolutely bound to obey the categorical imperative in our moral actions, even if we were not guaranteed eternal rewards for obedience and eternal punishment for disobedience. For Kant, deontology has absolute priority. Indeed, if we obey because of fear of hell, not because we stand in awe of the categorical imperative, then we are acting heteronomously, not autonomously, and so not strictly morally.

Rousseau rarely expresses himself with the precision of Kant. Yet we can say that the difference between his moral theology and Kant's is not so much one of 'inversion', but more a difference of emphasis. Like Kant, he starts with reflections about the moral agent and finishes with assertions about religion. He differs from Kant because he does not radically divorce questions about our psychology from questions about our moral duty. For Kant, in contrast, rational persons, whether believers or unbelievers, are driven to the categorical imperative because they see that the immoral course of action is inconsistent. In that sense, for Kant, psychological questions, though important, must always be secondary to deontological ones.

Concluding Reflections

As I suggested in Chapter I, and as I have attempted to show in the book as it has unfolded, Rousseau is driven by two opposing visions of what it is to lead a perfect life.

The first is a *naturalist* vision of the world. In terms of this vision, human beings are unique, endowed with properties which are not reducible to the properties of their material bodies, but at the same time, since they are always situated in an environment, they should strive to realize an ideal of integrity, which can be attained only when an equilibrium is established (or re-established) between the individual and its environment, something which has been gradually lost since the emergence from the pure state of nature, and which can be retrieved in society only when social relations have been radically transformed.

The second is a *deontological* vision of duty and virtue, according to which the human being is an essentially divided creature, and the division within human nature is something to be mastered rather than transcended. How does this vision relate to the first one? Sometimes Rousseau suggests that it is a second best, that self-mastery is a *pis-aller* when the goal of integrity cannot be attained. But at other times, and these are the times when he most clearly anticipates Kant, he values the second more highly than the first. At these times, Rousseau sees the moments of correspondence between duty and interest, between reason and feeling, between particular interest and public interest as mere coincidences, moments contingent on circumstances which vary according to time and fortune. In the words already cited in Chapter I, 'there is no virtue in following your inclinations and indulging your taste for doing good just when you feel like it; virtue consists in subordinating your inclinations to the call of duty . . .' (Reveries VI.1052–3/96). From this perspective,

271

Rousseau not only presupposes a duality that is incompatible with the goal of integrity, but also values that duality more highly than integrity, since only a divided creature is truly moral, and so truly human.

The second vision is characteristic of a particular religious frame of mind, for which fallen human beings are always in conflict with their base, bodily instincts, which they can control only by the force of virtue. In the concluding chapters of the book we have examined the depth of Rousseau's unconventional religious sensibility. But it would be a facile solution to the problem of his divided thought to claim that Rousseau the religious thinker was a deontologist, whereas Rousseau the 'scientist' was a naturalist. The truth is that Rousseau's approach to religion is as divided as his approach to other questions. His rejection of the doctrine of original sin lies at the heart of his quarrel with the established churches. But, as I argued in Chapter XI (D), he is drawn in two different directions when he comes to propound his own explanation of the depravity of his fellow human beings. According to his first, naturalistic vision, that depravity comes from 'the contradictions of the social system . . . *man* is naturally good and . . . it is by these institutions alone that *men* become wicked' (LMa 1135–6/575, italics added). According to his second vision, the vision of irreducible inner conflict, the spiritual element within us is enslaved by the physical, and then 'I become depraved and finally prevent the voice of the soul from being raised against the law of the body' (Em IV.586/280).

The unresolved tension between these two visions provides the motive force of much of Rousseau's creative work. Always on the horizon there lies a third vision, the vision of radical retreat, to the inner world of the pure heart, a world of solitude, which expands at the limit into a world of direct communication between initiates without the 'cold intermediary of words' (JNH V.3.560/459). It stands beyond the tension of the first two visions, not as a synthesis of them, but as a mode of escape, when the first vision appears to be unrealizable, and the second imposes too energetic demands on the individual. I suggested in Chapter I that the third vision represents a moment of resignation, when Rousseau despaired of the possibility of re-ordering our environment, as the first vision requires, or of mastering our passions in a disordered world, as the second requires. To do justice to that third vision, which came increasingly to dominate Rousseau's last works, would require the writing of another book, and it would be as long as the one just completed.[1]

Notes

Introduction   Rousseau: the life and the work

1   This sketch is based on the magisterial biographies of Guéhenno and Cranston and on the 'Chronologie' of Gagnebin and Raymond (OC 1.ci-cxviii). My periodization of Rousseau's life was based on that in *La route Rousseau*, pp. 75–7 ('*Quelques dates*'), but ended up somewhat different from it.

2   Gagnebin and Raymond (OC 1.1264) and Cranston, *Jean-Jacques, the Early Life and Work of Jean-Jacques Rousseau, 1712–1754*, London: Allen Lane, 1983, p. 17, note that Jean-Jacques pretended, in the opening pages of the *Confessions* (Conf I.6/7), that his mother was the daughter, rather than the niece, of a pastor.

3   For this phrase and for this understanding of Rousseau's relationship to the *philosophes* I am indebted to Hulliung, *The Autocritique of Enlightenment: Rousseau and the Philosophes*, Cambridge, MA: Harvard University Press, 1994.

4   Condorcet, *Esquisse d'un tableau historique des progrès de l'esprit humain* (10e. période), Paris: Éditions Sociales, 1966, p. 274 (English translation, p. 193). On the significance of Condorcet's slogan, see Hollis, *Trust within Reason*, Cambridge: Cambridge University Press, 1998.

5   On this, see especially Hulliung, op. cit.

6   Quoted by Guéhenno, *Jean-Jacques Rousseau*, vol. 2, 1758–1778, London: Routledge & Kegan Paul, 1966, pp. 165–6.

7   Osmont, Introduction to RJJJ in OC 1.lv.

8   See Kelly, *Rousseau's Exemplary Life: the 'Confessions' as Political Philosophy*, Ithaca: Cornell University Press, 1987, p. 240, for the relationship between the *Confessions* and *Rousseau, Judge of Jean-Jacques*.

9   See Rousseau, 'History of the Preceding Writing', OC 1.978/CW 1.248. For the most sensitive analysis of these strange events, see Starobinski, *Jean-Jacques Rousseau: la transparence et l'obstacle*, Paris: Gallimard, 1970, pp. 270–3.

10 This section is based on Starobinski, 'La maladie de Rousseau', ibid., pp. 430–44.

11   Ibid., p. 438.
12   Admittedly this includes some duplicated material, drafts of the *Emile* and the *Social Contract*, for instance, as well as Rousseau's laundry lists and bakery bills. But the volume of work is still daunting.
13   Hume, *The Letters of David Hume*, ed. Greig, Oxford: Clarendon Press, 1932, vol. 2, #314, p. 313.
14   In particular those of Goldschmidt, Masters and Dent.
15   There are several gaps in my book. In particular I make no attempt to treat Rousseau's writings on music, the most enduring and important love of his life. This deprives the reader of an analysis of some of Rousseau's most important work and it distorts the exegesis of the *Essay on the Origin of Languages*. Insofar as Rousseau's thoughts about music are an integral part of his critical reaction to contemporary culture, in ignoring his musicology, I am ignoring a major part of that critique. My only excuse for this omission is my incompetence in this field and my inability to add anything to the outstanding work on the subject that is readily available. See in particular Wokler's magnum opus *Rousseau on Society, Politics, Music and Language: an Historical Interpretation of his Early Writings*, New York: Garland, 1987, and his brief, elegant summary in *Rousseau*, Oxford: Oxford University Press, 1995. See also the works of Starobinski and Kinzler referred to in Chapter IX below.
16   Hume, op. cit., vol. 1, #196, p. 364.

Chapter I   *Rousseau's Divided Thought: the Morality of the Senses and the Morality of Duty*

1   Locke, *An Essay Concerning Human Understanding* IV.3.6.
2   For the classic statement of the problem of interaction, see Descartes' letter to Princess Elisabeth (28 June 1643) (AT III.691–2/CSMK III.227). For a remarkable and sympathetic interpretation of Descartes' theory, see Baker and Morris, *Descartes' Dualism*, London: Routledge, 1996.
3   Gauthier gives a luminous account of Rousseau's strategies in 'The politics of redemption', in *Moral Dealing*, Ithaca, NY: Cornell University Press, 1990; '*Le Promeneur Solitaire*: Rousseau and the emergence of the post-social self' in Paul, Miller and Paul (eds), *Ethics, Politics, and Human Nature*, Oxford: Blackwell, 1991; 'Making Jean-Jacques', in O'Hagan (ed.), *Jean-Jacques Rousseau and the Sources of the Self*, Aldershot: Avebury, 1997.
4   Starobinski, *Jean-Jacques Rousseau: la transparence et l'obstacle*, Paris: Gallimard (Collection Tel), 1971 (1970), p. 256.
5   Ibid., p. 254.
6   Gagnebin and Raymond, whose notes to the *Confessions* provided the starting point of my discussion of bad faith, commented: '[Starobinski's] criticism [of Rousseau] is impeccable from an intellectual point of view. But one might object that in reality it is not at all the same man who first organizes his environment, and then gives way to his action. It is possible to be *successively* the mystifier and the mystified. Is there bad faith in deliberately submitting

274

to a régime which one expects will provide one's salvation? The better part of us (according to our choice) decides somehow to exorcize the worse, with the help of things' (OC I.1470). I agree with them that people engaged in the morality of the senses are not necessarily involved in bad faith. But I differ from them since I hold that such moral agents are neither mystifiers nor mystified. They arrange their environment in such a way that they can lead a life which is both spontaneous and good.

7   See Schwartz, *The Sexual Politics of Jean-Jacques Rousseau*, Chicago: Chicago University Press, 1984, p. 139.

8   Cf. the letter to Franquières, 15 January 1769: 'This word virtue means *force*. There is no virtue without combat . . .' (CC 37#6529, p. 21). At Em V.817/ 444 Bloom translates the French *force* as 'strength', and that is indeed its primary meaning. I prefer 'force' to bring out the connection with struggle or combat, since that seems to be at the heart of this strand of Rousseau's thought.

9   Indeed the definition of political virtue in the *Third Discourse* suggests an ideal of harmony rather than domination: 'as virtue is only this conformity of the particular will to the general will, make virtue rule' (3D 252/149).

10 Cranston, *The Noble Savage: Jean-Jacques Rousseau, 1754–1762*, London: Allen Lane, 1991, p. 265.

11 The Abbé's letter is at CC 8#1331, pp. 184–95, 27 February 1761. Readers who are disturbed by the moral blackmail, laced with a whiff of incest, are right to be so. For an illuminating reading of *Julie, ou la Nouvelle Héloïse*, see Tanner, 'Julie and "La Maison Paternelle": another look at Rousseau's *La Nouvelle Héloïse*,' in *Daedalus*, 105, 1976.

12 OC 1.1725.

13 Gilson, 'La méthode de M. de Wolmar', in *Les idées et les lettres*, Paris: Vrin, 1932, pp. 283–4.

14 Cassirer, *The Question of Jean-Jacques Rousseau*, trans. Gay, New York: Columbia University Press, 1954 ('Das Problem Jean-Jacques Rousseau', first published in *Archiv für Geschichte der Philosophie*, 1932).

15 Cassirer, op. cit., p. 99.

16 Cassirer, op. cit., p. 104.

17 Ibid.

18 Cassirer, op. cit., p. 118.

19 Kant, *Critique of Practical Reason* (1788), trans. White Beck, Indianapolis: Bobbs Merrill, 1956, p. 129. On this see O'Hagan, 'Hegel's critique of Kant's moral and political philosophy', in Priest (ed.), *Hegel's Critique of Kant*, Oxford: Clarendon Press, 1987, pp. 147–9.

20 There is a duty to be happy in Kant, but it is a secondary one: 'To assure one's own happiness is a duty (at least indirectly); for discontent with one's state, in a press of cares and amid unsatisfied wants, might easily become a great temptation to transgression of duty'. (Kant, *The Moral Lane: Kant's 'Groundwork of the Mataphysic of Morals'*, trans. H.J. Paton, London, Hutchinson, 1961 (1785), p. 67.)

21 Cassirer, *Rousseau, Kant and Goethe*, trans. Gutmann, Kristeller and Randall, New York: Harper and Row, 1963 (1945), p. 42.

Chapter II *The* Discourse on the Origin of Inequality Among Men

1 Oddly, Masters and Kelly alter *Origin* to *Origins* in the short title of their translation (CW 3). Since the full title includes the plural, *Foundations*, alongside *Origin*, it might be argued that *Origins* covers the two words. I am unconvinced. Little hinges on it. But why make the change? If Rousseau had wanted to use the plural he would have done so.

2 See Cranston, *Jean-Jacques: the Early Life and Work of Jean-Jacques Rousseau, 1712–1754*, London: Allen Lane, 1983, ch. 12.

3 See Hulliung, *The Autocritique of Enlightenment: Rousseau and the Philosophes*, Cambridge, MA: Harvard University Press, 1994.

4 Lévi-Strauss, 'Jean-Jacques Rousseau, founder of the sciences of man', in *Structural Anthropology*, vol. 2, trans. Layton, London: Allen Lane, 1977, p. 35 (originally 'Jean-Jacques Rousseau, fondateur des sciences de l'homme', Neuchâtel: la Baconnière, 1962, p. 240).

5 Plato, *Republic* X.611. I am indebted to Tim Chappell for help with the translation.

6 I am indebted to David O'Brien for pointing this out to me.

7 I learnt all this from Sève, 'Rousseau et l'esprit du droit romain', in Terrasse (ed.), *Etudes sur les 'Discours' de Rousseau*, Ottawa: Pensée Libre, no.1, 1988. For the connection with the Stoics see Sorabji, *Animal Minds and Human Morals*, London: Duckworth, 1993.

8 In this reading of Rousseau's methodological remarks at the start of the *Second Discourse* I am following Goldschmidt, *Anthropologie et politique: les principes du système de Rousseau*, Paris: Vrin, 1983, pp. 107–67.

9 Lévi-Strauss, *Anthropologie structurale*, Paris: Plon, 1958, ch. 15, p. 314.

10 See Baczko, *Rousseau: solitude et communauté*, trans. from Polish by Brendhel-Lamhout, Paris: Mouton, 1974 (1970). Baczko gives the subtlest account of the multiple meanings of 'denaturation' in Rousseau.

11 This follows from the consensus which has now emerged that 'we should attribute a date later [than the *Second Discourse*] to Chapter IX of the *Essay on the Origin of Languages*, which has many resemblances to the *Emile*. We should stress the great resemblance between the theory of pity enunciated in the [latter] two texts. Pity is a feeling which the first human beings did not develop: it needs the intervention of the reflective faculty and the imagination' (Starobinski, OC 5.ccii).

12 In Graham Greene's novel the quiet American describes his squeamishness (as opposed to compassion) like this: 'I know myself, and I know the depth of my selfishness. I cannot be at ease (and to be at ease is my chief wish) if someone else is in pain, visibly or audibly or tactually. Sometimes this is mistaken by the innocent for unselfishness, when all I am doing is sacrificing a small good – in this case postponement in attending to my hurt – for the sake of a far greater good, a peace of mind when I need think only of myself' (*The Quiet American*, London: Heinemann and Bodley Head, 1979 (1955), pp. 124–5.

13 Starobinski, OC 3.1310–1.

14 See Starobinski's note to EOL ch.9.395 at OC 5.1559–60.

15 See Starobinski, 'Le remède dans le mal: la pensée de Rousseau' in *Le remède dans le mal: Critique et légitimation de l'artifice à l'âge des Lumières*, Paris: Gallimard, 1989.

16 This section is based on Hobson, ' "Nexus effectivus" and "nexus causalis" in the *Inégalité* and in the *Essai sur l'origine des langues*', in Hobson, Leigh and Wokler (eds), *Rousseau in the Eighteenth Century: Essays in Memory of R. A. Leigh*, Oxford: the Voltaire Foundation, 1992, pp. 225–50. Louis Althusser drew a version of Figure 2 on the blackboard during a lecture on the *Second Discourse* delivered at the Ecole Normale Supérieure, rue d'Ulm in the year 1971/2. I was able to convert my version of it into a computer graphic thanks to Topher Wright.

17 Starobinski notes (OC 3.1294–5) that Rousseau is following Buffon particularly closely here, echoing his very words *'le concours de causes extérieures et accidentelles'*. Rousseau is centrally interested in the transformation of the mind and morality of humanity, only marginally in the evolution of natural species. Rousseau's debt to Buffon is examined in detail in Marian Hobson's article.

18 I owe this thought to Peter Greenspan, a student at the State University of New York, Binghamton.

19 This important word is omitted by the translators in CW 3.46.

20 The chronology of the *Essay on the Origin of Languages*, Chapter 9, diverges in some important respects from that of the *Second Discourse*. In the *Essay* version the elaborate construction of the pure state of nature is lacking, and the state of war occupies a different point in time and is not explicitly condemned as it is in the *Discourse*:

> These times of barbarism were the golden age, not because men were united but because they were separated. Everyone, it is said, considered himself to be master of everything; that may be so; but no one knew or desired more than was ready to hand; his needs, far from drawing him closer to those like himself, drew him away from them. Men may have attacked one another on meeting, but they rarely met. Everywhere the state of war prevailed, yet the whole earth was at peace. (EOL ch.9.396/262)

In this passage, the state of war is treated lightly, ironically. It is transposed to a stage like the youth of the world, in which societies are not yet sufficiently organized for a true state of war to exist.

21 For this reading of the two contracts, see Starobinski, 'Du *Discours de l'inégalité* au *Contrat social*', in *Etudes sur le 'Contrat social' de Jean-Jacques Rousseau*, Actes des Journées d'étude tenues à Dijon, les 3, 4, 5, 6 mai 1962, Paris: Société des Belles Lettres, 1964.

22 Ibid., p. 103.

23 Following Derathé, quoted by Starobinski, OC 3.1355–6.

24 Rawls follows Rousseau in holding that inequalities based on 'contingent' differences between people, that is on their socially determined starting points in life, are not morally justified. The 'democratic' version of 'fair

equality of opportunity' which he advocates is designed to work against the unfairness of unequal starting points in the societies we inhabit (see *A Theory of Justice*, Cambridge, MA: the Belknap Press of Harvard University Press, 1971, §13, pp. 75–83). In *Anarchy, State, and Utopia*, Oxford: Blackwell, 1974, Nozick rejects the view of both Rousseau and Rawls that we are not entitled to any benefits which come to us through a series of historical accidents.

Chapter III   *The* Emile

1   Jimack has analysed these two components of the *Emile* in his two great commentaries, *La genèse et la rédaction de l''Emile' de J.-J. Rousseau*, in *Studies on Voltaire and the Eighteenth Century*, vol. 13, Geneva: Institut et Musée Voltaire, 1960, and *Rousseau, 'Emile'*, London: Grant & Cutler, 1983.

2   The latter topics will be treated in separate chapters of this book.

3   See Introduction (E) above.

4   Quoted by Grimsley, *Rousseau's Religious Writings*, Oxford: Clarendon Press, 1970, p. 214.

5   Reprinted in Grimsley, ibid., pp. 216–29.

6   For a summary of these events, see Dent, *A Rousseau Dictionary*, Oxford: Blackwell, 1992, under *Emile, or on Education*, p. 106. While both the great texts of 1762 received censure in both countries, Rousseau's local correspondents suggested that the Genevan authorities were more outraged than the French by the *Social Contract*.

7   See Jimack, *La genèse et la rédaction de l''Emile' de Jean-Jacques Rousseau* in *Studies on Voltaire and the Eighteenth Century*, vol. 13, Geneva: Institut et Musée Voltaire, 1960, pp. 178 ff.

8   Jimack, *Rousseau, 'Emile'*, London: Grant & Cutler, 1983, p. 11. Jimack (ibid., p. 9) notes that Rousseau, who can never resist a paradox, would on occasion even deny that the *Emile* was a work of pedagogy: 'I can't believe that you would take the book which bears that name ['on Education'] for a real educational treatise. It is a quite philosophical work [*un ouvrage assez philosophique*] on the principle propounded by the author in other works that man is naturally good' (Letter to Cramer, 13 October 1764, CC 21#3564, p. 248). But this looks like provocation, for, at least in its systematic sections, the *Emile* evidently advances the 'quite philosophical' position by means of the educational programme.

9   See Chapter XI (D) below.

10   The fundamental principle of all morality/moral philosophy [*toute morale*], one on which I have reasoned in all my writings . . . is that man is a being who is naturally good and who loves justice and order; that there is no original perversity in the human heart and that the first movements of nature are always right . . . I have shown that all the vices that are imputed to the human heart are not natural to it; I have told how those vices are born; I have so to speak followed their genealogy; I have shown how, by the successive deterioration of their original goodness, men finally become what they are. (LdeB 935–6)

I have already touched on this theme in Chapter I (B) above. It will be treated in more detail in Chapter XI (D) below.

11   The Index to the *Emile* shows that Rousseau uses the term 'internal' [*interne*] only five times in the whole of the work: twice in Book I, as cited here; once to describe the 'purely internal sensations' available to the 'sixth sense' (Em II.417/157); 'inner pains', arising from 'moral distress' (Em IV.511/227); and, in a religious context, where 'a thousand ardent passions absorb the inner feeling' (Em IV.591/283). The quasi-technical use of the term at the start of Book I is thus not sustained beyond it. In Book I it seems to stand for something like Hobbesian 'vital motions'.

12   In the more apocalyptic words of the *Manuscrit Favre*:

> When man once encroaches on the care which nature takes of him, she then abandons her work and leaves everything to human art. Those same plants which flourish in the wasteland die in our gardens when we neglect them. An animal, once it is domesticated, loses its instincts along with its liberty, and does not ever regain them when once more released. It is the same with our species; we can no longer do without the institutions which produce our miseries. Natural man has disappeared, never to return, and the one who is furthest from his natural state is he whom art has most neglected, for his only education is a worldly one, the worst which one can receive. (FM 57)

13   The tutor in the *Emile* and the Lawgiver in the *Social Contract* have much in common:

> He who dares to undertake the institution of a people should feel that he is capable of changing human nature, so to speak; of transforming each individual, who by himself is a perfect and solitary whole, into a part of a larger whole from which this individual receives, in a sense, his life and being; of altering man's constitution in order to strengthen it; of substituting a partial and moral existence for the physical and independent existence we have all received from nature. (SC II.7.381/151)

14   In the former case a highly idealized model of reality and in the latter a projected schema, as described in the *Letter to d'Alembert*, the letter to Tronchin and the *Government of Poland*: see Jimack, *Rousseau, 'Emile'*, London: Grant & Cutler, 1983, p. 20.

15   Jimack, ibid.

16   Jimack has pointed out (ibid., p. 10) that Rousseau is prone to apocalyptic rhetoric when he describes the catastrophic effects of bad timing: 'if he [the infant] once knows how to make you take care of him at his will, he has become your master. All is lost' (Em I.291/68). Later, if the tutor allows himself to become embroiled in futile arguments with the child, the latter soon 'gains . . . [the] advantage and notices it'. At that point, 'farewell to education. Everything is finished from this moment' (Em II.327/96).

17   See Chapter I (F) above, and Chapters V (C) and VI (F) below.

18 See *Social Contract* I.9, discussed at Chapter IV (G) below.

19 Burgelin has meticulously analysed Rousseau's writings on reason and reasoning in his note to Em II.317, OC 4.1350–3.

20 When Rousseau criticizes the use of reason in the natural law tradition it is often on the grounds that natural lawyers fail properly to distinguish reasoning from reason, and wrongly imagine that individuals, even in our corrupt societies, will, by reasoning, automatically arrive at outcomes which would be truly rational, that is in accordance with reason, as understood in its normatively charged fashion.

21 'Intellectual reason', in the terminology of the *Emile* (Em II.370/125).

22 The idea of the sixth sense, whose history goes back to Aristotle, was taking on a new lease of life among the sensationist philosophers of the eighteenth century. See Burgelin, note to Em II.417 at OC 4.1406–7.

23 OC 4.1414.

24 Bloom gives a clear account of the origin and nature of the distinction at p. 487 of his translation of the *Emile*.

25 Caygill focuses on this story in 'The master and the magician', in O'Hagan (ed.), *Jean-Jacques Rousseau and the Sources of the Self*, Aldershot: Avebury Press, 1997, pp. 16–24. He condemns Rousseau for advocating an education of deception and manipulation.

26 It is significant that the three anecdotes discussed in this chapter, the gardener Robert, the running race and the conjuror, all make use of the structure of social classes into which Emile is born. It is accepted that the services of members of subordinate classes are simply there to be exploited for the sake of furthering Emile's education. Jimack points out how closely Sophie's family of 'country gentry-folk' resemble the Wolmar household in *Julie, ou la Nouvelle Héloïse* (Jimack, *Rousseau, 'Emile'*, London: Grant & Cutler, 1983, p. 24).

27 See Burgelin, OC 4.1421–2.

28 Eigeldinger discusses this passage at *Jean-Jacques Rousseau et la réalité de l'imaginaire*, Neuchâtel: la Baconnière, 1962, p. 48.

29 Noted by Eigeldinger, ibid., p. 104, who glosses: 'The health and enchantment of love reside in the ideal representation which we make of the beloved object.'

30 Quoted by Eigeldinger, ibid., p. 52.

31 See Eigeldinger, ibid., p. 58 for the analysis of Em IV.501/219.

32 See Eigeldinger, ibid., p. 68.

33 In the *Manuscrit Favre* version: 'The first of all goods is freedom and the free man wants to do only what he can, that is my fundamental maxim' (FM 88).

34 See Jimack, op. cit., p. 56.

35 We have glanced briefly at this passage in Chapter I.

36 Highlighted by Jimack, ibid., p. 53.

37 If we can take *Emile et Sophie, ou les solitaires* as Rousseau's serious verdict on *Emile* Book V.

38 See Freud's notorious view that women never achieve this, remaining always in some degree of *dépendance personnelle* in their moral lives. In them 'the formation of the super-ego must suffer; it cannot attain the strength and independence which gives it its cultural significance, and feminists are not

pleased when we point out to them the effects of this factor upon the average feminine character.' (*New Introductory Lectures on Psychoanalysis*, Lecture 33 ('Femininity'), Pelican Freud Library, vol. 2, p. 163, Harmondsworth: Penguin, 1973 (1933).)

39 For a meticulous exposition of the Vicar's epistemology and philosophy of mind, see Gouhier, *Les méditations métaphysiques de Jean-Jacques Rousseau*, Paris: Vrin, 1984, ch.2, 'Ce que le Vicaire doit à Descartes'. François Quesnay: 'That the being endowed with senses [*l'être sensitif*] distinguishes the sensations one from another by the differences which those sensations have between each other. Thus discernment [*le discernement*], or the function whereby the soul distinguishes the sensations from the objects represented by the sensations, is executed by the sensations themselves ... judgment operates in the same fashion; for judging is no different from perceiving and recognizing the relations, quantities and qualities (i.e. ways of being) of things ...' (*Encyclopédie*, 'Evidence', vol. 6, p. 148). Helvétius: passage quoted in text is from *De l'esprit* (1758), Paris: Fayard, 1988, Discourse I, ch.1, p. 22. He continues: '... all our false judgments and errors are related to two causes which presuppose that there is in us only the faculty of feeling ... I maintain that all our false judgments are nothing but the effect of our passions or our ignorance' (pp. 24–5).

40 Descartes, *Discourse on the Method* (1637), Part 4, AT VI.31/CSMK I.126–7.

41 Descartes, *Meditation* II, AT VII.28/CSMK II.19.

42 Descartes, *Meditation* III: 'Now as far as ideas are concerned, provided they are considered solely in themselves and I do not refer them to anything else, they cannot strictly speaking be false; for whether it is a goat or a chimera that I am imagining, it is just as true that I imagine the former as the latter ... the only remaining thoughts where I must be on my guard against making a mistake are judgments' (AT VII.37/CSMK II.26). Descartes devotes *Meditation* IV to showing that I make mistakes when I misuse my God-given freedom and 'make judgments about matters which I do not fully understand' (AT VII.61/CSMK II.42).

43 But, as Burgelin has noted, the paradox hinges on a slip [*glissement*] from one meaning of sentiment to another:

> Truth is in things in the sense that they really are the way they present themselves to sensibility. Judgment can go wrong when it seeks relations between sensations. Reason, even the reason 'of the senses' [*raison 'sensitive'*], is the source of error. That is why, at the beginning, he advocates the method of sticking to sentiment ... But one cannot help thinking that Rousseau is here slipping from a notion of the 'sensitive', which is passivity, to one of 'sentiment', which already involves a certain activity on the part of the self. (OC 4.1524)

Chapter IV The Social Contract: *Principles of Right*

1   The reconstruction follows Derathé, *Jean-Jacques Rousseau et la science politique de son temps*, Paris: Vrin, 1988 (1950), pp. 52 ff.

2   Derathé has examined the 'missing' section on international relations in detail and explained Rousseau's terminology in SC IV.9 (see Derathé, op. cit., pp. 59–60, 395–6). I have followed his conclusion that without that section, 'the *Social Contract*, in the form in which it was published is . . . only a fragment'. Derathé has also shown that Rousseau regarded international relations as variable, contingent and not derivable from natural law. In that sense, Rousseau seems to have held that they could not be fully theorized in the way that the order of a particular state could be. That may explain why he never managed to complete the missing section. But it does not mean that he regarded international relations as unimportant. Indeed, if the axis of the *Social Contract* is the intersection between principles of right and maxims of politics, between normative questions of legitimacy and practical questions of feasibility, and if the feasibility of a state depends on its ability to sustain itself in the world, then its relations to other states, even if not fully theorizable, must be central to Rousseau's concerns. In taking this line, I am following Masters rather than Derathé.

3   J. S. Mill, *Essay on Liberty* (1859), in *Utilitarianism*, ed. Warnock, London: Fontana, 1962, p. 174.

4   See Blum, *Rousseau and the Republic of Virtue: the Language of Politics in the French Revolution*, Ithaca, NY: Cornell University Press, 1986.

5   Schama, *Citizens: a Chronicle of the French Revolution*, New York: Vintage, 1989, pp. 746, 748.

6   See *La route Rousseau*, Geneva: Editions Transversales, 1991, p. 63. Also quoted in Blum, op. cit., pp. 280–1.

7   Constant, *The Spirit of Conquest and Usurpation and their Relation to European Civilization* (1814) in *Political Writings*, ed. and trans. Fontana, Cambridge: Cambridge University Press, 1988, pp. 108–9. The classic modern statement of Rousseau's totalitarianism is Talmon, *The Origins of Totalitarian Democracy*, London: Sphere Books, 1970 (1952), ch. 3. Isaiah Berlin brought Constant to English speakers' attention in 'Two concepts of liberty' (1958), reprinted in *Four Essays on Liberty*, Oxford: Oxford University Press, 1969. The most recent collection of essays, many addressed to this topic, is Wokler (ed.), *Rousseau and Liberty*, Manchester: Manchester University Press, 1995.

8   Indeed, in a bitter comment to the rulers of Geneva, he suggests that his text was all too near to reality, not a utopia like Plato's *Republic*, but a picture of a real social order, now betrayed by an oligarchic faction (LMt 6.810).

9   I think Masters is right to translate '*les loix telles qu'elles peuvent être*' as 'laws as they *can* be', rather than '*might* be'. Masters' translation brings out the realistic, non-utopian theme. For more on this see O'Hagan, 'On Rousseau's *Social Contract*: translation and exegesis', in *History of Political Thought*, 3.2, 1982, p. 255.

10 This is one of the few points on which Hulliung is misleading. He glosses the phrase like this: 'Citizens and natural men living in society can learn to

will the necessity that for the original natural man simply is. It must be remembered that the *Social Contract* attempts to legitimize our "chains", not to remove them' (*The Autocritique of Enlightenment, Rousseau and the Philosophes*, Cambridge, MA: Harvard University Press, 1994, p. 197). But the grammatical object of '*rendre légitime*' is '*le*' (singular), referring to the change, not '*les*' (plural), referring to the chains.

11 Masters and Kelly have refused to reach a conclusion, and have left the ambiguity unresolved with the help of the '/' sign: 'Man was/is born free' (CW 4.131). Cole-Brumfitt-Hall translate 'is', noting that 'This is the consecrated translation of one of Rousseau's most famous phrases, though "man *was* born free" is arguably more accurate. Either translation fits Rousseau's general meaning, which is both historical and moral' (Cole-Brumfitt-Hall-Jimack 349). The *Déclaration des droits de l'homme et du citoyen* of 1789 would use the present tense in asserting: '*Les hommes naissent libres et demeurent libres, et égaux en droits*' (Godechot, *Les constitutions de la France depuis 1789*, Paris: GF-Flammarion, 1979, p. 33): see Derathé's note at OC 3.1433. So if Rousseau had intended 'man is born free' at this dramatic moment in his work, he would have written '*l'homme naît libre*', rather than '*l'homme est né libre*'.

12 The table of contents is printed in Vaughan (ed.), *The Political Writings of Jean-Jacques Rousseau*, Cambridge: Cambridge University Press, 1915, vol. 2, pp. 21–2, but not in OC 3. For this reference, and for the discussion of the distinction between principles of right and maxims of politics, see Masters, 'The structure of Rousseau's political thought', in Cranston and Peters (eds), *Hobbes and Rousseau: a Collection of Critical Essays*, Garden City, NY: Anchor Books, 1972, p. 415. Masters' starting point is Rousseau's comment that 'the established Government must never be touched until it becomes incompatible with the public good. But this circumspection is a maxim of politics and not a rule of right [*une maxime de politique et non pas une regle de droit*]' (SC III.18.435/196). I assume that a 'rule of right' would formulate one of the 'principles of right' of the subtitle of the *Social Contract*.

13 Masters and Kelly divide up the chapters of the *Social Contract* at CW 4.xxii. According to them, right is the subject matter of I.6–9, II.1–7, II.11–12, III.16–17, IV.1–2; and fact is the subject matter of II.8–12, III.1–15, III.18, IV.3–7. They leave unallotted I.1–5 and IV.8–9. The former are the opening chapters of the book, in which Rousseau subjects his predecessors to critical examination before embarking on his own system. I assume they are concerned, albeit negatively, with right rather than fact. The latter are the concluding chapters of the *Social Contract*, IV.8 on civil religion and IV.9, entitled 'Conclusion'. IV.9 is a mere envoi, but in IV.8 questions of fact and questions of right intersect, as Rousseau considers religion instrumentally, as a means to sustain the political order, but also makes normative judgments on the limits of religious toleration.

14 Summarized for him in Book V of the *Emile* (Em V.836–49/458–67).

15 Rousseau had bitter personal experience of *dépendance personnelle* and derived his hatred of the *Ancien Régime* from that experience. The elaborate theoretical structure of the *Social Contract* is not of course logically dependent on that experience, but it draws some of its passion from it.

16　Rousseau's use of the terminology of convention is examined in O'Hagan, op. cit., pp. 258–61.

17　Another passage which challenges the translator. The problem word in this one is '*convenances*': 'matters of expediency' (CW 4.163); 'what is proper' (Cole-Brumfitt-Hall-Jimack 226); 'the conventions' (Bondanella 117).

18　Both components of traditional naturalism had been under attack since Hobbes. According to Strauss, Rousseau's *Second Discourse* radicalized that attack and brought to its conclusion the 'crisis in natural right' (*Natural Right and History*, Chicago: University of Chicago Press, 1971 (1950), chapter 6.A).

19　See Locke, *First Treatise of Government* (1689), in *Two Treatises of Government*, ed. Laslett, New York: New American Library, 1965, and Derathé, OC 3.1434.

20　Hart argued in a similar way that the existence of a legal system depends on the *fact* that the citizens of a legal order adopt, however patchily, an 'internal point of view', that is a normative attitude, towards its laws. See Hart, *The Concept of Law*, London: Oxford University Press, 1961, Chapter 6.

21　See Derathé, OC 3.1437–8. Rousseau had already rejected Aristotle's view at SC I.2.

22　It is an important part of Rousseau's criticism of Hobbes that there can be no such thing as a state of war between individuals. He rejects Hobbes's idea of the 'war of all against all' as conceptually, not just empirically, mistaken. See '*Etat de guerre*' in SP607–8/41, and Masters, *The Political Philosophy of Rousseau*, Princeton: Princeton University Press, 1968, p. 282.

23　See Masters, ibid., p. 281.

24　This follows Starobinski, 'Du *Discours de l'inégalité* au *Contrat social*', in *Etudes sur le 'Contrat social' de Jean-Jacques Rousseau* (Actes des journées d'études tenues à Dijon, 1962), Paris: Société des Belles Lettres, 1964.

25　To be subject to *dépendance personnelle* is to be at the command of the arbitrary will of another individual and to have no appeal against that will to a higher tribunal. It results from unequal power, whether social, psychological, legal or political. The twin vices of the *Ancien Régime*, arbitrariness and inequality, express themselves in *dépendance personnelle*.

26　Though not from private life, as we saw in the *Emile*.

27　Hollis, 'Honour among thieves' (1990), in *Reason in Action: Essays in the Philosophy of Social Science*, Cambridge: Cambridge University Press, 1996, Chapter 8.

28　See Derathé, OC 3.1451.

29　See above, Chapter III (D).

30　Locke, *Second Treatise of Government*, paras 27, 46.

31　The latter is Rawls's difference principle: see *A Theory of Justice*, Cambridge, MA: the Belknap Press of Harvard University Press, 1971, §11. Intensive cultivation, the result of the privatization of agriculture, in particular the enclosure of common land, brings it about, according to Locke, that 'a Day Labourer in England' is better off than 'a King of a large fruitful Territory' in undeveloped America (*Second Treatise of Government*, para. 41).

32　See Em III.475ff./195ff. in which Emile is to be taught a trade. For the argument that agriculture is superior to commerce in promoting the moral and demographic health of a country, see PCC 904ff./282ff. For anecdotal comment (whether real or imaginary!) on the virtues of the small peasant and the vices of the tax régime which oppressed him, see Conf IV.63/139–40.

33   This reading of SC I.9 could be called 'marxist'.

34   In a footnote to the *Geneva Manuscript* Rousseau quotes an ironic comment from the *Dutch Observer*, a contemporary satire aimed at French colonial claims, in which he 'saw a rather amusing principle, which is that all land inhabited only by savages should be considered vacant, and that one may legitimately seize it and drive the inhabitants away without doing them any wrong according to natural right' (GM 301/92). Masters (CW 4.238) notes that Rousseau prudently omitted this note from the published version, apparently because it would have been taken as a subversive comment on the land claims then being made by France in the Seven Years War.

35   Grotius and Pufendorf had required that compensation be paid to owners whose private property was taken over by the state exercising the right of eminent domain in emergencies, whereas there is no mention of compensation in Rousseau. (Derathé, OC 3.1451).

Chapter V   *The Empire of the Laws: the General Will and Totalitarianism*

1   This eulogy is repeated verbatim in the concluding chapter of Book I of the first version of the *Social Contract*, of which the whole of Book II is devoted to 'The Establishment of the Laws' (GM 10/99).

2   Another rhetorical flourish which Rousseau liked to repeat, this time in the *Emile* (Em IV.600/290), though there, with unusual restraint, he removed the reference to the 'sublime emanation'!

3   This despite the fact that he held that the well-ordered society would need few laws, being integrated by its *moeurs*, the internal laws which bind our hearts: see Sève, 'Rousseau et l'esprit du droit romain', in Terrasse (ed.), *Etudes sur les 'Discours' de Rousseau*, Ottawa: Pensée Libre, no.1, 1988.

4   Strauss, *Natural Right and History*, Chicago: University of Chicago Press, 1971 (1950), Chapter VI (A).

5   Derathé, *Jean-Jacques Rousseau et la science politique de son temps*, Paris: Vrin, 1988 (1950), p. 158.

6   See O'Hagan, 'Aristotle and Aquinas on community and natural law' in Bellamy and Ross (eds), *A Textual Introduction to Social and Political Theory*, Manchester: Manchester University Press, 1996, ch. 2.

7   Masters, *The Political Philosophy of Rousseau*, Princeton, NJ: Princeton University Press, 1968, pp. 321–3.

8   Aquinas, *Summa Theologiae* 1a.2ae.21.4, vol. 18, trans. Gilby, London: Eyre & Spottiswoode, 1966, p. 119.

9   Constant, *Principles of Politics*, Chapter 1, in *Political Writings*, ed. Fontana, Cambridge: Cambridge University Press, 1988, p. 177.

10   Rawls distinguishes this substantive, even 'metaphysical', idea of liberalism, expounded in different idioms by Kant and J. S. Mill, from what he now holds to be the only defensible form of liberalism, the purely 'political' one.

If we cannot agree on a philosophical anthropology, then there may be only two remaining options: Rawls's political liberalism, lacking metaphysical foundations, or some version of Rousseau's voluntarism. (See Rawls, 'Justice as fairness, political not metaphysical', in *Philosophy and Public Affairs*, 14.3, 1985 and *Political Liberalism*, New York: Columbia University Press, 1993.)

11 For the 'right to be let alone', see Warren and Brandeis, 'The right to privacy' (1890), in Schoeman (ed.), *Philosophical Dimensions of Privacy*, Cambridge: Cambridge University Press, 1984. J. S. Mill combined the positive and negative versions of liberalism in his *Essay on Liberty*, which contains a stirring manifesto for the positive component in Chapters 2 and 3, and specifies the negative conditions for its flourishing in Chapter 1.

12 These comments on natural law and liberalism are brief and schematic, designed to highlight the distance between both those traditions and Rousseau's absolutism.

13 Constant, *The Spirit of Conquest and Usurpation and their Relation to European Civilization* (1814) II, ch.7, in Fontana (ed.), *Political Writings*, Cambridge: Cambridge University Press, 1988, p. 106. Constant's thought was developed by de Tocqueville, who denounced as 'impious and detestable that in matters of government the majority of people has the right to do everything . . . It is important to make the distinction between arbitrary power and tyranny. Tyranny can use even the law as its instrument, and then it is no longer arbitrary; arbitrary power may be used in the interest of the ruled, and then it is not tyrannical . . .' (*De la démocratie en Amérique*, t.2 (1840), eds. Lamberti and Mélonio, Paris: Laffont, 1986, pp. 242, 244–5). It might be argued that de Tocqueville has wilfully ignored Rousseau's distinction between the people, which is always sovereign, and which alone can legislate (SC III.1), and the government, which consists of the people's 'deputies', who 'are only its agents' (SC III.15), but which have executive power.

14 This chapter was finished before I had absorbed three important recent books: Spitz, *La liberté politique*, Paris: Presses Universitaires de France, 1995; Pettit, *Republicanism: a Theory of Freedom and Government*, Oxford: Clarendon Press, 1997; and Skinner, *Liberty before Liberalism*, Cambridge: Cambridge University Press, 1998. In the light of their work, I may have to reconsider my understanding of the 'liberal' critique of Rousseau mounted by Constant and Tocqueville.

15 On this see Derathé, OC 3.1455.

16 The words '*en secret*' appear in the *Geneva Manuscript* (GM 306/96) but not in the published version.

17 Philonenko argues that Rousseau had a serious grasp of the calculus, and used it to effect in this and other passages. See Philonenko, *Jean-Jacques Rousseau et la pensée du malheur*, Vol. 3, Paris: Vrin, 1984, ch. 2.

18 I owe this formulation to Martin Hollis.

19 See the discussion of voting in Weintraub, *Conflict and Co-operation in Economics*, London: Macmillan, 1975, ch.7. The Irish government recently put to a referendum draft legislation to introduce divorce into the Republic. Supporters of the reform were anxious that the government's proposal could be defeated in the referendum by the combined opposition of the traditional anti-divorce lobby and the new radicals who opposed the draft legislation on

the grounds that it was not sufficiently liberal. In the event those twin peaks did not combine to produce a majority and the 'yes' vote was victorious.

20 In the texts of applied political theory Rousseau stresses the integrative role of these 'smaller societies', like the *cercles* of Geneva, which he praises in the *Letter to d'Alembert*. Trachtenberg has highlighted the importance of this part of Rousseau's political theory in *Making Citizens: Rousseau's Political Theory of Culture*, London: Routledge, 1993.

21 See Derathé, OC3.1492.

22 Anyway, as Burgelin points out in his note to this passage,

> the text is somewhat weakened, since the idea is proposed only as a theme for reflection, and leaves the door open for the wronged citizen to withdraw, if his conscience tells him that he has indeed been wronged. But that hypothesis is in principle absurd if the general will cannot err. (OC 4.1690)

23 For Masters (op. cit., p. 275) 'the tension between Rousseau's political teaching [in the GM] and his conception of natural sentiment [in the *Emile*] illuminates the paradoxical character of his thought'. I interpret the 'tension' in terms of the morality of the senses.

24 For Rawls, 'pluralism' means the coexistence within a society of a multiplicity of different, and often opposed, views of what is fundamentally good. Modern, liberal societies are, through their historical evolution, all pluralist in this sense. On this view of Rawls, a general will, a cohesive ideology concerning shared goals, might exist in 'pre-modern' societies, but is now extinct. Any attempt to reimpose such shared goals, over and above the minimum commitment to 'justice as fairness', would constitute a dangerous, authoritarian archaism.

25 Arrow, *Social Choice and Individual Values*, New Haven: Yale University Press, 1963, pp. 81–2, 83, 85. Rawls holds the same view of majority rule in *A Theory of Justice*, Cambridge, MA: the Belknap Press of Harvard University Press, 1971, §54.

26 Runciman and Sen, 'Games, justice and the general will' in *Mind*, 74, 1965, p. 557.

27 SC IV.2 provides the clearest evidence for Arrow's view that Rousseau's general will entails 'two orderings' of preferences.

28 Boudon, *Effets pervers et l'ordre social*, Paris: Presses Universitaires de France, 1977, pp. 20–2.

29 Lewis, *Convention: a Philosophical Study*, Cambridge, MA: Harvard University Press, 1969, p. 90. The words 'a certain state of general nonconformity' in the definition of 'social contract' are important in Lewis's analysis, but do not concern us here.

Chapter VI   The Social Contract: *Maxims of Politics*

1   Rousseau denies that the *Social Contract* is a pure utopia more than once. In the *Letters from the Mountain*, he claims, provocatively, that it was realized in the constitution of Geneva before that constitution had been subverted by oligarchs. The latter, he holds, were aware that in previous times Geneva had been ruled by 'an existing government on my model'. It was because they recognized in the *Social Contract* a model of what they had betrayed that they reacted with such hostility to it. Otherwise, they would have been 'content to relegate the *Social Contract*, along with Plato's *Republic*, [More's] *Utopia* and [Vairasse's] *Sévarambes*, to the land of chimaeras' (LMt 6.810) (quoted by Masters, *The Political Philosophy of Rousseau*, Princeton, NJ: Princeton University Press, 1968, p. 304). Rousseau criticizes Plato in particular because he

established an ideal Republic in which he proves very well that each person will be valued in proportion to his worth and the most just will also be the happiest. So, virtuous people in search of a society, go and live in the one devised by Plato. But all those who are content to live among the wicked should not hope to find a good life there. (MP #22.1125)

2   Derathé supports Vaughan's view that these chapters are an irrelevance (OC 3.1464.n.4). Masters takes the opposite view, holding that Rousseau is equally concerned with the conditions in which a legitimate order may flourish. I have followed Masters' lead in taking the two components of the Proem ('legitimate and sure') as equally important.

3   Derathé, OC 3.1466.

4   I am following Masters' interpretation of this sentence, which links it closely to the discussions of demographic ratios in Book III. See Masters, *The Political Philosophy of Rousseau*, Princeton, NJ: Princeton University Press, 1968, pp. 394ff.

5   The difference was noted by Vaughan, and then by Derathé at OC 3.1527: 'the happiest nation is one that can most easily do without all the others, and the most flourishing is the one others can least do without' (PolFr VI.8.512/ 42).

6   On SC II.11, see Chapter V (C) above.

7   This is my speculation. Rousseau does not describe the range of civil laws, since, as he says, his interest in the *Social Contract* is confined to 'political laws'.

8   The subordination of government to sovereign people is an inference drawn from a principle, rather than a maxim. The chapter devoted to it (SC III.15, 'Deputies or representatives') contains a mixture of principles and maxims.

9   Masters, op. cit., pp. 340–8 and CW 4.254–5.

10 This, correct, translation of '*tout compensé*' is Bondanella's (see Bondanella 119). It is mistranslated at CW 4.167.

11 Masters, op. cit. p. 340 and CW 4.254.

12 See Masters, CW 4.255.n.76.

13 Earlier, in the Dedication to the *Second Discourse*, his terminology was different. There he says:

> I would have wished to be born in a country where the Sovereign and the people could have only one and the same interest, so that all movements of the machine always tended to the common happiness. Since that would not be possible unless the people and the sovereign were the same person, it follows that I would have wished to be born under a democratic government, wisely tempered.

Though he does not quite do so, he here comes close to identifying democratic government and popular sovereignty (2D 112/14)

14 P. Berthier, *Observations sur le Contrat Social*, published in 1789, but written soon after 1762, quoted by Derathé, OC 3.1477.

15 The final clause, that aristocracy is 'the worst of sovereignties' is also found in the *Judgment on the 'Polysynodie'* of the Abbé de St. Pierre (SP 645), to which he appends a footnote, apparently written after the publication of the *Social Contract*, predicting that superficial readers will take it that that phrase contradicts SC III.5 (see note by Stelling-Michaud, OC 3.1564).

16 In another idiom, governments are a superstructure on an economic base.

17 Here, and elsewhere, Masters translates '*s'altérer*' and '*altération*' as 'alter' and 'alteration'. Though the French words can have the neutral meanings, they normally have the negative ones.

18 Vaughan's description of the claim, cited by Derathé, OC 3.1486.

19 Rousseau's terminology has shifted here from the beginning of the chapter, where 'deputies' had a negative sense. Now that the distinction between deputies and representatives has been made, 'deputies' stands for the legitimate function, 'representatives' for the illegitimate function of magistrates.

20 See Derathé OC 3.1489.

21 Derathé OC 3.1490.

22 Derathé agrees with Vaughan's negative judgment of the excursus (OC 3.1495).

23 The laws of Geneva, at least when Rousseau was writing the *Letters from the Mountain*, were little better:

> The Council [of Geneva] pronounces that my Books tend to destroy Governments. The Author of the Letters [to whom Rousseau is replying in the *Letters from the Mountain*] says only that Governments are subjected in my books to the most audacious critique. That is something quite different. A critique, however audacious it may be, is not a conspiracy. To criticize or blame some Laws is not to overthrow all Laws. It would be the same as accusing someone of murdering the sick when he pointed out the faults of doctors. (LMt 6.804–5)

Here Rousseau's response is more candid. There is no talk of 'respect' for unjust laws, only a distinction between subversion and criticism, a claim that Rousseau is a critic, not a conspirator.

24 In a note to SC IV.5 (OC 3.1496) Derathé cites the *Letters from the Mountain* 9: 'I do not excuse the faults of the Roman People. I spoke of them in the *Social Contract*. I blamed it for having usurped executive power, which it ought

only to restrain . . .' There Rousseau attributes popular usurpation to misuse of the rules determining the office of tribune of the people (LMt 9.880).

25 Derathé note, OC 3.1497.

26 Rousseau stresses the need for good *moeurs* to guarantee the emergence and preservation of the general will. See especially SC IV.1. For the importance of *moeurs* in Rousseau's political thought, see Trachtenberg, *Making Citizens: Rousseau's Political Theory of Culture*, London: Routledge, 1993.

27 We shall return to the conflict between patriotism and cosmopolitanism at (F) below. There we shall see that Rousseau's hostility to cosmopolitanism is not absolute, and that 'great cosmopolitan souls' are not necessarily hypocrites.

28 Sève brings out the Lawgiver's role as inculcator of good *moeurs*. See 'Rousseau et l'esprit du droit romain', in Terrasse (ed.), *Etudes sur les 'Discours' de Rousseau*, Ottawa: Pensée Libre, no. 1, 1988.

29 Burke, *Reflections on the Revolution in France*, ed. O'Brien, Harmondsworth: Penguin, 1969 (1790), p. 135. On the close kinship between Burke and Rousseau on this and much else, see Cameron, *The Social Thought of Rousseau and Burke*, London: Weidenfeld & Nicolson, 1973, particularly Chapter 3, part IV.

30 See in particular Leduc-Fayette, *Rousseau et le mythe de l'antiquité*, Paris: Vrin, 1974.

31 Is there a discrepancy between this passage and SC I.2: 'The family is, . . . if you wish, the first model of political society'? I think not. On my reading, SC I.2 forms part of the critical rendering of accounts with previous attempts to theorize the basis of political obligation. Patriarchalism would then be the 'first model', but only the first of several erroneous models.

32 Quoted by Derathé, OC 3.1397.

33 This definition of virtue brings it closer to the morality of the senses than the picture of virtue as 'a state of war' discussed in Chapter I.

34 Quoted by Derathé, OC 3.1414.

Chapter VII Amour-propre

1 Dent, in *Rousseau*, Oxford: Blackwell, 1988, gives the definitive account of *amour-propre* in Rousseau. He demolishes the received wisdom that Rousseau sees *amour-propre* as simply a vice. He distinguishes between 'inflamed' *amour-propre*, which is vicious, and 'normal' *amour-propre*, which is the appropriate vehicle of socialization. In this chapter I develop this central insight of Dent, while putting more stress than he does on the underlying tensions between Rousseau's positive and negative images of *amour-propre*.

2 Rousseau held an ambivalent view of sexual passion throughout his work. It is an irreducible surd in his system, an essential moment in the formation of the child into a morally autonomous adult, but also capable of producing all the evil effects of deformed *amour-propre* even in an ideal social setting.

3 In his analysis of this passage in the *Second Discourse*, Starobinski sees inequality and *amour-propre* developing in parallel (OC 3.1349). I think the connection is clearly a causal one.

4   Rousseau's most consistent critic on this front is Crocker. He is one of those who notes how closely the Polish utopia resembles the 'idyll' of the de Wolmar estate in *Julie, ou la Nouvelle Héloïse*. They are identical in that both call for a transparency, an absolute exposure of the individual's behaviour to public scrutiny. They differ in that de Wolmar exercises an allegedly enlightened despotism over the members of his extended household, whereas the constitution of Poland will be relatively democratic. (Crocker, 'Rousseau et la voie du totalitarisme', in *Annales de la philosophie politique*, 5, 1965, 'Rousseau et la philosophie politique', pp. 122 ff.).

5   Shklar, *Men and Citizens: a Study of Rousseau's Social Theory*, Cambridge: Cambridge University Press, 1969, p. 202.

Chapter VIII   Men and Women

1   Wollstonecraft, *A Vindication of the Rights of Woman*, ed. Brody, Harmondsworth: Penguin, 1992, p. 129.

2   Masters translates it as 'the ascendancy of women' (CW 2.15), which wrongly suggests that Rousseau is criticizing women for dominating men.

3   In a previous version of this chapter, I suggested that the changed account of men and women is simply part of a change in all of Rousseau's views between 1755 and 1762, during which time the sceptical *Encyclopédiste*, having regained his religious faith, jettisoned the radical lessons he had once learnt from Buffon and Diderot. According to that version, Rousseau changed from seeing sexual inequality as the outcome of chance to seeing it as ordained by divine providence. But that interpretation is simply wrong, since the anti-feminist current was already running strongly in the *Third Discourse*, published in the same year as the *Second*. I still maintain that there are strains within Rousseau's writings on women, but I no longer think that they can be explained (or explained away) by reference simply to the chronological development of his thought.

4   Locke, *Second Treatise of Government* §80, in *Two Treatises of Government*, ed. Laslett, New York: New American Library, 1965.

5   An anonymous reader has impugned this interpretation on the grounds that Note XII constitutes a criticism of Locke's argument, not of his conclusion. On re-reading the Note, I find that in it Rousseau evidently criticizes both argument and conclusion.

6   Voltaire, *Voltaire's Marginalia on the Pages of Rousseau*, ed. Havens, New York: Haskell House, 1966, p. 12.

7   Rousseau returns to this theme in both the *Letter to d'Alembert* and the *Emile*.

8   In the nobility, widows and other independent women, like Rousseau's beloved 'maman', could be heads of households.

9   In the *Emile*, Rousseau returns to these themes, the claim that wives are more guilty than husbands in committing adultery, and the fear that men become enslaved by women in the play of sexuality. See (E) below.

10   Quoted by Burgelin, OC 4.lxxx, translated by Bloom, *Emile, or on Education*, pp. 488–9.

11   On this see Schiebinger, *The Mind Has No Sex? Women in the Origins of Modern*

Science, Cambridge, MA: Harvard University Press, 1989. She describes the emergence of 'complementarism' in the eighteenth century, a doctrine which gave a causal explanation of moral and psychological differences between the sexes in terms of supposed physiological differences, and then called for different, allegedly complementary, but in fact radically unequal, social and political roles for the two sexes on the basis of those supposedly 'scientific' findings. She shows how Rousseau popularized 'complementarism' in his political and educational writings. In *Julie* he gave the doctrine the added cachet of a literary masterpiece.

12 My students at SUNY-Binghamton clarified this point to me, and made me realize that Rousseau's argument depends on the demographic imperative, which in turn has biological implications. His argument can be defended in terms of the imperative, though not through to its outrageous conclusion.

13 My colleague Kate Nash emphasized Rousseau's unbalanced tone in this passage.

14 Wollstonecraft, op. cit., p. 176.

15 On this see Schwartz, *The Sexual Politics of Jean-Jacques Rousseau*, Chicago: Chicago University Press, 1984. Rousseau's concerns about demography in general and about the use of wet nurses in particular may not have been paranoid or far-fetched: see Badinter, *L'amour en plus*, Paris: Flammarion, 1980.

16 The unwary reader should not be deceived by the fragments in Rousseau's hand entitled 'On women' and 'Essay on important events of which women were the secret cause' (OC 2.1254 and 1257). Though their dating has been disputed, it is clear that they were written when Rousseau was employed by the formidable Madame Dupin, probably in 1754. Cranston says that what the manuscript

> contains is clearly the work of Mme Dupin's brain and not Rousseau's; it represents her ideas, not his. He penned the words as the employee, the secretary, the amanuensis of another. His experience with Mme de Warens had taught him to admire remarkable women, but it is plain from all his published writing that he was never a feminist . . . Mme Dupin wanted to prove that women were as good as if not better than men in every respect, including physical prowess, and that women had done prodigious deeds in the few societies where they were allowed equality with men . . . [Rousseau's] duties included searching through books to find evidence for Mme Dupin's theses . . . (Cranston, *Jean-Jacques: the Early Life and Work of Jean-Jacques Rousseau, 1712–1754*, London: Allen Lane, 1983, p. 206)

Chapter IX   *Language*

1 The dating of the *Essay on the Origin of Languages* has been a matter of immense scholarly debate. Kintzler's bibliography to the GF-Flammarion edition of the *Essai* lists the most important contributions, including Wokler's magnum opus, *Rousseau on Society, Politics, Music and Language: an*

Historical Interpretation of his Early Writings, New York: Garland, 1987. I have accepted Kintzler's conclusion (Introduction to the *Essai*, p. 9) that 'the most probable hypothesis is that ... we can date [its] composition to between 1756 and 1761, and even more probably between 1758 and 1761 ...' Aarsleff, *From Locke to Saussure: Essays on the Study of Language and Intellectual History*, London: Athlone, 1982, shows how the problematic of *origins* was a popular theme in linguistics at the time. It should be emphasized that the present chapter is devoted entirely to problems of language. It ignores the subtitle of the *Essay*, namely *in which melody and musical imitation are discussed*. All the scholars cited above are in agreement that the topic that preoccupied Rousseau in the *Essay* was music, in particular the dispute with Rameau concerning melody and harmony. I have ignored this most important topic in Rousseau's *oeuvre* only because I have nothing to add to the outstanding work of those scholars.

2 On this see Wellman, *La Mettrie: Medicine, Philosophy and Enlightenment*, Durham: Duke University Press, 1992, pp. 164–5 and 191–2.

3 See Eigeldinger, *Jean-Jacques Rousseau et la réalité de l'imaginaire*, Neuchâtel: la Baconnière, 1962, p. 344.

4 Condillac, *Discours préliminaire*, I.403b, quoted by Aarsleff, op. cit., p. 164.

5 See Saussure, *Course in General Linguistics* (1916), trans. Baskin, Glasgow: Fontana/Collins, 1974.

6 Condillac, *Essai sur l'origine des connaissances humaines*, II, Chapter 4, §§ 35,38,46. This paragraph, and these references, are due to Aarsleff, op. cit., p. 170.

7 Condillac, ibid., §102, quoted by Starobinski, OC 3.1326.

8 Condillac, *Essai* II, Chapter 1, §60.

9 On this see Starobinski, OC 3.1328.

10 The title of Condillac, op. cit. Chapter 15. The following quotations are from §143 and §148 of that chapter.

11 Rousseau holds that you need to learn Latin to understand French (Em IV.675/342). On comparison, see Burgelin, OC 4.1375.

12 On Rousseau's approach to metaphor, see Starobinski, OC 5.1545. He points to Condillac, *Essai* II.1.ch.14.§140 as Rousseau's source on this question.

13 For this historical story of the origin of the opposition between the literal and the metaphorical see Lloyd, *Demystifying Mentalities*, Cambridge: Cambridge University Press, 1990.

14 On eloquence, new and old, see Starobinski, OC 5.1584.

15 See Eigeldinger, op. cit., pp. 130–1.

16 Aarsleff gives an illuminating account of the historical context. He is particularly critical of Chomsky's version of the history in *Cartesian Linguistics*.

17 Taylor made much of the romantic turn to 'expressivism' in linguistics in 'Language and human nature', *Philosophical Papers*, vol. 1 (*Human Agency and Language*), Cambridge: Cambridge University Press, 1985, ch. 9. On my reading, Rousseau is part romantic, part rationalist in his approach to linguistics.

Chapter X   Religion and Politics

1   Derathé, OC 3.1499.

2   Derathé, OC 3.1498.

3   See Derathé, OC 3.1503, for a discussion of Rousseau's responses to those protests.

4   Rousseau makes the same point in the first *Letter from the Mountain*, in which he defends SC IV.8 at length. (LMt 1.703-6).

5   See Rawls, *A Theory of Justice*, Cambridge, MA: the Belknap Press of Harvard University Press, 1971, §35, pp. 216-21. Rawls holds that holders of even outrageously intolerant views should be tolerated unless the expression of those views constitutes a 'real and present danger' to the maintenance of the just, tolerant society.

6   See Gouhier, note to the LdeB in OC 4.1746.

7   See J. S. Mill, *Essay on Liberty* (1859), ed. Warnock, London: Fontana, 1962, ch.1, p. 135.

8   This is the position of Lord Devlin in his famous debate with Hart, 'Morals and the criminal law' in *The Enforcement of Morals*, London: Oxford University Press, 1977.

Chapter XI   Negative Theology: Revealed Religion Criticized

1   See Cranston, *Jean-Jacques: the Early Life and Work of Jean-Jacques Rousseau, 1712-1754*, London: Allen Lane, 1983, ch.12 'The Encyclopaedist'.

2   See Hulliung, *The Autocritique of Enlightenment: Rousseau and the Philosophes*, Cambridge, MA: Harvard University Press, 1994 for the most brilliant presentation of this theme. Hulliung shows that even when Rousseau was closest to the *philosophes* he was always more radical than they in his criticism of inequality. In the *Second Discourse* he combined the most complete naturalism with the most radical egalitarianism.

3   When was this dramatic moment? In the Third Walk Rousseau says it was when he was forty, i.e. in 1752 (Reveries III.1014/50-1). He continues: 'I put this plan into effect slowly and haltingly [*à diverses reprises*], but I devoted to it all the effort and attention of which I was capable' (Reveries III.1016/53). The wording is close to the Savoyard Vicar's as he starts his 'Profession of Faith'. It is agreed by commentators since Masson that Rousseau composed the latter between 1757 and 1762. Perhaps 1757 represents a '*reprise*' after an interruption.

4   Rousseau puts it even more strongly in the *Confessions*: 'the two parties resembled rabid Wolves, desperate to tear each other to pieces, rather than Christians and philosophers who reciprocally wish to enlighten, convince, and restore each other to the path of truth' (Conf IX.435-6/366).

5   We shall consider Rousseau's hesitant use of this idea at (E) below.

6   Jimack points out that the order of the two parts of the 'Profession of Faith' is significant:

The usual version of deism started from the challenging and rejection of

... fundamental features of Christian revelation ... and then proceeded nevertheless to defend the existence of God ... the starting point was the dissociation from Christianity. In Rousseau's version the same elements are differently combined: he begins with the proof of the existence of God and expresses his reservations about Christian revelation only in the second half of the 'Profession'. His starting point thus appears to be the rejection not of Christianity but of atheism. (*Rousseau, 'Emile'*, London: Grant & Cutler, 1983, pp. 39–40)

7   Voltaire, letter to Etienne-Noël Damilaville, 14 June 1762, in *The Complete Works of Voltaire*, vol. 109, ed. Besterman, Banbury: The Voltaire Foundation, p. 31.

8   See *Voltaire's Marginalia on the Pages of Rousseau*, ed. Havens, New York: Haskell House, 1966, pp. 93–109.

9   P.-M. Masson, edition of *La profession de foi du Vicaire savoyard*, Paris, 1914, p. xxxix, quoted by Raymond, OC 1.1783. For the dating of the first draft, see Masson, *La religion de Jean-Jacques Rousseau*, t.II, ch. 2, Geneva: Slatkine Reprints, 1970 (1916), quoted by Raymond, OC1.1781.

10   OC4.1587.

11   Charles de Beaumont, *Mandement, portant condamnation d'un livre qui a pour titre* EMILE, OU DE L'EDUCATION *par J.-J. Rousseau, citoyen de Genève*, 1763, in Grimsley, *Rousseau's Religious Writings*, Oxford: Clarendon Press, 1970, pp. 217–18.

12   OC 4.1567.

13   Ibid.

Chapter XII   Positive Theology: Natural Religion Defended

1   See Chapter II (C) above, and Hobson, ' "Nexus effectivus" and "nexus causalis" in the *Inégalité* and the *Essai sur l'origine des langues*", in Hobson, Leigh and Wokler (eds), *Rousseau in the Eighteenth Century: Essays in Memory of R. A. Leigh*, Oxford: the Voltaire Foundation, 1992.

2   See Starobinski, OC 5.cxcix-cc.

3   See Hobson, op. cit.

4   See Starobinski, 'L'inclinaison de l'axe du globe', in EOL-Folio 168.

5   In EOL-Folio 178 Starobinski explains the context of this debate. Theologians and 'naturalists' were discussing the status of Old Testament narratives. In the case of the Flood, the former attributed its cause to God, the latter to nature. Starobinski suggests that Rousseau is entering that debate obliquely, siding here with the theologians on this relatively trivial point, while siding with the 'naturalists' in the all-important denial of the reality of the Fall and the expulsion from the Garden of Eden.

6   See Chapter II above.

7   For the changed '*mise-en-scène*', see Hobson, op. cit., Starobinski, EOL-Folio 166 and Cranston, *Jean-Jacques: the Early Life and Work of Jean-Jacques Rousseau, 1712–1754*, London: Allen Lane, 1983, Chapter 17, p. 331. I follow their view that Rousseau's return to religion, his own minimalist

version of theism, was sincere, and marks an important shift in his worldview.

8 Diderot, *Pensées philosophiques*, no.21, in *Oeuvres philosophiques*, ed. Vernière, Paris: Garnier, 1964, pp. 21–3.

9 This passage, not included in the version of the letter published in *Oeuvres de M. Rousseau*, Neuchâtel, 1764, was published first by G. Streickesen-Moultou, *Oeuvres et correspondance inédites*, Paris, 1861. It has been authenticated by R. A. Leigh in 'Rousseau's letter to Voltaire on optimism', *Studies on Voltaire and the Eighteenth Century*, vol. 30, 1964, pp. 269–70.

10 See Diderot, *Le rêve d'Alembert* (written 1769), in *Oeuvres philosophiques*, ed. Vernière, Paris: Garnier, 1964, p. 276 (Penguin translation, p. 159).

11 See e.g. the letter to Jacob Vernes, 18 February 1758 (CC 5#616, p. 33) and the letter to Franquières, 15 January 1769 (CC 37#6529, p. 17). The latter is also printed in OC 4.1139.

12 See Vartanian, *Diderot and Descartes: a Study of Scientific Naturalism in the Enlightenment*, Princeton, NJ: Princeton University Press, 1953, pp. 310–11, and Ehrard, *L'idée de nature en France à l'aube des lumières*, Paris: Flammarion, 1970, p. 139.

13 Other arguments in the article concern speculations about evolution. Rousseau holds that the lack of signs of 'imperfect species' counts against Diderot's thesis, and he sides with Voltaire against Diderot in maintaining that the species are immutable. That too, he thinks, is a demonstration of God's intelligence in maintaining harmony.

14 Burgelin, note to Em IV.590 (OC 4.1546).

15 Madame de Warens, recalls Rousseau, 'was a good Catholic, or claimed to be one, and it is certain that she claimed it in very good faith.' Yet

> the whole doctrine of original sin and redemption is destroyed by [her] system, and the whole basis of vulgar Christianity is shaken by it . . . Maman did not lie to me, and that soul without bitterness, which could not imagine God as vindictive and always wrathful, saw only clemency and mercy where the devout saw only justice and punishment. She often said that it would not be justice at all for God to be just with regard to us, because – since he had not given us what we needed to be just – it would be asking for a return of more than he had given us.' (Conf VI.229/ 192)

As we saw in Chapter XI, Rousseau's view of original sin was identical to Maman's.

16 Burgelin, OC 4.1550.

17 For the professional treatment of this device, see Thomas Aquinas, *Summa Theologiae*, vol. 3, trans. McCabe, London: Eyre & Spottiswoode, 1964. The whole of Part 1, Question 13 is devoted to 'Theological Language'. See in particular Article 5: 'are words used both of God and of creatures used univocally or equivocally?' and Article 6: 'given that they are in fact used analogically, are they predicated primarily of God or of creatures?'

18 See Chapter III (E) above.

19 Here is Russell's brutal dismissal of Rousseau's philosophy of religion:

The rejection of reason in favour of the heart was not, to my mind, an advance. In fact, no one thought of this device so long as reason appeared to be on the side of religious belief. In Rousseau's environment, reason, as represented by Voltaire, was opposed to religion, therefore away with reason! . . . [T]here are two objections to the practice of basing beliefs as to objective fact upon the emotions of the heart. One is that there is no reason whatever to suppose that such beliefs will be true; the other, is that the resulting beliefs will be private, since the heart says different things to different people . . . However ardently I, or all mankind, may desire something, however necessary it may be to human happiness, that is no ground for supposing this something to exist. There is no law of nature guaranteeing that mankind should be happy. Everybody can see that this is true of our life here on earth, but by a curious twist our sufferings in this life are made into an argument for a better life hereafter. We should not employ such an argument in any other connection. If you bought ten dozen eggs from a man, and the first dozen were all rotten, you would not infer that the remaining nine dozen must be of surpassing excellence; yet that is the kind of reasoning that 'the heart' encourages as a consolation for our sufferings here below. For my part, I prefer the ontological argument, the cosmological argument, and the rest of the old stock-in-trade, to the sentimental illogicality that has sprung from Rousseau. The old arguments at least were honest: if valid, they proved their point; if invalid, it was open to any critic to prove them so. But the new theology of the heart dispenses with argument; it cannot be refuted because it does not profess to prove its points. At bottom, the only reason offered for its acceptance is that it allows us to indulge in pleasant dreams. This is an unworthy reason, and if I had to choose between Thomas Aquinas and Rousseau, I should unhesitatingly choose the Saint. (Russell, *History of Western Philosophy*, London: Allen & Unwin, 1946, pp. 720–1)

20 There are evident similarities between Rousseau's religious vision and Wittgenstein's. See, for example: 'It strikes me that a religious belief could only be something like a passionate commitment to a system of reference. Hence, although it's *belief*, it's really a way of living, or a way of assessing life . . .' (Wittgenstein, *Culture and Value*, trans. Winch, Oxford: Blackwell, 1980, p. 64e). For the most illuminating account of religion and *seeing as* in Wittgenstein, see Monk, *Ludwig Wittgenstein: the Duty of Genius*, New York: The Free Press, 1990, especially Chapter 24, 'A change of aspect'. See also Wisdom, 'Gods' (1944), in *Philosophy and Psycho-Analysis*, Oxford: Blackwell, 1953.

21 Burgelin, *La philosophie de l'existence de J-J. Rousseau*, Paris: Vrin 1973, p. 455.

22 Kant, *Critique of Practical Reason* (1788), trans. Beck, Indianapolis: Bobbs-Merill, 1956, II.2.6, p. 137.

23 Kant, op. cit., II.2.4, p. 127.

24 Ibid.

25 Kant, op. cit., II.2.5, p. 129.

26 Kant, op. cit., II.2.5, p. 130.

Concluding Reflections

1   For an exquisite presentation of this third vision, see the eloquent papers of David Gauthier: 'The politics of redemption', in *Moral Dealing*, Ithaca, NY: Cornell University Press, 1990; *'Le Promeneur Solitaire* and the emergence of the post-social self', in Paul, Miller, and Paul (eds.), *Ethics, Politics, and Human Nature*, Oxford: Blackwell, 1991; 'The making of Jean-Jacques', in O'Hagan (ed.), *Jean-Jacques Rousseau and the Sources of the Self*, Aldershot: Avebury, 1997. A powerful recent work on the theme of integrity is Grant, *Hypocrisy and Integrity: Machiavelli, Rousseau, and the Ethics of Politics*, Chicago: University of Chicago Press, 1997.

Bibliography and Reference
Conventions

(A)   *Rousseau's works*

Citations in the text

With the exception of the correspondence, citations in the text to Rousseau's works are to abbreviated titles (abbreviations listed below), followed in most cases by two sets of page references, separated by '/', the first to the French, the second to the English translation. Although I have not always used a published translation, I have always given a page reference to one, where available.

The first page reference is standardly to the relevant volume of:
Jean-Jacques Rousseau, *Oeuvres complètes*, 5 volumes, Paris: Gallimard (Bibliothèque de la Pléiade), general editors Bernard Gagnebin, Marcel Raymond, vol. 1, 1959; vols 2 and 3, 1964; vol. 4, 1969; vol. 5, 1995 (OC).

The second is to the relevant volume of the *Collected Writings*, where available:
Jean-Jacques Rousseau, *Collected Writings*, series editors Roger D. Masters and Christopher Kelly, Hanover, NH: University Press of New England, vol. 1, trans. J. R. Bush, C. Kelly and R. D. Masters, 1990; vol. 2, trans. J. R. Bush, C. Kelly and R. D. Masters, 1992; vol. 3, trans. J. R. Bush, R. D. Masters and T. Marshall, 1992; vol. 4, trans. J. R. Bush, R. D. Masters and C. Kelly, 1994; vol. 5, trans. C. Kelly, 1995; vol. 6, trans. P. Stewart, J. Vaché, 1997 (CW).

References to Rousseau's correspondence are to:
Correspondance complète de Jean-Jacques Rousseau, 49 volumes, ed. R. A. Leigh, vols 1–15, Geneva: Institut et Musée Voltaire, 1965–71; vols 16–49, Banbury: the Voltaire Foundation, 1972–89 (CC). References to volume, letter number and page (e.g. CC 21#3564, p. 248 = volume 21, letter number 3564, p. 248).

Other French editions and English translations used are listed below.

Other collections in French

Jean-Jacques Rousseau, *Oeuvres complètes*, 3 volumes, Paris: Seuil (Collection 'L'Intégrale'), general editor Michel Launay, vol. 1, 1967; vols 2 and 3, 1971 (Seuil).
Rousseau's Religious Writings, ed. Ronald Grimsley, Oxford: Clarendon Press, 1970.
The Political Writings of Jean-Jacques Rousseau, ed. C. E. Vaughan, 2 volumes, Cambridge: Cambridge University Press, 1915.

Other collections in English

Jean-Jacques Rousseau, *The First and Second Discourses, together with the Replies to Critics, and Essay on the Origin of Languages*, ed. and trans. Victor Gourevitch, New York: Harper and Row, 1986 (highly recommended).
Jean-Jacques Rousseau, *The Social Contract and Discourses*, trans. G. D. H. Cole, revised J. H. Brumfitt and J. C. Hall, updated P. D. Jimack, London: Dent (Everyman Library), 1993 (Cole-Brumfitt-Hall-Jimack).
Rousseau's Political Writings (*Discourse on Inequality, Discourse on Political Economy, On Social Contract*), trans. J. C. Bondanella, eds. A. Ritter and J. C. Bondanella, New York: Norton, 1988 (Bondanella).

Individual works by Rousseau (with abbreviated titles)

A Discourse on the Sciences and the Arts (*First Discourse*), 1750. **1D**
OC 3/CW 2 (cited by page number).

Preface to *Narcisse*, 1753. **PN**
OC 2/CW 2 (cited by page number).

A Discourse on the Origin of Inequality among Men (*Second Discourse*), 1755. **2D**
OC 3/CW 3 (cited by page number).

A Discourse on Political Economy (*Third Discourse*), 1755. **3D**
OC 3/CW 3 (cited by page number).

Letter to Voltaire, 1756. **LV**
OC 4 (cited by page number).

Lettres morales (written 1757–8, published posthumously). **LMor**
OC 4 (cited by Letter and page number).

Letter to d'Alembert, 1758. **Ld'A**
OC 5/trans. Allan Bloom in *Politics and the Arts: Rousseau's Letter to d'Alembert*, Ithaca, NY: Cornell University Press, 1960 (cited by page number).

Essay on the Origin of Languages (probably written between 1756 and 1761, published posthumously). **EOL**
OC 5/trans. V. Gourevitch in *The First and Second Discourses, together with the Replies to Critics and the Essay on the Origin of Languages*, New York: Harper and Row, 1986 (cited by chapter and page number). (Reference is also made to the following: Jean-Jacques Rousseau, *Essai sur l'origine des langues*, with 'Etudes annexes': 'Les pérégrinations de Cadmus' and 'L'inclinaison de l'axe du globe', ed. Jean Starobinski,

Paris: Gallimard (Folio-essais), 1990; Jean-Jacques Rousseau, *Essai sur l'origine des langues*, ed. C. Kintzler, Paris: GF-Flammarion, 1993.)

Julie, ou la nouvelle Héloïse, 1761. **JNH**
OC 2/CW 6 (cited by Part, Letter and page number, e.g. III.5.315 = Part III, Letter 5, OC 2, p. 315, CW 6, p. 258).

Emile, or on Education, 1762. **Em**
OC 4/trans. Allan Bloom, New York: Basic Books, 1979 (cited by Book and page number, e.g. Em V.692/357 = *Emile* Book V, OC 4, p. 692, Bloom translation, p. 357)
Emile et Sophie, ou les solitaires (published posthumously).
OC 4 (cited by page number).
Manuscrit Favre (Favre Manuscript) (published posthumously). **FM**
OC 4 (cited by page number).

Letters to Malesherbes (written January 1762, published 1779). **LMa**
OC 1/CW 5 (cited by page number).

Social Contract, 1762. **SC**
OC 3/CW 4 (cited by Book, chapter and page number, e.g. SC I.6.360/138 = *Social Contract* Book I, chapter 6, OC 3, p. 360, CW 4, p. 138).
Political Fragments (published posthumously). **PolFr**
OC 3/CW 4 (cited by Fragment number and page number).
Geneva Manuscript (first version of the *Social Contract*) (published posthumously). **GM**
OC 3/CW 4 (cited by page number).

Letter to de Beaumont, 1763. **LdeB**
OC 4 (cited by page number).

Letters from the Mountain, 1764. **LMt**
OC 3 (cited by Letter number and page number).

Project for a Constitution for Corsica (written 1763–5, published posthumously). **PCC**
OC 3/trans. F. Watkins in Rousseau, *Political Writings*, Edinburgh: Nelson, 1953 (cited by page number).

Considerations on the Government of Poland (written 1771–2, published posthumously). **GP**
OC 3/trans. W. Kendall, Indianapolis and New York: Bobbs-Merrill, 1972 (cited by chapter number and page number).

Confessions (written c. 1766–71, published posthumously). **Conf**
OC 1/CW 5 (cited by Book and page number).
Mon portrait ('Fragments autobiographiques' III, date of writing uncertain, published posthumously) **MP**
OC 1 (cited by page number).

Rousseau, Judge of Jean-Jacques: Dialogues (written 1772–6, published posthumously). **RJJJ**
OC 1/CW 1 (cited by Dialogue and page number, e.g. RJJJ 1Dial.672/12 =

Rousseau, Judge of Jean-Jacques, First Dialogue, OC 1, p. 672, CW 1, p. 12).

Reveries of the Solitary Walker (written 1776–8, published posthumously). **Reveries** OC 1/trans. P. France, Harmondsworth: Penguin, 1979 (cited by Walk number and page number, e.g. Reveries VI.1059/103 = *Reveries*, Sixth Walk, OC 1, p. 1059, France's translation, p. 103).

(B)   Biography

Cranston, Maurice, *Jean-Jacques: the Early Life and Work of Jean-Jacques Rousseau, 1712–1754*, London: Allen Lane, 1983.
Cranston, Maurice, *The Noble Savage: Jean-Jacques Rousseau, 1754–1762*, London: Allen Lane, 1991.
Cranston, Maurice, *The Solitary Self: Jean-Jacques Rousseau in Exile and Adversity*, London: Allen Lane, 1997 (appeared after this book was completed).
Guéhenno, Jean, *Jean-Jacques Rousseau*, vol. 1, 1712–1758; vol. 2, 1758–1778, trans. J. and D. Weightman, London: Routledge & Kegan Paul, 1966 (1962).

Guidebook and biography

La route Rousseau (Guide régional Rhône-Alpes/Suisse romande), Rémy Hildebrand, Jean-Jacques Monney and Alain Schneider (eds), Geneva: Editions Transversales, 1991

(C)   Reference Works

The most useful reference work available in English is:
Dent, N. J. H., *A Rousseau Dictionary*, Oxford: Blackwell, 1992.

There is a concordance, an invaluable aid to tracking Rousseau's terminology:
Etudes rousseauistes et index des oeuvres de J.-J. Rousseau, Geneva: Librairie Slatkine, Paris: Librairie Champion, 1978 ff. It covers the following texts: *Rêveries*; *Fragments autobiographiques et Lettre à Voltaire*; *Emile* (two volumes); *Emile et Sophie*; *Discours sur les sciences et les arts et Discours sur l'inégalité*; *Essai sur l'origine des langues*; *Julie, ou la Nouvelle Héloïse*; *Lettre à de Beaumont*; *Lettre à d'Alembert*.

(D)   Other works

(Only items referred to in the book and a few others are listed here. There is an excellent bibliography of the primary and secondary literature in N. J. H. Dent, *A Rousseau Dictionary* (see (C) above).)

Aarsleff, Hans, *From Locke to Saussure: Essays on the Study of Language and Intellectual History*, London: Athlone, 1982.
Aquinas, Thomas, *Summa Theologiae*, vol. 3, trans. Herbert McCabe, London: Eyre & Spottiswoode, 1964.
——, *Summa Theologiae*, vol. 18, trans. Thomas Gilby, London: Eyre & Spottiswoode, 1966.

Arrow, K. J., *Social Choice and Individual Values*, New Haven: Yale University Press, 1963.

——, 'Values and collective decision-making', in P. Laslett and W. G. Runciman (eds), *Philosophy, Politics and Society*, 3rd Series, Oxford: Blackwell, 1967.

Baczko, Bronislaw, *Rousseau: solitude et communauté*, trans. from Polish by Claude Brendhel-Lamhout, Paris: Mouton, 1974 (1970).

Badinter, Elisabeth, *L'amour en plus*, Paris: Flammarion, 1980.

Baker, Gordon and Morris, Katherine J., *Descartes' Dualism*, London: Routledge, 1996.

Berlin, Isaiah, 'Two concepts of liberty', in *Four Essays on Liberty*, Oxford: Oxford University Press, 1969 (1958).

Blum, Carol, *Rousseau and the Republic of Virtue: the Language of Politics in the French Revolution*, Ithaca, NY: Cornell University Press, 1986.

Boudon, Raymond, *Effets pervers et l'ordre social*, Paris: Presses Universitaires de France, 1977.

Burgelin, Pierre, *La philosophie de l'existence de J.-J. Rousseau*, Paris: Vrin, 1973.

Burke, Edmund, *Reflections on the Revolution in France*, ed. Conor Cruise O'Brien, Harmondsworth: Penguin, 1969 (1790).

Cameron, David, *The Social Thought of Rousseau and Burke*, London: Weidenfeld & Nicolson, 1973.

Cassirer, Ernst, *The Question of Jean-Jacques Rousseau*, trans. Peter Gay, New York: Columbia University Press, 1954 (1932).

——, *Rousseau, Kant and Goethe*, trans. J. Gutmann, P. O. Kristeller and J. H. Randall, intro. Peter Gay, New York: Harper and Row, 1963 (1945).

Caygill, Howard, 'The master and the magician', in Timothy O'Hagan (ed.), *Jean-Jacques Rousseau and the Sources of the Self*, Aldershot: Avebury Press, 1997.

Condillac, Etienne Bonnot de, *Essai sur l'origine des connaissances humaines* in *Oeuvres philosophiques de Condillac*, vol. 3, ed. G. le Roy, Paris: Presses Universitaires de France, 1947 (1746).

Condorcet, Antoine-Nicolas de, *Esquisse d'un tableau des progrès de l'esprit humain*, Paris: Editions Sociales, 1966 (English translation: *Sketch for a Historical Picture of the Progress of the Human Mind*, trans. J. Barraclough, Westport, CT: Greenwood Press, 1955) (1795).

Constant, Benjamin, *The Spirit of Conquest and Usurpation and their Relation to European Civilization*, in *Political Writings*, ed. and trans. B. Fontana, Cambridge: Cambridge University Press, 1988 (1814).

——, *Principles of Politics Applicable to All Representative Governments*, in *Political Writings*, ed. and trans. B Fontana, Cambridge: Cambridge University Press, 1988 (1815).

Crocker, Lester, 'Rousseau et la voie du totalitarisme', in *Annales de la philosophie politique*, 5, 1965 ('Rousseau et la philosophie politique').

Dent, N. J. H., *Rousseau*, Oxford: Blackwell, 1988.

Derathé, Robert, *Le rationalisme de J.-J. Rousseau*, Paris: Presses Universitaires de France, 1948.

——, *Jean-Jacques Rousseau et la science politique de son temps*, Paris: Vrin, 1988 (1950).

Derrida, Jacques, *De la grammatologie*, Paris: Minuit, 1967.

Descartes, René, *Oeuvres de Descartes*, eds Charles Adam and Paul Tannery

(11 volumes), Paris: Vrin, 1996 (English translation: *The Philosophical Writings of Descartes*, trans. John Cottingham, Robert Stoothof, Dugald Murdoch and Anthony Kenny (3 volumes), Cambridge: Cambridge University Press, 1984, 1985, 1991).

Devlin, Lord Patrick, 'Morals and the criminal law', in *The Enforcement of Morals*, London: Oxford University Press, 1977.

Diderot, Denis, *Pensées philosophiques*, in *Oeuvres philosophiques*, ed. Paul Vernière, Paris: Garnier, 1964 (1746).

——, *Le rêve d'Alembert*, in *Oeuvres philosophiques*, ed. Paul Vernière, Paris: Garnier, 1964 (English translation by Leonard Tancock, Harmondsworth: Penguin, 1966) (written 1769).

Ehrard, Jean, *L'idée de nature en France à l'aube des lumières*, Paris: Flammarion, 1970.

Eigeldinger, Marc, *Jean-Jacques Rousseau et la réalité de l'imaginaire*, Neuchâtel: la Baconnière, 1962.

Freud, Sigmund, *New Introductory Lectures on Psychoanalysis*, Lecture 33 ('Femininity'), Pelican Freud Library, vol. 2, Harmondsworth: Penguin, 1973 (1933).

Gauthier, David, 'The politics of redemption', in *Moral Dealing*, Ithaca, NY: Cornell University Press, 1990.

——, '*Le Promeneur Solitaire*: Rousseau and the emergence of the post-social self', in E. F. Paul, F. D. Miller and J. Paul (eds), *Ethics, Politics, and Human Nature*, Oxford: Blackwell, 1991.

——, 'Making Jean-Jacques', in Timothy O'Hagan (ed.), *Jean-Jacques Rousseau and the Sources of the Self*, Aldershot: Avebury, 1997.

Gilson, Etienne, 'La méthode de M. de Wolmar', in *Les idées et les lettres*, Paris: Vrin, 1932.

Godechot, Jacques (ed.), *Les constitutions de la France depuis 1789*, Paris: GF-Flammarion, 1979.

Goldschmidt, Victor, *Anthropologie et politique: les principes du système de Rousseau*, Paris: Vrin, 1983.

Gouhier, Henri, *Les méditations métaphysiques de Jean-Jacques Rousseau*, Paris: Vrin, 1984.

Grant, Ruth W., *Hypocrisy and Integrity: Machiavelli, Rousseau, and the Ethics of Politics*, Chicago: University of Chicago Press, 1997.

Greene, Graham, *The Quiet American*, London: Heinemann and Bodley Head, 1979 (1955).

Grimsley, Ronald, *Rousseau and the Religious Quest*, Oxford: Clarendon Press, 1968.

——, *The Philosophy of Rousseau*, London: Oxford University Press, 1973.

Hart, H. L. A., *The Concept of Law*, London: Oxford University Press, 1961.

Helvétius, *De l'esprit*, ed. Jacques Moutaux, Paris: Fayard, 1988 (1758).

Hobson, Marian, '"Nexus effectivus" and "nexus causalis" in the *Inégalité* and in the *Essai sur l'origine des langues*', in M. Hobson, J. T. A. Leigh, and R. Wokler (eds), *Rousseau in the Eighteenth Century: Essays in Memory of R. A. Leigh*, Oxford: the Voltaire Foundation, 1992.

Hollis, Martin, 'Honour among thieves' (1990), in *Reason in Action: Essays in the Philosophy of Social Science*, Cambridge: Cambridge University Press, 1996.

——, *Trust within Reason*, Cambridge: Cambridge University Press, 1998.

Hulliung, Mark, *The Autocritique of Enlightenment: Rousseau and the Philosophes*, Cambridge, MA: Harvard University Press, 1994.

Hume, David, *The Letters of David Hume*, 2 volumes, ed. J. Y. T. Greig, Oxford: Clarendon Press, 1932.

Jimack, Peter, *La genèse et la rédaction de l'*'Emile' de J.-J. Rousseau, in *Studies on Voltaire and the Eighteenth Century*, vol. 13, Geneva: Institut et Musée Voltaire, 1960.

——, *Rousseau, 'Emile'*, London: Grant and Cutler, 1983.

Kant, Immanuel, *The Moral Law: Kant's 'Groundwork of the Metaphysic of Morals'*, trans. H. J. Paton, London: Hutchinson, 1961 (1785).

——, *Critique of Practical Reason*, trans. Lewis White Beck, Indianapolis: Bobbs Merrill, 1956 (1788).

Kelly, Christopher, *Rousseau's Exemplary Life. The 'Confessions' as Political Philosophy*, Ithaca: Cornell University Press, 1987.

La Mettrie, J. O. de, *Man a Machine* (French text with English translation by G. C. Bussey), La Salle, Ill. : Open Court, 1912 (1748).

Leduc-Fayette, Denise, *Rousseau et le mythe de l'antiquité*, Paris: Vrin, 1974.

Leigh, R. A., 'Rousseau's letter to Voltaire on optimism', in *Studies on Voltaire and the Eighteenth Century*, vol. 30, 1964.

Lévi-Strauss, Claude, *Tristes Tropiques*, Paris: Plon, 1955.

——, *Anthropologie structurale*, Paris: Plon, 1958.

——, 'Jean-Jacques Rousseau, fondateur des sciences de l'homme', in *Jean-Jacques Rousseau* (collection of essays published by the Université Ouvrière et Faculté des lettres de l'Université de Genève), Neuchâtel: la Baconnière, 1962 (English translation: 'Jean-Jacques Rousseau, founder of the sciences of man', in *Structural Anthropology*, vol. 2, trans. M. Layton, London: Allen Lane, 1977).

Lewis, David, *Convention: a Philosophical Study*, Cambridge, MA: Harvard University Press, 1969.

Lloyd, G. E. R., *Demystifying Mentalities*, Cambridge: Cambridge University Press, 1990.

Locke, John, *An Essay Concerning Human Understanding*, ed. J. W. Yolton, London: Dent (Everyman's Library), 1961 (1689).

——, *Two Treatises of Government*, ed. Peter Laslett, New York: New American Library, 1965 (1689).

Masson, Pierre Maurice, *La religion de Jean-Jacques Rousseau*, Geneva: Slatkine Reprints, 1970 (1916).

Masters, Roger, *The Political Philosophy of Rousseau*, Princeton, NJ: Princeton University Press, 1968.

Masters, Roger, 'The structure of Rousseau's political thought', in M. Cranston, and R. S. Peters (eds), *Hobbes and Rousseau: a Collection of Critical Essays*, Garden City, NY: Anchor Books, 1972.

Mill, John Stuart, *Essay on Liberty*, in *Utilitarianism*, ed. Mary Warnock, London: Fontana, 1962 (1859).

Monk, Ray, *Ludwig Wittgenstein: the Duty of Genius*, New York: The Free Press, 1990.

Nozick, Robert, *Anarchy, State, and Utopia*, Oxford: Basil Blackwell, 1974.

O'Hagan, Timothy, 'On Rousseau's *Social Contract*: translation and exegesis', in *History of Political Thought*, 3. 2, 1982.

O'Hagan, Timothy, 'On Hegel's critique of Kant's moral and political philosophy', in Stephen Priest (ed.), *Hegel's Critique of Kant*, Oxford: Clarendon Press, 1987.

——, 'La morale sensitive de Jean-Jacques Rousseau', in *Revue de théologie et de philosophie*, 125, 1993.

——, 'Aristotle and Aquinas on community and natural law', in R. Bellamy, and A. Ross (eds), *A Textual Introduction to Social and Political Theory*, Manchester: Manchester University Press, 1996.

—— (ed.), *Jean-Jacques Rousseau and the Sources of the Self*, Aldershot: Avebury, 1997.

Pascal, Blaise, *Les pensées*, in *Oeuvres complètes*, ed. Louis Lafuma, Paris: Seuil, 1963 (English translation by A. J. Krailsheimer, Harmondsworth: Penguin, 1966) (1670).

Pettit, Philip, *Republicanism: a Theory of Freedom and Government*, Oxford: Clarendon Press, 1997.

Philonenko, Alexis, *Jean-Jacques Rousseau et la pensée du malheur* (3 volumes), Paris: Vrin, 1984.

Plato, *Republic*, with translation by Paul Shorey, London: Heinemann (Loeb Classical Library), 1935.

——, *Meno*, with translation by W. R. M. Lamb, London: Heinemann (Loeb Classical Library), 1924.

Quesnay, François, 'Evidence', in the *Encyclopédie*, vol. 6 (*Encyclopédie, ou Dictionnaire raisonné des sciences, des arts et des métiers, par une société de gens de lettres, mis en ordre et publié par M. Diderot . . .*), Lausanne, Berne: chez les Sociétés Typographiques, 1779–82.

Rawls, John, *A Theory of Justice*, Cambridge, MA: the Belknap Press of Harvard University Press, 1971.

——, 'Justice as fairness, political not metaphysical', in *Philosophy and Public Affairs*, 14. 3, 1985.

——, *Political Liberalism*, New York: Columbia University Press, 1993.

Riley, Patrick, *Will and Political Legitimacy*, Cambridge, MA: Harvard University Press, 1982.

——, *The General Will before Rousseau*, Princeton: Princeton University Press, 1986.

Runciman, W. G. and Sen, A., 'Games, justice and the general will', in *Mind*, 74, 1965.

Russell, Bertrand, *History of Western Philosophy*, London: Allen & Unwin, 1946.

Saussure, Ferdinand de, *Course in General Linguistics*, trans. Wade Baskin, Glasgow: Fontana/Collins, 1974.

Schama, Simon, *Citizens: a Chronicle of the French Revolution*, New York: Vintage, 1989.

Schiebinger, Londa, *The Mind Has No Sex? Women in the Origins of Modern Science*, Cambridge, MA: Harvard University Press, 1989.

Schwartz, Joel, *The Sexual Politics of Jean-Jacques Rousseau*, Chicago: Chicago University Press, 1984.

Sève, René, 'Rousseau et l'esprit du droit romain', in Jean Terrasse (ed.), *Etudes sur les 'Discours' de Rousseau*, Ottawa: Pensée Libre, no. 1, 1988.

Shklar, Judith, *Men and Citizens: a Study of Rousseau's Social Theory*, Cambridge: Cambridge University Press, 1969.

Skinner, Quentin, *Liberty before Liberalism*, Cambridge: Cambridge University Press, 1998.

Smith, Barry, 'Textual deference', in *American Philosophical Quarterly*, 28. 1, 1991.

Sorabji, Richard, *Animal Minds and Human Morals*, London: Duckworth, 1993.

Spitz, Jean-Fabien, *La liberté politique*, Paris: Presses Universitaires de France, 1995.

Starobinski, Jean, *Jean-Jacques Rousseau: la transparence et l'obstacle*, Paris: Gallimard (Collection Tel), 1971 (1970).

——, 'Du *Discours de l'inégalité* au *Contrat social*', in *Etudes sur le* 'Contrat social' *de Jean-Jacques Rousseau*, Actes des journées d'étude tenues à Dijon, les 3, 4, 5, 6 mai 1962, Paris: Société des Belles Lettres, 1964.

——, 'Le remède dans le mal: la pensée de Rousseau', in *Le remède dans le mal: critique et légitimation de l'artifice à l'âge des Lumières*, Paris: Gallimard, 1989.

——, 'L'inclinaison de l'axe du globe', in Rousseau, *Essai sur l'origine des langues*, ed. Starobinski, Paris: Gallimard (Folio-Essais), 1990.

Strauss, Leo, *Natural Right and History*, Chicago: University of Chicago Press, 1971 (1950).

Talmon, J. L., *The Origins of Totalitarian Democracy*, London: Sphere Books, 1970 (1952).

Tanner, Tony, 'Julie and "La Maison Paternelle": another look at Rousseau's *La Nouvelle Héloïse*' in *Daedalus*, 1976.

Taylor, Charles, 'Language and human nature', in *Philosophical Papers*, vol. 1 (*Human Agency and Language*), ch. 9, Cambridge: Cambridge University Press, 1985.

Tocqueville, Alexis de, *De la démocratie en Amérique*, eds J.-C. Lamberti, and F. Mélonio, Paris: Laffont, 1986 (1835, 1840).

Trachtenberg, Zev, *Making Citizens: Rousseau's Political Theory of Culture*, London: Routledge, 1993.

Vartanian, Aram, *Diderot and Descartes: a Study of Scientific Naturalism in the Enlightenment*, Princeton, NJ: Princeton University Press, 1953.

Voltaire, *Poèmes sur le désastre de Lisbonne et sur la loi naturelle* (1756), in Voltaire, *Mélanges*, ed. J. Van den Heuvel, Paris: Gallimard, 1961.

——, *Candide, ou l'optimisme* (1759), in *Romans et contes*, Paris: Gallimard (Folio), 1972 (English translation by John Butt, Harmondsworth: Penguin, 1947).

——, *Voltaire's Marginalia on the Pages of Rousseau*, ed. G. R. Havens, New York: Haskell House, 1966.

——, *The Complete Works of Voltaire*, ed. Theodore Besterman, Banbury: the Voltaire Foundation, vol. 109, 1973.

Warren, S. D., and Brandeis, L. S., 'The right to privacy' (1890), in F. D. Schoeman (ed.), Philosophical Dimensions of Privacy, Cambridge: Cambridge University Press, 1984.

Weintraub, E. R., *Conflict and Co-operation in Economics*, London: Macmillan, 1975.

Wellman, Kathleen, *La Mettrie: Medicine, Philosophy and Enlightenment*, Durham: Duke University Press, 1992.

Wisdom, John, 'Gods', in *Philosophy and Psycho-Analysis*, Oxford: Blackwell, 1953 (1944).

Wittgenstein, Ludwig, *Culture and Value*, trans. Peter Winch, Oxford: Blackwell, 1980.

Wokler, Robert, *Rousseau on Society, Politics, Music and Language: an Historical Interpretation of his Early Writings*, New York: Garland, 1987.

———, *Rousseau*, Oxford: Oxford University Press (Past Masters), 1995.

———, (ed.), *Rousseau and Liberty*, Manchester: Manchester University Press, 1995.

Wollstonecraft, Mary, *A Vindication of the Rights of Woman*, ed. Miriam Brody, Harmondsworth: Penguin, 1992 (1792).

Index of Citations

Name Index

Subject Index